Louise Booth

A LITTLE BUD.
Katharine Elizabeth Gamble, Granddaughter of the Author.

THE

STORY OF CAMP CHASE

A HISTORY OF THE PRISON AND ITS CEMETERY,
TOGETHER WITH OTHER CEMETERIES
WHERE CONFEDERATE PRISON-
ERS ARE BURIED, ETC.

BY

WILLIAM H. KNAUSS

**WITH NEW INTRODUCTION
BY DAVID E. ROTH**

————

NASHVILLE, TENN., AND DALLAS, TEX.
PUBLISHING HOUSE OF THE METHODIST EPISCOPAL CHURCH, SOUTH
SMITH & LAMAR, AGENTS
1906

THE *General's* BOOKS

PUBLISHER
David E. Roth

PUBLISHER'S ADVISORY BOARD
Albert Castel
Ronald T. Clemmons
Stephen Davis
Gary Kross
William Marvel

SPECIAL ACKNOWLEDGMENT
The New Coonskin Library
Columbus, Ohio

This reprint edition by THE *General's* BOOKS
is printed on acid-free paper.

ISBN: 0-9626034-0-6

Printed in the United States of America

New Materials Copyright 1990 by
THE *General's* BOOKS
an affiliate of *Blue & Gray Magazine*
522 Norton Rd., Columbus, OH 43228
(614) 870-1861

THE *General's* BOOKS
Columbus, Ohio
1990

Introduction to the Reprint Edition

Camp Chase is gone. It has disappeared without a trace. The great camp from Civil War days that served numerous roles, from a recruiting post to a prison, has simply been allowed to slip away. Nothing remains of the old compound—nothing. Even the several creeks and ditches, big and small, that drained the camp were obliterated by the flurry of residential development that swept West Columbus in the 1930s and 1940s.

And of course the government really didn't build Camp Chase to last. All the buildings were constructed of wood planks, without foundations of formidable substance, if any, on leased property. After the war the buildings were auctioned off, and the ones that survived this sale were dismantled to build the first fence around the only reminder of the place, the Camp Chase Confederate Cemetery. The cemetery occupies about two and a half acres and is located a short distance south of where the compound was situated. If not for the cemetery, all would be lost.

It's all a very sad tale. And because of that, as well as the glut of legends, hearsay and misinformation that comprises the local reference base on Central Ohio's greatest Civil War connection, a few historically-minded folks have undertaken the reprinting of this book.

William H. Knauss was a Union veteran who had been left for dead on the frozen Fredericksburg battlefield in December 1862. Ironically, it was William Knauss who years later would make it a life-passion to aid in preserving the memory of those who nearly killed him. He fought local public opinion and managed to assemble enough supporters to undertake a complete restoration of a cemetery that had become a weed-choked eyesore along Sullivant Avenue, forgotten even by Southerners.

This book is by no means a definitive history of Camp Chase. It is more a volume in memoriam to Confederates who died there, and at Ohio's other important prison on Johnson's Island in Sandusky Bay, and, as Mr. Knauss seemed to lose focus and direction just a bit, to Confederates who were buried on South Mountain, and at Antietam and Monocacy battlefields, and at Shepherdstown, West Virginia. For you see, William Knauss became a Dixie-phile. Because of his efforts to preserve the Camp Chase burying ground he was welcomed all over the South as a great hero. *Confederate Veteran Magazine* carried countless references to his good works, and its editor, S.A. Cunningham, traveled to Columbus on several occasions to attend memorial ceremonies. Knauss was awarded medals by Southern organizations and received high praise from such high placed ex-Confederates as General John B. Gordon of Georgia. Kentucky's Bennett Young, best known for his work in the Confederacy's Canadian operations, but also a former Camp Chase inmate, became Knauss' friend and spoke at memorial events at the cemetery.

Meanwhile, many people in Columbus, Union veterans or folks who still held bitter memories of loved ones lost in the war or who had suffered in Rebel prisons like Andersonville, with no barracks over their heads, disapproved of Knauss and his memorial programs and all he stood for. Newspaper editors found plenty to editorialize about, old wounds were opened, and guards had to be posted in some cases. In particular, threats of destruction were numerous when the cemetery memorial arch was dedicated in 1902. William Knauss, a hard-bitten veteran in his own right, never faltered in his mission to preserve the final resting place of his one-time enemies. He paid little mind to his critics in the North. He wrote this book in spite of them.

The fascinating thing about Camp Chase is the many roles it served during the Civil War. It was not really intended to be a prison, which resulted in its uniquely inefficient prison layout. At least four different parts of the compound served as three different prisons. Prison #1 included a section reserved for officers (not all of whom were sent to Johnson's Island, as is generally believed). Prison #2 included the Confederate hospital. And Prison #3, the largest stockade, at one time occupied the barracks of the 88th Ohio, which was forced to move outside and a high plank fence was put up around the buildings; later a new Prison #3 was built in anticipation of the large influx of prisoners after the discontinuance of prisoner exchanges.

Camp Chase served three other purposes, non-prisoner related. These roles were less intriguing than a prison and Mr. Knauss chose, rightfully so for his purposes, to ignore them. The camp's first purpose was as a gathering place for units organizing for military service, similar to a modern-day "boot camp." It also served as a mustering-out post for units being discharged at the expiration of their enlistments. And third, Camp Chase became a parole camp. This means that Union soldiers who had been captured by the Confederates and released "on parole" (their promise not to serve in the military or give information to Union authorities) were detained at Camp Chase awaiting "exchange" (notification that an equivalent number of Confederates on parole were allowed to return to combat).

Still, it was the prisons at Camp Chase that naturally drew the most attention to the place. There, despite the sedentary lifestyle of incarceration, was the "drama" of Camp Chase. In the prisons was where men died far from home and loved ones and filled the camp cemetery. This William Knauss wrote about.

Disregarding his slight focus problems and his somewhat folksy presentation—he included photos of his whole family in this book—there is a wealth of good information here about the prisons in Ohio during the Civil War. Knauss consulted the archives of local newspapers for colorful information about Camp Chase, written while it was in operation. He sought out ex-Confederates for their reminiscences of prison life, and rather than paraphrase their comments he let them tell their stories in their own words, uninterrupted, for better or worse. He uncovered a cache of undelivered letters written by inmates in the early spring of 1862. Many appear herein, some in facsimile. He even turned up a former spy. All in all, William Knauss did a commendable job.

The reprinting of this book is the first step in what promises to be a revival of interest and scholarship on Camp Chase. *Blue & Gray Magazine* headquarters is a mere three miles from Camp Chase Cemetery. An archival file is being collected from a multitude of different sources, to be housed at *Blue & Gray* and made available to all interested parties as a sort of informal visitors center. With the help of many interested people, including Paul Clay, John Duncan, Lois Neff and Don Selvage, and volunteers from the Ohio Historical Society, Martha Burk and Miriam Simmons, this material is being gathered, catalogued and indexed. Also, great strides have been made in identifying the location of the camp. While it's true that the entire site is now criss-crossed with residential streets and alleys, we have gotten close to being able to pinpoint the blocks of houses now sitting atop what once was, say,

Prison #3, and telling some homeowner that it was his front yard where the post flagpole stood. With any luck, historical markers will be placed throughout the area, now known as the Westgate section of town, and a walking tour is definitely feasible.

Those of us working on the project like to think that the same wonderful spirit that possessed William Knauss in the 1890s has captured us in the 1990s. Camp Chase can only be a little better for it, and the dead in the cemetery along a busy Columbus street will be just a little less forgotten.

David E. Roth
Columbus, Ohio
May 1990

NOTE: The only part of the 1906 edition not included in the reprint edition is a useless handwritten spreadsheet of the grave numbers in Camp Chase Cemetery. Today the graves are marked with government issue stones with grave numbers clearly indicated on them.

THE *General's* BOOKS

is an affiliate of

CONTENTS.

CHAPTER IX.

VISITING THE SOUTH. PAGE

CHAPTER X.

CAMP CHASE IN 1861.

CHAPTER XI.

INCREASING NUMBERS.

CHAPTER XII.

THE YEARS CREPT SLOWLY ON.

CHAPTER XIII.

AFTER FORTY-TWO YEARS.

CHAPTER XXIII.

THE END AT LAST.

INTRODUCTION.

In this volume the author seeks to give to the survivors of the Southern army such data as may be of interest to them and their friends, and it is his earnest prayer that this story, however imperfect, may be kept somewhere in Southern homes, Southern societies, and by patriotic associations, to keep green the memory of their heroes, when they and he shall have passed into the silence.

More than forty years ago the story began, and it is not yet ended, nor can it end while there are human hearts to thrill at deeds heroic. When there is left in this fair land not one person to remember or care for the mighty deeds of the sixties, or for the men who went down to death, will the story be concluded.

The cemetery at Camp Chase has received regular care since 1894. Those who went to sleep so far away from home were, in the main, plain, simple folk, and the world knew little about them. Here and there in the South a heart ached because a man in gray marched away from home and never returned. The names of most of these men were marked on boards at the heads of the graves, but have been destroyed by storms and by time. For thirty years God only has known just where they are.

Time, the great healer, had almost ceased to dress the festering wounds that war had left, when He who doeth all things well caused Henry Briggs to place in the hands of the author a little paper-covered book containing the names of the Confederate dead in Ohio. It was not to be that their names should perish from off the earth, for the annual report of Adjt. Gen. B. R. Cowen, submitted to Governor Cox, of Ohio, in 1868, contained the list of the dead in Camp Chase.

Prisoners of war did not die amid the roar and crash of battle, where soldiers go to death with heart aflame and blood on fire; but, heart-sick and weary, they sank to rest far from home, far from shrill of fife or beat of drum. It is not the purpose of this volume to compare the prisons North and South.

Prison and paradise are not synonymous terms. There was

suffering, there was death, where the Southern sun blistered and burned in the shadeless prisons; there were months when the cold blasts of the North chilled to death, and stilled the heart throbs of the soldiers of the South.

A chivalrous man prefers to forget the things that rankle, and remember instead the deeds that thrill. With this idea ever in view, a soldier of the Union, wounded in its defense, seeks to tell in a simple and unharrowing manner the story of Ohio's military prisons, and the incidents pertaining to the care of the same since 1894. This story might come from some one else with better grace; but as the author's work is a part of its history, he will tell it plainly and with sincere regard for the conditions to all concerned.

In 1868 business called the author to North Carolina and Virginia, at which time a friendship was formed between himself and an ex-Confederate who was acting as a guide. By comparing notes, the fact developed that both were wounded in the same battle—Fredericksburg. The Confederate lost a leg. Through a bond of the friendship then formed, we mutually agreed to assist the comrades of the other, as best we could, whenever opportunity occurred.

A few months later, while visiting the battlefields of Antietam and South Mountain, the writer found a graveyard where a number of Confederates had been buried. It was upon the side of a hill, and uninclosed. Having in mind the agreement with his Confederate friend, he hired a farmer living near by to build a log fence around the graves of those soldiers who had fallen in battle. Thus he became impressed with the belief that some good might be done, and, perchance, some persons be made happy should they learn that a stranger respected the resting place of their loved and lost.

Upon coming from New Jersey to Columbus in 1893, he learned of the Confederate cemetery west of the city, where there are buried more than two thousand ex-Confederates who had died while prisoners of war in Camp Chase, and that the burial place was in a very bad condition. The gate and gateposts of the stone wall inclosing the cemetery were down, the ground overrun with briers, bramble bushes, and weeds, and it had become a resort for animals.

Shortly afterwards he arranged with Mr. Henry Briggs, who owns a farm opposite the cemetery, to have it cleaned up; and in the spring a few friends distributed some flowers about the place.

GEN. GEORGE MOORMAN.

During the following year (1895) efforts were made to find some ex-Confederates in Columbus. A meeting of some gentlemen was called at his office, and it was agreed that we inaugurate a memorial service and contribute *pro rata* to the expense. A programme was arranged, and steps were taken to have the place grubbed and thoroughly cleaned, have the trees trimmed, the gate and gateposts reset, and other necessary work done.

Within three days of the time arranged for the services the speakers all backed out, concluding that it would be unpopular and injure them as professional men. This action was a source of deep regret, but he determined to have the service and pay the expenses himself. All of the newspapers were visited and requested to say nothing about the matter except that services were to be held there, and to have their reporters present to report in a fitting manner what occurred.

As the street cars at that time ran only within a mile of the cemetery, wagons were hired to convey the people from the terminus of the street railway to the cemetery. Lumber was sent out to build seats, and arrangements were made for comfort. The result was a nice service with about fifty people present. The proceedings of that day are given in Chapter I.

During the year he ascertained that Capt. W. B. Allbright, a Confederate, had been a resident of Columbus for several years, but had not let himself be known as such. He consented to join in the service the coming year, for which quite extensive preparations were made, with the result that probably a hundred people were present. About this time five or six friends in sympathy with the cause paid for some shrubbery and young trees, which were placed in the cemetery.

While riding in a carriage with Gen. J. B. Gordon during one of his visits to Columbus the writer asked if, in his opinion, the Southern people would appreciate the service and care of the ground enough to send some flowers for the following spring ceremony, when with a comrade's demonstration he said: "My dear friend, my people in the South would be happy to have the pleasure of sending their choicest flowers for the purpose of decorating those graves. Through my Adjutant General Moorman I will see that the people of the South are made acquainted with your desires, and you will have the flowers and the prayers of them all." At the proper time a request was made of General Moorman, and the flowers came in large quantities for the service in 1897. On this occasion there were present 1,000 to 1,500 persons. The principal addresses were made by Judge David F. Pugh, an ex-Union soldier, and Col. Bennett H. Young, an ex-Confederate. Both addresses were highly appreciated, and published in the newspapers here and throughout the South.

The writer emphasizes the fact that the newspapers of Columbus not only treated that first meeting with great consideration, but the same attention has been given to each succeeding year on the Memorial Day at Camp Chase as to the annual decoration exercises over the graves of the Union dead.

The author was subjected to much unkind criticism by his Northern comrades, so that this public indorsement by the press was very gratifying. Time, which softens the heart's bitterness by the harsh deeds of war, has failed to remove all the enmities born of that first service at Camp Chase. The author does not seek sympathy from his friends in the South because of this, for he undertook the work keenly alert to the fact that there would be opposition.

On one occasion—the presentation of a floral piece—a committee, self-constituted perhaps, sent for him to appear at the Statehouse, where meetings of the committee were being held. He did not go, but a member of the committee came to his office and proceeded to lecture him on the error of his ways, demanding to know who paid for the design in question, and that he desist from conducting these memorials for the Southern soldiers. In reply he made a few remarks expressive of his indignation, and then promptly left.

Following the service of 1897 some eight or ten ex-Confederates in the county were found, who, with the exception of one or two, united with us. These thought it would injure their business to be known. That the graves might be shaded by trees from their native land, application was made to the different States in the South for a donation, and each State contributed ten trees, but unfortunately very few of them lived.

The G. A. R. Drill Corps, the Uniform Company of Veterans, which had assisted year after year at Camp Chase, as at the Union Cemetery, firing salutes, were at last requested by the Adjutant General of the Department of Ohio, G. A. R.—prompted by certain G. A. R. men of Columbus—not to attend the Confederate services. Colonel Coit, commanding the Fourth Regiment Ohio National Guard, hearing of the action, tendered a company of his and a regimental band for the occasion; the services of which were gratefully accepted.

Notwithstanding the opposition, the work went on each year. The interest grew, the crowds came, and the people of the South sent flowers to place upon the graves of their dead heroes.

In 1898 the presence of the Confederate Glee Club from Louisville, Ky., added greatly to the interest of the services. Col. Bennett Young, of the same city, was again one of the orators of the occasion, and so well was he gratified that he planned to have presented to the G. A. R. upon the following year the floral design symbolic of the peace and harmony existing between the sections. The design, a most beautiful and expensive one, was ready for May 30.

The writer attended a meeting of a joint committee in charge of the Memorial Day exercises at Post Hall for the purpose of having the design accepted and placed on the lot known as the "Circle," where the ritualistic services of the G. A. R. are conducted. The joint committee was in session when he arrived, and had drawn up resolutions condemning the acceptance of such an emblem. After listening to the reading of the resolutions, he asked the chairman if the sentiments expressed were those of the committee, and all answered in the affirmative. He then expressed disgust at their unsoldierlike action. Arrangements were then made to have the design placed in a wagon and follow the parade, with printed banners, telling the people of Columbus what it was and what it meant. This plan did not carry, however, because the Ex-Soldiers and Sailors' Association, hearing of the action of those G. A. R. men, said: "Put that floral piece on the Ex-Soldiers and Sailors' lot; we will be pleased to accept it."

Leaning against the splendid monument erected by the county upon their lot the beautiful floral picture was placed. From out of a bed of immortelles came an arm with a sleeve of blue holding a flag of *Our Country,* and from the other side was an arm with a sleeve of gray extended to receive the flag. The emblem was one of the most elaborate floral pieces ever seen in this city, and was the sensation of the day. At the proper time it was presented to the ex-soldiers and sailors of Franklin County, Ohio, in the following words: "You see, my comrades, this beautiful design which is the gift of Southern friends who wore the gray, to be placed over the graves of men who wore the blue. It is fit that it should be here, for the sons of the North and South are marching under one flag. I feel, my comrades, that the men who knew the least of war's hardships are the bitterest to-day. There are exceptions, I admit. We do not envy that man who, in the face of this expression of unity, seeing the grand uprising of the North and South for the glory and honor of America, can coldly turn his back upon the outstretched hand of his brother. In the name of the donor, my friend in the South, I present to you this emblem of a reunited people, wishing that it may be received in the spirit in which it is offered."

The Ex-Soldiers' Society has selected Col. S. N. Cook to formally accept the design, who said: "We receive this most beautiful token of a new and splendid era in the history of our country when on Northern graves lie fragrant blossoms of the South, and on graves of Southern soldiers rest Northern blossoms. With pride and thankfulness the oldest veteran organization in the city of Columbus, born before the Grand Army was, accepts this beautiful gift from brave men. If there was no other reason for accepting this gift than the mere fact that Fitzhugh Lee, the Virginian, is wearing to-day a uniform of blue, and soldiers from North and South vie with each other in doing honor to him, we should accept it. We should place it where it is, and treasure it afterwards as a gift beyond price. The gift reminds us also that Gen. Joe Wheeler is in the saddle again. When I see the men of the South marching with steady tread under the folds of our glorious banner, then it is indeed a pleasure and an honor to accept such a token of esteem from the South."

The newspapers spoke enthusiastically of this event, and the only criticism came from the few who seemed to forget that they had fought no man in gray for over forty years.

We turn with pleasure from this unpleasant side of the subject to the erection and unveiling of the monumental arch, an event of great pleasure to the author. Elsewhere this event is narrated in detail. In that part of the history devoted to the year 1902, Mr. W. P. Harrison is given credit for his generous donation toward the arch and monument, which came unsolicited and unexpectedly, and for which the author will ever feel grateful.

The monument would have been erected had no generous friend been found, and not a dollar would have been asked or accepted from the South. The writer felt it a duty that he owed his friends, as well as a testimony to the dead, for he has found in the last eight years that no matter where he has met a Southerner he met a friend.

The unutterable loneliness and shameful disorder of Camp Chase Cemetery as it was when first seen by the writer moved his heart to pity, and he felt impelled to do what has been done, and the result has been that the monumenal arch was built to the perfect satisfaction and gratitude of the delegations from West Virginia, Kentucky, and other portions of the South, and of all who have seen it.

The events just related lead to a time after the ex-Confederates in the county had formed a Confederate Camp, and the Southern ladies a Chapter of the Daughters of the Confederacy here in Columbus, and this having been done, he concluded, when the monument was unveiled and presented to the Confederates, that his work was completed.

The presentation of the monument was made by a G. A. R. comrade, Judge David F. Pugh, and received by an ex-Confederate Congressman, David E. Johnston, of Bluefield, W. Va., Gen. J. B. Gordon, who was to receive it, being unable to be present. With the presentation of the monumental arch the care and charge of the cemetery was turned over to the Daughters of the Confederacy.

The monument was unveiled by the writer's daughter, Elizabeth May (John T.) Gamble, and Florence Tucker (John H.) Winder, assisted by Mrs. David Lindsey (T. M.) Worcester. From the beginning his wife and children, together with Miss Sadie Stimmel, Mr. Charles Roth, and Mr. Thomas J. Davies, gave him constant assistance in the work.

There was opposition to the erection of the monument, notwithstanding the greatly improved sentiment, and threats were made that if done it would be blown up. Two men were employed to stay at the grounds during its erection, and to guard it at night for some ten days after the unveiling, but no one attempted to molest it. It may have been because the Governor of the State of Ohio, Hon. George K. Nash, had been present, and had made a speech full of sympathy for the occasion, or it may have been because of fear of the Northern soldiers guarding it. When the storm was most bitter, the gentle-hearted McKinley, at Atlanta, spoke words that well might silence the criticism that followed my every attempt to honor the last resting place of the Confederate dead, and it is fitting that in this personal chapter this splendid sentiment be repeated: *"Every soldier's grave made during the unfortunate Civil War is a tribute to American valor;* and while when these graves were made we differed widely about the future of the government, those differences were long ago settled by the arbitrament of arms—and the time has now come in the evolution of sentiment and feeling, under the providence of God, when, in the spirit of fraternity, we should share with you in the care of the graves of the Confederate dead."

The President had uttered these words in 1898. Some of the seeds of kindness fell upon stony places. There were some even in 1902 who hated the sight of that arch.

At this point, even though good taste offending, the writer quotes from Circular Letter No. 86, United Confederate Veterans, May 20, 1898, the words of Adjutant General Moorman, published in the *Confederate Veteran:*

To All Commanders and Confederate Veteran Camps.

At Camp Chase, Ohio, where 2,260 Confederate soldiers are buried, that noble "American," Col. William H. Knauss, a brave Union soldier, and his grand coworkers have designated June 4 next as the date for Decoration Day, when ceremonies will be observed and flowers will be strewn over these 2,260 long-neglected graves, where rest the heroes, sleeping far away from homes, kindred, and loved ones.

It is well known that the cemetery which contains the remains of these Southern soldiers was rescued from decay and neglect, repaired, a stone wall built around the place, trees and shrubbery planted, the grounds cleaned up, and an annual Decoration Day observed, through the humanity and patriotism of Govs. R. B. Hayes and J. B. Foraker, the golden-hearted William H. Knauss, Mr. Henry Briggs, a farmer living near, Capt. W. B. Allbright, an ex-Confederate soldier, and a few other friends.

By order of   John B. Gordon, *General Commander.*

The Heaven-gifted orator, the knightly soldier, the splendid gentleman has gone from us, but the perfume of his good deeds remains to make the world sweeter. In life his hand clasped the writer's and somewhere and sometime our hands will clasp again.

In telling the story of Camp Chase and Johnson's Island much information was secured through the courtesy of others. The author has drawn liberally upon the *Confederate Veteran,* Nashville, upon all of the Columbus papers, the Sandusky *Register,* and other Ohio newspapers. He desires to express his gratitude also to Captains McNeil, Dinkins, Herbert, Lieutenant Mitchell, D. H. Strother, and Majors Wilson and Marlowe for interesting reminiscences, and Mr. C. B. Galbraith, Ohio State Librarian, for the long-lost letters given. The author is impressed with the idea that such a history as this should be given before all those who had a part in it were dead, and many Southern friends have urged it. It is a simple story of men who endured much, who fought bravely, and they who survived went back to their commands and fought again, and when it was all over went home—generally speaking to desolate homes—but one rich in love and affection, if there was a Southern woman in that home. Those who died here went to their final rest as became brave men.

The history of these prisons of Ohio has been gathered from various sources—from survivors who remember well the time of their captivity, from diaries kept by prisoners, and from histories of regiments, etc.

With no thought but that of pride and admiration for the great American people, regarding no North or no South, but a land rich in memories of its brave dead, this volume is offered.

THE STORY OF CAMP CHASE.

CHAPTER I.

DECORATING THE GRAVES—1896.

After Long Years Strangers Pay Tribute to the Valor of the Southern Dead—The First Programme at Camp Chase—What Was Said That Day and Who Said It—A Stranger from the South Had Something to Say—An Afternoon Where Tenderness Reigned—More Than Two Thousand Flags Fluttering over Low Green Mounds—The Setting Sun Stoops to Kiss the Little Banners as It Sinks to Rest—Left Alone in Their Slumbers.

IN the Introduction the reader was enabled to see the beginning of an annual event, uncommon in the North. When those who began this work shall have gone to their rest, the service will continue.

Because of the uniqueness of its beginning, opposition to it from unlooked-for sources, and because of the warm hand-clasps and tender words of commendation from the South, the history of these events is given. The press, both North and South, have published columns, making the telling less difficult than if one told the story of this simple work from memory. Necessarily the author draws upon these detailed facts, and thus the friends of those who sleep at Camp Chase, Ohio, may see how the strangers, at last, after long years, came to pay reverence to their memory as American soldiers, whether or not in sympathy with the cause in which they were engaged.

The first complete programme of exercises at Camp Chase Cemetery was held upon the afternoon of June 5, 1896. A small service was held there in 1895.

The day was beautiful, and the little cemetery was decorated with two thousand two hundred and sixty American flags waving over the dust of mortals who nearly forty years before had fought bravely, during the battle storm, under the "Stars and Bars."

Quiet, orderly, and reverential were the fifty or more persons
who gathered to take part in or listen to the services. Hushed
were the voices, as though the sleeping ones might be awakened
from their rest.

Speaking of this occasion, the *Press-Post,* of Columbus, said:

The little Confederate Cemetery at Camp Chase, with its
green, waving elm trees, its long grass rank with the richness
of the graveyard, its birds the only creatures that until yesterday
ever sang a hymn over the last resting place of over two
thousand brave men, its deathlike peace—the little cemetery, with
its long ranks of the dead, was the scene of one of the most
remarkable events ever witnessed in this country. It was a sight
that proved that the bitterness of war time can die away even
with those who experienced all the heat and passion of the
battle, who went through the long, weary marches, who lay in
the mud of the trenches under the fire of the enemies' guns, and
who froze or famished in dreary camps. Veterans of the Union
army were assisted by veterans of the Southern Confederacy
in the beautiful work of laying flowers upon the graves of two
thousand two hundred and sixty Confederate dead who lie under
the grass and in the shade of the trees in the stone-girdled
cemetery.

No scene could have been more impressive, especially to
those who knew from experience the sadness of the fate of those
who had given up their lives and had died in a strange country
for that which they believed to be right. For many years the
graves were overrun with weeds and brambles, and the cattle
of the country wandered over the heads of the men whose valor
was greater than that of Spartan. With the exception of the
towering elms, which were bushes when the sleepers went to
their final rest, only noxious plants grew there. To-day there
are flowers and flags and women's tears. Grizzled warriors of
the Union stood with bared heads, reverent at the graves of men
once foes. Men who had stood guard with loaded muskets over
these long-departed enemies paused to drop a tear and lay a
flower full of meaning upon their graves. A few scarred ex-
Confederates, silent, solemn, and wondering, looked on at the
strange sight.

The speakers' stand was a cart brought there by some
farmer in the neighborhood; and when the hour for the beginning was reached, the Chairman, W. H. Knauss, mounted the
cart and, after a song, delivered the following address:

My friends and American citizens, about us and within this
inclosure are buried American citizens. For many years this
burial ground was open commons, overgrown by briers and

brush, until about ten years ago, when Governor Foraker in his message referred to it as a disgrace and unworthy of a Christian people. From his interest in the matter the government built this wall and the place was cleared of brambles; but from that time until last year no attention had been given to it other than occasionally by individuals, when Governor Hayes secured an appropriation of twenty-five dollars a year from the contingent fund to cut away the briers, bushes, etc.

We will commence these humble exercises without apologies, other than to say that we wish to pay respect to some unknown dead who were American citizens and who died in a cause which they believed was right; and I ask each of you present not to judge or criticise our motives or actions until we are through. If we have done that which is unbecoming American citizens, we are willing to be censured for the act of decorating these men's graves. This movement is not gotten up by any association or society. I take all the responsibility as a citizen and a soldier.

As our Heavenly Father set for us in the sky a rainbow in remembrance of the storm, so our forefathers left us this beautiful flag, whose colors were taken from the heavens in remembrance of the stormy battles where they shed their blood for liberty and freedom—for free schools, free speech, and free ballot. I have been to this place a number of times, and each time I have said to myself: "They were American citizens, they were men, they had mothers and sisters, some had wives and children, all praying to one God and Father; and O how many a prayer went up that these unfortunate dead might be returned to their homes!"

Alas! the fate of war decreed otherwise, and where their bodies lie is in many instances unknown to their loved ones. There has been a patriotic revival during the past few years among American citizens. Societies have been formed to expound American principles, to impress upon the young what it has cost to perpetuate these principles.

Being a descendant of soldiers from Revolutionary times, my great-grandfather having been in that war, my two grandfathers in the War of 1812, my father in the Mexican War, and my only brother and myself in the War between the States, I cannot help having respect for conscientious soldiers. I fully believe we should never be timid in a matter of honor or where an expression of our patriotism is needed.

Therefore my conclusion is that it is not unpatriotic or un-American to do what we are doing here to-day. If I were in the South and saw an ex-Confederate do honor to an unknown soldier's grave, I would say with all my soul: "God bless you and yours forever!"

One hundred and twenty years ago three or four thousand

PRISON STOCKADE, CAMP CHASE, COLUMBUS, OHIO, 1862.

half-clad, shoeless, depressed, and dispirited patriots, made up
of the then thirteen colonies, marching under the scowling December sky, pelted by the pitiless storm of sleet and rain, crossed
the Delaware and before daybreak drove in the British sentinels.
The enemy had spent the night in drunkenness and revelry, but
Washington led his tattered legions on.   The commanding officer
of the enemy and many of his men were killed and wounded,
and a thousand were captured.   The surviving British galloped
away, leaving their allies to the mercy of their foe.   If Washington and his army had been destroyed, there would have been
an end to the war.   Victory crowned his efforts; and the battle
of Trenton, measured by its results, was the decisive battle of
the Revolutionary War.

Who composed this army of men from the colonies?   Who

FOUR-MILE HOUSE, OPPOSITE CAMP CHASE.

were these patriotic soldiers?   Men from the North and South.
Who was this man Washington, upon his knees in the snow at
Valley Forge praying to God for guidance and for victory?   He
was a Virginian and a patriot.   Who were his soldiers in that
war?   Men from the North and South who fought for liberty.
Who said: "My life you can have, but never my loyalty and my
principles for freedom and my country?"   They were American
citizens from the North and the South.   These dead soldiers
lying here should not have tried to overthrow this grand republic
that cost such sacrifice.   Though we do not seek to justify their
cause, to place flowers on their graves is Christianlike.   "Charity
is the true spirit of Christianity," and charity prompts our acts
to-day.   These symbols of purity we offer at these lowly graves;
these American flags are given that future generations may

emulate the unselfish devotion of even the lowliest of these dead soldiers.

At the conclusion of this address the Chairman introduced Gen. E. J. Pocock, who said:

With malice toward none, with charity for all, we come here to-day to decorate the graves of those known only as deceased prisoners of war. Under the sod of this field, once a military prison, are buried two thousand and more Confederate captives. Sickness and disease carried them to a grave in this inclosure, known in history as Camp Chase. The soldiers here buried have gone to where no man returns. In meeting here these men are not enemies, but brothers of a common country blood. They took up arms against this grand government. The government conquered, the South is reconciled; we are a common country and common fellow-men. For a moment let us forget the battles of Stone River, Chickamauga, Nashville, Gettysburg, Antietam, the Wilderness, the sieges of Vicksburg and Petersburg. Let us forget the cry of "On to Richmond!" the march to the sea, and the thought of Andersonville and Libby. Let us think of the unknown dead lying here, of the mothers, wives, and children who mourn their loss, and of the homes made desolate by the cruel fate of war. These men died for a cause that we thought was wrong, but they gave up their lives believing they were right in their cause. To-day we are to think of them as the brave men who fought on many bloody battlefields, as the men in Pickett's charge at Gettysburg and in Cleburne's and Cheatham's charges at Franklin. This hour we are to forget the past and think of the sad hearts who in the many years since the war have mourned for their dear ones who lie here in unknown graves.

Rev. Dr. T. G. Dickson, pastor of the King Avenue Methodist Episcopal Church, was called from the audience. The Doctor had not been in either army, being a mere boy during the war. After making some appropriate remarks, he closed by saying: "May the roots of the tree of Liberty entwine the bowels of the earth and its branches tower among the clouds."

Gen. Thomas E. Powell, who enlisted as a boy sixteen years old, was present and was called unexpectedly to say something. He said that he was glad to join in this tribute to his old foes. He was glad to see the spirit exhibited on both sides. Peace had brought its blessings, and the men of the South were as loyal after the war as the men of the North. The General spoke of the Cuban struggle for independence, and said that if it became necessary Ohio and Virginia would combine and send enough men to the field to establish the independence of the brave little island. He considered this occasion second in importance as an indication of the good feeling between the North and the South only to the mingling of the blue and the gray at the Gettysburg meeting.

"America" was sung by all present, led by Mr. Nolan. Then Col. S. N. Cook was called out. He told of his experience as a guard at Camp Chase, of his suffering in Southern prisons, and of acts of kindness done him by Confederate soldiers. He told of his boyish captor and the boy's wish that the war would end, that he might see his home once more. He said: "I am only fifteen, and I am so tired of this fighting and marching all the time. My mother would shut the door in my face if I went home before the war is over—unless I am wounded."

"This was in 1862, at Harper's Ferry, Va.," the speaker continued, "and I wonder if he is lying asleep here now, or did he at last get home? It was a long road from Harper's Ferry to Appomattox."

The services were about to be concluded, when a fine-looking, elderly gentleman, with a snow-white mustache, an imperial of the Southerner, stepped forward and said with marked accents of the South: "I beg your pardon, sir, but may I say something?" He was asked his name, but at first declined to give it, until a prominent railroad man and a friend of his introduced him as a Mr. W. H. Gardner, a business man of Union City, Tenn. Mr. Gardner said he came to the service as a Southern man. He had fought for more than four years in the Southern army, and he wanted to thank these men of the Northern army for this demonstration. Politicians had tried to make the South believe that there was bitterness in the North against that section, but he knew better and so did the other Southern people. He wished that the mothers of the brave boys who slept in that cemetery could look down and witness the magnificent tribute paid them by men who fought against them and won. The war was over, and all were proud to know that Ulysses S. Grant was an American citizen. So were all proud of the glory of Robert E. Lee and Stonewall Jackson. He was glad to be among such people as he had met there. He would carry back with him most pleasant recollections of his short sojourn in the capital of Ohio, and he would devote himself to telling his neighbors of the touching tribute paid to the Southern dead. Mr. Gardner said that it was the first speech that he had ever made in his life, but he felt impelled to express his appreciation of this beautiful action. At the close of his remarks he was trembling like a little girl. The veterans of the armies of Grant and Lee crowded around to shake his hand, and he received an ovation.

Everybody joined in singing the doxology, and Dr. Dickson pronounced the benediction.

Some of the incidents of that day and the reminiscences that occasion revived are worth telling. Some of the veterans present remembered the story of one marked grave. Just within the shadow of the inclosure stood a simple stone on which was a plain inscription telling that the body that had moldered in the earth beneath was that of George Raney, who was born in Livermore, Ky. There was never a better exemplification of the honors of the war in which brothers fought against brothers. George Raney was a Southern sympathizer, a believer in the greatness of the State over the Nation. His brother loved the flag of the Union and enlisted to defend it. George was wounded and made a prisoner of war. He was brought to Camp Chase. His brother was there as a Union soldier and had to stand guard over him. But blood was thicker than water. All that brother could do for brother was done, but the boy in gray was dying. The struggle was over—only peace now. The simple shaft standing to-day was the tribute of love—the Blue and the Gray.

Many lingered in the grounds until the sun was far down the western sky—lingered and talked in subdued tones. The birds ceased wondering at the thousand little flags which grew so suddenly on the low mounds, and began their evening songs of praise. The cattle in the fields were going home as the last participant in the services turned away. The leaves upon the elms were whispering as though something unseen was asking what these flags and flowers meant. It meant much to one man who is yet thankful.

So closed the first public ceremony for the Confederate dead at Camp Chase. Nature smiled upon it all, the day had been perfect, and the sun as it sank behind a slow-rising cloud kissed tenderly the waving flags.

CHAPTER II.

CARING FOR THE GRAVES—1897.

A Larger Crowd—A Southern Orator, Colonel Bennett H. Young, Addresses the People Assembled—Address of Judge David F. Pugh, a
Northern Veteran—The Chairman Reviews the History of the Cemetery—The Mayor of the City Speaks Briefly—Some Letters from the
South; Also Cash—The Second Memorial Service over the Confederate Dead a Success.

THERE is of necessity some similarity in such services as these
memorial events, but it will interest those for whom this volume
is written.

The preceding chapter relates at length the details of that
first decoration. Through the newspapers the South learned that
there were Union soldiers who were pleased to show a gentle
courtesy to the dead. In the introductory chapter mention was
made of the fact that there was an unpleasant side to these
events—the criticism of friends and comrades. But when one
has done as conscience dictates, prompted by the charity taught
by the lowly Nazarene, the criticisms fall harmless. One can
easily forget the unpleasant side when he reads the letters from
warm-hearted friends that he has not and possibly will never see
on earth.

Many of these letters will be reproduced here, that the writers
may know that the wastebasket did not receive them.

To-day Confederate comrades are performing the work begun
by the Union soldier who tells this story.

When the time came to prepare for the next decoration services
there were many to assist. Those who took part in the services
of 1896 were men unknown to the people of the North or South,
or, for that matter, to the public at large of Columbus.

At the 1897 memorial, however, a brilliant Southern orator was
present, and thrilled the assembled multitude with his impassioned eloquence; also a distinguished jurist, a Past Post Commander and Past Department Commander of the G. A. R., delivered an address at once interesting and able. The Southern

DECORATION SERVICE, CAMP CHASE, 1897.

soldier was Col. Bennett H. Young, of Kentucky, and the North- ern soldier was Judge David F. Pugh, of Columbus. The exer- cises were held at Camp Chase Cemetery June 6; and again, as on the year before, nature was benign and the day was as fair as the occasion was pleasing. At the first service the flowers were from the lawn and gardens of Columbus and from the dooryards of the farmers living near by, but in 1897 there came loads of flowers from the South. The people of the South as well as our home citizens became interested in the almost forgotten graves—graves of the dead so long asleep here. So many were the questions asked, and so few seemed to remember anything about Camp Chase Cemetery, that the following facts were gath- ered, some of which have been incidentally mentioned, but being a part of the exercises of that day, they are here presented.

The land was leased by the government during the war and continued to April 23, 1879, when it was bought by the govern- ment and described as the Confederate cemetery formerly occu- pied by the Camp Chase rebel prison. At the close of the war the barracks were torn down and the old lumber used to build a fence around the cemetery.

There was a wooden headboard with name and number of company, State, and date of burial inscribed, placed at each grave. Subsequently the government replaced this with a substantial plank, with the same inscription, but in a few years all decayed. Eventually, because of neglect, the ground became a bramble patch.

When Ex-President Hayes was Governor, Mr. Henry Briggs, a farmer in the neighborhood, was employed to clean up and take care of the cemetery and to be paid $25 per year out of the contingent fund. This was continued until Mr. Bishop was elected Governor, when he ordered it stopped. The place became a wild waste again until Hon. J. B. Foraker became Governor. He then caused Adjt. Gen. Axline to correspond with the general government and explain the condition it was in and the disgrace it was to the State, urging that it be given attention. The action resulted in an appropriation sufficient to build a substantial stone wall around Camp Chase Cemetery and an iron fence around the Confederate burial ground at Johnson's Island.

A large bowlder was procured and bears the inscription: "2,260 Confederate soldiers of the war 1861-65 buried in this inclosure.'"

There were from Virginia, 337; Kentucky, 158; Tennessee, 239; Alabama, 431; Texas, 22; Georgia, 265; South Carolina, 85; North Carolina, 85; Arkansas, 25; Mississippi, 202; Florida, 62; Maryland, 9; Missouri, 8; Louisiana, 52; and unknown, about

HON. J. B. FORAKER.

280. Of these, 135 were buried in the City Cemetery, southeast of Columbus, and afterwards removed to this inclosure.

At Camp Dennison, near Cincinnati, there are buried 116 Confederate soldiers—from Alabama, 7; Arkansas, 2; Mississippi, 4; Texas, 5; Louisiana, 11; Tennessee, 1; and unknown, 36. Many of these were taken home by their people, and the others were brought to Camp Chase.

At Johnson's Island there are buried 206 Confederate soldiers—

from Alabama, 19; Arkansas, 16; Virginia, 20; Georgia, 12; North Carolina, 17; Louisiana, 3; Mississippi, 16; Tennessee, 20; Missouri, 5; Kentucky, 7; South Carolina, 4; Florida, 5; Choctaw Cavalry, 3; John Dow, from Pulaski, Ohio, a citizen; and unknown, 57—making a grand total in Ohio of two thousand five hundred and eighty-two.

With the work last year you are all familiar; the newspapers gave us credit as Americans doing honor to our great country. I would like for you to read some of the many letters received from the friends and relatives of those buried here. I will give a few extracts from a letter received from Gen. George Moorman, of New Orleans, La., Adjutant General of the Confederate organization:

It will be a revelation to many, and will come in the nature of a surprise and benediction, that, while kindred and loved ones are scattering flowers over the graves of their dead on Southern soils, strangers—aye, our former foes—are decorating with spring's choicest flowers the graves of our known and unknown dead who sleep upon Northern soil, so far from home and kindred, but who, as you justly say, will always live in history as patriots. God bless you and Gov. J. B. Foraker and Mr. Henry Briggs, and all honor to the memory of Ex-President Hayes, for the noble Christian spirit you have displayed in the preservation of these neglected graves of the dead from every Southern State!

All that was said that day cannot be reproduced, but the story of the occasion would not be complete if passages from the addresses of Colonel Young and Judge Pugh were omitted. Colonel Young said:

We are gathered this afternoon to contemplate one of the sequences to the happenings of that crucial period in human history. I should be wanting in a conception of the proprieties of this occasion if any reference were made to the cause of that great struggle upon which the people of the North and South entered at that hour. These braves over which you are here to scatter these beautiful flowers—heaven's sweet messengers—are peaceful but eloquent witnesses of the awful sacrifice the war entailed. The struggle lasted fifteen hundred days, the deaths from all causes averaged three hundred every twenty-four hours. In the South, whence these dead warriors came, there were no exempted communities and but few unstricken households, and the tidings from the front came freighted with woe and sadness. Every breeze that sighed in the trees was a requiem for some one's dead, and every rustle of the wind among the pines was a mourning song for that Southern land.   If we had some quantity by which we could measure grief, or figures by which we could calculate the worth of sobs or the value of woman's tears, what

COL. BENNETT H. YOUNG.

countless treasures the people of America could lay aside as the possession of those who bore the trial of the war of the sixties!

The scene which we witness here to-day in the great State of Ohio, which also made tremendous sacrifice in the war and gave much of its best and noblest blood to maintain the Federal cause, has but few parallels in the history of the world.   It is nearly thirty-four years since, as a prisoner of war, I was confined in Camp Chase, and at the moment I recall with vivid recollection the surroundings where several hundred Confederates were summoned from the inclosure for transportation to Camp Douglas, at Chicago.

We had come in a few months to realize some of the most distressing phases of war. The excitement, commotion, and the din of a great war then encompassed the city on every side, and the uppermost thought in every mind was the prosecution of hostilities and the enforcement of Southern submission,

That great contest, the most stupendous the world ever saw, is ended. There are none but freemen in this great land. The shackles of the slaves have been broken, and the principles for which the Federal army fought have prevailed. But though Federal armies triumphed and the doctrines maintained by the North have become the accepted law of the land, yet the magnanimity and the humanity of a few people remain untouched and undimmed, and I defy human history to produce a record of an event similar to this.

Surely there can be no higher testimonial to republican institutions or to the breadth and nobleness of American manhood and womanhood than that I, as one who fought those you loved and sent to do battle for your cause, should on this beautiful afternoon find you decorating the graves of those who opposed you and listening to the kindly words which I speak at the sepulchers of departed comrades.

It would be untrue to the great Confederate host whom I represent if there were expressions of sorrow or regret for the loyalty and faithfulness of the Southern people to their section in that conflict; but it would be equally untrue to the highest sentiments of a brave and chivalrous people if I did not with the most grateful words and with the highest admiration and profoundest gratitude offer sincerest praise and unmeasured thankfulness for such magnanimity to the Southern dead. . . .

They made the costliest sacrifice man can make for any cause, and the mournful fact that few who loved them have come to weep at their sepulchers or place fresh flowers on their graves pleads with irresistible eloquence the generosity of those within whose gates they died and so sadly found a place of burial. Somewhere in the stricken land whence they came loving hearts mourn their loss. There are vacant chairs that will never be filled, there are firesides which will never be the same, because these warriors never will return, and there are those who will love on in silence and in tears until the end.

The mothers who mourn these sons here buried in your midst, the sisters who weep for the return of brothers who here went down to the oblivion of unknown sepulcher, and all who long for the sight of vanished forms and the sounds of silenc'd voices, which found the end in these Confederate graves, will rise up and call you blessed, and somewhere in the register of heaven there will be a place to record the graciousness and mercifulness of these unselfish and benignant acts.

At the conclusion of his oration Colonel Young unfolded a faded gray jacket and recited two verses of the touching poem,

JUDGE DAVID F. PUGH.

"The Jacket of Gray," and when he had finished the entire audience broke forth in one great shout.

Space forbids and the reader would doubtless weary if all the speeches of all the years were reproduced in this volume, so it is that only portions of even such excellent addresses as those of Colonel Young and Judge Pugh are given.

Judge Pugh on this occasion said:

The poverty of human language is such that the heroism of

both Union and Confederate soldiers cannot be described. They fought honorably and died honorably. These men whose graves are being decorated were not victors: their cause failed, but their failure was a priceless blessing to both South and North. Both Blue and Gray can clasp hands and rejoice over that common victory.

The whole land was made to blush with blood and was drenched with tears; peace, happiness, and joy fled from thousands of firesides; the land was filled with cripples; the wail of the orphans crying to heaven and the moans of the widows saddening the earth were over all the land.

These were the immediate results of the war. But, in obedience to the great law of compensation, labor was emancipated, our prosperous activities quickened and deepened, the energy and skill which had been used in destructive war were turned into peaceful and constructive industries, making a splendor of national progress which was unparalleled. It is doubtful if the four years of blood and unspeakable anguish were not, after all, more noble and glorious than have been the thirty succeeding years of peace.

It is honorable to come here and decorate the graves of these men. It is convincing evidence that the Union in its sublimest significance is established when such events as this occur.

Carrying two wounds made by Confederate bullets, I am perfectly willing that their graves may be decorated, and even to participate in it when their survivors are not numerous enough to do it. I am willing to admit that their heroism is a part of our national heritage. I am willing that their survivors or admirers may erect monuments to perpetuate their memories. I am willing that their surviving comrades may be elected to as high an office as Vice President of the United States. I am willing on proper occasions to meet with them and celebrate the valor of both the Blue and the Gray. I am willing to join in prayer to our Heavenly Father that he will watch over and bless the veterans of both armies. This sort of fraternal forbearance and generosity is, in my humble judgment, one of the surest guarantees of stability for the future of our common country.

Mayor Black spoke briefly and recited the poem entitled "The Blue and the Gray."

Chaplain DeBruin pronounced the benediction, and the second memorial service or Confederate Decoration Day at Camp Chase was near the end and but little else was said.

The voice of an officer dressed in blue was heard to say: "Ready! Aim! Fire!" Captain Bidwell's company of the Fourteenth Infantry, Ohio National Guard, firing the salute.

(Later, when the war with Spain came, this company went with its regiment to the front, and there and since has been known as the Fourth Ohio.) Then, when the sun was low, there came pealing forth that most plaintive call on bugle: "Lights out!" Long ere this the South knew what had been done the year before; and as the crowd left, the odor of Southern flowers followed them as blessings follow righteous deeds.

That the letters received in response to notices sent to Confederate camps by direction of General Gordon may be fully understood I will state that I believed that the veterans of the Confederacy, with hearts as liberal as they were brave, might wish to aid in this work, and through Adjutant General Moorman the matter was explained to the various Camps, and the responses showed the unanimity of sentiment which prevailed throughout the South.

From the letters received each year it will be seen that the ex-Confederate has not ceased to remember that his Northern friends wished to pay loving tribute to his comrades so long asleep.

The statement of receipts and expenditures for 1897 shows thirty-two Camps and individuals responding, and the list of expenses shows that they responded to some purpose. Amount received, $142.50; amount expended, $145.30.

In a great scrapbook all the letters received are filed, and when this story has been told they will be there—there to remain until the work is done and the laborer has gone to his rest. All itemized receipts and expenses were sent to George Moorman, Adjutant General of the United Confederate Veterans, and *The Confederate Veteran*, published at Nashville, Tenn.

CHAPTER III.

THE INTEREST GROWING—1898.

Again Orators of the North and the South Pay Tribute to the Silent Dead—Patriotic Lessons Taught—The Confederate Glee Club from Louisville Is Present—Colonel Young, Captain Leathers, and Mr. Osborne the Southern Speakers, Captain G. H. Bargar Representing the North—Letter from a Texas Veteran—A Lady from Atlanta Writes Encouragingly—"You Will Be Gratefully Remembered by Us; Yours for America on Land or Sea."

Welcome.

Here's to the Veterans of the South.
   They fought, it is true, in gray;
But the heart goes out in the word of mouth
   To greet them in love to-day.

The strife is ended, and now we stand,
   United in love's sweet thrall;
And we look aloft, as the hand clasps hand,
   To the one flag over us all.
                                        —Columbus Dispatch.

ON Saturday, June 4, 1898, there was held the annual decoration service at Camp Chase Cemetery. Col. Bennett H. Young came again and was most heartily welcomed by both Blue and Gray. Those who had heard his eloquent and patriotic address the year before wished to hear the music of his voice again.

Ex-Gov. Robert Taylor, of Tennessee, came also and delivered a most feeling address. With Colonel Young came the Confederate Glee Club of Louisville, Ky., which organization attracted a great deal of attention both from the public and the press. Capt. John H. Leathers, of Louisville, was also present, and spoke with great earnestness and feeling.

The chief addresses were by Colonel Young, of Louisville, and Capt. Gilbert H. Bargar, of Columbus. Each of these gentlemen fought in the war of 1861-65, Colonel Young with the South and Captain Barger on the side of the North.

PREPARING FOR DECORATION SERVICE, CAMP CHASE, 1898.

DECORATION SERVICE, CAMP CHASE, 1898. SHOWING GLEE CLUB FROM LOUISVILLE, KY., TO LEFT OF BOWLDER.

Only one sentiment prevailed through the entire occasion—the dead were honored as men who fought bravely, and by Americans was their bravery recognized. In recording the events of that occasion it is fitting to quote from the *Press-Post* of June 5 the sentiments uttered so happily in keeping with the day:

There may be found within the pages of fiction a more thrilling scene than that witnessed at Camp Chase yesterday afternoon when the veterans who wore the blue stood side by side with the veterans who wore the gray, and strewed flowers upon the graves of the unknown dead buried at Camp Chase, yet in reality such another beautiful picture will hardly ever be witnessed.

To those who stood by the graves of the known and unknown Southern dead, and saw the battle-scarred soldier of the North slowly and reverentially advance to the little green-covered mounds and tenderly lay upon them garlands of roses or fresh and fragrant cut flowers, there was a lesson engraved upon their minds that the ravages of time can never erase. It was the act of a hero to the memory of a fallen and defeated foe; an acknowledgment to his Southern brother, whom he respected for his convictions and honored for the bravery he displayed in offering his life for what he considered was right.

From the sunny Southland came the men who had fought while wearing the gray and against the glorious old flag to lay upon the silent sepulcher of their fallen brother and comrade a token of remembrance in the shape of a floral offering and live over in memory the terrible scenes of war and conflict through which they had passed side by side with those who fell on Northern soil, and whose ashes repose in Northern dust far from the land they loved.

Soldiers, your brothers in arms and kindred by birth, it is true, rest far from home; but their graves are not neglected, nor are they permitted to go unwatched and unattended. The men of the North were your foemen during the dark days of war, when brother was arrayed against brother and father did battle against son; but all feeling of animosity and revenge has long since been buried, and to-day they are your brothers in all that sacred name implies, and as years roll by and seasons come and go the little green mounds in Camp Chase, where your dead are sleeping their last long and eternal sleep, will each year be decorated by the hands of the children of the men who fought your dead in honorable warfare. The graves of your loved ones are in the keeping of men and women of the North whose pleasure it will be to each year visit their lonely and narrow habitations and, as the song birds sing their carols from the treetops, deposit on those graves flowers pure and sweet, and tenderly care for them.

To those who journeyed from the South to be present at the beautiful ceremonies held at Camp Chase no words are necessary to remind them of the lesson taught by the single act of strewing the graves with flowers. They are silent witnesses to the act declaring that in the Northern breast there remains no sectional hatred; that all grievances of the past were buried in the graves of the heroes whose little cells were covered with flowers, and that no more shall there be heard, North or South, that this is a divided country. It was a symbol that there is no North or South, but that we are all a united and solid country now and forever.

With what feelings of pride and gratification must those people of the South have turned from the graves of the Southern dead, realizing that their loved ones were in the tender care of friends and that hands which at one time were hostile to them will each year cover these lowly mounds with nature's offerings and moisten the gift with a tear. Such scenes as that witnessed yesterday are the little oases in the desert of life, and serve to make all happier and more content.

The *Columbus Dispatch* on that occasion said:

The taking part in the exercises, not alone in Columbus, but in all places where there are buried Confederate soldiers, by the boys in blue is not considered by either the Blue or the Gray as the sacrificing of thought or conviction as to the issues of the war.

By recognizing in this manner the bravery of the dead, they gladden the heart of many a Southern man or woman who knew and loved these men in life. Such deeds knit closer the bonds of unity between the North and the South. Particularly at this time is the act of to-day significant, when the boys of the Northland and the Southland are standing shoulder to shoulder under one flag fighting for a common cause. Think of it a moment— Michigan and Georgia in the same brigade; Illinois and Florida in another; a Confederate General commanding a corps and the boys from the North envious of those so fortunate as to be in his command. The whirligig of time works wonders which are hard to understand, but in this day and age the fights are all toward harmony and peace; the soldiers of the two sections long ago learned that the war is over, and the exhibition of to-day was only a manifestation of that return of peace at which all the world wonders.

Thus it will be seen that papers differing politically were pleased to express upon one subject the same sentiments. In no other land could this happen—and if we linger long over these scenes, who but a soured pessimist can complain, so full of peace and joy were they—and to-day these scenes and memories, to an American who loves his country, are inexpressibly beautiful. Without hindrance of nature or fault of man the programme was carried out as planned, and, as was the case the year before, the entire event was interesting.

At two o'clock the Chairman called the assembly to order and in concluding his remarks said: "We may shout, 'Blow, bugler, blow!' but the shrillest note can never, no never, again call the matchless armies of Lee and Grant to carnivals of death."

The programme proceeded as follows: Song, "My Country, 'Tis of Thee," by the Confederate Glee Club of Louisville, Ky.; prayer by Rev. John Hewett, an ex-Confederate, pastor of St. Paul's Episcopal Church, Columbus, Ohio. This prayer, rich in its tenderness, was as follows:

O God, who art everywhere and over all, the same yesterday and to-day and forever; the Creator of all nations, the Father of all families, and the Friend of all enemies; as we stand by the graves of soldier brothers we lift up our souls to Thee and invoke Thy spirit of love to direct and rule our hearts.

Remembering Thy great goodness to us as a nation, we repent of the sins of former days which brought us in fratricidal strife. We forget the heat of anger which raged in the hearts of men of a common blood in a common country and threatened our national ruin, and here in the presence of the living and the dead we lift our minds in united prayer and thanksgiving to our common Father and God.

Beneath the shadow of years that are past we behold to bless the outstretched hand of a power divine bestowing love for the healing of our nation's wounds, causing the Blue and the Gray to blend in harmony with a will divine in loyalty to a common flag.

O God, we thank Thee for this revelation of national unity and human fraternity which Thou hast made, and we pray Thee to give it the quality of permanence; and in token of the sincerity of our gratitude we here clasp hands over the graves of our American brothers and dedicate ourselves anew to the service of Thee, our common Father, and of this, our common country. Let this occasion be, indeed, a true Mohanism—a place of the meeting of two hosts; not merely of two hosts—the living and the dead—but of two hosts that once were enemies, but now are friends, whose spirit now as one beholds the face of our Father which is in heaven. Having come here as a representative of the Blue and the Gray to strew flowers upon these graves in loving memory of those who counted not their lives dear unto themselves in the defense of disputed rights, may the varied and mingled fragrance which these flowers shed abroad ascend to heaven as the incense of the fraternal feeling which fills our breasts and claim a blessing for our united country! In the faraway homes from which our brothers came to find their graves here lift Thou up the light of Thy countenance, and let the peace of God which passeth all understanding settle and gladden the souls whose longing eyes look for the day when there shall be a restitution of all things and a union of hearts and of lives which neither war nor death can ever dissolve.

O Thou who maketh men to be of one mind in a house, put far away from us all pride and prejudice and all causes of dissension and discord, that our land may bring forth that increase of truth and justice whereby all nations of men shall be made to live. To all who sigh for freedom grant that we may be the instrument in Thy hands for the fulfillment of their desires now on this earth and hereafter in the new and permanent glory of heaven.

Hear our united prayers also in behalf of our soldier brothers, North and South, who in the service of our country and in the cause of humanity and freedom go forth against the enemies of both. Give them faith, courage, and endurance, patience, gentleness, and obedience. Preserve them in the midst of the temptations of the camp and of the field, from the perils of the ocean and of the land, from the pestilence that walketh in darkness and the sickness that destroyeth in the noonday. Keep them under the shadow of Thy wing and restore them to their homes in safety. And so such as may fall in battle or by sickness do Thou, O Lord, graciously grant the preparation of repentance unto eternal life, where the flowers of love are forever strewn and never fade or change; through the infinite love and merits of the Saviour of all men, and unto Thee shall be the praise forever and ever. Amen.

Song, "Rest, Comrade, Rest," by Confederate Glee Club. Colonel Young was then introduced, and spoke as follows:

Friends and fellow-countrymen, we have come from the Southland to spend this day with our dead; and narrow must be the heart which would limit our love, our praise, our honor for these, our comrades, who sleep so far away from their homes in unmarked and unknown graves.

More than a third of a century has elapsed since the last grave was opened for the sepulcher of a Confederate soldier at Camp Chase; and during this period, with one exception, none have come from the homes of these dead to lay a flower on the sod that covers their ashes, to offer prayer for those who were bereft, or to speak generous words of those who, isolate and separate, found their last resting place here.

CAMP CHASE, 1898. LOUISVILLE (KY.) GLEE CLUB IN CENTER.

CAMP CHASE SERVICES, 1898. THE BENEDICTION BY REV. JOHN HEWITT.

We Confederates at this hour would be unworthy of our manhood if we did not recognize with grateful tribute the kindness and nobleness of those who, though opposed to us in conflict, unite with us in this day in these simple and beautiful ceremonies which bespeak in wonderful eloquence the victories of peace.

It hath been said that peace hath her victories no less renowned than those of war; and this victory of human kindness, human sympathy, and human generosity, which has been manifested on this day and at this hour by the people of Columbus, surpasses in grandeur and glory the victories of the war.

The passions and prejudices of the great struggle in which on one side a nation's integrity and the freedom of more than three millions of people were involved, and on the other side the defense of homes and firesides and a nation's life, are all blotted out and remembered no more; and you come as citizens of a great nation, forgetting the past and looking only to the future, and in this magnanimous and splendid way to show true chivalry and true humanity.

There is no heart in all the Southland to-day that does not go out in affection, in admiration, and in thankfulness to you, people of Columbus, who have thus again remembered our Confederate dead; and I repeat: Of all the messages that were ever sent from one people or section to another, this which you this day send to those who have died here—that you are keeping watch over these sepulchers and keeping green these graves—is the sweetest and most grateful.

In this narrow inclosure sleep heroes. There are no cowards here. They were men who were worthy not only of the country, but of the age in which they lived, and with unselfish patience, unfaltering fortitude, and magnificent courage laid their all upon what they believed to be the altar of right.

The world looks with wonder and admiration upon the soldiers, both North and South, who made Gettysburg famous as one of the most momentous of the world's battles. No man who has the heart of a soldier or the impulse of a freeman could fail to feel admiration for those Confederates who on that July day charged up the heights of Gettysburg, and who, amid shot and shell, never faltered in the discharge of duty. There were heroes meeting heroes on the crest of that hill, and the men who gave the shock and the men who received the shock command alike reverence and plaudits. Some of those who fought there rest here. There are men sleeping death's sleep in this inclosure who made splendid the glories of Cold Harbor, and who, like some grand and mighty fortress, withstood the shock of the legions of Grant as again and again they rushed against its ramparts, only to be laid low by the terrible storm of shot and shell that came from those in gray who manned the Confederate works.

There are men, too, sleeping here who in the mighty rush of

Gen. Albert Sidney Johnston's army at Shiloh swept before them the Federal hosts, and who in return on the morrow were compelled to retire before the onslaught of Grant and Buell.

There are some buried here who charged the works at Franklin, and whose chivalry and bravery, as again and again, even amid the darkness of the night, assailed the Federal breastworks, only to fall in the trenches or on the crest, elicited applause from their enemies who were waiting to stay them.

These were not unworthy of honor; they are part and parcel of that superb host which in the Civil War created American manhood—a manhood which commands the world's highest admiration, and which stamps this people as the most patriotic, most enlightened, and most powerful nation the world has ever seen.

It was the lessons at Chickamauga, at Chancellorsvile, at Cold Harbor, at Gettysburg, at Franklin, at Resaca, at Shiloh which contributed to make American manhood and patriotism what it is, and which give power and stability to our country and its people and quiet those disturbing fears which sometimes arise in the hearts of people when they would doubt the perpetuity of American institutions.

The people of Ohio, in honoring these dead as Americans, only add luster to their own renown and to their splendid history; for as you magnify and glorify Confederate courage and chivalry, you only make more resplendent the courage and chivalry of those armies who overcame the magnificent hosts who once rallied beneath the Confederate ensign.

In the name of all that is good and kind and true, and with hearts full of the profoundest gratitude, we come to thank you for this offering to our fallen friends and comrades; and we shall carry back with us sweet assurance of your splendid generosity and your superb humanity.

The lessons of this hour are teaching us the splendor and the grandeur of republican institutions. You do not love the flag of this country because it won in the great contests which were waged in 1812 and 1813 for the redemption of Ohio and the States in the Northwest, or because of its superb triumphs on the plain of Buena Vista, or in the battles in which your own people were engaged in the great Civil War. It is not the victories that the armies which followed this flag have achieved, but it is what this flag represents that makes it the object of love and admiration of all the people of the world, and that makes all this American nation ready to lay down their lives and sacrifice their fortunes in defense of its honor and glory. That flag represents the best principles of government and noblest teachings of liberty.

If, by some divine power, I could bring to life the dead who lie beneath this sod, they would spring forth into a patriotism as true as any the nation has ever seen.

The sons and grandsons of the men who sleep here are to-day part and parcel of the defenders of the glory of the American people. General Lee, General Wheeler, and General Butler, Confederates though they be, can be trusted to lead your sons to battle and to maintain on any field the illustrious courage and heroic manhood of the American nation.

There is something peculiarly touching in the conditions which surround these Confederate dead at Camp Chase. They died far away from their homes, amid the privations, the sufferings, of prison life.

War always has its barbarous features. Within the walls of Camp Chase I lay by night and heard the groans and sobs of my comrades without power to help. I saw their pale, emaciated forms carried forth to sepulture in this cemetery. I saw them die without that care, tenderness, and watchfulness to which I thought, as men, they were entitled; but this was only the war's results, and war is always organized barbarism.

Your sons and brothers and friends have had the same experience in Southern prisons. We are not now here to argue as to who was right or wrong; we are here simply to say that we mourn our dead, that we love their memories, that we venerate their courage, their heroism. They died for what they believed was right; they made the costliest sacrifice or offering man can make— they laid down their lives to testify their devotion and sincerity for the cause for which they fought; and the man who thus dies honestly and courageously never dies in vain.

Our friends who went down to death here have no monuments. It were better so. The green grass grows above them. All who knew them will in a few years be dead. It is enough to know that their dust rests here, where they died for the cause to which they consecrated themselves.

It was a custom among the Greeks to bring back the bones of their dead from their battlefield and inter them in a common sepulcher in their capital cities; but in one great battle (that of Marathon) the Grecian soldiers were buried where they fell. Their fidelity had been such that it was deemed fitting to sepulcher them where they died. And so, if we could, we would not disturb this dust that sleeps here.

The Great Teacher said that one who should give a cup of cold water in his name should have an everlasting reward. You, friends and fellow-countrymen, have done far more than give a cup of cold water in your splendid and magnanimous generosity to these Confederate soldiers who rest in your midst.

You have spoken kindly of their courage; you have spoken generously of their gallantry; you have spoken justly of their sacrifices; you have scattered flowers over their resting places; you have remembered them after long years have passed since they were placed in these humble and unmarked tombs; and I tell you that, in the eyes of God and of the angels who stand around his throne, such kindness, such sweet remembrances, shall not be forgotten, but somewhere in God's book there is a place to record this superb and splendid work.

I thank God we do not offend you when we come into your midst and, looking up to heaven, ask him to bless our dead and those they represent; and we should be ungrateful if we did not ask our God to bless you and to reward you for this kindness which you have shown to those we love.

In a little while those of us who participated in that greatest of all wars will have passed away. We imagine we can commune with the spirits of our dead as we stand here about their graves to-day. We are not ashamed of them nor of the cause for which they died. We loved them, and we love their dust. We shall join them in a little while.

We shall not come long to pay this tribute to those we love.

> "They hear a voice we cannot hear,
>   Which says we must not stay;
> They see a hand we cannot see,
>   Which beckons us away."

We will follow them in a little while; but while we do live we come in reverence and tenderness to bless this spot, which contains for us "war's richest spoils, the ashes of the brave."

And again, in the name of our people, in the name of all these generous, manly, magnanimous acts, we thank you for your kindness to our departed comrades. To them there is no longer clash of arms; the conflict is over. The living speak for them, and we speak gratefully for these renewed evidences of your nobleness.

Death sheds a solemn halo over these mounds. Peace and good will only abide here.

> "The foeman need not dread
>   This gathering of the brave,
> Without sword or flag and with soundless tread.
> We muster once more our deathless dead
>   Out of each lonely grave.
>
> The foeman need not frown,
>   These all are powerless now.
> They gathered them here and laid them down;
> Love, tears, and praise are the only crown
>   We bring to wreathe them now."

Colonel Young's address was followed by another song by the Glee Club, entitled "Blessed Be the Ground." Remarks were made by local members of the G. A. R.; and the school children, under Miss Maud E. Fleming, of Avondale School, rendered in a most beautiful manner the song "Cover Them Over."

Capt. John H. Leathers, President of the Confederate Association of Kentucky, was introduced, and said:

CAPT. JOHN H. LEATHERS.

Fellow-citizens, ladies and gentlemen, and comrades (I think I can use the word "comrades" on this occasion), I rejoice to see this day. I rejoice that the day has at last come when we can in truth and sincerity say no East, no West, no North, no South, but one country and one flag, and that flag the flag of a fully restored and glorious Union.

For years the burden of my song has been the words of the

immortal Webster: "Liberty and Union, now and ever, one and inseparable."

Whatever difference of opinion there might have been in the minds of many of us concerning the necessity for our present war with Spain, one thing is certain: it has demonstrated to the world that sectionalism is dead in this country, and that we are now one people, with one common name and one common destiny.

The war between the North and South was a most remarkable war, as well as the greatest war recorded in history, of either ancient or modern times. It was remarkable in that it was not a war between two different countries or people speaking different languages, waged for conquest, but was among people of the same country, who spoke the same language, and who were bound together by the strongest ties of blood and kindred. Both followed their convictions of what they believed to be right. Both fought with a valor unparalleled in the annals of warfare, and the bones of both lie mingled on every battlefield, from Bull Run to Appomattox, as the bones of their common ancestry lie mingled on every battlefield of the American Revolution, from Lexington to Yorktown.

It was a remarkable war in that when the war ceased the vanquished immediately accepted the results of the war and renewed their allegiance to the Union, while the victorious extended the right hand of peace and good fellowship, and they both immediately commenced repairing the waste places made desolate by war.

Passion and prejudice have long since gone with the flight of years, and each of us is now doing what we can to unify and develop this great country. The name and fame of the heroes of the war on both sides are now the common heritage of our children and children's children.

As one who for four years wore the gray, I stand here to-day on this happy occasion to avow my love and my allegiance to the flag of my country. "Long may it wave o'er the land of the free and the home of the brave!"

The Glee Club sang "Tread Lightly, Ye Comrades," and Miss Annie Williams recited that glorious poem, "Blue and Gray." The Glee Club sang "Tell the Boys I'm Coming Soon," and Thomas D. Osborne, Secretary of the Kentucky Confederate Association, spoke as follows:

To-day I feel like an Ohio man—the man from Columbus who went South during the war, and who, meeting with a warm reception, was so pleased that when peace came he moved down South to make it his home.

Ohio men go everywhere and get everything. This man chose to live in Arkansas. He had often heard the Rebel yell, and could imitate it admirably; so much so that it was his boast that he could shout longer and louder than any man in Arkansas.

One day, when the White River was higher than ever known, a steamboat came there and tied up under a bluff near the Ohio man's town. He didn't know the boat was there. The captain came to town and heard the boaster brag that he could shout longer and louder than any man in Arkansas.

After a talk, a bet of ten dollars was made. The captain, being allowed to select the time and place of contest, had chosen a distant stump and had instructed his mate to watch his hand—when he lifted it to his mouth, to pull the steam whistle and let it go till his hand fell. The captain's turn came first, and when his hand went to his mouth there came a shouting noise that almost split the leaves of the trees. After the deafening sound had got well under way, the Ohio man raised his hand to his vest pocket, took out his money, walked to the steamboat captain, and said: "Hold on. I could yell louder than that, but here's your money; I don't want to strain myself."

So to-day, like the Ohio man, I could make a longer and louder speech, but I don't want to strain myself.

Recently, when Ex-Confederate General Joseph Wheeler, through the magnificent kindness of that great Ohio man, President McKinley, put on the blue uniform of the United States of America, he was asked how he felt. He replied: "I feel like I have been off on a furlough and am now back in the ranks again."

Back in the ranks again—that's it. That's where we all are under one flag—the most famous flag ever floated by any government.

We always had a claim on Old Glory. At the beginning of the war many in the South wanted to fight under it. Our forefathers had followed it when it floated on the breeze of battle.

My grandfather, Lieut. Bennett Osborn, marched with Washington under it. My father's brother went through the Mexican War with it. My son followed it three years in the Louisville Legion.

Like General Wheeler, we can all gladly say: "Back in the ranks." On this happiest occasion, when through your magnificent kindness our heroes sleep in flower-garmented graves, we tender you unspeakable thanks.

Ex-Governor Taylor, of Tennessee, spoke briefly but eloquently, and was listened to with deep attention by all present. Capt. Gilbert H. Barger, of Columbus, made an interesting address, alluding to the unity of sentiment between the sections in all things pertaining to the honor and glory of our common country.

Chaplain Winget, a member of the G. A. R., offered prayer, and a gun squad from the McCoy G. A. R. Drill Corps fired a military salute over the graves, and the flowers were strewn by the loving hands of Union and Confederate veterans.

Before closing the exercises the Chairman, in making some acknowledgments he thought proper, stated that during the last three years Mr. T. J. Davies had helped with his horse and wagon and many days of labor, free of charge; Mr. Charles A. Roth, a Columbus (Ohio) florist, had been of great assistance, without cost. Thanks were extended to W. H. Grub for use of organ, to G. A. R. comrades of the McCoy Post Drill Corps for their presence and participation, to the Fourth Ward Columbus (Ohio) Republican Club for the use of their chairs, and to the dear little girls of Avondale School for the music of their sweet voices; also to many that had helped on decoration days and to others that had stood ready to assist.

Continuing, the Chairman said that until 1898 no contributions had been accepted from any person in Ohio, but that Comrade R. M. Rownd had expressed his sympathy and tendered financial aid, being told that under no circumstances could any money be accepted.

Afterwards, however, payment for planting shade trees and shrubbery was accepted from Mr. W. D. Brickell, Comrade Thomas E. Knauss (G. A. R.), Comrade Rownd (G. A. R.), and Confederate Comrades J. Y. Bassell and Rev. John Hewitt, all of Columbus, Ohio. Other contributions were received from Dr. Thomas P. Shields, J. B. Darling, and J. W. Carroll. No money had been asked for at any time from any person in the city of Columbus or State of Ohio.

An itemized report was rendered to Gen. George Moorman and the *Confederate Veteran* of all donations received.

So ended the service for 1898.

The conveyances running from the terminal of the street car line carried free of charge all who wished to go to the cemetery. Four to five thousand people were present to participate, standing throughout the exercises in the shade of the trees, made cool by the gentle June breeze, which seemed to whisper, "Peace on earth, good will toward men."

Many of the choicest Southern flowers were received for the

occasion, and their fragrance that evening seemed to linger with almost human sympathy over the graves of the Southern dead.

The feeling in the South regarding the care of the graves of the Confederate dead in the North cannot be better expressed than to quote extracts from some of the letters received by me.

CAMP CHASE SERVICES, 1898. AN EMBLEM FROM THE SOUTH.

DEAR SIR: I notice in *The Veteran* the interest you have taken in caring for the Confederate dead at Camp Chase. I was in Camp Chase prison from August, 1864, to March, 1865; therefore it is my privilege to acknowledge the obligations that all, especially those who were prisoners of war at that place, are under to you and your associates in the work.

You will pardon me if I say that it is humiliating to acknowledge the fact that it remained for a Federal soldier thirty years after to have the manhood to step to the front and do what the Confederates should have done long ago.

But this manhood is not born of sections; no arbitrary lines,

DERORATION DAY, CAMP CHASE, 1898. EMBLEM ON THE LEFT PRESENTED BY EX-SOLDIERS' AND SAILORS' ASSOCIATION, FRANKLIN COUNTY, OHIO.

no uniform, no cause, no line of battle, no flag mark the higher type of man.

Much of the bitterness of life in Camp Chase will be blotted out by works such as this. I hope you will receive such assistance as will enable you to permanently mark the resting place of the bodies of those who, summoned to the other great army mustered under "The Bonnie White Flag," peacefully wait the comrades yet in ranks.

By the way, "The Bonnie White Flag" was written by Colonel Hawkins, of our mess in Camp Chase.

That was a typical mess—colonels, captains, border men, and way-down-South fellows. Organized to escape, we worked day and night under many disappointments; but all the same that old mess went to work again, determined to get away. But only through the gates and by parole did we turn our backs on the horrors of Camp Chase, and thirty-two years after the first bright spot in that dark memory appears. May it spread until all the nightmare of the past is forgotten in the brightness and rest of the present!

A letter from Mrs. J. S. Raine, Secretary of Atlanta Chapter, Daughters of the Confederacy, is reproduced to show the spirit of the time, and the kindly help we received at the hands of that chivalric gentleman and friend, S. A. Cunningham, of Nashville:

Col. W. H. Knauss.

Dear Sir: At a recent meeting of Atlanta Chapter we had the pleasure of an address from Mr. S. A. Cunningham, proprietor of *The Confederate Veteran*, in which he spoke of his complimentary and most delightful reception tendered by a number of citizens of Columbus, Ohio, at your suggestion. He spoke very feelingly of your noble and successful efforts that proper care should be taken of the graves of our unforgotten dead buried at Camp Chase Cemetery.

I have before me a picture of the ceremony of decoration which occurred in 1897. I trust it may be my pleasure to see the sacred inclosure. The Atlanta Chapter of Daughters of the Confederacy desire to express their sincere thanks and appreciation for your generous and loving attentions to our dead. On this occasion of your decoration we will be happy to assist with our floral offerings.

A letter from William H. Herbert, of Sandusky, Ohio, 1898, gives an insight to matters relating to decoration services in that city, and it shows that another Ohio city is not forgetful of courtesies to dead foes. The letter states that the cemetery in which are buried the Confederates who died in prison is in a good state of preservation and has been well taken care of since about eight years ago, when an association of Georgia editors was in the vicinity and made a pilgrimage to Johnson's Island and cemetery. At that time the graves were marked with wooden head-pieces, giving the name, regiment, etc. Some of the boards were very much decayed and the names scarcely legible; so the editors, when they returned home, made a request through their papers for contributions to replace the boards with marble, also to build a fence around the cemetery. The result was that they collected enough in a short time to do the work nicely.

In Sandusky, Ohio, it has been the custom for eighteen years to send a delegation from the G. A. R. Post on the morning of decoration day to the Confederate cemetery at Johnson's Island and hold a short service. They are always joined by a large number of men, women, and children.

Mr. Herbert was a prisoner at Camp Chase (Prison 2, Mess 12) in the fall of 1862, and left there the latter part of November, 1862, in company with some 200 Confederate prisoners, who were taken by rail to Cairo, Ill., and thence by boat to Vicksburg, Miss., thence to Jackson, Miss., where they were exchanged and furnished transportation to the Army of Northern Virginia.

A letter from a Mr. McClellan, of Athens, Ala., glowing in patriotic sentiment and beautiful Christian charity, will be treasured by the one who received it until blotted out by the final call:

What a privilege to be an American! M. Lester says: "God has given us a grand mission."

The war with Spain was on and the Southern boys were marching away under the Stars and Stripes. Sons of heroic men who fought to tear its stars from the azure field were bearing it proudly against a foreign foe who could not know the magnificent strength of a united North and South. . . . You can understand how busy are our women with their needles these bright days, ministering to our absent soldier boys. The sewing machine, instead of the parlor instruments, makes the music of the hour.

You will not know until the struggle is over the strong ties between the North and South born of this comradeship—whose sons, the descendants of patriots, could mingle their blood and tears for principles dear to them, under opposing standards, and blend their dust under a common banner against a merciless foe on alien shore. Let us keep their graves green.

We will send flowers for the Southern Memorial Day, and may God bless the hands that place them over our silent heroes!

As the promoter of this fraternal observance, you will be gratefully remembered by us. Yours for America on land and sea.

DECORATION SERVICES, CAMP CHASE, 1898. THE BLUE AND THE GRAY.

CHAPTER IV.

The Services of 1899.

The Children of Avondale School Sing—Orations by Judge David E. Johnson, of Bluefields, W. Va., and by General W. D. Hamilton— Tableau of Blue and Gray with Hands Clasped—An Impromptu Service Some Days before the Regular Decoration Exercises—The Southern Members of Waterworks Convention Pleased and Impressed—They Stood with Uncovered Heads—The Mystery of the Broken Tombstone.

> True to the South, they offered free from stain
> Courage and faith; vain faith and courage vain.
> For her they threw lands, honors, wealth away;
> And one more hope that was more prized than they.
> For her they languished in a foreign clime,
> Gray-haired with sorrow in their manhood's prime;
> Beheld each night their homes in fevered sleep,
> Each morning started from their dreams to weep;
> Till God, who saw them tried too sorely, gave
> The resting place they asked—an early grave.
> O, then,
> Forget all feuds, and shed one manly tear
> O'er Southern dust—for broken hearts lie here.
> —*Columbus (Ohio) Press-Post.*

Again there were flags and flowers at Camp Chase Cemetery. Again the Blue and the Gray walked side by side through grass-grown paths and scattered flowers upon pathetic heaps of earth.

There were not so many ex-Confederates present as the year before, but all who came were made welcome by their Ohio friends. If at first the friends seemed few, that time was past, and a multitude was present for the exercises in 1899. Among the number again taking melodious part were the pupils of the Avondale School of Columbus; and if the souls dwelling in God's eternal somewhere revisit earth, two thousand spectral forms stood reverent as the sweet, fresh, young voices of the children sang.

The exercises began by bugle call. Then the long roll was sounded by the G. A. R. Veteran Drum Corps. The audience joined with the school children in singing "America," after which there was presented, on behalf of the Ex-Soldiers' and Sailors' Association, by Comrade D. M. Brelsford, for many years its secretary, a large and handsome floral piece, received by that courtly representative of the South, Rev. John Hewitt, in a graceful speech of thanks, voicing the gratitude of the Southerners toward the ex-soldiers and people of Columbus.

The "Blue and the Gray" was then sung by the Misses Maud and Sophia Fleming in a sweet and charming manner, after which prayer was offered up to the Divine Being for his blessing upon so auspicious and important event in the advance of his kingdom and love.

The invocation was followed by the pupils of the Avondale School singing "To-Day This Hallowed Place We Seek," in which the sweet young voices, rising amid a hushed and sacred silence, moved many to tears.

The opening address, by Judge D. F. Pugh, was listened to with deep attention and interest. At its conclusion the school children sang "Cover Them Over with Beautiful Flowers."

Col. David E. Johnson, of Bluefield, W. Va., spoke briefly in response to the address of Judge Pugh. He thanked the soldiers' organization which presented the floral piece, also the ladies' societies auxiliary to the Union Veteran Legion, and the Ex-Soldiers' and Sailors' Society.

He expressed the thanks of the South for the thoughtful regard which inspired these services and the men and women who took part in them, concluding in a most touching manner by picturing scenes in Southern homes where women were thinking tenderly of those flower-strewn mounds beneath which the dust of their loved ones lay.

The concluding address was delivered by Gen. W. D. Hamilton, of Zanesville, Ohio, whose speech the Louisville *Courier-Journal* published in full and said of the speaker: "He was during the Civil War one of the noted cavalry leaders on the Federal side, and the sentiments that he expressed were so manly, brave, and patriotic that they reflect great credit on his head and heart; and the people of the South will pleasantly remember General Hamilton for his generous and noble address."

My friends, it is easy to hate our enemies. It is natural to retain a spirit of enmity against those who have injured us.

It is a mission of Christianity to give us lessons of forgiveness,

and the Son of God came from heaven to teach us not only to forgive our enemies, but to love them.

In this there is an inference that we ourselves may have given
some cause to make enemies, and that there is something good
and lovable even in those who differ from us.

It is not our province to discuss the cause of our Civil War.
It is enough for us to know that these men buried here were innocent. It cannot be traced to the men who took to the field on

GEN. W. D. HAMILTON.

either side. Its origin was embodied in the Constitution and
grew out of the unfortunate existence of slavery when it was
formed, and came down to us through nearly a century of bitter
legislative contention, and was finally disposed of in that bloody
court of which we formed a part.

During all this time the social relation between the sections
became less and less cordial, and the business interests more and
more strained. We cultivated the habit of belittling all that was
good and magnifying all that was bad in each other.

War brought destruction and untold sorrow, but it cleared away the obstacles to a better knowledge of the people toward each other. Our former impressions were entirely upset by the wonderful courage and nobleness of character displayed on both sides.

Never were armies composed of men more earnest in their efforts, intensified, if possible, during the last two years as the forces of the South were driven back to become the defenders of their homes against the increasing strength of a powerful invading army.

It is little wonder that the women of the South, whose homes were ruined, and the women of the North, whose sons lie scattered in unknown graves, should retain a feeling of bitterness. Heart wounds were given which saddened the life of a generation and have magnified the task of conciliation which the best men and women of both sides have undertaken and which these floral tributes to the Confederate dead to-day are designed to promote.

On occasions like this we feel that there is a holiness in flowers. They are the mute companions of our purest thoughts and give expression to our tenderest sympathies. They are angels from the realm of nature employed to bear our message of affection to the dead.

The fraternal spirit which prompts our presence here to-day is the harbinger of a time when the people of the United States will gather annually, bringing the roses of the North and the magnolia blossoms of the South as a tribute to American valor to trim the graves of every soldier who fell in battle or died in prison for a cause he had been taught from pulpit and from family altar to believe was right. . . .

In the better light of a third of a century both sections are learning to look upon the Civil War as thoughtful students of its results.

We can now see that God was preparing the nation through a sacrifice of blood to become his consistent agent in the difficult task of advancing civilization in the dark places of earth and in extending Christian liberty among the islands of the sea.

It was the training of the Civil War that made recent unparalleled achievements possible.

The sons of the Blue and the Gray fulfilled the promise of their fathers when they fell into line side by side to test the power of Spain. And they have divided the honors of a most brilliant campaign on land and sea.

The daring spirit of Lieutenant Hobson, of Alabama, is the pride of the North as well as the South.

The dashing courage of Colonel Roosevelt, of New York, with his Rough Riders from both sections, has won the admiration of us all, and we old soldiers of the cavalry recognize a gallant brother in Gen. Joe Wheeler, that ubiquitous trooper of Alabama, who used to bother us so much when we wore the blue and he

DECORATION DAY, CAMP CHASE, 1899. SCHOOL CHILDREN OF AVONDALE SCHOOL, COLUMBUS, OHIO, WHO SANG AT THE SERVICES.

the gray; and a startled world joins us with uncovered heads in paying homage to that phenomenal hero of the Asiatic seas, George Dewey, of Vermont.

It is time that we bury the bitterness of the past when we reflect that in the scales with which anxious nations are weighing us to-day not only will these names be placed, but the character and ability of Robert E. Lee, Joseph E. Johnston, and Stonewall Jackson will be estimated side by side with that of Grant, Sherman, and Sheridan, and the soldierly qualities of both armies will be equally considered in determining the nation's place among the powers of the earth.

My fellow-citizens of the gray and the blue, as we distribute these flowers on the graves of more than two thousand of the nation's Confederate dead I feel that we should thank God that we and they were permitted to belong to that generation of soldiers who were selected to work out his plans, however mysterious, for the republic.

In closing I quote the language of General Gordon at a Confederate reunion in Charleston, S. C., when he said: "I feel the power of your confidence to pledge in the name of every Confederate and son and daughter of Confederates the South's eternal loyalty to every cause for the upholding of American manhood, the perpetuity of American freedom, the unity of the American people, and by all these agencies we may accelerate the onward march of the American republic in its benign progress."

Men and women of the North, we should be encouraged to pay some regard to the graves of their comrades, which the fortunes of war have placed in our keeping, to hear such sentiments expressed by the foremost living Confederate and indorsed by that great assembly of his comrades.

"The Soldier's Farewell" was sung by the school children, followed by a tableau in which Blue and Gray clasped hands. At the conclusion of the exercises J. C. McCoy Post Drill Corps fired a soldier's salute, and the graves were decorated by the representatives of the two armies present, assisted by the ladies of the U. V. L. and ladies, and Society of the Ex-Soldiers' and Sailors' Association.

In addition to the flowers sent from the South, several wagon loads of flowers were sent by local friends. Not a grave of the two thousand two hundred and sixty was slighted; on each were flowers from the old home and from the North.

So ended the services of 1899.

Some twenty days prior to the events just narrated an impressive and impromptu little service was held at Camp Chase Cemetery, and it came about in this way:

A national convention of waterworks superintendents was being held in the city of Columbus, and among the number were many Southern men. Some of these gentlemen bore a part in the memorable struggle of the sixties, and naturally desired to see the cemetery that was attracting so much attention North and South.

These gentlemen, together with the ex-Confederate soldiers and ladies of the South then residing in Columbus, by invitation of the writer visited the cemetery for the purpose of seeing how well and with what tender devotion the mounds covering the last resting place of the Confederate dead were cared for by the people of the North in whose keeping the destinies of war had placed them. The party was made up of Rev. John Hewitt, rector of St. Paul's Episcopal Church; Hon. H. C. Erwin, Atlanta, Ga.; Mr. W. J. Milne, Birmingham, Ala.; Mr. Charles A. Bolling, Richmond, Va.; Judge J. A. Anderson, Atlanta, Ga.; Col. L. H. Goodman, New Orleans; Gen. Waller S. Payne, Fostoria, Ohio; Mr. H. C. Campbell, Charlotte, N. C.; Mr. W. H. Rapp and Col. J. B. Travis, of Atlanta; and others.

The trip to Camp Chase was made in carriages, kindly furnished by Chief Lauer, of the Columbus Fire Department, Judge D. F. Pugh, A. W. Shields, W. B. Potts, H. N. P. Doyle, and myself.

Arriving at the burial grounds, Rev. Dr. Hewitt offered an invocation in which he eloquently and beautifully referred to the noble cause promoting the gathering, and invoked the blessing of the Supreme Ruler of all in the exercises to be performed.

The members of the party were provided with potted flowers by Mrs. Knauss to be planted upon graves of the heroic dead. The ladies who had assembled at the grounds before the arrival of the visitors requested the honor of planting the flowers, and that pleasant task was submitted to their willing hands. The scene presented after the graves had been decorated was beautiful and impressive. Around and above the silent mounds of earth stood with uncovered heads the persons mentioned. The fresh, green grass waved gently to and fro, swayed by the gentle spring breeze, while the wind breathed a solemn requiem through the trees overhead. As each one of the party spoke tenderly of the silent heroes buried there, and uttered words of commendation and praise for the men and women of the North, the eyes of the visitors from the South filled with tears of emotion as they beheld the graves of their dead.

For years there stood in the cemetery a broken tombstone, and its loneliness made it conspicuous. The top of the stone, through some unknown cause, had been broken off and in the lapse of years had been lost. On the remaining portion of the stone remained the inscription: "Third Miss. Batt. Resident Osyka, Miss. Died Jan. 16, 1865. Aged 37 yrs. Erected by his wife." The lost portion evidently contained the husband's name. The stone was broken long before the decoration services caused the briers to be torn away and flowers placed thereon.

The story of these exercises reached the Southland, and a Union soldier placed there a box of flowers which came with the request that they be strewn over this unknown grave.

W. Y. Smith, who had been a bugler in the Second Ohio Volunteer Cavalry, was present at the exercises in 1898, and when he learned the story of the broken stone said he would replace it if the name of the Confederate buried there could be ascertained. Eventually word reached a far-away home in Mississippi, and in due time a letter came containing a strip of muslin yellow with age, on which was an impression of the face of the broken stone as it was when originally put up. The impression showed the words and their alignment, as follows:

IN MEMORY OF

I. L. CAUSEY,

ORDNANCE SERGT.

The stone was broken through the line "Ordnance Sergt."

Smith made good his promise, and when the graves were decorated in 1899, there stood a marble slab and the name of the dead soldier was a mystery no longer.

CHAPTER V.

CAMP CHASE IN 1900.

Ohio's Governor Present at the Services at Camp Chase—He Makes a
Wise and Patriotic Address—The Ex-Confederates Pleased with His
Kindly Expressed Sentiments Concerning the Dust of the Lonely Dead
—General Arnold, of Kentucky, Delivered an Eloquent and Touching
Speech—Mrs. T. W. Rose, President of the Ladies' Society of the
Union Veteran Legion, Spoke with Much Tenderness—Dr. Thomas P.
Shields, an Ex-Confederate of Ohio, One of the Speakers—What South-
ern Governors Said.

THE slanting rays of the setting sun were tinting the flowered
graves as, leaving the cemetery, the people turned to catch a last
look at the peaceful scene and breathe once more the floral Southern fragrance.

It had been a successful day, and for the first time in the history of the exercises there was an Ohio Governor present. Year
after year the chief officer of the State Government had been
invited to be present, and year after year the invitation was declined. One Governor said frankly he was not in sympathy with
the work and did not think it right. The kind-hearted McKinley
was in doubt as to the propriety of decorating these graves and
declined attending with the gentleness and dignity that character-
ized his dealings with his fellow-men. Afterwards, when he became President of the United States, his feelings underwent a
change, as was evidenced by his Atlanta speech, mentioned in the
introductory chapter of this volume.

When the invitation was extended to Governor Nash he at once
accepted, saying with decided emphasis: "I am in sympathy with
this work and will join you willingly in paying tribute to the
memory of these men."

Not only the ex-Confederates, but all who took part in the exercises, were pleased because of his views upon this and kindred
subjects.

The address delivered by Governor Nash was as follows:

This is a strange scene. We are assembled about the graves

of more than two thousand soldiers who perished from 1861 to
1865. At that time the men buried here were a part of that
great army engaged in civil strife. More than thirty-five years
have passed since that great conflict ended, and we are here to do
honor to them by bestowing loving tributes upon their graves.
They were once our enemies, but we now look upon their brave
deeds as a part of our history.

GOV. GEORGE K. NASH.

As I said in the beginning, this is a peculiar situation, and yet
it is no more so than the conflict in which these men fell. In
his second inaugural President Lincoln said: "Neither party expected for the war the magnitude or the duration which it has
already attained. Neither anticipated that the cause of the conflict might cease with it, or even before the conflict itself should
cease. Each looked for an easier triumph and a result less fun-
damental and astounding. Both read the same Bible and prayed
to the same God, and each invoked his aid against the other."

It was strange, indeed, that two parties through whose veins flowed the same blood should inaugurate and carry on for four years a conflict the most destructive conflict in life and property which is recorded in modern history. . . .

It was most fortunate that both parties read the same Bible and prayed to the same God, because such peoples could not remain hostile to each other. With the lapse of time all the peoples of this country have again become loyal to the government founded by a common country. All have again learned to love the same flag, and have been, and will be, its ardent supporters when danger threatens. When engaged in a foreign war the sons of the South and the sons of the North again became loyal soldiers of the republic and demonstrated that we are a reunited people—in heart, in soul, and in every aspiration of patriotism.

The ceremony in which we have engaged to-day is not a useless nor a meaningless one. It shows that we of the North have no hatred for the brave men who were once our foes. On the other hand, it demonstrates that for those who fell in an unavoidable conflict we have respect and honor and love, and that with those who still live we join hands in loyal support of the matchless government whose foundations were laid by their fathers and ours,' and cemented by their blood in the days of the Revolution.

It is hoped that as the years go by our children and our children's children may unite in showing honor to the soldiers of the Confederacy as well as to the soldiers of the Union. All fought most honorably in a conflict which, it seems, could not have been avoided. To their names no dishonor should be attached. By thus honoring all, love for a great republic will be strengthened and her flag will be followed as the guiding star for all the people for all time to come.

Again I quote from the local daily papers:

Over the graves of the fallen Southerners floated a tiny red, white, and blue banner of the United States, while the memorial shaft and the speakers' stand were decorated in the same colors. The remarks of Governor Nash were so well received by the Confederate veterans that Rev. Dr. Hewitt moved a vote of thanks be tendered. This was carried by—as Col. Knauss put it—a vote of two hundred thousand to one, the Governor voting "no." "The Governor has expressed," continued Dr. Hewitt, "a sentiment that is as broad and liberal as it is possible for any one who had fought either for or against the South to express. Any one who could stand there and express the sentiments the Governor has done would be worthy the recognition and thanks of those against whom he had fought."

Mrs. Alice M. Rambo and Miss Edna Smith sang the duet, "Forget Not the Day," after which General Arnold, an ex-Confederate, whose son was in one of the Kentucky regiments in the Spanish-American War, made a beautiful and touching speech. He told of the gratitude of the Southern wives and mothers toward the noble Northern men and women who had reclaimed the burial grounds and strewed flowers over the mounds of the sleeping veterans of the South, adding:

When my countrymen and my countrywomen read of your acts, the fragrance of your good deeds is like the dew on the blossom, and the rain of their blessing is upon you.

The General told of the bloody day at Perryville, Ky., when the home of his widowed mother was turned into a hospital and she administered alike to those who wore the blue and those who wore the gray. God created the world, the flowers, and the birds; then he created man after his own image; and then, best of all, he created woman.

General Arnold, continuing, said:

For four years I was a Confederate soldier, and as such I have no regret. With the memory of those days upon me, I desire to thank Governor Nash for his patriotic address. Both sides built monuments of bronze and stone, but those crumble. The names, however, will be handed down as a heritage as long as language is a vehicle of thought between man and man.

The Chairman, at the conclusion of Gen. Arnold's address, introduced Mrs. T. W. Rose, National President of the Union Veteran Legion, a ladies' society, who said:

I have been asked to represent the Woman's Soldiers' Aid Society and the ladies of the Union Veteran Legion, which duty I feel myself incompetent to perform adequately. I feel it my sacred duty, however, to come and assist in strewing flowers over these brave men who lie here, so far from home and kindred. These were men who fought bravely for their convictions. They left their loved ones as did our own brave boys. We come remembering the mothers, wives, and sisters who sent them and prepared them for war with their own hands, and we know they would gladly strew with their own hands these flowers.

Sisters of the South and sisters of the dead in our keeping, as long as we are permitted to come here we will cover these green graves with your flowers; and with our own loved ones we hope to meet after the last bugle calls to the other shore. God bless the Blue and the Gray!

Dr. Thomas P. Shields, of Union County, an ex-Confederate,

DECORATION DAY, CAMP CHASE CONFEDERATE CEMETERY, 1900.

Gov. George K. Nash (Ohio) second from the right; Mrs. Mary Rose, National President U. V. L., Woman's Relief Corps, in center;
Dr. Thomas P. Shields, President Confederate Veteran Camp, Columbus, Ohio, to the left of Mrs. Rose,

was introduced; and though at first he was overcome by emotion, he made an eloquent speech. Among other things, he said that he always marched with the boys in blue on their memorial day and helped to strew the flowers.

The *Daily Press-Post,* of Columbus, which has always treated the Confederate Memorial Day with great consideration, asked the Governors of many Southern States, particularly those who had been in the Southern army, to express their views upon the memorial services conducted at Camp Chase each year, outlining the interest taken by Col. W. H. Knauss and the Columbus people in this Confederate burying ground and how in recent years veterans of both armies have gathered around the graves and obliterated the old hostilities forever in the ceremonies of fraternal forgetfulness.

The responses, some of which are quoted, tell eloquently of national rejuvenation, for which the people of Columbus are profoundly grateful, since they have so earnestly promoted the new era of fellowship between the sections.

Gov. Joseph D. Sayres, of Texas, wrote:

The intelligence conveyed in your telegram of this date is indeed gratifying. Such action cannot fail to receive the sincere and hearty approbation of every true American. I wish that I could be present to participate.

Gov. J. Hoge Tyler, of Virginia:

The occasion mentioned in your telegram is of special interest to me, because of loved ones resting beneath the sod at Camp Chase.

May the fragrance and sweetness of flowers from Union and Confederate hands be a token of that love and friendship which now unites our country!

Gov. A. D. Candler, of Georgia:

It is to me a beautiful sentiment which prompts the action of those who wore the blue and those who wore the gray in the work of doing honor to their dead comrades who fought on both sides in the fratricidal conflict from 1861 to 1865. I have said— and I have been criticised for saying—that, next to my brother Confederate soldier who fought for his convictions, I have the greatest admiration for the good Federal soldier who fought for his convictions; and it speaks well for our civilization and well for our glorious Union that those arrayed in deadly conflict a generation ago can now unite as a band of brothers in doing honor to the memory of their dead comrades, without regard to the flag under which they fought.

As an American citizen, proud of the country in which he lives, I am thankful that I have lived long enough to see the asperities of that sanguinary conflict largely disappear, and I feel confident that in less than another generation they will have entirely disappeared from the minds and hearts of all unbiased and intelligent men. Each side had convictions and each side was brave enough to fight for its convictions. That is the whole case in a sentence.

With love for my old comrades who wore the gray, and the highest admiration and esteem for the men who wore the blue.

Gov. J. F. Johnston, of Alabama:

Every flower laid on the graves of our dead soldiers, sleeping so far from their homes and loved ones, by the gallant comrades of the Grand Army and by the Confederate Veterans, fellow-citizens of the North, will be fragrant in our memories for years to come.

Such acts show that the American soldiers are the bravest and gentlest in all the world.

Gov. Daniel W. Jones, of Arkansas:

I congratulate the veterans of the Civil War, and the nation, upon the state of feeling which makes it possible to witness the decoration of Confederate graves by veterans of both sides, as I am informed is to be done in your city to-morrow.

Gov. Daniel L. Russell, of North Carolina:

Your communication, conveying to me the pleasant intelligence that the Federal and Confederate veterans of your city will unite this year to adorn the graves of the Confederate dead who sleep at Camp Chase, is gratifying to me.

It indicates that the unpleasant sentiments which so long and so disastrously divided our country are passing away, and that we are to have not only a union under our Constitution and laws, but also a reunited people, exhibiting a willingness to forget the past and determined to unite in securing the future good government and glory of our common country.

Please convey to the veterans, Confederate and Federal, my appreciation of their generous and patriotic behavior, and allow me to express the hope that the time may not be distant when the last vestige of passion that accompanied and followed the struggle which threatened the destruction of the republic shall have passed away and have been entirely forgotten.

The sentiments expressed by these distinguished gentlemen are treasured in the hearts of those who took part in the service at Camp Chase, not only that year, but the preceding years when there were few to do honor to these sons of the South at rest upon Ohio soil.

CHAPTER VI.

The Memorial of 1901.

Arm in Arm the Men of the South and North Marched into the Cemetery Where Sleep the Dead of Camp Chase Prison—Commander Shields, of the Confederate Camp, and Commander Grim, of McCoy Post, G. A. R., Leading the Way—Children of Avondale School Sing—Rev. John Hewitt Delivers an Address—Hon. Emmet Tompkins, Then Republican Member of Congress, Delivers an Oration—Remarks by Rev. Howard Henderson, Ex-Confederate—Captain Rogers, an Ex-Confederate, Places Southern Flowers on Graves of the Union and Confederate Soldiers.

THE services of 1901 were successfully carried out, nothwithstanding the fact that at a late hour changes in the matter of transportation from Columbus were made that required prompt action. The arrangements made with the Columbus, London, and Springfield Interurban Line tò use a locomotive to haul the people who proposed to attend had to be canceled at the moment, owing to the possibility that it might endanger the company's franchise to use a locomotive. The nearest approach by rail at that time was the Camp Chase terminus of the West Broad Street Line, and from that point to the cemetery was about three-quarters of a mile. As hurriedly as possible cars were secured and great crowds filled them as fast as they came. Carriages and omnibuses were ordered posthaste for the school children and invited guests. The people of Columbus and near-by towns walked from the end of the street car line to the cemetery, and the crowd was the largest that had thus far attended the exercises.

The veterans of McCoy Post, G. A. R., and the ex-Confederates in attendance, together with the school children, formed outside the grounds, and arm in arm the Southern and Northern men marched to the platform, where, side by side, sat T. P. Shields, Commander of Confederate Camp No. 1181, of Columbus, and John Grim, Commander of J. C. McCoy Post No. 1, G. A. R.

Again the children of Avondale School, under the direction of their teacher, Miss Osgood, daughter of a Union soldier, sang "The Star-Spangled Banner," while Commanders Grim and

Shields drew the starry banner to its place upon the tall flagstaff that I erected in the cemetery. A burst of cheers greeted our national flag as it floated in the breeze, waving joyously as though instinctive with knowledge that old-time foes were united in making it the emblem of one country and for one people.

Rev. John Hewitt delivered an address that was listened to

REV. JOHN HEWITT.

with deep appreciation. The name of this gentleman and Southern soldier appears quite frequently in this story, and it is unnecessary to repeat to the reader again who he is. When the Fourth Ohio Infantry returned from Porto Rico at the close of hostilities, he was made Chaplain; so much for the peace and harmony demonstrated since the men of Camp Chase prison went to their sad and lonely rest. Dr. Hewitt concluded his address by saying:

They are no longer prisoners of war. If they could know all that has happened since they died, and see what we see to-day, I

venture to believe that they would think and feel about what we
are doing to-day as we ourselves do—would think and feel about
the flag as we do.   And hence it cannot be as some have hinted—
that it was an offense to their memory to raise that flag where
they now sleep.   It seems fitting, therefore, that such who recall
the conflict that proved them the bravest of brave soldiers and
learned to respect them for valorous deeds when living should
gather about their graves when dead and join in ceremonies such
as these in testimony of the fact that they won this respect—
worth the winning, worth remembering, and worth being kept
alive.

You Ohio comrades of the Blue will not deny that when we
laid down our arms and again raised the Stars and Stripes over
the capitols of our Confederate States, by those acts the nation
began to grow stronger and the flag to take on greater glory.

The Hon. Emmet Tompkins, Republican Member of Congress
from the Columbus district at the time, delivered an oration, in
which he said:

Friends and fellow-citizens, we are assembled to-day for the
purpose of laying flowers on the graves of dead Americans.   The
children have come with their beaming faces and clothed in bright
summer garments to sing with sweet and innocent voices songs
of praise and patriotism.   Among you I behold men crowned
with the frost of time and even bent with the weight of years.   It
seems to me that all the stages and all the walks of active life
have here their representatives, mingled as they are into a har-
monious whole, while over all, stretched by a friendly breeze,
floats the flag of our nation—the Star-Spangled Banner.   The
scene is novel and affecting to me because these dead Americans
gave up their lives for their convictions, and one might well wonder that at the capital of the great State of Ohio there would
ever assemble such a body as this to perform the simple and
tender acts of to-day.

But during the long stretch of years since the Confederacy
dissolved wondrous changes have been wrought and many wounds
have been healed by the touch of time.   I am not here for
the purpose of paying tribute to or manifesting concurrence in
that war which dug these graves.   But I am here for the purpose
of indicating my willingness to adopt the admonition of General
Grant when he said, "Let us have peace!" and to bury in these
graves along with the bones of soldiers the animosities which for
four dreadful years held the North and the South in their deadly
grasp.

To the Confederates who accept the results of that war and
now join in devotion to the Union I give the right hand of fellowship; to those of them who still linger amid the ashes and

A GROUP OF SOUTHERN MEMBERS OF THE WOODMEN OF THE WORLD AT CAMP CHASE CEMETERY, 1901.

nourish in their bosoms the bitterness of the past I can only express the hope that they will ere long realize how vain all such thoughts are and how far better it is to dwell together in peace and harmony.

To the words of General Grant, already quoted, "Let us have peace!" we add the sentiment of President McKinley when he expressed the wish that the government would take charge of and care for the final resting places of Confederate soldiers. Both these are the manifestations of the spirit of forgetfulness, and they lead to the high plane of universal brotherhood among all Americans. If we imbibe this spirit, then will this nation reach the full orb of its possible greatness.

The late war with Spain has done much to close the breach between the North and the South. Upon the land and upon the seas the sons of the North mingled their blood with that of the sons of the South, and the two made a common and a glorious sacrifice. It was an inspiring spectacle to behold the heroic youth of the land of flowers marching by the side of the youth of the land of the snow—each wearing the blue, each keeping step to the "Star-Spangled Banner," and each lifting his cap to the emblem of liberty and equality. Earnest and patriotic men find much hope in that spectacle.

To-day we are in the presence of the dead. The edge of the grave is no place for bitterness. Let us be just and concede that these dead while in life believed they were engaged in a righteous cause. Let us acknowledge that they were courageous adversaries. The uncounted heaps of earth dotting this fair land bear witness to these facts. Let us hope that from these graves the settled conviction may be drawn that it is all in vain to attempt the dissolution of this Union, and that the God of battles directs the armies of the nation. From these ceremonies may we catch increased inspiration to move forward in the great mission allotted to the American people, and may the century just dawning to be filled with peace and happiness and the uplifting of mankind everywhere throughout the universal earth!

Rev. Howard A. M. Henderson, an officer in the Confederate service and special commissioner of exchange, delivered an address, in which he said, in alluding to the Union soldier who began these services, that "his acts, even more than the lapse of years, did that which went to wipe out the bitterness between sections."

Gen. J. A. Arnold, of Kentucky, was again present and spoke briefly in renewed appreciation.

After the services were over several incidents occurred worthy to be related. A battle-scarred veteran of the North, approaching General Henderson, recalled that the General had exchanged him out of Libby Prison. The General, of course, did not remember the man personally.

An old lady, three of whose sons had given their lives for the Confederacy and one of whom slept in the shade of the inclosure, sat on the platform and witnessed the tributes to his memory.

Dr. T. P. Shields, who met at a reunion in Memphis, Tenn., his old comrade, Col. D. B. Baldwin, of Virginia, prevailed upon him to attend these exercises, and he introduced him, stating that they met as strangers in Memphis and the fact developed that the Colonel was from the Doctor's old home in Virginia. The acquaintance was brought about in this way:

The Doctor asked the Colonel: "Do you know D. B. Baldwin there?"

"That's my name," was the answer.

The Doctor then recognized him, and demanded: "Don't you know me?"

But the old comrade could not see through the veil that the years had hung, and Dr. Shields had to reveal his identity.

The *Columbus Dispatch* relates how Mr. W. T. Rogers, of Chattanooga, accompanied by his beautiful daughter, came to Columbus with flowers sent by the N. B. Forrest Camp No. 4, U. C. V., and arrived too late for the decoration services. However, the following day the flowers were divided and some of them were placed by Miss Rogers on the graves in the Confederate Cemetery and the rest were taken by Captain Rogers to Green Lawn Cemetery and laid at the base of the monument raised to the memory of the brave men in blue who have obeyed the last signal.

CHAPTER VII.

The Monument Unveiled—1902.

What Southern Writers Who Were Present Said about the Occasion—
The Chairman Tells Who Helped so Liberally with the Arch—The
Oration of Governor Nash—The Reply of Judge D. E. Johnston, of
West Virginia—The Speech of Judge D. F. Pugh—Captain Dinkins, of
New Orleans, Delivers an Eloquent Speech—The Story of the Colored
Men—Letter from Mrs. Randolph—Invitation to Go to Nashville—The
Monument Turned Over to the Ex-Confederates—Happy Ending of
the Author's Work at Camp Chase.

THE memorial arch, an enduring monument to the memory of
these Southern Americans, had been completed and the day for
its unveiling was at hand.

The *Columbus Dispatch* of April 13, 1902, said of it:

The arch which will be unveiled June 7 will be the first to be
constructed by Northern people to mark the final resting places
of Confederates who fought bravely for their convictions.

Colonel Knauss's idea is to have an arch that will be an everlasting monument to designate the location of the graves. It will
be situated seventy-five feet from the entrance to the grounds,
which fronts on Sullivan Avenue. As shown in the cut, the memorial will arch the large bowlder which for many years was
famous as the only headstone for the two thousand two hunded
and sixty bodies buried within the inclosure. Several years ago
Colonel Knauss had a wooden arch placed over the bowlder, and
on it was painted "Americans."

The bowlder referred to above is seven feet in diameter and
weighs approximately sixteen tons. It extends seven and one-
half feet above the ground and several feet below the surface.
From the top of the bowlder to the bottom of the keystone it is
over eight feet. On top of the keystone of the arch is the statue
of a Confederate private soldier in gray bronze. On each side
of the arch there are large flower urns which set off the masonry
in a very pleasing manner.

There was great disappointment by the citizens of Columbus
that Gen. J. B. Gordon could not be present to receive the monument, but his place was ably filled by that eloquent Southern gentleman, Hon. David E. Johnston, Member of Congress from West

Virginia, and the ceremonies of the day were a source of pleasure to many people throughout the broad land.

If we dwell upon the incidents of that day, if the orations are considered at greater length, the reader will realize that the work of years was near the end; and one cannot refrain from dwelling in the happiness of realized hopes.

To those of us who bore a part in the war of the sixties the afternoon of life is well on. It will not be long until "taps" sound, and it is natural, therefore, that when memory leads us out where we see the panorama of the past we look first at the morning view, where are charging squadrons and smoking cannon and dying men. Then we turn away to a scene far different —a graveyard, low-lying mounds, bands playing softly, men who had charged upon each other with bayonets red-stained standing side by side with uncovered heads, placing flowers on the graves of the lonely dead. This last is the picture of our afternoon, and we love to linger over this event of 1902. If the first simple, unheralded service was creditable, then in this event modesty gave way to pride, and he who tells it gloried in the day.

There is a Camp of Confederate Veterans in Columbus named for the immortal Lee, and no one protests; there is a Chapter of United Daughters of Confederacy who wear tri-colored ribbons, and no one shudders. These organizations are ready to take up the work and care for the graves of their dead.

It is well that others tell the story of that day, and it is not necessary to draw exclusively upon home journals for the details. From Southern periodicals and papers we can learn all that is necessary to prove that the Southerner, who loves his friend as few people love and hates his enemies with unconcealed intensity, has overpraised the work done at Camp Chase. At the same time, the recipient of this praise cannot help but appreciate the kindly words and own that deep in his heart he is prouder of them than he can tell.

A Huntington (W. Va.) paper says:

The exercise incident to the unveiling of the arch erected at Camp Chase to the memory of Confederate soldiers buried there were simple, but beautifully impressive.

Within the graveyard, which is surrounded by a stone wall, more than twenty-two hundred Confederates are buried, and this inclosure is all that visibly remains of the once terrifying prison camp. For a number of years Col. W. H. Knauss, a Union veteran residing at Columbus, has taken care of the ground and annually decorated the graves. He was almost mortally wounded at the battle of Fredericksburg and carries in his face a conspicuous scar of battle.

The war has long been over to the gentleman whom General
Gordon was pleased to designate as the "golden-hearted Knauss,"
who honors the Confederate dead as his countrymen.

The memorial is a stone arch surmounted by the bronze figure
of a Confederate soldier looking toward the South, and is a handsome tribute.   In the smooth surface of the keystone appears the

MRS. J. H. WINDER,
of the U. D. C., who, with Mrs. John T. Gamble, assisted in unveiling
the arch and statue.

word "Americans."   A profusion of flowers from different sections of the South were distributed on the graves, which were also
ornamented by small flags.   The ceremonies were conducted by
Col. Knauss and consisted of songs, martial music, and addresses.
The vocal music was delightfully rendered by a chorus of young
ladies from the Columbus schools.   Among the speakers were
Judge Pugh, Governor Nash, and Col. Kilbourne.   Nothing occurred to mar the harmony and sympathetic good feeling man-

ifested by the assembled thousands. Gen. John B. Gordon was
on the programme to accept the monument on behalf of the South,
but in his absence Judge David E. Johnston, of West Virginia,
made a short impromptu address of acceptance. His words were
from the heart, however, and thrilled the audience with their
earnest and felicitous simplicity.

MRS. JOHN T. GAMBLE.

Grasping the hand of Colonel Knauss at its conclusion, he led
that fine old soldier to the front of the stage and in loving and
impassioned words told how now and forever hereafter the people of the South would cherish and revere his memory.

This was the most charming and affecting incident of the day,
and was immediately followed by the hymn, "Asleep in Jesus,"
led by Mrs. Winder. The services were marked by a feeling
as spontaneous as though the dead of yesterday were being
buried. The whole affair was a unique expression of a reunited

country from which the last vestige of sectionalism is swiftly passing.

Mr. J. A. Allen of the Cynthiana (Ky.) *Democrat,* wrote of the event:

If Col. W. H. Knauss, of Columbus, Ohio, had not already established a strong hold on the hearts and affections of the Southern people, the unveiling of the statue and arch at the Camp Chase Cemetery would have settled the matter. For years past we have been reading of Colonel Knauss and his patriotic and unselfish care of the graves of the Confederate dead near the site of the old prison, and the services Saturday furnished an opportunity for the *Democrat's* representative to be on the ground and see for himself.

The crowd at Camp Chase, viewed from its proper standpoint in the conferring of honor upon alien dead in a territory whose people were hostile to the principles for which men fought and fell, was most impressive. Thousands of persons gathered within the gray stone walls inclosing the dust of the "Flowers of the South." It presaged that not impossible day when the Blue and the Gray will be honored alike, North and South; and, as a Columbus paper put it, there will be mingled "love and tears for the Blue, tears and love for the Gray."

The ceremonies were simple. Colonel Knauss, the father of the movement, acted as master of ceremonies, and from the stand which had been erected to the east of the arch explained briefly his connection with the work and introduced the different people on the programme, which follows:

Assembly bugler, D. McCandlish, ex-Federal; "Star-Spangled Banner," Normal School; prayer, Rev. John Hewitt, ex-Confederate; music by Fourth Regiment Band; unveiling address, Hon. D. F. Hugh, ex-Federal; "America," Fourth Regiment Band; address of presentation, Gov. George K. Nash, ex-Federal; address of acceptance, Judge D. E. Johnston, ex-Confederate; song, "Lead, Kindly Light," Normal School; address, Dr. Darlington Snyder; song, "Asleep in Jesus;" address, Capt. James Dinkins, ex-Confederate; poem, Mrs. Thomas Worcester, U. D. C. of Cincinnati; music, "Dixie," Fourth Regiment Band; address, Marcus B. Toney, ex-Confederate; music, "Nearer, My God, to Thee," Normal School; firing salute, details from three companies, Fourth Regiment, O. N. G., Capt. A. C. Reynolds; strewing flowers by the Daughters of the Confederacy and ladies of the U. V. L. and G. A. R.; taps by D. McCandlish, ex-Federal; Visitors' Escort, Ex-Federal Soldiers' Drum Corps, Gus Johns.

Of the decoration attractions, it is noted that in the arch hung four baskets of living vines and a large floral piece sent by the Robert E. Lee Chapter, United Daughters of the Confederacy, in Columbus. A circular bed of geraniums in bloom was planted in front of the arch, and on each side were almost numberless boxes and baskets of flowers sent from the South. The speakers' stand was also lavishly ornamented with wreaths and other designs. From all of the trees and shrubs within the cemetery inclosure depended strings of the famous gray moss that is peculiar to the Southland.

No tribute is too splendid to pay this noble ex-Federal soldier for the work he has done at Camp Chase for the people of the South. One who has not been on the ground and talked with Colonel Knauss can have no idea of the obstacles which have confronted him and the obstructions that have been thrown in his way. But with a stout heart and a courage that marked his career at the front till "shot out of service at Fredericksburg," he has bravely, dauntlessly marched on and on until this latest splendid achievement is placed to his eternal credit in the hearts of the South and of every man everywhere who has a spark of patriotic pride and tenderness in his soul. Col. Knauss's work has required a strong moral courage united with an enduring physical strength.

In the Jackson (Miss.) *Evening News* Clay Sharkley writes:

I set out to tell you of the unveiling of a monument at Columbus, Ohio, to the Confederate dead of old Camp Chase.

Well, I found the North fully reconstructed. I had my doubts, from the legislation that has burdened the statutes of the United States in discriminating against the South, whether they were genuinely reconstructed, but they are. . . .

Among the many friends who have aided in every manner possible the work at Camp Chase, no one has been more untiring than Mr. S. A. Cunningham, proprietor of the *Confederate Veteran.* In the July number for 1902 there appeared an article covering several pages giving a complete description of the affair. Although no doubt it has been widely read in the South, and by friends of the South elsewhere, the story of that day cannot be told without quoting from that issue. . . .

Governor Nash, of Ohio, who presented the monument, said:

Mr. Chairman, ladies and gentlemen, and fellow-Americans, this is truly a happy day with me, when I can address you upon this sacred ground as fellow-Americans. Forty years ago we were divided into two hostile camps. To-day the scene is changed. We are not here as Federals, we are not here as Confederates; we are all here as Americans to do honor to our heroic dead and to do something, if possible, to make our country greater and better in the years to come. [Applause.]

It is indeed a pleasure to be here. The ground upon which we now stand is sacred. In it lie the remains of two thousand who were of the bravest and best of the sons of the South, and here they have peacefully slept during all these years. It is a sacred duty which we perform when we come here to honor their memories and to do homage to their brave deeds. It is not only a sacred duty, but it seems to me that in doing this we are doing a splendid work for this reunited country. When the people of the North show their esteem for the brave men of the South who sleep in their midst, they are teaching a splendid lesson in patriotism.

The days of strife are over, they are gone forever, and nevermore will they disturb our peace and harmony. I believe that it will be your aim [addressing the Confederates present] in all the days to come to aid in all ways possible the glory of the beautiful flag which we all love to-day. [Applause.] I know it will ever be your pleasure to uphold law and order in this country, and thus make greater and stronger the splendid institutions founded by our fathers. Whenever we unite in meetings like this, we come together not as men who were once hostile but as men and women who love and honor this great republic and who will forever uphold its beautiful banner. [Applause.] This is no idle prediction. Less than four years ago our country was called upon to engage in war with a foreign foe. The sons of the Confederate soldiers rallied to the defense of our threatened flag and upheld her honor and glory just as bravely and just as readily as did the sons of the North. The sons of the North were rejoiced to have the sons of the old Confederates at their sides doing valiant service for their country. Some people at times despair of the future of this republic, but I have no such misgivings. I know that for the last thirty years the old Confederate soldiers of the South have faithfully taught the story of patriotism to their children. I know that the old Union soldiers of the North have been just as patriotic in their teachings to their children, and from these sources has grown throughout this nation a wonderful patriotism, a wonderful love for our country. This spirit will forever guard the honor of my country and my flag.

I am rejoiced that we have among us to-day many ex-Confederate soldiers and their friends. To them I bid a most hearty welcome. I am glad that you are here, because you can see from this splendid assemblage that the people of the North honor with you the memory of your old soldiers who sleep in this cemetery. [Applause.] I hope that you will take the story of it back to your Southern homes, and inform your friends that the remains of the ex-Confederate soldiers in the State of Ohio are honored by the people of this State. [Applause.] In this sacred connection it gives me pleasure to present, on behalf of the State of Ohio, this splendid monument to the memory of your soldiers. This monument, builded of stone and bronze, will last for many years, but it will not outlive the memory of the brave deeds and the heroic men whose sacred ashes repose in this cemetery.

Judge David F. Pugh, Past Department Commander of the G. A. R. of Ohio, said in the unveiling address:

The beautiful and impressive custom of decorating the graves of the soldier dead originated after the Civil War and was inaugurated in several Southern States, I believe, in the year 1866 or 1867, by Southern ladies; and the fact that they decorated graves of unknown Union soldiers, as well as their own Confederate soldiers, gives it an additional historical and sentimental interest. They went out into the cemeteries and scattered flowers impartially over the unmarked graves of the Union dead and upon the graves of their own soldiers. The hearts of Northern people were touched and thrilled by this kindly act. We of the North are to-day merely following the unselfish and noble example of those women. Five or six years ago a fair was held in the city of Wheeling, W. Va., to raise money for the erection of a home for dependent Confederate soldiers of West Virginia. A Captain Johnson, an ex-Union soldier and officer, contributed a Chinese sword of curious workmanship, to be sold for the benefit of the home. In sending it to the managers he said it was all he was able to do for the home, and expressed the hope that God would bless the surviving veterans, both Blue and Gray. We here to-day, in our participation in this solemn and decorous ceremony, are moved by the same spirit which inspired and actuated Captain Johnson.

The ablest, most skilled of the Union generals, General Grant, occupied a portion of his last days on this earth urging and impressing his countrymen to restore fraternity and love between the North and South; and this advice was illustrated and illuminated by the unspeakable pathos of his death chamber. When he was serving his first term as President, Gen. Robert E. Lee visited the White House. He honored his old antagonist by giving him audience in preference to the Senators and Representatives in Congress who were in waiting and had preceded Lee under the inspiration of his motto, "Let us have peace!" When Lee surrendered, he refused to imitate the example of the Roman and Grecian generals by making a triumphal entry into Richmond. He would not permit any celebration of the victory by the Union army in the presence of the Confederates. He spared the latter every humiliation. He knew that it was necessary to the consummation of the victory that the surrendered Confederate soldiers should become loyal citizens. He knew that the republic could not hold vassal provinces by the bayonet and survive. We simply honor his memory and observe his dying precept to-day by participating in the decoration of these graves and the dedication of this statue.

One of the wisest acts—certainly the most magnanimous act— of President McKinley was his advocacy of a plan for the

National Government to maintain the Confederate cemeteries.
and at its expense.   It was only a reiteration of what he had said
twenty years before at Oberlin, Ohio.   In a memorial address
there, speaking of the duty of the people of Ohio with respect
to the graves of the dead Confederates in Camp Chase, he said:
"On us, too, rests the responsibility of caring for their graves.
If it was worth while to bury each man in a separate grave, or
give him an honorable interment, is it not worth while to preserve
the grave as a sacred trust, as it is, and as it is to us alone?"
The line of action for us is, fortunately, simple.   In the office
of the Adjutant General of the State is a record of all these
dead, with a diagram of the grounds, each grave being numbered.
From this it is possible to find the grave of each man and to
arrange the grounds in proper manner.   Let this be done by the
State.   Let the Legislature provide for the oversight and care
of these graves.

President McKinley made two extended tours through the
Southern States.   The ex-Confederates by the thousands attended his meetings and receptions, and cheered and applauded him.
Nowhere in the South was he threatened by anarchists.   His life
was safer than in the North.   When it became necessary to make
additional major and brigadier generals for the Spanish War,
this broad-minded President did not hesitate to put the stars upon
the shoulders of those old graybacks, Generals Wheeler, Lee, Butler, Oates, and Rossiter.   When McKinley died, not the North
alone, but the North and South—the whole nation, reborn, reunited—mourned his death and shed tears over his grave.   The
"kindly light" of his magnanimous example and teaching encour-
ages and cheers us on to-day in paying tribute to the heroic Confederate dead who sleep in this Confederate cemetery.

Just fresh from the battlefield of Shiloh, where I witnessed and
heard two ex-Confederates, one representing the State of Tennessee, participate in the dedication of the Ohio monuments to
the heroic Union dead who sleep there, and where I was thrilled
by the royal eloquence of one of them, in which he honored our
dead comrades, I have no doubt either of the propriety or the
duty of an ex-Union soldier participating in the ceremonies of this
occasion.   We decorate these graves to-day, and we dedicate this
statue, because the men who sleep here were brave men, because
they nobly illustrated American skill and valor on the battlefields
of the Civil War.   Although one side was thought to be right
and the other considered wrong, yet both sides were inspired by
similar impulses and actuated by the same sincerity of conviction.
The Civil War is without its twin in history.   For the grandeur
of its impost, the vastness of its resources, and the tenacity of
the combatants it has no parallel in the annals of war.   Fought
by men of the same blood, it demonstrated the endurance, the
prodigious power, and the vast resources of the republic.   It was

not a war by either side against Chilians or Italians, Spaniards or Filipinos. It was only Americans who could hope to successfully overthrow the Union, and it was only Americans who were qualified to successfully defend it. The Civil War showed what kind of people inhabit this continent—all brave men and women. It demonstrated that the Anglo-Saxons on this continent, whatever might betide them on the other side of the ocean, had not degenerated. Bunker Hill was easier to climb than Cemetery Ridge, Missionary Ridge, or Lookout Mountain. During those four years Washington, sleeping on the banks of the Potomac, often heard martial footsteps like those of its own soldiers. On both sides there was unparalleled endurance, with fortitude and unselfishness, through a long and exhausting conflict. Such armies as were raised and maintained on both sides were wonderful in their exhibition of soldierly attributes. That the Confederate soldiers were gallant, that they were hard fighters, can be proved by every Union soldier who struggled against them in the fiery front of battle.

After the battle of Missionary Ridge I was attracted by the extreme youthful appearance of a dead Tennessee Confederate soldier who belonged to a regiment of Cheatham's Division, against which we had fought the day before. He was not over fifteen years of age and very slender. He was clothed in a cotton suit and was barefooted—barefooted on that cold and wet twenty-fourth day of November, 1863. I examined his haversack. For a day's rations there were a handful of black beans, a few slices of scrghum, and a half dozen roasted acorns. That was an infinitely poor outfit for marching and fighting, but that Tennessee soldier had made it answer his purpose. The Confederates who, half fed, looked bravely into our faces for many long, agonizing weeks over the ramparts of Vicksburg; the remnants of Lee's magnificent army, which, fed on raw corn and persimmons, fluttered their heroic rags and interposed their bodies for a year between Grant's army and Richmond, only a few miles away—all these men were great soldiers. I pity the American who cannot be proud of their valor and endurance.

All the bitterness has gone out of my heart, and, in spite of a Confederate bullet in my body, I do not hesitate to acknowledge that their valor is part of the common heritage of the whole country. We can never challenge the fame of those men whose skill and valor made them the idols of the Confederate army. The fame of Lee, Jackson, the Johnstons, Gordon, Longstreet, the Hills, Hood, and Stuart, and many thousands of noncommissioned officers and private soldiers of the Confederate armies whose names are not mentioned on historic pages, can never be tarnished by the carping criticisms of the narrow and shallow-minded. On both sides the Civil War was prolific in that heroic excellence of human character which some people had supposed was the monopoly of ancient history, tradition, and poetry. Hereafter it will not be necessary for any American, whether he be Blue or Gray, to read the stories and legends of Grecian and Roman glory to inflame his imagination about heroes and heroism. There are other trophies than those of Miltiades, as some

W. P. HARRISON.

one has said, to keep him awake at night. He can set his imagination on fire and keep himself awake by reading stories of equal interest and of equal valor about a hundred crimson battlefields of the Civil War.

More than thirty-seven years have passed away since Lee and Grant met at Appomattox. Thirty-six seedtimes and harvests have distributed their benedictions to the Blue and Gray alike. After going through ordeals which we were spared and through privations of which the North has no conception, the Southern people rebuilt, rehabilitated, their part of the country in a most phenomenal way. The waste places have been made to blossom like the rose, and old battle grounds are covered with verdure. Northern capital and vigor have married Southern energy and capital, their sons and daughters have intermarried, and the South is sharing in the universal prosperity.

Much has been done for the burial of ancient grievances and old grudges and for the cultivation of thoughtful love of country. We are in the midst of an epoch of fraternal love and peace. The final victory at Appomattox was not a victory of the North over the South, but of the North and South over the South. it was as much their victory as ours. They were, equally with us, beneficiaries of that victory; and its blessings are just as precious to them as to us. The North and South have been welded into a more homogeneous nation by a common grief. Our nation has been made richer by the blood and tears mingled together from both sides. What we thought and said of each other in the war times is now forgotten. Our flag, with not one star dropped from it, waves over both Blue and Gray.

On Decoration Day the flowers of the earth, so blue and golden, make no distinction between the Blue and the Gray, but freely give their fragrance to both. No mother weeps the less fervently because her boy wore blue or gray. To-day in this cemetery the flowers will be scattered on the graves of Americans. Thirty-eight years have stilled the bitterness of the conflict. To-day we stand immeasurably above all resentment or revenge.

I have just returned from a visit to two of the great battlefields, Chickamauga and Shiloh, and it is no extravagance to say that no Union soldier who sleeps in the cemeteries on those battlefields speaks to-day from his grave of wrath or hatred toward the South, but their voices would mingle with ours for peace, fraternity, and a reunited country.

To-day, standing upon the serene heights of love and forgiveness, and with an implicit faith in the Divine Forgiver of all, we can see in this joint participation, and we can see in this coöperation of Blue and Gray in paying tribute to the heroic Confederates sleeping here, a symbol of the true American—the Union for which we have been hoping and praying for many years.

In this final resting place of over two thousand Confederate dead Mr. W. P. Harrison has assisted Col. William H. Knauss to erect this memorial arch and statue of a Confederate soldier. Both Mr. Harrison and Colonel Knauss should be honored for this appropriate monument. It is their votive offering to that brotherly kindness, peace, and love, and forgiveness for which there has been pleading and praying for years all over this country. Only a few of us know how Colonel Knauss has toiled, struggled, and endured to make this monument and these conditions a success. He has braved the criticism and censure of a few but bitter opponents of reconciliation. He has resisted the advice of those who have told him that it was not expedient and good policy for him to manage and superintend the decoration of these graves from year to year; and I repeat that he should be honored for what he has done.

Let the statue be unveiled!

HON. D. E. JOHNSON.

Judge D. E. Johnson, of Bluefield, W. Va., on behalf of his Southern comrades, made a worthy speech of acceptance:

Mr. Chairman, unexpectedly and without preparation, I am called upon to respond to the patriotic and eloquent speech of the distinguished Governor of the Commonwealth of Ohio, presenting, on behalf of his people, to our Southern people this splendid monument erected to the memory of more than two thousand brave men who wore the gray and whose ashes repose in this area.

These men who sleep here were Confederate soldiers (Americans), who dared to "do the right as God gave them to see the right;" and so seeing and believing, they consecrated their lives, their all. They suffered and died for their convictions rather

BOWLDER AND MEMORIAL ARCH.

than prove false to the cause which they had espoused. Right or wrong, they suffered the horrors of prison life, eked out a miserable existence, and died in the belief of the justice and righteousness of principles which they had been taught to hold as sacred and dear to them as life itself. I accord to those who wore the blue the same right I here to-day claim for those who wore the gray—that is, that we believed we were right; and, whether right or wrong, the fierce and bloody struggle of four years, the terrible sufferings and sacrifices which we made, the memories of our honored dead, their splendid deeds of valor and heroism, we would not forget if we could, and we could not forget if we would. In calling to mind our own sufferings and the great sacrifices we made to maintain our cause it is evident that those who opposed us were no less in earnest than we. They expended millions of treasure and poured out rivers of blood to uphold and maintain the principles for which they battled and contended. And, above all things else, we must not forget that in that great contest we were, and are still, all Americans, and that the splendid courage and gallantry, heroism and valor displayed by the men who sleep here are the common heritage of our American people.

In accepting, on behalf of our people, this monument erected to the memory of these men, after listening to the patriotic and tender speech of Governor Nash, I am happy to say that I rejoice to find that, in a great measure at least, if not altogether, the bitterness and prejudice engendered by the strife between the sections have passed away, and we are again one and the same people, with one common flag, hope, and destiny, and that this monument is one among many tokens of that evident good feeling of patriotism and fraternalism that will forever bind us together in one common bond of affectionate brotherhood.

I cannot close without saying that he who above and beyond all others is more absolutely entitled to the lasting gratitude of our people, on account of his great love for our common humanity, and who by his earnestness and activity in procuring the erection of this monument has endeared himself to our people by "ties stronger than hoops of steel," is a grand old veteran who wore the blue, and who for the cause he espoused spilt his blood and suffered all things, endured all things, even unto death—his coffin ready—and when the war closed devoted his life not only to peaceful pursuits, but out of the love of his great soul and a heart filled with good red blood has worked earnestly and faithfully to bridge the chasm that so long had separated the North and South, and has labored unceasingly for the restoration of harmony, peace, and fraternal relations between our countrymen. He to whom I refer now stands by my side. I grasp his hand as an indication of what I have said, and as a token of my love and esteem; and now, on behalf of my people, who owe him a debt of gratitude perhaps greater than to any other man living north of Mason and Dixon's line, I, from the depths of my heart [turning to Col. W. H. Knauss] thank you; and now here with clasped hands we declare to this large assemblage, composed in part of those who wore the blue as well as those who wore the gray, that the war is over and that lasting peace is here to stay.

Colonel Knauss, allow me to say in conclusion—and I say it believing that I bespeak the honest, sincere sentiments of our people —that they will not only to their latest day honor you and hold you and your kindly deeds in grateful remembrance, but that our children's children and generations yet unborn will bless your memory.

Following the hymn, "Asleep in Jesus," Capt. James Dinkins,

CAPT. JAMES DINKINS.

of New Orleans, delivered an address which in eloquence is worthy to live after him:

Although the people of the South did not bid me come, I know that I represent them to-day when I extend the hand of kinship and express my pleasure in meeting the people of the great State of Ohio—valiant in war and progressive in peace. The nation knows you well and has called your sons to high places on field and in council.

The South shares the pride in your achievements and testifies to the quality of your manhood—first to pay the tribute of courage to those who once opposed, first to hail the grander brotherhood of the stronger Union, first to raise the rainbow arch above the sacrifice of strife.

Our comrades dead are the living fire upon the altars of memory, and your tender solicitude has taught all Americans that immortality's light perpetually hallows every grave where heroes lie, and that every death for duty was a hero's death.

The beautiful custom of keeping green and glorious the sacred spots where soldiers sleep stirs patriotism wherever practiced. No section monopolizes it; no sectional lines divide the reverence paid.

In our own fair Louisiana are two national cemeteries: one at Baton Rouge, where rises the Capitol; the other at New Orleans, close to Chalmette field, where Jackson gave undying force to the American doctrine to which Monroe afterwards gave undying fame. Our flag is still here. Under its folds sleep Union soldiers from many fields; under its folds for twenty years and more have women—our Southern women—strewn the flowers of love. Mothers and sisters there are in Ohio, Iowa, Illinois, Wisconsin, and other States whose hearts lie buried there—too far away for them to place their tokens upon the biers of their beloved. Mothers and sisters there are in Louisiana who say: "These are our own; their graves shall not be neglected." Their magnolias transplant the message of your lilies; their roses clasp yours in the wreath of a nation's mourning, dewed perennially by a nation's tears.

Confederates have gathered annually upon this spot, marching beside the other Grand Army, proud that the women of New Orleans have set the example to which more men bow their heads each year in the sight of the God whose blessings our banner begs. Only a few days ago we said "Amen" over your prayers there; to-day you share our sorrow above the buried Gray.

The people of the North and South have often held different views and opinions in the past, and will continue to do so in the future; but the only serious disagreement between them was forever settled by war thirty-seven years ago.

I am not one of those who tell you there is no East, no West, no North, no South; but, on the other hand, I am proud of the distinctiveness of our separate sections, whose friendly rivalry is the corner stone upon which the nation's greatness rests. Deprive the Puritan in the East of his reverence for his ancient laws, and you destroy his happiness and his usefulness. Take away from the South her traditions, ideals, and legends, and you rob her of much of her glory.

I would not change the well-defined accent of the Northern people, nor lose the soft, musical sound of the Southerner's voice. Each section represents a member of the family, but each has its individuality. They argue and quarrel, and have been known to fight; but when one of our ships sank in a treacherous harbor, an electric spark flashed over all the land—one message, one signal, and that was "Union." The speed, the strength, the soul of that response blazed upon the world warning for all the future and settled forever any doubt that the scattered sons have come together.

Forty years ago the Southern States, by common impulse, withdrew unto themselves apart. They believed that right and honor compelled them to do so. They upheld that opinion as long as their means and resources permitted; but when the Confederate soldiers laid down their arms and returned home to begin life anew, they did so with the firm resolve to support the standard they had fought and which was their own again.

They were not understood, however, and were compelled to bear and suffer in silence for many years; but, thank God! we stand to-day with our brothers of the other section, on equal grounds for a common cause in freedom's name.

I believe I speak for the whole South when I say: "My head and my heart for my country—one people, one language, one flag." All nations may well envy the patriotic spirit, boundless as the air and resistless as the bounding oceans, which fills every home in the South. And every Southern home takes pride in the fact that this spirit is the spirit of the land.

In an emergency never prophesied nor anticipated the United States was called on to lend a hand for humanity. We undertook to relieve the oppressed and to punish the oppressor, and the South was not backward in rallying to the call. Her sons supported the starry ensign with all their might, bravely and gloriously, and the stars shone together as they ever will, lending liberty new beauty, giving brotherhood a new name and government a new lesson.

Martyrdom was the crown the angels placed upon McKinley's brow, a sign high in the heavens that bids our manhood break the bonds of self and hasten the radiance of a world redeemed. It is beside his grave as well as the burial place of these, my brethren, that I stand to-day and repeat again the lesson of our poet, Father Ryan, gathered from the war-bruised flowers of faith:

> Give me the land of the wreck and the tomb;
> There is grandeur in graves, there is glory in gloom.
> For out of the gloom future brightness is born,
> As, after the night, comes the sunrise of morn.
>
> And the graves of the dead, with the grass overgrown,
> May yet form the footstool of Liberty's throne;
> And each single wreck in the warpath of night
> Shall yet be a rock in the temple of Right.

We have taught it to our children. Your children, strewing their wreaths above the heroes to-day, are planting the same seed of everlasting loyalty to principle. It was for principle, not for dissension nor for conquest, that these men gave their lives. It was this complete renunciation for country's sake that McKinley is pointed to as worthy our veneration and as insuring the nation's indissolubility.

Capt. Marcus B. Toney, of Nashville, Tenn., delivered an address replete with patriotic sentiment and abounding fraternity. The speech is not in print or obtainable, or it should appear with the other notable addresses of that occasion. The same is true of the speech of General Arnold, of Kentucky, who spoke tenderly and beautifully, as befitted the occasion.

A detail from the Fourth Regiment, Ohio National Guard, fired the soldiers' salute; the Ladies of the Union Veteran Legion and the G. A. R. accompanied the Daughters of the Confederacy and assisted in the pleasing and merciful duty of strewing the flowers. Presently Bugler McCandlish sounded taps, and the drum rolled. The drum corps was of old soldiers under the direction of Gus Johns, of the One Hundredth Pennsylvania. So ended that day, the memory of which lives and is as though it were yesterday. One can well believe it will not be forgotten even in that endless to-morrow that lies beyond life's sundown.

An interesting letter and newspaper clipping were received from Clarksville, Tex., from M. L. Sims, First Lieutenant of Company D, Forrest's Original Battalion of Cavalry, in which he expresses the highest appreciation of what has been achieved for the Camp Chase Confederate dead. He had arranged with Miss Mary Logan, of Louisville, Ky., to procure the flowers in that city and express them in time for the dedicatory ceremonies.

The flowers were sent as a tribute to all Confederate soldiers buried there, but especially to be placed at the graves of two faithful and unfortunate colored men—Haywood and Walters—if their graves could be identified.

The following clipping from the *Dallas News* will be interesting reading to all Confederates:

The only company from Texas in Forrest's Original Battalion was captured at the battle of Fort Donelson in February, 1862. The noncommissioned officers and men were sent to Camp Douglas, near Chicago, and the commissioned officers were sent to Camp Chase. These officers were L. L. Bailey, R. G. Lane, and

M. L. Sims. With them were two negroes—Haywood Goodloe and Walter ——. Haywood was the servant of John J. Goodloe, and Walter the servant of Sergt. John L. Jamison.

Lieutenant Sims states: "After the surrender I advised these negroes and Ben, my servant, that we were prisoners; that we no longer had the right to control them and could not protect them, and that they might make their escape either then or in the near future. Ben took my advice and succeeded in reaching his home. Haywood and Walter seemed terrorized by the situation and remained with us. At St. Louis I again tried to get them to work their way home. They refused to do so and went with us to Camp Chase and were treated as other prisoners. In a few days they both died with pneumonia and were buried in the same cemetery in which the Confederate officers were buried. I went to the graves with the funeral party and chaplain and made a statement as to who they were and how they came to be there, a record of which was made, I think, by the Federal chaplain. Burial services were held and a headboard with the name placed by a Federal officer at each grave. When these men took sick they were placed in the prison hospital; were given clean clothing, good beds, and received the same medical attention and nursing that the Confederate officers received. Lieut. (Dr.) R. G. Lane gave each of them his special attention, and Lieutenant Bailey and myself assisted in nursing them until they died.

On June 25 a letter was received from Miss Mary Logan, of Louisville, explaining that she had sent the flowers.

Among the many noble Southern women who have labored unceasingly for the Confederates the name of Mrs. N. V. Randolph, President Richmond Chapter, U. D. C., is prominent. To this daughter of Virginia the author is indebted for many encouraging and helpful words. Mrs. Randolph was invited to attend the unveiling service, but could not be present. She wrote from Virginia Beach, saying:

I am sure every Southerner, especially the women who have struggled so long to keep green the graves of their dead, will bless you for your beautiful tribute to our prison dead. The Chapter will take official action as soon as I return. You must feel proud that you have trampled prejudice under your feet; and no one knows better than I what you have had to contend with, and how bravely you have stood up for the Confederate prison dead.

After Capt. Marcus B. Toney returned to Nashville he wrote:

Dear Colonel: I want to express to you and to the G. A. R. boys my appreciation of the hearty reception given me. To say I enjoyed my visit would be putting it mildly. I was delighted.

While General Gordon was deeply interested in the work at Camp Chase, all correspondence upon the subject was conducted by Adjutant General and Chief of Staff Gen. George Moorman.

The letter received from him just after the ceremonies, and perhaps one of the last written to the author before he died, is reproduced, with tender recollections of the friendly associations through the years of work in caring for the graves at Camp Chase. He wrote:

I received a letter from General Gordon saying he was disappointed about perfecting some matters at the last moment so that he could go to Columbus, and very much regretted that he was unable to attend.

I was very sorry I could not be present, as I was myself one of the Camp Chase prisoners, and was paroled awhile in the city of Columbus, and afterwards sent to Johnson's Island. I knew Governor Todd well, and reported to him every day while I was on parole in Columbus. During that time I boarded at Mr. Harper's, just back of the Governor's mansion. He had two daughters, whom I remember well—Misses Hattie and Mary.

I was paroled by order of Hon. Edwin M. Stanton, Secretary of War, for having given water to a wounded Federal soldier on the battlefield at Fort Donelson.

I could have given you some reminiscences of Columbus at that time which would have been good reading for the present generation, and particularly so, as I was one of the leaders in decorating the Federal graves at Chalmette sixteen or seventeen years ago. The matter of decorating the graves of the opposing army is not new to me.

The decoration of the graves of Northern soldiers was first done by our Confederate Veterans in New Orleans. With every good wish, your friend and comrade.

Not only is the illustrious soldier, so long the Commander in Chief of the Confederate Veterans, gone to the bivouac eternal, but his chief of staff also. On account of our relations, his enthusiastic helpfulness, his great ability, and splendid patriotism, the writer unites with the soldiers of the South in paying tribute to Gen. John B. Gordon, and withholds not his hand from writing of General Moorman. As one of you, men of the South, this friend who signed himself comrade shall not soon be forgotten.

General Moorman's letter was answered by the writer as follows:

The exercises were perfectly satisfactory. All regret the absence of General Gordon and yourself. All pronounce the arch

very fine and the statue as perfect as they ever saw. Two gentlemen from Mississippi, members of a committee looking for a
statue for their home country, declared it to be nearly perfect.

I think I have done my work, and will now turn the matter over
to the Confederate Camp and the U. D. C. Chapter. The cemetery is in good condition, and there is an appropriation, recently
made by the government, to rebuild the stone wall. The cemetery will be in such condition, when repaired, that it will be an
honor to the present generation; and I think now is the proper
time for me to withdraw and leave it in the hands of the local
Camp and Chapter.

The Southern poet, Robert Loveman, has written:

"Wrath is a wrinkled hag, hell-born;
Her heart is hate, her soul is scorn.
Blinded with blood, she cannot see
To do a deed of charity.

Love is a maiden, young and fair;
She kissed the brow of dumb despair,
Till comfort came. O, Love is she
Whose other name is Charity!"

In that stormy long ago we were "blinded with blood," but to-
day we can see once more "to do a deed of charity."

As we linger at the graves of those we love, loath to leave
them in their loneliness, so we leave this portion of our subject
with regret.

It has been a labor of love, but it has been misunderstood, even
in the South, in some instances. At home and abroad men have
wondered at the purpose back of it all.

It was unforeseen that the impulsive and warm-hearted people
of the South would feel so deeply upon the subject. If criticised
at home, the words of appreciation from unknown friends have
more than repaid. The prayers of one widow, sorrowing yet in
her Southern home, are more than recompense for the time and
money spent. When alone oftentimes in the little cemetery to
see if all is well, there is a feeling of comfort and content which
forces the thought that unseen sentinels are whispering, "All is
well; all is well!"

"We put fresh flowers on forgotten graves,
We, who once wore the Union blue;
O'er their low tents the old flag waves—
O'er these men of the South, so true.
Oft were our blooms bedewed with tears;
Unnoted they slept through all the years,
Until at last the lone, dank banks
Were garlanded by old-time "Yanks.""

CHAPTER VIII.

Odds and Ends.

Planting Trees at Camp Chase Cemetery—An Incident of Concord, N. C.—Confederate Dead at Gallipolis—Official Correspondence Concerning the Cemetery—A Few of the Many Friendly Letters—The Return of a Confederate Flag—A Speech That Caused Comment—Insinuating Postal Cards—The Visit of Editor Cunningham—Visiting Camp Chase Cemetery in Winter.

MENTION is made in the Introduction relative to the idea of planting trees in the cemetery at Camp Chase, and that these trees should come from the Southern States. This suggestion was made to Gen. George Moorman, General Gordon's chief of staff, who issued a circular letter which was sent to each Camp of Confederate Veterans. The trees came; some were in good condition, while others were doubtless improperly removed from the native earth, so that they died soon after being replanted. Even if many of the trees died, however, the idea of having Southern trees to shade the graves of the men who died for the South was well worth trying.

There being a Camp of Confederate Veterans in Columbus at this time, the work of planting them in the cemetery was turned over to them.

Many beautiful and tender letters were received in this connection, worthy of a place in this book. That the reader may enjoy the sentiments expressed, some of them are here quoted.

Supt. C. S. Douglas, of the Gallatin (Tenn.) Public Schools, wrote:

In the Nashville *American* of February 27 Maj. G. B. Guild, U. S. A., who is now located in Columbus, graphically describes his visit to the Confederate Cemetery near Columbus. To you he ascribes all praise and much honor for the care and protection of the graves of the Confederate soldiers who lie slumbering in your midst. This letter was read at our last meeting of Cheatham Bivouac, and so magical was its effect, so grateful did the old comrades feel toward you, and so ready were they to assure you of their appreciation of your magnanimity that your humble servant was commissioned to write you our sincerest thanks.

Your name is written on the register of our bivouac, your nobleness of heart will be embalmed in our souls, and of your character we would write in living letters, "How true, how beautiful!"

Gen. J. J. Dickison, Florida Division, U. C. V., Ocala, writes of flowers sent, and adds:

May God bless you and yours! is not only the beautiful prayer in our division, but every one's heart in the Southland rings out a benediction for you.

R. B. Coleman, Major General Indian Territory Division, U. C. V., wrote from McAlester, Ind. T.:

Your name shall be a household word for all Southerners as a token of the service you have rendered the North as well as the South in caring for the Confederate graves at Camp Chase. Nothing could please me more than to shake the hand of one who is free from malice toward the men who fought for the right as their consciences understood it.

From Greenville, S. C., James A. Hoyt wrote:

The ten trees which we send you for Camp Chase have been taken from the grounds here by an ex-Confederate private, who with his own hands wished to render homage to the memory of his fallen comrades. With kindly regards and appreciation of your fraternal solicitude for our dead soldiers' graves, etc.

A letter from Asheville, N. C., says about the trees:

With a hope that may live and grow to be an honor to the Tar Heel State, from which they are sent, and to the generous projectors of the plan of maintaining the hallowed ground into which they are to be planted, I am, yours most sincerely,

JAMES M. RAY,
Brig. Gen. Comdg. Fourth Brigade, N. C. Div., U. C. V.

From Richmond, Va.:

I deeply appreciate the sentiments expressed by you in your request for trees from this State. R. E. Lee Camp No. 1 of the Confederate Veterans of Richmond, Va., has received from the city of Richmond fifteen trees, which have been shipped to your address. THOMAS A. BRANDER,
For R. E. Lee Camp No. 1.

From Booneville, Mo.:

Let me assure you, my dear sir, that you have the sincere thanks of every ex-Confederate Missourian for your noble work in caring for the graves of the ex-Confederates buried at Camp Chase. ROBERT McCULLOCH,
Major General Missouri Division, U. C. V.

From Dallas, Tex.:

The trees went forward yesterday. The express company forwarded them free of charge.   BEN M. MELTON,
For Camp Stirling Price of the U. C. V.

From Bluefield, W. Va.:

I sent you by express twenty white pine trees for the Confederate Cemetery at Camp Chase. Best wishes for your success and long life.   DAVID E. JOHNSTON.

Some sending trees did not describe them, but as they grow many who visit Camp Chase can do so.

On another occasion trees and shrubbery from the nursery were purchased by business friends in Columbus. On all occasions, when permitted, Mr. R. M. Rownd, postmaster at Columbus, and who was a member of the Ninth Ohio Cavalry, gave money to assist in paying the expenses of the memorial services, and others offered to help; but in most cases financial aid, except that received from the South, was declined.

From Washington, D. C.:

Thank you for your noble and generous interest and zeal in the care of the graves of the Southern dead at Camp Chase. Very truly,   THOS. W. HUNGERFORD,
Chairman Ex. Com. Camp 171 of the U. C. V.

From Lexington, Ky.:

Your generous care of our dead heroes will give you a warm place in the hearts of all of our Confederate Veterans. Fraternally,   JOHN H. CARTER,
Adjutant General Kentucky Division, U. C. V.

A little story that is known to but a few at present is considered of sufficient interest to be told here. It gives an insight into the character of one mentioned here and demonstrates the good work done long ago.

In 1865, during the time that Lee and Johnston's heroic but defeated legions were going home as best they could, a young cavalryman sought credit in the village store at Concord, N. C. The proprietor looked at the young man sharply, saying: "I have many requests from your people for credit."

"I'm honest, sir, and I'll pay you," said the young man.

"They all say so," answered the storekeeper.

It looked as if the incident was closed, but the cavalryman, after a pause, said: "You may not believe it, but I'll pay you every cent if you let me have the things I want. I have no money nearer than Ohio, and unless you trust me I must do without."

"How much do you want?"

"I do not know how long we will stay here; it may amount to $20."

"What is your name?"

"Robert M. Rownd, of the Ninth Ohio Cavalry, sir."

"I'll trust you."

The regiment left Concord before being paid off, going to Lexington, some thirty miles distant. Pay day came at last, and Rownd went to Concord with the money to pay his debt. A friendship was born that day that meant something to the storekeeper in after years.

The North Carolinian and the Ohio soldier corresponded with each other at long intervals. Finally the Concord merchant moved to Richmond, Va., and engaged in a manufacturing business. During the dark financial days in 1893 the manufacturer found himself in great need of money to tide through a crisis. He found that if he could weather the gale at that particular time he would be in easy circumstances; and if not, he would be a bankrupt.

With gentlemanly delicacy he spoke of the past and of his present situation. "I need very much more than twenty dollars," he wrote; "but if you could see your way clear to lend me the amount, I can say as you did, I am honest and will pay you every cent."

It does not matter about the amount—it is told in four figures anyway—but a New York draft went to Richmond by return mail.

Learning from one who had been in the Gallipolis (Ohio) Cemetery that there were some of General Morgan's men buried there, a letter was written to a gentleman, J. M. Alexander, of that city, about the matter, to which he replied:

. . . I have spent a good part of the day investigating the matter. I have known for years that three Confederates lie in the Pine Street Cemetery, but the old record before me fails to make any mention regarding them. I find that one hundred and fifty-eight Union soldiers have been buried in this cemetery, according to this record, yet one-half of those are marked "Unknown" and only three of them have the year in which they were buried; so it is no wonder the Confederate graves have been neglected. Yet it is understood that three Confederates were buried in the southwest corner of the cemetery. Two of them, I find, died from wounds in the general hospital at this place, and it must have been in 1861. I am sorry there are no means of further identification. When we consider that so very many of the Union dead are marked "Unknown," we cannot wonder that, as the Confederates were strangers, no record was made.

At the last decoration, on May 30, I was in charge. After all the Union graves had been strewn with flowers, I marched the column to the place desigated as Confederate graves and had them covered with flowers, and, standing in the drizzling rain, made a talk of several minutes—not because they had been Confederate soldiers, but because they were patriots and brave men. None but brave Americans could have fought and held out against such odds as did the Confederate army. I believe the feeling of the old soldiers of the Union army is of the kindest toward the Confederates.

Should you want to send markers for these three graves at any time, I will see them put in place.

We find by reference to some old files that it was in 1886 that an effort was made to have Camp Chase Cemetery receive some care and attention. The correspondence was as follows:

ADJUTANT GENERAL'S OFFICE, STATE OF OHIO,
COLUMBUS, June 2, 1886.

To His Excellency, J. B. Foraker, Governor.

SIR: I have the honor to submit the following report concerning the condition of the Confederate Cemetery at Camp Chase, near Columbus.

As requested by you, I have made a careful examination of all the records accessible pertaining to this burial place.

The cemetery contains the remains of the Confederate soldiers who died while prisoners of war at Camp Chase, during the years of 1863, 1864, and 1865. About twenty-one hundred interments were made during that period. A few bodies were removed immediately after the war by friends to Southern burial grounds. A complete list of the names of the dead, with the numbers of the graves to correspond to the plat of the cemetery, together with said plat, are found among the records in this office.

The ground which comprises the cemetery was deeded to the United States Government by the executors of John G. Holloway, April 23, 1879, and the deed for the same is recorded in Volume

141, page 528, Records of Deeds of Franklin County, Ohio, and contains two and one-half acres.

On May 15, 1886, I wrote the Quartermaster General, United States Army, concerning the condition of the cemetery, and submit herewith copy of my letter and his reply:

"ADJUTANT GENERAL'S OFFICE, STATE OF OHIO,
COLUMBUS, OHIO, May 15, 1886.

"To the Quartermaster General, U. S. Army, Washington, D. C.

"SIR: There is located near Columbus an old Confederate burial ground, in which were buried those who died while in prison at Camp Chase. These grounds have been neglected for years. The fences are all down; the headboards have been displaced.

"The ground is owned and controlled by the United States Government. I write this communication to inquire if there is not some provision by which the ground can be restored to proper condition.

"Very respectfully, your obedient servant,
"H. A. AXLINE, Adjutant General."

"WAR DEPARTMENT, QUARTERMASTER GENERAL'S OFFICE,
"WASHINGTON, D. C., May 20, 1886.

"Gen. H. A. Axline, Adjutant General, Columbus, Ohio.

"GENERAL: I have the honor to acknowledge the receipt of your letter of the 15th instant, calling attention to the condition of the Confederate Cemetery at Camp Chase, near Columbus, Ohio, and asking if provision cannot be made for the improvement or restoration of these grounds, etc.

"In reply, I beg to say that there is no appropriation that can legally be applied to the care and maintenance of this cemetery, and the Department has, therefore, no means with which to make the improvements suggested.

"Very respectfully, your obedient servant,
"S. B. HOLABIRD,
"Quartermaster General, U. S. A."

With an acknowledgment, I replied:

"I quite agree with Your Excellency that the present condition of the cemetery is a disgrace to civilization, and that humanity requires that even the burial places of our enemies in war should not be thrown into the commons and left for briers and brambles.

"Very respectfuly, your obedient servant,
"H. A. AXLINE, Adjutant General."

It will be observed that the government had no money to repair the place where rests the dust of those who died at Camp Chase Prison. But the then Governor and his Adjutant General did not let the matter rest until a bill was prepared, introduced in Congress, and finally passed authorizing a stone wall to be built around the cemetery.

As sometimes happens with government work, the wall was a poor job and soon began to crumble. There was no one to look after it, and many administrations came into power in Ohio and passed away, none seeming to think of the lonely cemetery where lay the Southern dead.

As already stated, it was in 1895 that the writer became interested in the place, and, among other things, called the attention of Mr. Foraker, after he became Senator, to the condition of the wall, with the result that an appropriation at first of two thousand dollars was secured to rebuild it. At a subsequent session of Congress, this sum being too little, it was increased to three thousand six hundred dol!ars. A contract was made for the work, under direction of Colonel Yeatman, Commander of the Columbus Barracks, and was completed by the middle of November, 1904.

The wall, which is four feet high in front and five feet above the two and one-half feet of concrete foundation on the north, is built of Ohio limestone and cement, surmounted by a broad coping of sandstone. It presents a strong, fine appearance, giving the impression of stability that will stand well the storms of time. Mr. Grant, the government inspector, says there need be no new wall built around the cemetery for three hundred years.

In the fall of 1900 there occurred a pleasing event in which the writer participated; and while not germane to the text, it was one of those incidents that made friends of old-time enemies, and thus fits in here.

Judge D. F. Pugh prepared a bill, and procured its passage, authorizing the Governor to return the Confederate flags and banners. The act is as follows:

Whereas, The animosities of the Civil War are forgotten by the people of this nation, sectionalism is dead, and fraternity and good will prevail everywhere; therefore,

Be it resolved, That the Governor of Ohio be, and is hereby, authorized and empowered to withdraw from the relic room of the Capitol building, from time to time, the Confederate flags and banners there stored, and return the same, or cause them to be returned to the survivors of the military organizations of the late Confederate army from whom they were respectively taken and captured.

The reunion of the Forty-Sixth Ohio was held in the town hall of Worthington, near Columbus, at which time the tattered battle-flag of the Thirtieth Louisiana was put into the keeping of those who had fought for it. The story is told by the New Orleans *Picayune* as follows:

With other battle-marred and bullet-pierced relics of the Confederacy reposing in Memorial Hall, there was deposited last evening the battle flag of the Thirtieth Louisiana Regiment. This sacred memento of the fighting days of 1861-65 was for thirty-six years in the possession of its captors, the Forty-Sixth Ohio Volunteers, who recently sent a gracious invitation to the "Boys in Gray" of the Thirtieth Louisiana to send a delegation to Columbus, Ohio, for the purpose of being guests of the Forty-Sixth and at the same time receiving their old flag, as a token of the esteem, unity, and harmony which now prevail over all parts of the United States.

The Louisiana veterans sent their delegates to Columbus, and the flag was returned to them and brought back to this city. The cherished colors were formally presented to the Army of Tennessee for deposition in Memorial Hall.

Secretary Brown read the minutes of the meeting of the Thirtieth Louisiana survivors held September 14.

At that meeting the invitation of the Forty-Sixth Ohio was read and accepted, and a committee was appointed to act in all matters pertaining to the proposed trip to Ohio.

J. H. Brown, Judge J. U. Landry, and —— Harrison were appointed to receive the flag.

Mr. Brown then read the report of the flag committee, giving the particulars of the trip and of the reception, paying special tribute to such gallant Ohioans as Judge D. F. Pugh, Col. Wm. H. Knauss, Governor Nash, and Dr. Thos. P. Shields. The committee was enthusiastic about Ohio and her generous, hospitable people.

The meeting adjourned to Memorial Hall, where the Army of Tennessee was in session. Business was suspended as the survivors of the brave old Thirtieth Louisiana entered the hall with martial tread and erect bearing, headed by Major Trepagnier and Private John M. Coos, bearing the flag.

In giving a lengthy account of the engagement wherein the flag was lost by the Louisianians, Major Trepagnier says:

. . . This position of the enemy's line was occupied by the Forty-Sixth Ohio Regiment, one of the best veteran commands in the Federal army, all being armed with murderous Spencer six-shooting rifles. They wisely reserved their fire until we were close to their line, when they poured such a terrific and destruc-

tive fire at short range into our line that our men were actually
mowed down without being able to do much injury to them, they
being concealed from view by the thick underbrush in front of
their works.   In a short time the Thirtieth Louisiana was fear-
fully cut up by this hailstorm of lead.   Our gallant field officers,
Lieut. Col. Thomas Shields and Maj. Charles J. Bell, had fallen,
both shot dead; fourteen line officers out of twenty present had
also fallen, either killed or wounded.   The color bearer and all
the color guards were shot down; only six members of the color
company and only three members of the company on the left
of the colors were uninjured.   All of the officers of these two
companies were either killed or wounded; and when the brigade
was ordered to retire from the field, the Thirtieth Louisiana could
muster only six officers and about sixty men.

This flag, whose staff had been shattered by bullets, had
changed hands as often as its defenders had fallen, until there
was no one left around to protect it, and it remained on the
bloody ground, close to the enemy's works, surrounded by the
bodies of its defenders, and thus became a prize in the hands of
the Forty-Sixth Ohio Regiment.

We feel keenly the loss of our colors, and our only consolation
lies in the fact that they fell without dishonor.   We also derive
great satisfaction from the spontaneous action of the members
of the Forty-Sixth Ohio in their anxiety to return us our flag as
a testimonial to the soldierly conduct of its defenders.   These
brave and chivalrous soldiers of the Forty-Sixth Ohio Regiment
many years ago desired to return this flag, and were prevented
from doing so only because they could not legally obtain possession of it.

It was the fixed intention upon the part of the writer to cease
active work regarding the care of Camp Chase Cemetery at the
conclusion of the unveiling of the arch and statue in 1902; for, as
has been said, the care of the cemetery and the arrangements for
memorial services were placed in the hands of the Daughters of
the Confederacy and the local Camp of Confederate Veterans.
In 1903 and also in 1904 the ladies in charge of the exercises
called upon me for an address, to which I responded.   There
had been mischievous endeavors to prevent my further service
in these Confederate memorial exercises.   It is amusing to recall
efforts by narrow-minded and prejudiced Federal comrades to
prevent my being present on that occasion.   For instance, one
wrote: "Don't forget the 30th of May in your anxiety to decorate
and care for the Confederate dead."   Rude cartoons of me were
sent by anonymous persons, but none of this interfered with my

even tenor. I considered the sources and took fresh courage with an approving conscience. It is most gratifying to have the approval, years afterwards, of distinguished and noble men, of which the following is an illustration:

President McKinley, in an address at Atlanta, Ga., about the close of the Spanish War, said:

Every soldier's grave made during the unfortunate war is a tribute to American valor. And while, when those graves were made, we differed widely about the future of the government, those differences were long ago settled by our arbitrament of arms; and the time has now come, in the evolution of sentiments and feeling under the providence of God, when, in the spirit of fraternity, we should share in the care of the graves of the Confederate soldiers.

Those men and their true followers who fought the battles of the war on both sides were glad the war was over. But those of both armies who managed in various ways to get on detail duty in the rear or around headquarters, so that when the army moved they could remain behind, were the ones to disapprove.

It is good to be alive to-day; good to be able to look into the eyes and to grasp the hands of each other—the Blue and the Gray—when we recall how, a generation ago, we strove with each other under the lightning and the dim clouds of battle. Together the two armies—the Federate and Confederate—embrace the choicest of American men, and together they built high the standard of American courage. I think that we can claim that there are no better warriors in the wide world than in America, and no emblem of grander principles ever designed by man or God than our flag—the flag of our fathers.

In several Southern places the Confederate Camps have joined with the G. A. R. organizations on May 30, our Memorial Day, and assisted in doing honor to our dead heroes.

Allow me to announce that on May 29 I received from Mrs. E. K. Fritzlin, of Denton, Tex., a box of Southern Cape jasmine buds, to be given to the women of the Union Veteran Legion, who have in the past assisted with the Confederate memorial services in this city, for them to wear while on their blessed work of strewing flowers over the graves of our Union dead on our Memorial Day. She said: "As a token of my respect for their noble and Christian work."

I received also a box of white carnations from Mrs. Florence Tucker Winder, President of R. E. Lee Chapter, U. D. C., for our services at Greenlawn Cemetery in doing honor to our dead.

Would to God there were more of this feeling, and that we, as Americans, could go arm in arm to these sacred places! We hope that when we join that brotherhood beyond, and meet the Commander of the great majority, we will see more clearly. Just now an instance of the battlefield occurs to me: The dead and wounded were lying together. One boy thought he was dying. His thoughts going back to his home in the North, he saw his mother on her knees praying for him. He asked the one by his side to pray for him. The reply was: "I have never prayed in my life—don't know how." The dying fellow turned to the other side and saw that the one lying there was shot through the head and was speechless, but he said to him: "Can you pray for me?" The dying man slowly laid his hand on his heart, and then as he raised it slowly he pointed up, up to heaven, implying: "God is there. Give your heart to him!" Then both died. The one who never prayed lived and became a Christian man, and said he there gave his heart to God. May that same God who has spared us to this time bless you all!

Another event that I cannot refrain from mentioning was the large informal banquet, at the Great Southern Hotel in Columbus, to Mr. S. A. Cunningham, of Nashville, Tenn., editor of the *Confederate Veteran*. Besides the guest of honor, Mr. Cunningham, there were present: Dan Emmett, of Mt. Vernon, author of "Dixie;" John Y. Bassell, Judge D. F. Pugh, Gen. H. A. Axline, Col. R. M. Rownd, Mayor Sam Black, Judge Todd Galloway, Thomas E. Knauss, W. H. Holliday (County Auditor), S. N. Cook, D. B. Ulrey, J. L. Porter, C. A. Roth, Rev. T. G. Dickson, Henry Briggs, Capt. W. B. Albright, Dr. Thos. P. Shields, John H. Levy, John Grim, S. A. Humphries, Thos. J. Davies, W. J. Snyder, J. H. Crampton, and representatives of the city papers. Several of the foregoing were prominent Union veterans, while several others were much-esteemed Confederates.

The inner man having been satisfied, the toastmaster said:

The Camp Chase Association was formed by a few men, some of whom fought in the Union army and some in the Confederate army, and some of them are here to-night to break bread with our friend and guest from the South.

S. A. CUNNINGHAM, EDITOR CONFEDERATE VETERAN.
(Showing the Sam Davis overcoat.)

The object of our association is to take care of the neglected graves of Americans who fought for what they thought was right and, as American heroes, sacrificed their lives for their principles. They prayed to the same God that we did, and in the judgment day must answer to the same God.

It is a token of our good will toward and respect for our Southern friend that we come together to spend a social hour in getting better acquainted.

Our guest, the editor and publisher of the *Confederate Veteran*, is not here to increase his subscription list, but to visit the burial place where many of his comrades rest. I am sure he will tell his people at home that we are civilized and live in the Lord's land, and show respect to the living and the dead.

Among those who spoke that evening were Mayor Samuel Black, Gen. Axline, J. Y. Bassell, Dr. Dickson, and Judge Pugh. In response, Mr. Cunningham graciously thanked those present for the honors conferred, and said that it had impressed him more than any other incident in his life. His work for the last five years had been in the line of this meeting. He was grateful for the spirit manifested by the Union soldiers.

He said no section could have regretted the death of Lincoln more than the South, and he knew that many Southern men and women shed tears at the death of Garfield. He was profoundly impressed with the attention given the graves of the soldiers at Camp Chase, and expressed the gratitude of his people for it, knowing that the South would thoroughly appreciate it. He appreciated the fact that the Federal Government had built the wall around the cemetery, and said that it must be repaired. While the Southern people revered the Confederate flag, yet it should be draped in crape, as he had it in his publication—the *Confederate Veteran.* He was glad that the war was ended, and said that all the South would be grateful to the Northern people just as long as they realized that the war ended in 1865.

In the *Confederate Veteran* for December, 1897, there is a complete and perhaps flattering account of the event, which was well appreciated by every Northerner who read it. We will conclude the story of that evening by quoting from the *Confederate Veteran.*

When the guests had dined in the superb hotel, the Great Southern, Col. Knauss, the master of ceremonies, startled nearly everybody by stating that there was present a gentleman who was a soldier in the United States Army before any one at the table was born—Daniel Decatur Emmett, the author of "Dixie." The applause was so general that Mr. Emmett rose to his feet when called upon for a speech, but he said he must be excused. The writer, knowing how exquisitely he could sing "Dixie," urged that he sing a stanza of it. He said he could not unless all joined

DAN EMMETT, AUTHOR OF "DIXIE."

in the chorus. There was a quick, hearty assent, and the Grand Army veterans joined with the Confederates in the spirit of the great tune. General Axline showed his appreciation of "Dixie" by saying: "We should never have let you Southerners have 'Dixie.' It added fifty thousand soldiers to your army."

Mr. Cunningham went to Camp Chase Cemetery, but the chill of our winter lay over it. The stately elms waved their bare limbs helplessly in the blast from the northwest. One could wish that it had been summer when he first looked upon the spot where

these men of the South had slept so long.   Nature smiles even in
the graveyard in summer, and it would not have seemed so lone-
some.   The birds would have kept the dead company.

> "We care not whence they came,
>   Dear in their lifeless clay!
> Whether unknown or known to fame,
> Their cause and country still the same;
>   They died—and wore the gray."
>   —*Father Ryan.*

Many letters have been received by the writer from friends
throughout the South, dating back to 1897, and each year growing
in number.   The later letters are not less interesting than those
received in the beginning.   The earlier friends wrote again, and
new friends added strength and cheer by their expressions of appreciation.

Many and cordial have been the invitations for the writer to
visit the South, and he regrets having been unable to show his
appreciation.   He quotes testimonials from Tennessee:

From L. T. Dickinson, Adjutant N. B. Forrest Camp No. 4,
U. C. V., Chattanooga, Tenn.:

Col. W. H. Knauss, Columbus, Ohio.

DEAR COMRADE: Your name has been a household word in our
company for several years.   As the years roll by we appreciate
more keenly the noble and patriotic work done by you for our
sacred dead.   In recognition of your generosity, we have made
you an honorary member of our company.   I take pleasure in inclosing your certificate of membership.

The papers you sent, giving an account of the dedication of
your arch, were duly received and presented before the Camp
last night; also the picture of the arch and a portrait of yourself, for which I am instructed by the Camp to thank you.   Your
picture will be framed and hung upon the wall.

From Nashville, Tenn.:

At a regular meeting of Frank Cheatham Bivouac, Association
of Confederate Soldiers, a circular from the headquarters of the
United Confederate Veterans was read, calling attention to the
fact that on Saturday, June 14, 1902, Col. Wm. H. Knauss, of
Columbus, Ohio, would have unveiled and dedicated a monument
over our Confederate soldiers who are buried at Camp Chase;
moreover, that he had for years had these graves annually strewn
with flowers.

Thereupon the president appointed a committee, which submitted the following preamble and resolutions, which were unanimously adopted:

"Whereas Col. Wm. H. Knauss, by his acts, has proven himself to be a true Christian gentleman and patriot, and has cared for the graves of our comrades when no one else dared do so; therefore,

"Be it resolved, by Frank Cheatham Bivouac, That the thanks of this association be, and are hereby, extended to Colonel Knauss for his noble and self-sacrificing acts in honoring our Confederate dead.

"In testimony whereof the Bivouac has caused these presents to be signed by its president and secretary, and attested with the seal of the State Association.

GIDEON H. BASKETTE, *President;*
JOHN P. HICKMAN, *Secretary;*
M. B. TONEY, *Recording Secretary."*

CHAPTER IX.

VISITING THE SOUTH.

A Trip to New Orleans Mardi Gras Time—An Unlooked-For Reception
—What the Crescent City Papers Said—Great Bouquets of Roses by
the Ladies—The Confederates Present the Stranger with a Fine Gold
Badge—Eloquent Speech of Captain Dinkins—-An Editorial—Going to
Nashville—A Fourth of July Event—Meeting Friends Both Blue and
Gray—Guests of Mr. and Mrs. M. B. Toney—A Remarkable Camp
Fire—Well Repaid.

I WOULD be ungrateful and unworthy of the high honor paid
me by my Southern friends at various times and places did I not
make public recognition of their cordial greetings and unstinted
hospitality. I regret exceedingly that I could not accept many
invitations to visit the homes of friends whom I have never met.
I shall mention an invitation that I accepted for myself and wife—
to spend the 4th of July, 1902, in Nashville, Tenn. I had made
a visit to New Orleans, the quaint old metropolis of Louisiana, in
February, 1902. I did not anticipate the reception I met; it was
overwhelming. There is a foolish song that most of us have
heard that runs: "There are moments when we wish to be alone."
There were moments at New Orleans on the evening of February
13 when I wished to be alone—alone until I could find voice,
which somehow had left me; alone until I could see without blind ·
ing tears. Not until I leave earth will I forget that night, and
not then if I am permitted to think of things terrestrial. How
could I be expected to forget such a night as that, at Memorial
Hall, when eloquent words laden with affection, when armfuls of
magnificent roses and other fragrant flowers, were showered upon
me, a stranger within their gates?

Registered at the St. Charles, I met General Moorman just as
he was leaving the city; but he had evidently posted a number of
his comrades, for it was not long until inquiries were being made
at the hotel for "the man from Columbus, Ohio." At dinner a
gentleman informed me that a crowd of both ladies and gentlemen were waiting to meet me. I explained that I was weary,
but that I would be pleased to meet them the next day.

I hesitate to tell of that next evening at Memorial Hall. To the plain business man, plodding on in the usual prosaic way, ovations are rare. I may be forgiven, then, for the seeming vanity of telling the story. It is also due the splendid men and glorious women of New Orleans, and I desire that those who live after me shall know of that eventful evening which is as indelible with me as is the event of the bloody battle of Fredericksburg (where I was shot down). And this is the part of it so beautifully strange: it was men of the South who put a bullet through my face that marked me for life, and it was Southern men and women who forty years after wove garlands for me and made a night of hand-clasps, of flowers, and of welcoming words. Such is the character of this nation of ours; such is this land of ours.

It was Mardi Gras week, and the city was full of joyous people watching the ever-shifting but ever-brilliant pageant. In every city there is a trust, a close corporation, known as society, and in New Orleans this unincorporated corporation was busy about Mardi Gras time. In that proud old city there were none nearer the throne of that mystical monarch, the ruler of society, than the majority of those in Memorial Hall. They had turned aside, however, from courtly gayeties to visit for an hour with a plain old "Yank." What is written is written; if to my confusion, it is for their glory. Even in the midst of that crowded, joyous time the New Orleans *Daily Picayune* gave, on the morning of the 14th, nearly one entire page to the event at Memorial Hall.

With the egotism of love—love for these warm-hearted strangers—I copy the headline of the *Picayune* that morning:

CONFEDERATES HONOR A HERO WHO FOUGHT THEM

But Who Recognized His Foes as Americans Who Became His Brethren Again, and Made the Care of the

Graves of Southern Soldiers in Neglected Places His Special Care Until Others Rallied to the Cause of Proper Protection. Colonel Knauss, of Columbus, Ohio, Given a Reception at Memorial Hall and Presented with a Medal.

Mrs. W. J. Behan, President of the Ladies' Confederated Memorial Association, called the meeting to order. The hall was filled with ladies and ex-Confederate soldiers when one of the ladies asked Capt. J. C. Dinkins to escort me to the platform. As we walked up the aisle the audience applauded heartily. The Captain presented me to Mrs. Behan, Mrs. Aldin McLellan, and Mrs. J. Pinckney Smith. On the platform with the ladies were Gen. W. L. Cabell, of Texas, and others.

MRS. W. J. BEHAN.

Mrs. Behan delivered a brief and most generous address. She concluded by saying: "He did this work, and now we feel that he is one of us." Taking me by the hand and turning to the audience, she continued: "I now take pleasure in introducing to you William H. Knauss, of Ohio." I was about to reply when she placed in my hand a magnificent bunch of flowers, at the same time alluding to the flowers placed on the graves of the dead at Camp Chase.

MRS. J. PINCKNEY SMITH.

The proceedings had reached that point where I began to feel that there was something the matter with my throat when, happily, Mrs. J. Pinckney Smith arose and claimed the right to address me, as she was the first woman in New Orleans to send flowers from that city to me for the Camp Chase Cemetery. Then she presented me with a large bunch of American beauties.

Captain Dinkins came forward then and said:

During the four years of desperate struggle between the North and the South there died in the Federal prison at Camp Chase, Ohio, 2,260 Confederate soldiers, who were buried within the prison limits. Those devoted men, separated from comrades and friends, could have regained their liberty, and doubtless many of them would be living to-day, had they taken the oath of allegiance to the Federal government; but, rather than yield the opinions which they believed were guaranteed by the Constitution, they gave up their lives as a sacrifice to principle. Their bodies lie in Northern soil, and for thirty years we had no record of their resting place. Far removed from those whose love and teachings made them what they were, their graves remained unmarked until finally one of that mighty host which opposed them (ah, I may say, the greatest of that mighty host), regardless of the jealousies and prejudices of his neighbors, determined to perpetuate their deeds and their glory; and to-day, thanks to his courage, his munificence, and his patriotism, it is his pleasure to have sweet flowers tenderly placed on them every year.

They were Americans, who, believing they were right, did not hesitate between sacrifice and personal safety. Having that sense of appreciation which only a patriot can feel, that great soul present here to-night began the work which he has so successfully pursued. We are assembled to do him honor, and to acknowledge the obligations we feel for his unselfish deeds, and his noble example of an American which we are proud to recognize and to follow.

It has been truthfully said that the greatest happiness is derived from contributing to the pleasure of other people; therefore Colonel Knauss must enjoy much satisfaction, because the people of the South will ever hold him in grateful remembrance. And I can assure you, my dear Colonel, that these people, representatives of the best social condition, whose guest you are to-night, convey the sentiments of all the Southern people in tendering to you the warm and sincere expressions of admiration and love.

It may be justly said that the Southern people are generous in their love. No section is superior to them in devotion to duty; and as patriotic American citizens, whose record in war and in peace will forever be maintained, whose conduct on the battlefield can never be excelled, whose love for the traditions of the South will continue to descend from parents to children, and whose loyalty to the flag is unsurpassed, they are deeply sensible of the obligations they owe Colonel Knauss.

Then addressing him directly, Captain Dinkins continued:

These obligations they have no desire to cancel; but, moved by a common impulse, the Confederate soldiers of New Orleans, their wives and daughters, created this beautiful memento which they now present to you, sir, with the hope that your life may be spared for many years, and with prayers that finally the great Captain may crown you with a wreath immortal.

A New Orleans daily paper, in describing the event and the badge, said:

All of the Confederate Veteran Camps participated in the reception and presentation of the medal, which is a very handsome and costly one. It is made of 16-carat gold, about the size of a silver dollar, and suspended from a crescent, to which is attached the coat of arms of Louisiana, and on the face of the medal is the Confederate flag, stars and bars beautifully enameled, with "W. H. Knauss" on the bar between the crescent and the medal. On the reverse side is the inscription: "In appreciation of the notable care of our comrades' graves at Camp Chase, Ohio, the Confederate soldiers of New Orleans present this memento to Col. W. H. Knauss, February 13, 1902."

Finally the time came when I had an opportunity to thank them for their graciousness and their great kindness. It matters not what I said. I recall that I reviewed what had been done at Camp Chase, and that they were pleased when I told how Miss Osgood, a teacher in the public schools, had trained one hundred and fifty children to sing on one memorial occasion, and how the little girls took flowers from the platform and strewed them upon the graves of men who had died far away from home, far from those they loved. From the audience came bouquets until they were piled around me. There were many kind and beautiful things said and many gracious attentions shown me. I mentally see the picture of that scene over and over, with its soldierly men and beautiful women, and I catch the perfume of the flowers, and with its glamour I wonder how and why it all came about.

The New Orleans daily papers commented upon the event editorially. Without comment on my part, or apology for doing so, I reproduced the sentiments expressed by the *Picayune* and *Times-Democrat.*

In the introduction to a five-column article descriptive of the meeting at Memorial Hall, the *Picayune* says:

The reception given Col. W. H. Knauss, of Columbus, Ohio, last night by the ladies of the various Confederate associations of the city, which was participated in by the Confederate veterans of the various Camps, was a notable affair. Though the attendance was confined almost, if not quite, to the members of the Confederate organizations, there was a large gathering, and it represented the best social and intellectual elements of the city.

Colonel Knauss has been so long honored and admired for his care of the graves of Confederate dead at Camp Chase and Johnson's Island, in Ohio, that many have desired to show their appreciation of his service to the South, and he has been known as a friend, even though never seen. He came to New Orleans to the carnival, but has been so quiet that not many people knew of his presence; but after the veterans and the ladies found it out, he was "captured by the ladies," as he expressed it.

One of the chief incidents of the evening was the presentation of a beautiful gold medal by the veterans of all the Confederate associations. Colonel Knauss did not know about that part of the programme, and it was hard to decide whether he was most delighted with that or the magnificent bouquet of white roses presented by the Daughters of the Confederacy.

The *Times-Democrat* editorial of February 15 said of "An American Patriot:"

We had occasion a day or two ago to emphasize the point made recently by Senator Hoar, of Massachusetts, that there are various, though in no sense conflicting, ways in which men who love their country may manifest their patriotism. "Some men show their love for the flag of their country by protecting it from violence," said Senator Hoar; and it is a noble thing to do. Other men show their love for the flag of their country by keeping it pure and preventing it from becoming a symbol of tyranny and injustice. The Senior Senator from Massachusetts was inclined to think that the latter phase of patriotism was quite as honorable as the former. It is certain that all temperate, thinking American citizens will sustain him in the admirable point he makes. It may be said, indeed, that patriotism in its highest and best form is that intelligent love of one's country which supplements the willingness to die that the nation may live with the determination that the nation's life shall be animated by the philosophy that "He who ruleth his own spirit is better than he that taketh a city." It is only when the positive force is supplemented by what might be called the negative force that love of country becomes a passion the noblest known to the human heart.

There are millions of men in this country of ours who, aroused by the ardor of conflict, would step with jubilant feet the moment the war drum might throb; and there are millions of other citizens who, in the quiet of peaceful industry, each day illustrate the virtues of courage and constancy, which only and which alone make a people great. The citizen of finest fashioning, however, is he who may pass from the calm of peace into the storm of war and from the storm of war return once more to quieter days, and withal keep his conscience unseared, his mind unprejudiced, and his spirit sweet and unspoiled. The kind of patriot we have in mind it has been the pleasure of the people of New Orleans to welcome here within the last few days and, out of the abundance of their kindly hospitality and fraternal feeling, to honor with a tribute of their respect and their affection.

It is hardly necessary to add that the gentleman to whom we refer is Col. William H. Knauss, who while in the Federal army almost lost his life on the battlefield of Fredericksburg, and who after the close of war devoted his time and his attention to an unsolicited labor of love in caring for the graves of Confederate soldiers who during the conflict died at Camp Chase and were buried in a cemetery near Columbus, Ohio. The simple story told by Colonel Knauss in his talk of Thursday evening at the Memorial Hall was one which, so long as man is man, can never fail to move the human heart. It was eloquent of the one touch of nature that makes the whole world kin. It illustrated the larger significance of Appomattox. It taught that the surrender of the Confederate soldier meant more than the emancipation of a race, more than the political welding together of separate and individual States. It meant that with the echo of the last gun should die every ignoble prejudice and memory; that beneath the repelling features of war should be discerned the redeeming nobleness of both Federal and Confederate; that a reciprocal confidence should solidify and purify our political life; and, finally, that as one nation we should become one people.

This is the message fresh brought to us from Ohio by this gallant Union soldier; and in contemplating not only the words spoken by Colonel Knauss, but also the man who spoke, the people of New Orleans pause for a moment to listen and to applaud— "to do him honor," as Captain Dinkins said, to acknowledge the obligation we feel for his unselfish deeds and for his noble example of an American which we are proud to recognize and to follow." We are quite sure that among the men who wore the gray or among their children may be found not one whose heart does not echo another sentiment perfectly expressed by Captain Dinkins in presenting Colonel Knauss with a gold medal.

When I visited my good Southern friends at Nashville in July of that same year, in the beautiful capital of Tennessee, every courtesy that generous hearts could conceive or willing hands execute awaited me at all times. Mrs. Knauss and myself were the guests of Mr. and Mrs. M. B. Toney, at Vauxhall Place, and enjoyed the hospitality of these good friends during our stay. Our friend and comrade, Mr. S. A. Cunningham, of the *Confederate Veteran,* Mr. Toney, and others met us at Bowling Green, Ky., escorting us to Nashville.

MARCUS B. TONEY.

When these gentlemen explained what had been planned for our entertainment, I was deeply moved. Not only did the ex-Confederates seek to make this one of the most beautiful visits of my life, but my comrades of the G. A. R. also joined heartily in making the occasion pleasant.

A Nashville paper of June 29 said:

It will be a pleasure to old Confederates generally, and especially to the committee of Frank Cheatham Bivouac appointed to invite the Union soldier, William H. Knauss, of Columbus, Ohio, to their Fourth of July celebration at Cumberland Park, to know that he has decided to come. He wired his acceptance yesterday. Colonel Knauss is now looked upon as guardian of the graves of all Confederate dead buried at Camp Chase. He comes to join the camp fire to be held at Cumberland Park, and will be the guest of the Confederate Bivouac.

The Nashville G. A. R. Posts are, however, claiming the right to show their esteem and affection for Colonel Knauss, and with this end in view the Commander of George H. Thomas Post, N. D. Higley, has appointed a committee to join the Bivouac and meet him at the depot on arrival.

The following programme will be carried out at the camp fire: The Blues—"The Confederate Dead at Camp Chase," Col. W. H. Knauss; "The Army of Tennessee," Dr. N. D. Higley; "Gen. George H. Thomas," Gen. G. P. Thruston; "Nashville During the War," A. W. Wills; "Nashville After the War," John Ruhm. The Grays—"The Confederate Private," G. H. Baskette; "Prison Life in the North," B. M. Hord; "Reminiscences—Generals Lee and Jackson," M. B. Toney; "The Twentieth Tennessee Infantry," Dr. W. J. McMurray; "The Tactics of 1861," Theo. Cooley; "The Confederate Veteran," S. A. Cunningham.

The Nashville *Banner* of July 4 said:

Col. W. H. Knauss, of Columbus, Ohio, the Federal veteran who is to-day the guest of Frank Cheatham Bivouac, U. C. V., and George H. Thomas Post, G. A. R., arrived last night, accompanied by Mrs. Knauss. He was driven to Mr. Toney's home, in Vauxhall Place, where he was accorded a Southern welcome.

Colonel Knauss has endeared himself to every Southerner by his generosity and magnanimity in caring for the graves of the Confederate dead at Camp Chase, Ohio; and by his splendid war record on the Federal side he is a hero in the North. He will be the principal orator at the camp fire of the Confederate and Federal veterans to be held at Cumberland Park, and will respond to the toast, "The Confederate Dead at Camp Chase."

He was indeed accorded a "Southern welcome." As in New Orleans, so it was in Nashville—kindness and friendship everywhere. There was the satisfactory knowledge that these attentions proved the nobility of character of the Southerner and his quick appreciation of a friendly act. The *Banner* of that date told the story (already alluded to) of the battle at Fredericksburg, Va., in which a piece of shell came near finishing my life work.

The Fourth of July celebration was gotten up by the Frank Cheatham Bivouac at Cumberland Park for the purpose of raising money to erect a monument to the private Confederate soldier. The Post of the G. A. R. at Nashville gave them cordial assistance, and a feeling of good will seemed to pervade the atmosphere. All in all, it was a day of genuine enjoyment.

There was a sham battle that made the light of battle come again in the eyes of the veterans. In this case the defenses were rows of mown weeds. At a distance they looked impregnable, but when set on fire, accidentally, they disappeared faster than earthworks under masked batteries. The volumes of smoke, the roar of the artillery, and the spiteful crack of the rifles seemed like old times, particularly when a command in the old-time gray and with the old-time yell moved to the attack. That night the camp fire was an interesting occasion. It is ever interesting when men once foes meet together as though comrades always and talk of the battle days.

Before the great battles of the sixties it would have been considered an event worthy of world-wide note, could there have occurred a camp fire of Wellington's grenadiers and Napoleon's Old Guard. The world heard of Gettysburg as well as Waterloo. Meade's legions of blue were as terrible as Wellington's grenadiers, and Lee's old guards in gray under Pickett charged where Napoleon's men could not have gone. It was such soldiers who sat together and ate and drank together that night in Nashville.

In concluding this portion of the history of Camp Chase and its dead, I assert that, if I had hoped for any reward, I have had it abundantly; but I had no thought when I began the work that any such scenes as I have described would occur. At most I felt that if I could let it be known in the South that there was sleeping here some one who had left standing at the gate as he marched away a woman who could not see him through her tears—a woman who had left her farewell kiss upon his lips, a woman who knew not where he sleeps—I should be repaid. I was permitted to give this information, and they thanked me, and that was enough. But they have written that they prayed God to bless me, and that is enough, quite enough.

CHAPTER X

Camp Chase in 1861.

Once a Military Camp and Prison; Now a Fine Farm—The First Prisoners—A Confederate Pictures the Daily Grind of Prison Life—What a Texan Remembers of Camp Chase Prison—The Plot to Escape—The Spies' Report—Brutalizing Effects of Prison Life—The Man with the Poor Memory—The Deserter and the Prisoner—Strother's Story— Work on Camp Chase Begun in May, 1861.

To-day fruitful fields and comfortable homes take the place of the old parade grounds at Camp Chase, once worn bare by the tramp of men who had grown weary waiting for exchange. In the long stretch of years from '61-'65 to 1904 time has easily removed the traces of a prison from Camp Chase. Time softens memories, as "distance lends enchantment."

The first prisoners of war received at Camp Chase were a party of the Twenty-Third Virginia Regiment who had been captured in the Kanawha Valley. They were taken there July 5, 1861, and for a time were held as hostages for the Union soldiers captured by Confederates. They were not held long, but were returned to their homes. The names of these Virginians, as given by the local papers of that date and from official records, were as follows: R. B. Hackney, A. B. Dorst, A. Roseberry, H. J. Fisher, R. Knupp, J. A. Kline, Frank Ransom, J. W. McMollen, J. W. Echard, David Dong, G. B. Slaughter, A. E. Eastham, J. W. Diltz, Robert Mitchell, S. Harfiss, E. J. Romson, F. B. Kline, Sly McCausland, O. H. Selnll, James Johnson, W. A. Roseberry, B. Franklin, and James Carr. The high tide of prison population was reached in 1863, when there were confined at Camp Chase stockades about 8,000 Confederate soldiers. The majority of these were privates and noncommissioned officers. There were at times officers of the rank of colonel at this prison, but they were moved to Johnson's Island; if not exchanged.

The first military camp for the Union soldiers was Camp Jackson. It is a park now, called Goodale Park. A story extant is that a regiment stationed at Camp Jackson upon the occasion of an anticipated outbreak of prisoners at Camp Chase was "double-quicked" all the way from Camp Jackson to Camp Chase, a distance of five miles. It was a severe test of endurance, for not every man could run for five miles without resting.

When the call for 300,000 more men was made in 1862, Camp Chase was made the place of rendezvous for ten of the interior counties. There were large camps near Cincinnati and Cleveland —Camp Denison, near Cincinnati. Regiment after regiment was equipped and sent to the front from Camp Chase, and Confederate prisoners were received in great numbers.

The prisons neither North nor South were intended for "pleasure resorts," and the death rate at Andersonville, Millen, Camp Chase, and Johnson's Island is proof that none of them were desirable places.

One feature of Camp Chase, unchanged through all these years, is the old "Four-Mile" house. It appears now as it was then. (See page 5.) Some who were in prison at Camp Chase will remember the Confederate sutler store, where the prisoners secured rubber buttons and made rings, for which there was quite a demand from visitors, who were desirous of getting these souvenirs from the prisons. Many of these rings are still retained as mementos of this Federal prison.

A pen picture of a prison mess at Camp Chase or Johnson's Island is from Col. Barbiere's "Scraps from the Prison Table at Camp Chase and Johnson's Island," written soon after the war.

A prison mess contained from sixty to one hundred persons. They slept in two long rooms, in single bunks, but two were forced into each bunk. They were three tiers high. In the upper tier the occupants could barely turn over without brushing the ceiling. A cynical comrade who was at Millen Prison, Georgia, in October and November, 1864, remarked that he had not room to turn over without brushing the roof or ceiling, while I had all the room that was between the stars and that patch of sand—nothing above me but the clouds, not even a blanket.

Colonel Barbiere also adds:

One dining room, one side of which was arranged with bunks, rendered eating at all times disagreeable to a man of sensitive olfactories. In our room were ten plank tables, each adorned with ten plates, an equal number of tin cups, two pronged forks, a dull knife and an iron spoon, and a chunk of bread about the size of a man's fist to each plate, which allowance was all the bread one received at that meal. In the center of the tables there was meat or bacon. Coffee was poured into the cups previous to meals to cool. One stood to eat, and did not waste time at the table. Breakfast was served at six, dinner at half past eleven, and supper at half past five. Every one returned to his quarters at "retreat" and lights were extinguished at "taps," the former being at sundown and the latter at ten. Then everything was quiet until the treadmill of daily movements began with the next day's sun. . . .

Camp Chase is situated in a flat four miles from Columbus, with a high board fence around the cabins. There is an elevated plank walk within the yard, to keep us from falling in the mud while making a circuit of the prison. It is one of the filthiest of the many pens assigned for the confinement of the Confederate prisoners.

Col. W. H. Richardson, of Austin, Tex., in 1898 wrote the author of Camp Chase Prison:

It is but natural that you should like to know something of the life in Camp Chase and of those who fill the graves you have so kindly cared for. The story as it was written in hunger and suffering might bring to the surface bitter memories and be considered unseemly and out of place. I will therefore deal only in a general way.

Arriving in Camp Chase early in August, 1864, we found an order curtailing rations to the lowest minimum possible to sustain life. Therefore a constant want of necessary, healthy food to sustain life fast filled those graves. The weak went first, and the unfortunate ones who contracted diseases next; while strong men, inured to hardship and short rations, wore on.

All this time the sutler was not allowed to sell anything in the shape of food, not even pepper. It is little wonder, then, that any scheme to escape was readily entered into. Our mess, composed of officers only (mostly border men), organized for the purpose of escape. We occupied a room twenty-four by twenty-four feet, with twenty-four men in the room, in one end of a barracks shanty built on posts two and a half to three feet off the ground. With one blanket and one suit of clothes, cold and hungry, we dug and worked for eight long months, only to be disappointed again and again. Secret tunnels and charging combinations all failed.

I will give you one instance: After many failures through spies, and often by the failure of weak-kneed brothers, nine of us organized, pledged to one another by all we held sacred, our sole purpose being to get away. The wall of No. 1 on the side next to Columbus was moved farther out, making more room. A new sink was dug eight by sixteen feet and eight feet deep, and we conceived the idea of getting into it as soon as opened for use and tunneling out, as we had only about twenty feet to go. I volunteered to take up the planks and let down a detail to dig. Mine was the post of honor. Immediately in front was a street lamp, and on the wall a sentinel twenty-five feet away. I worked long and hard, for planks were double-nailed and tools were scarce. The faintest shadow hid the form of the prisoners from the aim of the sentinel, only too willing to fire, but the boldness of the thing was what counted. No one suspected us; not even the spy saw the dark outlines of that desperate soldier working for life and liberty. The planks were raised; the work progressed rapidly; two or three shifts were worked desperately. The ground was not frozen solidly enough where the new sewer led off, and when the tunnel reached the sewer it caved in, and the morning revealed the plot.

Then a howl went up under the very feet of the sentinel, and in the light of a street lamp a daring attempt to escape was made. The excitement in the Federal camp was great. It was ration day (rations were issued every two days), but instead of rations an order was posted which read: "Until the men concerned in the attempt to escape are brought forward, no more rations will be issued." Some of the prisoners were ready to sell us for a mess of pottage. But little we cared; we, the picked nine, were not making a circus of ourselves. That we would be betrayed and probably shot bothered us but little, for ·a hungry man cares not a great deal for life. Colonel Hawkins, a preacher and soldier, volunteered to go before the commander. He did this, and, eloquently presenting the case, showed how hundreds of men were being punished for the act of others. Then the rations were issued and the job ended. . . .

Thirty odd years is a long time, Colonel, and you and I are through fighting and can look back on the scenes of long ago without bitterness.

That there was unnecessary hardship in all prisons, North and South, goes without saying. Men in those days were ofttimes cruel to their comrades. An instance of this was related recently by a man who had been a prisoner of war for a time at Macon and Millen, Ga. This was a case of ingratitude by a comrade, and is told simply to show the brutalizing effects of a prison life.

These men belonged to an Ohio regiment. They were captured near Atlanta and taken first to Macon. The friend who tells the story had been a prisoner some time before the other men of his company were captured. It was a common thing that men were two days in the inclosure before they were marked for rations. There were not many prisoners from the North at Macon,

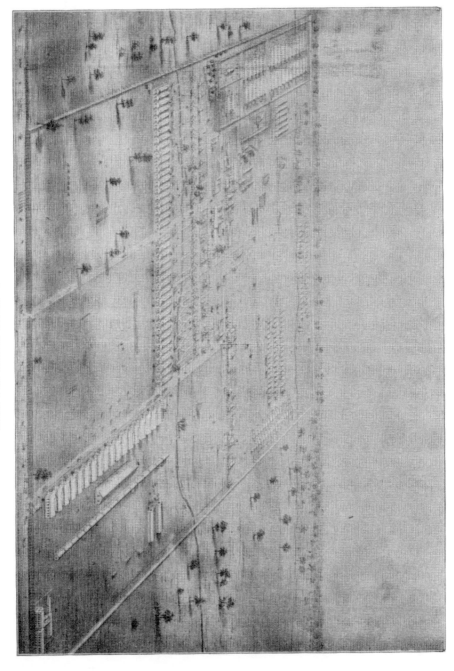

CAMP CHASE PRISON DURING WAR TIMES.

there being quite as many Confederate soldiers confined there as Union. The Confederates were charged with one offense or another, and were awaiting court-martial. Both Northern and Southern men drew the same amount of rations. During the time the two men were waiting to be named for rations they were fed by the comrade who arrived first. He not only shared his rations, but his bunk, for shelter or bunks at Macon were scarce. When they were shifted from Macon to Millen, they became separated. One of the two, who shall be called John B. (as he is yet alive and doubtless regrets his heartlessness), had traded a fine pair of boots for a large piece of rag carpet and a sum of Confederate money. With the money he had built a sod hut or cave. It was large enough for three, but he failed to remember the comrade that had befriended him. The latter was too proud to ask any favors, and managed to get an excavation in the sand, which protected him to some extent from the wind. His captors had taken his blankets, and the prison authorities furnished none. The bit of a boy slept in this alone. One raw November night, after the rain had fallen steadily all day and into the night, he went to the dry quarters of this man, John B. He was not welcomed, but he said: "I have come to say to you, John B., that when you had nothing to eat I fed you. I fed both you and Dave, and you shared my bunk; and now to-night it is cold and wet, and I am sick, and I want you to give me a place to sleep." John growled about it, and finally gave grudging permission that the boy who had befriended him might sit up all night by the door of the hut, but there would be no room to lie down. There was room, however; but the boy sat all night in a sort of kneeling position, while his comrades slept comfortably. This story illustrates that there were brutes in both armies.

In the South, as in the North, prisoners captured in battle were kindly treated by the men who stood upon the battle line. W. C. Dodson, of Atlanta, Ga., relates in the *Veteran* an incident which illustrates this admirably. When he was captured there was placed with him a deserter, or one who claimed he had deserted because he had been conscripted, and Dodson refused to share a bed with him.

There being for several days only the two of us, we were thrown together, but I persistently refused to associate with the deserter. The commissary respected my feelings, and issued my rations separately, remarking each time: "Now, Johnny, when you eat that up come back and get more." I had no blankets, having left mine under my saddle, and the first night I determined to sit up by the fire. A good-natured teamster asked me why I did not go to bed. I told him I had no blanket, and could not afford to sleep with a deserter. "Well, Johnny," said the teamster, "durn him, you needn't sleep with him. Come to my wagon, and I will lend you a blanket." There is not a living Confederate comrade whom I had rather meet than that big-hearted teamster. There are many other pleasant incidents connected with my stay with these brave men at the front, and I truly wish there was no other side to the picture, but there is.

Soon other prisoners came in, and we were sent back to Stevenson and turned over to some home guards, who made life almost a hell to us. At Louisville I got into an argument with one of this kind of sentry, and for saying nothing more offensive than that I had been fighting men in the front I found a bayonet at my breast. I still have the man's name, and it may be best for us both if we never meet again.

I remained six months at Camp Chase, but the policy of starvation did not commence until afterwards, though many kinds of petty tyranny were practiced. For some flagrant abuse (I forget now the circumstances) several of my mess addressed a note of protest to the commander. It was written and signed by gentlemen of intelligence and refinement, and was respectful. The response received was a squad of soldiers with handcuffs and balls and chains for the entire party. The younger men made light of the punishment, but among the victims was a gentleman (Capt. S. F. Nunelle, of Center, Ala.) much older than the rest, and who was disabled by a wound in the hip. The shackles of course rendered him practically helpless, and we younger ones had to wait on him. To those of us nearest naked were issued inferior Federal uniforms.

In the April *Veteran* for 1898 appears the following:

W. H. Lastinger writes from Waco, Tex., that among the dead Confederate prisoners buried at Camp Chase, as published in the January *Veteran*, is W. H. Leatinger, Twenty-Ninth Georgia Regiment, of which he was a member. Knowing nothing of this name "Leatinger," Mr. Lastinger supposes it was himself. He is glad to report that he is still on the top side of *terra firma* and enjoying good health. Mr. Lastinger wrote: "Until I read the magazine, I knew not where lay G. W. Bond, William Hodge, R. McKinney, John T. Simons, Elihu H. Tygart, and William Anderson—all my comrades of Company G."

The list of names published in the *Veteran* were from the Adjutant General's report for the year 1867. In that report are the names of Alex J. Smith, Company E, Twenty-Ninth Georgia Infantry, Grave No. 563, who died December 6, 1864, and S. S. or S. P. Smith, Company G, Twenty-Ninth Georgia Infantry, Grave No. 1800, who died March 31, 1865. So much for the printed record. Mr. Lastinger was doubtless correct, as he knew the names of his company by heart.

From the same source comes the story of W. O. Connor, of Cave Springs, Ga., who was for a short time a prisoner at Camp Chase. He was captured at Salisbury, N. C. One of the battalions defending Salisbury was composed of "galvanized" Yankees, as they were called in the South—men who, as prisoners of war, had taken the oath to support the Confederacy after they had enlisted in the Union army. The writer has tried to show in various ways his respect for the living and dead of the Confederate Army, but only one sentiment can be entertained for these creeping things. But to Mr. Connor's narrative:

Having no fortifications, of course this force offered but little resistance to the impetuous onslaught of General Stoneman's disciplined cavalry. Those "galvanized" Yankees threw down their arms and refused to fight as soon as the Yankees made the charge on our lines, and they, with nearly all the rest of the command, were captured.

We were then marched across the Blue Ridge and Alleghany Mountains to Johnson's Station, on the old East Tennessee and Virginia railroad, the first stretch being forty-eight miles before a stop was made, with the exception of two hours at Statesville. On the way we were told that General Lee had surrendered, but of course we did not believe it until we saw numbers of his soldiers on the way home. We were taken to Camp Chase, where we arrived May 3, 1865.

En route we were kept a day and a night at Nashville, being quartered in the Tennessee penitentiary. The "galvanized" Yankees who were held as prisoners with us had been very abusive in their treatment of the Confederates on this long and arduous march. When we were marched into the penitentiary they were placed in an upper story of the building, and boasted of their superior treatment; but when we were marched out the next day to take the train they were left locked up in the prison, and then it was our time to crow. We were told that every one of them would be shot for desertion.

Arriving at Camp Chase, we were marched into Prison No. 3. There were about one thousand of us, and as we marched in the roll was called, with instructions to answer either "Oath" or "Exchange." This meant that our names would be entered as being willing to take the oath of allegiance or to remain in prison until exchanged. Knowing that Lee had already surrendered, about half of the men signified by their answer that they were willing to take the oath of allegiance.

We found in Prison No. 3 from fifteen hundred to twenty-five hundred men, and but sixteen of the entire number answered "Exchange." When the roll of the prison was called, J. Courtney Brown, now a prominent Baptist minister of Aiken, S. C., and the writer were two of the sixteen. Each of the sixteen men who wanted to be exchanged was ordered to report at the gate, with knapsack and one blanket, prepared for marching. During these three weeks all sorts of rumors were circulated as to what would be done with us, one being that we would be put in irons in the Ohio State Prison for life, and another being that we would be shot in retaliation for something the Confederates had done. Every man who has ever been in military prison is familiar with the absurd rumors that will somehow be circulated.

Our comrades gathered around us and bade us farewell, many of them with tears streaming down their bronzed cheeks. We marched out the bluest-looking men that had ever been gathered together, and not one of us would have been surprised if we had been put in front of a file of soldiers and shot down. Instead of this, however, we were marched along the side of the prison wall a short distance, a gate was thrown open, and we were thrown into Prison No. 1. Here we found seventy-five or eighty Confederate officers and citizens, some of whom I knew. Instead of a barracks accommodating two hundred men, we were given rooms arranged for twelve men each. In each room was a cooking stove with necessary vessels, and our rations were issued directly to us, so that each man could prepare his food to suit himself. Hence we were much more comfortably situated and fared better than the men we left in Prison No. 3.

When the time came for liberating the prisoners, all the sixteen were liberated with the others except one little fellow from West Virginia (I never knew his name) who still refused to take the oath, giving as a reason that he had promised his father that he would never do so without his consent. No explanation was ever given why the change was made from Prison No. 3 to No. 1, nor was there a word spoken to us in regard to the matter.

An interesting story of an attempt to escape is told in the *Veteran* by R. H. Strother, of Milton, Ky., who served in the Fourth Kentucky Cavalry:

During the summer of 1864 a movement was started to organize the prisoners at Camp Chase into companies, regiments, and brigades. After the organization was effected instructions were secretly given in regard to how the break for liberty should be made. July 4 was the day selected, and the hour ten o'clock, as the bread wagon was leaving the prison. The prisoners were not allowed to assemble in crowds, so we had to be cautious in our movements. They were to take position in groups of three or four men, as near the gate as possible without causing suspicion. The signal agreed upon was to be "Fresh fish," which was to be given by the leader of the charging squad when the bread wagon went out. The leader with his group was to drop in behind the wagon just before it reached the gate, and as it was passing out the signal was to be given and the groups of the charging squad were to fall in rapidly, keeping up a continuous charge through the gate. Those nearest the gate were to rush out and fall immediately in the rear of the charging squad, and those of Barracks No. 2 to drop in behind those of No. 1, and so on, which would keep up a continuous charge, so that the gate could not be closed.

The Confederates were to have their pockets full of rocks, which was the only ammunition available. Everything seemed to be working all right, and there were no indications that the officers in charge of the prison had suspected anything wrong.

The morning designated came bright and beautiful. The prisoners were jubilant over the prospect of escaping, and every man was in his place, waiting for the time. All eyes were watching for the bread wagon to come and to make its exit. Confusion came, however, through the earlier and, as it proved, untimely arrival and departure of the wood wagon. This caused the charge to result in failure. The charging squad was so eager that they gave the signal as the wood wagon went out, and the main force were off guard, not expecting the signal at that time. Thus it was that the charging squad passed out through the gate, and, the main column not being in supporting distance, the gate was closed.

There was a picnic that day a few miles from the prison, and most of the Federal officers and soldiers not on duty were going to attend. In fact, when the charge was made a large number of them were mounted ready to start, so that all they had to do was to surround the little squad and march it to prison.

In corroboration of the story told by Mr. Strother, the *Ohio State Journal,* of Columbus, tells the following story:

On the morning of the 4th of July about twenty prisoners, taking advantage of the large gate being opened, gave a yell and broke for liberty. They were fired upon by the guard, two of them being severely wounded and the remainder captured. It is learned that as soon as the break was made the Eighty-Eighth Regiment formed and pursued the fugitives at double-quick, firing as they went. The prisoners in the meantime pulled off their hats and held them up in token of surrender. Colonel Richardson, who was in command, then ordered his men to cease firing.

The first public mention of Camp Chase, so far as the history of it can be gathered from the newspapers of that date, was on May 28, 1861, in the *Ohio State Journal,* the only newspaper in Columbus now that was in existence then, and was as follows:

Workmen were engaged yesterday in taking down the barracks at Camp Jackson, for the purpose of removing to a new camp to be organized four miles west of this city. It is to be a regular camp, and will contain one hundred acres. The land has been plowed, harrowed, and rolled smooth, and will make a good place for drilling purposes.

The following notices of arrivals of Confederate prisoners are from the same paper and quoted literally:

August 9, 1861.—Capt. J. W. Free arrived here at a late hour last night from Lexington, Perry County, Ohio, with a company of one hundred and fifty men. This company brought with them from Zanesville one hundred and ten Rebel prisoners, which the Seventeenth Ohio Regiment had sent to that place. Among the number were one preacher, one lawyer, and one doctor.

Under the date of August 19, same year, appears the following:

Twenty-eight prisoners arrived Saturday from West Virginia via Cincinnati; and of these, twenty-three are on parole. They will be immediately transferred to Richmond, Va. The reporter heard one of them remark that if they took Washington City they would not burn it, for there were too many good buildings there; and as they wished to make it the capital of the Confederacy sometime, these buildings would be needed.

August 20.—GONE. The secessionists who attracted eager crowds at the American Hotel yesterday left for their homes in Virginia to-day. They were released on parole not to take up arms against the government again.

The last lot of prisoners for Camp Chase in the year 1861 arrived on December 28 and consisted of eight captured Confederates.

CHAPTER XI.

Increasing Numbers.

The Indifference of Columbus toward the Soldiers—Southern Prisoners
Were Not the Only Men Neglected—A Wife Accompanies Her Husband to Prison—Arrival of a Number of Officers—A Kentuckian Expresses Himself—What the Raw Recruit Said—The Long Roll Beaten
—Almost a Riot.

It is remarkable that in all the official reports and records of
1861-65 of the Governor of Ohio, his Adjutant General, or his
subordinate officers no mention is made of the Confederate prison
at Camp Chase except a brief reference made in 1861 by Gov.
William Dennison, who in his annual report said:

In accordance with his request, instructions were some time
since given to General McClellan to send prisoners to Ohio. Regarding the jails of the State as being insecure and improper
places for confinement, I caused to be erected at Camp Chase a
prison of sufficient size for the accommodation of four hundred
and fifty inmates, and upon a plan capable of enlargement. A
considerable number have been and are there confined, and others
are continually arriving.

Columbus was indifferent to the men who had battled and
struggled for the cause in which the North was enlisted. For
years the men in blue marched in and out of the city. The citizens read of war, but felt none of it. They grew weary of the
drumbeat and of the glitter and glory of it all. The spirit of
commercialism was rampant, and there was a widespread desire
on the part of those not in business to organize schemes to get
the money of the soldiers. Camp Chase, being central and convenient, was made the depot for the Union paroled prisoners
in the North. Often they came here sick and in tatters and were
driven to Camp Chase like so many cattle, and when they got
there they were lucky to find an open shed to lie in,

In the spring of 1863 there came from a Southern prison a
squad of Union men who were almost naked. They were turned
into an open shed, without officers to see to their wants, and they
soon became a menace to the troops near by. Days went by

before these men drew rations. They were fed by men of another command who were fortunate enough to have something to spare. This condition of affairs lasted for some time; and the paroled prisoners, hungry, half-naked, and disgusted at the treatment accorded them, plundered the tents of their more fortunate comrades. The story of this situation at Camp Chase was found in the columns of the *Ohio State Journal.*

From January 1, 1862, there is no mention of the arrival of Confederate prisoners until on the 24th of February. A few Virginians had been sent back and forth, but nothing of note had occurred. On that date the *Journal* mentions the arrival of Robert J. Baldwin, who had been captured by General Lander at Bloomery, Ga., together with six captains, nine lieutenants, five first sergeants, six other sergeants, five corporals, and nineteen privates. No names were given except that of Colonel Baldwin. Continuing, the *Journal* stated:

Nine prisoners captured near Fayetteville, Ky., by Colonel Scammon, of the Twenty-Third Ohio, arrived Saturday last and "took lodgings" at Camp Chase. The visitors are to be increased soon by a fresh arrival of the Southern chivalry. The secession sympathizers, who hung their jaws on the reception of the Fort Donelson news, ought to turn out *en masse* and give their Southern brethren a cordial welcome. Names to-morrow morning.

The names did not appear the next morning. Instead, there was a notice of the arrival of another lot of prisoners, alluded to as follows:

Another detachment of one hundred and four Southern prisoners arrived about half past nine last night. They were all officers, including Buckner's staff, captured at Fort Donelson. They were generally fine-looking men; and, being all officers, are undoubtedly of the upper crust of chivalry of the South. There appeared to be no uniformity of dress; each seemed to consult his own taste or convenience—perhaps the latter.

The sympathies of the crowd were awakened by the appearance among the prisoners of a woman, the wife of one of the officers, who had clung to her husband in his reverses and was determined to share his captivity. She was sent in advance of the others in charge of a special guard. There were also several contrabands in the company, brought along as servants. We doubt very much, however, whether the contrabands will be held as prisoners, but rather as contrabands of war.

It is rumored that twelve hundred more prisoners will arrive at 12 o'clock to-day.

Of the noble woman whose unselfish love prompted her to to go to prison with her husband, no further record can be found. One can only wish that the love of such a wife, that such unbounded affection, was at last rewarded; that each lived to see the war end and, like the hero and heroine of the fairy tale, "lived happily ever after."

The *Journal* on Saturday, March 1, 1862, gave the following names of those who arrived the Thursday preceding. No doubt these men have friends in the North who will scan the list with eagerness:

Third Mississippi Regiment.—Col. T. J. Davidson, Lieut. Col. J. M. Wiltz, Chaplain J. H. Robinson; Company A, Capt. A. J. Gibson, Lieuts. E. M. Smith, J. W. Day, and H. B. Meneden; Company B, Capt. J. R. Hill, Lieuts. M. P. Harbin, V. B. Dixen, and J. B. Pennell; Company C, Capt. G. W. Garrett, Lieuts. N. L. Dazey, B. F. Darrod, and J. G. Moore; Company D, Lieuts. J. C. Tumer, W. H. Groyn, and B. H. Estes; Company E, Capt. J. H. Kennedy, Lieuts. A. D. Saddler, and E. Roberts; Company H, Capt. E. M. Wells, Lieut. J. W. Douglass; Company G, Lieuts. J. H. Keddlesperger, David Lewis, and J. W. Childs; Company 5, Capt. S. W. McWharter, Lieuts. C. N. Simpson, W. C. Swindale, and W. G. Young.

Twentieth Mississippi Regiment.—Maj. W. N. Brown; Company A, Capt. H. Canteg, Lieut. R. M. Wilson; Company B, W. A. Rover, Lieut. Thos. B. Sykes, R. S. Murff, and J. A. Roberts; Company C, Capt. J. Z. George, Lieut. J. M. Liddel, F. W. Keyes, and A. A. Staddord; Company D, Capt. O. K. Massey, Lieuts. J. C. Williams, P. L. Dotson, and R. C. McClelland; Company E, Lieut. William S. Champlen; Company F, Capt. Thomas B. Graham, Lieut. P. R. Sterling; Company G, Lieut. W. R. Nelson; Company H, Lieut. Thomas H. Harrison; Company I, Capt. W. M. Chatfield, Lieuts. F. W. Gale and J. V. Williams; Company K, Lieuts. S. L. Oldham and J. R. Henephile.

Seventh Texas.—Col. John Green, Maj. R. H. Graham, Adjt. H. Douglas, Asst. H. Beall; Company A, one lieutenant (name not given); Company B, Lieuts. Kemp, Covid, and Ford; Company C, Capt. Houghton, Lieuts. English and Henderson; Company E, Capt. E. M. Zaut, Lieuts. Donnelly, Martin, Lipscome, and Adams; Company F, Lieut. Moore; Company G, Capt. Moody, Lieuts. Callett and Tildwell; Company H, Lieuts. Fonest and Craig; Company 5, Capt. John Brown, Lieuts. Ballinger, White, and McDavid.

Third Battalion Alabama Infantry, Capt. D. T. Ryan; Twenty-Seventh Alabama, Capt. E. G. Wright; Tenth Tennessee, Capt. B. M. Cheatham.

The *Journal* of Monday, March 3, states that seven hundred and twenty prisoners arrived Saturday morning. "They were nearly all officers, many of them men of intelligence, some having held honorable positions under the government they are now endeavoring to destroy. Some of our citizens showed a disposition to quiz several of them, but their curt replies soon silenced such comment. The prisoners at Camp Chase now numbered some twelve hundred."

The following letter from a gentleman who had been a prisoner at Camp Chase for a time shows that there were some humane men in charge part of the time, at least:

HOUSE OF REPRESENTATIVES, FRANKFORT, KY., Feb. 10, 1862.
Mr. N. A. Gray.

DEAR SIR: The Cincinnati *Gazette* of yesterday, in a very untruthful notice of some remarks made by myself in the House on Saturday last in relation to my late arrest and imprisonment at Camp Chase, conveys the idea that I complained of bad treatment while there. This is not true; and for fear the article may place me wrong with several gentlemen whom I may never see again, but whose respect I wish to preserve, I bear public testimony to their uniform kindness and courtesy to me while a prisoner in their hands. Nothing was said or done by any one to insult me, and I acknowledge the gentlemanly and considerate treatment I received from Lieutenant Colonel Remple, Capt. A. V. Rice, Lieutenants Wright and Knauss, and Sergeant Buice. I remember also with satisfaction the friendly conduct of many members and officers of the Ohio Legislature (which of course includes yourself), and will frankly confess that an utter change of sentiment with them enabled me to return from Ohio with more hope for the future of our country than I felt before. The *Gazette,* however, quotes me correctly in that I called Camp Chase prison a "mudhole."

Your friend, S. B. CHAMBERS.

The Capt. A. V. Rice alluded to in the above letter afterwards became a brigadier general, and when President Cleveland was elected the second time he appointed him pension agent for Ohio, the salary being about $4,000 per year. He lost one leg in battle; and, while a Democrat, held office under Presidents McKinley and Roosevelt. He died recently.

A little incident occurred early in April, 1862, that caused much excitement in Camp Chase, but did no damage. A sentinel who had not soldiered long was on guard at one of the prisons, and as dawn approached thought he saw a man in gray trying to make his escape. He quickly drew aim and fired at the supposed Rebel. This alarmed other sentinels, and these, being new to the business, also fired, and the camp was alarmed. The long roll was beaten and the orderly sergeants shouted to their men to "fall in." The *Journal,* in speaking of the occurrence, said:

The guards turned out with commendable alacrity, thinking perhaps that the whole Rebel horde were at their heels and were about to take possession of the camp. They presented a ridiculous appearance as they crawled out in every condition—some without their coats and others with one boot or barefooted. When investigation was made, the prisoners were all there and the majority asleep. Only a few were aroused by the excitement. The sentinel shot a cow near by and nearly killed some of our men.

The *Journal* of April 9 said:

Yesterday morning Colonel Moody, commandant at Camp Chase, started thirty Confederate officers for Fort Warren. They included most of those on parole in this city. The Knights of the Golden Circle shed buckets of tears at parting with their Southern brethren.

The same paper on the morning of July 10 said:

The ingenuity of the Confederate prisoners confined at Camp Chase has been tested in a variety of ways in their efforts to see the outer world. Their latest was to dig out. It was discovered recently that two mines had been made, commencing underneath one of their quarters and running to within a few feet of the outside prison fence. Had they succeeded in reaching the outside, they would there have been met by the ground guard, whose attention they could scarcely have escaped.

The *Journal* of July 23 said:

Yesterday two squads of prisoners were taken to Camp Chase. The train from the East brought twenty bushwhacking Confederates captured in Virginia. Several of them were wounded and on crutches.

The afternoon train from the South brought twenty-eight more, captured recently in Kentucky, among them a Colonel Jones. They marched from the depot to Messrs. Hawkes & Company's stage office, where omnibuses were provided to carry them to the prison. Among the number attracted by them through curiosity were several paroled Union prisoners, who were not very choice in their language in denouncing the authorities for their accommodating spirit exercised toward these men.

The prisoners at Camp Chase are quiet and submissive since their attempt some days ago to dig out. The three prisons contain some 1,676 men. No one is permitted to see them without a special permit from the commandant.

On August 17 eleven hundred Camp Chase prisoners were sent South. They were to be exchanged at Vicksburg.

In 1862 there were many political prisoners at Camp Chase. A Columbus paper of November 22 says:

There have been examined up to this time three hundred and twenty-seven political prisoners by special commission, and two hundred and seventy of them discharged by order of the Secretary of War, together with fifty-seven others reported upon by the War Department. There are yet about four hundred prisoners confined at Camp Chase, anxiously waiting a hearing.

The following-named prisoners were released on the above-mentioned date: Wm. M. Butler, Davis County, Ky.; T. W. Hawthorn, Mercer County, Va.; George W. Demsey, Fayette County, Va.; John Oder, Campbell County, Ky.; W. L. Hontom, Mercer County, Va.; E. J. Ranson, Virginia; Walter, Brown County, Ohio; Thomas C. Read, Alleghany County, ——; Thomas Brigham, Mercer County, Ky.; W. H. Robertson, Robertson County, Ky.; James W. Evans, Grant County, Ky.; Charles Richard, Hampshire County, Tenn.; John N. Helmick, Calhoun County, Va.; John W. Campbell, Davis County, Ky.; A. H. Clement and James Lester, Pike County; J. D. Lillard, Calhoun County; Joseph Hicks, Owen County; John Roland and R. Smith, Swan County; Thomas J. Webster, Grant County; L. Slems, Campbell County; Solonion McDade and James Green, Gallatin County; Richard McGeness and John King, Harrison County; Z. Doly, Bourbon County; M. Jenkines, Pendleton County; John Dougherty, Bath County; B. R. Griffin, Henderson County; James Lafferty, Harrison County; Samuel Flowers, Champaign County, Ohio.

The *Ohio State Journal* of February 5, 1863, says:

The ten o'clock train from the South last night brought three women from Nashville who have elected themselves to a term of repose at Camp Chase. It seems that they were decidedly brisk in forwarding contraband information to Southern leaders and giving money and aid to their soldiers. They are of one family, being mother and daughters.

The Columbus *Crises,* speaking of the episode, says:

A few days ago a mother and two daughters, one sixteen and the other eighteen years of age, were sent to Camp Chase as political prisoners from Tennessee. They are very respectable and intelligent ladies. This act to outsiders seems very ungallant and has excited a good deal of talk, and a resolution was introduced in the Ohio Senate by Mr. Kenny, of Ashland County, himself a gallant soldier, inquiring into the facts.

Many Confederate officers in those days lived in Columbus. They had given their word of honor not to attempt to escape, and they kept their word. They were associates of the officers of the regular army, or such of them as were stationed in Columbus at one time or another. The Eighteenth United States Infantry was in that city for some time, and its officers and the paroled Confederate officers were conspicuous figures in the hotels and cafés. Among those whose intimacy was most marked were Captain Joyce, of General Buckner's staff, and Captain Dodge, of the Eighteenth Regulars. One day these gentlemen were dining and drinking at Wagner's, the leading café of Columbus, when a private soldier a little worse from drink entered and saluted Captain Dodge. The Captain paid no attention to the salute. The soldier paused and addressed some remark to him, when Captain Joyce sprang to his feet and struck the soldier in the face. With his mouth bleeding he went out of the place and, meeting a number of his comrades, told the story of the assault.

A crowd gathered, as many citizens as soldiers, and a riot was imminent. Threats were made that the Confederate must die, and the crowd assumed a moblike aspect. When a number of soldiers entered the restaurant Wagner managed to get the two officers out, but the crowd surrounded them upon the outside. "Kill the d—— Rebel!" came the cries from every side. "Kill the other ——; he is no better!" cried others. As readily would they have killed Captain Dodge as his Confederate friend; but when they began to crowd upon and jostle the officers about, waiting and wishing that the Confederate would strike again, the police appeared and the officers were hurried to the American house. Here the crowd followed, and it was with difficulty they were rescued and taken to a place of safety. The papers published the story, and both soldiers and civilians were excited; and had Captain Joyce appeared upon the streets again while the excitement was high, he would probably have been shot.

CHAPTER XII.

THE YEARS CREPT SLOWLY ON.

From 1863 to 1865—Gen. John Morgan and His Men—A Brief Review of His Famous Raid through Ohio—On the Road to Camp Chase—A Tennessee Judge Once a Boy Prisoner—The Boy and the Bowlder—A Conspiracy.

THE events at Camp Chase Prison were not narrated by the Columbus writers, for there was little to consider in the way of news in 1862. There was much transferring to Johnson's Island and to Camp Douglass, and occasionally to the Elmira (N. Y.) prison. The chief event of 1863 was the Morgan raid and its dramatic dénouement.

It was about the middle of July, 1863, that Gen. John Morgan and his faithful horsemen stirred Ohio from center to circumference. The first one of Morgan's men to arrive at Camp Chase was one Jacob Hix, a private, who, exhausted by the terrible march, fell asleep on his horse and rode for miles. Finally the horse wandered up a country lane far out of the line of march. When Hix awoke, there were no troops in sight, and he knew not which way to turn. He wandered on, however, and finally brought up in the little village of Richmond, some fifty miles south of Columbus. When the villagers saw a real, live Rebel riding leisurely along the streets, there was intense excitement. There was a hurried search for shotguns and the like, and one or two men more collected; then the rest demanded that Hix surrender, which the weary Confederate, knowing nothing of the country, did. After getting their prisoner something to eat, they took him to Chillicothe and delivered him to Deputy Provost Marshal Thomas J. Guin, who took him to Camp Chase.

Monday morning, July 27, 1863, the *Ohio State Journal* placed at the head of its editorial columns with big black headline the following: "John Morgan Captured." The editorial said:

The career of the great Rebel raider is ended. He and his whole force are now in General Shackelford's possession. Morgan surrendered unconditionally at three o'clock yesterday (Sunday) afternoon. All honor is due the gallant and hardy boys who have finally captured the reckless rider of Rebeldom. Morgan and his command will doubtless be brought to Camp Chase.

The *Journal* stated several days later:

The noted raider, John Morgan, received a very handsome reception yesterday afternoon at the depot—at least so far as numbers are concerned. The desire to see one who has given the citizens of Ohio as much trouble as this Rebel has could hardly have been greater than to see President Lincoln. The hero came on a special train, accompanied by General Shackelford and staff, and several other Union officers. The excitement ran high, and a rush was made for the train. The crowd in front feasted their eyes and made way for others eager to see him. The Governor, General Mason, and portions of their staffs were introduced to Morgan and shook hands with him, after which they paid their respects to General Shackelford.

The cell in which General Morgan was confined is yet marked and is pointed out to visitors to the Ohio penitentiary.

The Richmond *Enquirer* tells of how they managed to escape:

Their bedsteads were small iron stools fastened in the wall with hinges, which could be hooked up or allowed to stand on the floor. To prevent any suspicion, for several days before any work was attempted they made it a habit to let them down and sit at their doors and read. Captain Hines superintended the work, while General Morgan kept watch to divert the attention of the sentinel, whose duty it was to come around during the day and observe conditions.

One day the sentinel came in while Hokersmith was down under the floor boring away and, missing him, said: "Where is Hokersmith?" The General replied, "He is in my room sick," and immediately pulled a document out of his pocket and said to him, "Here is a memorial I have drawn up to forward to the government at Washington. What do you think of it?" The sentinel, who perhaps could not read, being highly flattered at the General's condescension, very gravely looked at the document for several minutes before he vouchsafed any reply; then, handing it back, he expressed himself as highly pleased with it. In the meantime Hokersmith had been signaled and came up, professing to feel very unwell.

This sentinel was the most difficult and dangerous obstacle in their progress, because there was no telling at what time he might enter in the day, and at night he came regularly every two hours to each cell and inserted a light through the bars of the doors to see that all were quietly sleeping, and frequently after his rounds he would slip back into the dark in India rubber shoes and listen. The General says that he would almost invariably know of his presence by a certain magnetic shudder it would produce; but for fear that his acute sensibility might sometimes fail him, he broke up small particles of coal and sprinkled them before the cell door, which would always announce the sentinel's approach.

About the latter part of October they began to bore. All were busy—one making a rope ladder by tearing and twisting up strips of bedticks, another making Bowie knives, and another twisting towels. They labored perseveringly for several days, and after boring through nine inches of cement and nine thicknesses of brick placed edgewise they began to wonder when they would reach the soft earth. Suddenly a brick fell through. What could this mean? What infernal chamber had they reached? It was immediately entered, and to their great astonishment and joy, it proved to be an air chamber extending the whole length of the row of cells. Here was an unexpected interposition in their favor. Heretofore they had been obliged to conceal their rubbish in bedticks, each day burning a proportionate quantity of straw; now they had room enough for all they could dig. They at once commenced to tunnel at right angles with this air chamber, to get through the foundation. Day after day they bored, day after day the blocks of granite were removed, and still the work before them seemed interminable.

After twenty-three days of unrelenting labor, and getting through a granite wall six feet in thickness, they reached the soil. They tunneled up for some distance, and light began to shine. How glorious was the light! It announced the fulfillment of their labor; they would soon be free. This was the morning of the 26th day of November, 1863. The next night at twelve o'clock was determined on as the hour at which they would attempt to get away. Each moment was filled with dreadful anxiety and suspense, and each time the guard entered their apprehensions increased. The General says that he prayed for rain, but the morning of the 27th dawned bright and beautiful. The evening came, and the clouds began to gather. How they prayed for them to increase! If rain should only begin, their chances of detection would be greatly lessened. While these thoughts were passing through their mind the keeper entered with a letter for General Morgan. He opened it, and what was his surprise and wonder to find it from a poor Irish woman of his acquaintance in Kentucky, commencing: "My dear Ginral, I feel certain you are going to get out of prison, but for your sake don't try it, dear Ginral. You will only be taken a prisoner again and made to suffer more than you do now." The letter then went on to speak of his kindness to the poor when he lived at Lexington, and concluded by again exhorting him to trust in God and wait his time.

What could this mean? No human being on the outside had been informed of his intention to escape; and yet just as all things were ready for him to make the attempt, here comes a letter from Kentucky advising him not to try it. This letter had passed through the examining office of General Mason, and then through the hands of the lower officials. What if it should excite their suspicion and cause them to exercise an increased vigilance? The situation, however, was desperate. Their fate could not be made worse, and they resolved to go. Nothing remained to be done but for General and Col. Dick Morgan to change cells. The hour approached for them to be locked up. They changed coats, and each stood at the other's cell door with his back exposed, and pretended to be engaged in making up their beds. As the turnkey entered they pulled their doors shut.

Six, eight, ten o'clock came. How each pulse throbbed as they quietly awaited the approach of twelve! It came; the sentinel passed his rounds. After waiting a few moments to see if he intended to slip back, the signal was given and all quietly slipped down to the air chamber, first stuffing their flannel shirts and placing them in the bed as they were accustomed to lie. As they moved quietly along through the dark recess to the terminus where they were to emerge from the earth, the General prepared to light a match. As the lurid glare fell upon their countenance a scene was presented which can never be forgotten. There were crouched seven brave men who had resolved to be free.

Fortunately—yes, providentially—the night had suddenly grown dark and rainy, the dogs had retired to their kennels, and the sentinels had taken shelter. The inner wall, by the aid of a rope ladder, was soon scaled, and now the outer one had to be attempted. Captain Taylor, a nephew of the illustrious Zack, being a very active man, by the assistance of his comrades reached the top of the gate and was enabled to get the rope extending all around, which the General immediately cut, as he suspected that it might lead into the warden's room. This turned out to be correct. Then they entered the sentry box on the wall, changed their clothes, and crept down the wall. The General skinned his hand very badly and all were more or less bruised. Once down, they separated, Taylor and Sheldon going one way, Hokersmith, Bennett, and McGee another, and General Morgan and Captain Hines proceeding immediately toward the depot.

The General had succeeded in obtaining a paper which informed him of the schedule time of the different roads. The clock struck one, and he knew that by hurrying he could reach the down train for Cincinnati. He got there just as the train was moving off. He at once ascertained if any soldiers were on board; and espying a Union soldier, he boldly walked up and took the seat beside him. He suggested to his seat companion that, as the night was damp and chilly, he join him in a drink. The hospitality was accepted, and the two soon became friends. The cars in crossing the Scioto had to pass in a short distance of the penitentiary. As they passed, the officer remarked: "There is the hotel where Morgan and his officers are spending their leisure. I sincerely hope he will make up his mind to board there during the balance of the war, for he is a great nuisance!" When the train reached Xenia, it was detained by some accident for nearly an hour. Imagine the anxiety as soldier after soldier would pass through the train, for fear that when the sentinel passed his rounds at two o'clock their absence might be discovered!

The train was due in Cincinnati at six o'clock. This was the hour at which they were turned out of their cells, and of course their escape would be discovered. In a few moments after that it would be known all over the country. The train was running rapidly to make up the lost time. General Morgan said to Captain Hines: "It is after six. If we go to the depot, we are dead men. Now or never." They then went to the rear and put on the brakes. Hines then jumped and fell heels over head in the mud. Another severe turn of the brakes, and General Morgan jumped. He was more successful, and lighted on his feet. There were some soldiers near, who remarked: "What do you mean by jumping off the cars here?" The General replied: "What is the use of my going into town when I live near here? And besides, what business is it of yours?"

They went immediately to the river and found a skiff, but no oars. Soon a little boy appeared, and seemed to be waiting. "What are you waiting for?" asked the General. "I am waiting for my load." "What is the price of your load?" "Two dollars." "Well, we are tired and hungry. We will give you two dollars, and you can put us over." So over they went. The house of a friend was reached and a fine breakfast was obtained. Money and horses were furnished, a woman's prayers were bestowed, and off they went, forward through Kentucky. Everybody vied with each other as to who should show them the most attention, even to the negroes. Young ladies of refinement even begged the honor of cooking their meals.

General Morgan remained in Kentucky some days, feeling perfectly safe and sending into Louisville for many little things that he needed. He went to Bardstown and found that a Federal regiment had just arrived there looking for him. His escort, with heroic self-sacrifice, refused to cross the river until he was safely over. He then hired a negro to get his horse over. The river was high and the horse came near drowning, but after more than an hour's struggle with the stream he was pulled out so exhausted that he was scarcely able to stand.

The Columbus (Ohio) *Crisis* had the following pleasant word to say about the raid:

We received a letter Monday from Batavia, Ohio, giving some rather laughable accounts of Morgan's passage through that place. The great scare did not last long—nobody hurt; but a good many horses were taken by Morgan's men.   Hobson's men, who were following Morgan, got the mail just in from Cincinnati and carried it off, but promised the ladies to return any letters for them, which was strictly complied with next day.   One lady begged of them not to take her pony.   They had the saddle on, but delivered it up.   They said they did not come to disturb the ladies.

Naturally the excitement was great in Ohio, and particularly in Columbus.   All sorts of rumors were in circulation about collusion from penitentiary officials or persons from the outside. General Morgan's story is corroborated by Governor Tod, as the following letter will show:

THE STATE OF OHIO, EXECUTIVE DEPARTMENT,
COLUMBUS, Dec. 11, 1863.

N. Merion, Esq., Warden of Penitentiary.

DEAR SIR: Deeply chagrined and mortified as I was to hear of the escape of General Morgan and six other Confederate prisoners, I am glad to know from the report of Messrs. Wright and Hoffman, just handed to me, that there is not the slightest evidence to be found of fraud and corruption on the part of the officers, either civil or military, in whose custody the prisoners were, nor on the part of any individual or citizen without or within the prison; but that the sole reason for their escape is to be found in the misunderstanding of General Mason and yourself as to which of you should be responsible for, and have the care and inspection of, the prison cells.

To avoid a like occurrence, I have now to request that you take upon yourself the entire charge and responsibility of the safe-keeping of the prisoners.   I have furnished Colonel Wallace, Commander of the Post, with a copy of this letter of instruction, and directed him to conform his actions thereto.

Respectfully yours,   (Signed) DAVID TOD, *Governor.*

The announcement was made in the Columbus papers of December 25, 1863, of the arrival at Camp Chase of Colonel Carter, late commander of the famous Black Horse Cavalry of Virginia, that made the famous charge on the Union lines at the battle of Bull Run.   "That redoubtable body of horsemen," said the *Ohio State Journal,* "which constituted the flower of Stuart's cavalry division, has been entirely used up. The Colonel Carter mentioned was one who in the Virginia Convention persistently opposed secession."

There arrived on May 13, 1863, a number of prisoners under charge of Lieutenant Thorpe, of a Michigan regiment, and a set of resolutions were presented by the prisoners that leave a bit of brightness on the usual somber canvas of the prison scene:

On the Road to Camp Chase.

Thinking as we do that justice should be done in all cases, we take this occasion to return our sincere and heartfelt thanks to Lieut. D. D. Thorpe for his kindness and gentlemanly treatment toward us. May he and the kind guards who accompanied him with us to Camp Chase continue to exercise their courtesies! for they will find that humanity is a great comforter in this vale of tears.

We hope to live and know that Lieutenant Thorpe shall wear an eagle on his shoulders.

With kind regards, J. H. Triplett, J. H. Thomson, J. R. Betteson, W. C. S. Wetmore, E. P. Smith, J. R. Smith, R. V. Hamilton, W. T. Drodley, J. Kindall, J. Meneer, S. Everman, H. C. Molen, B. Braidy, J. Giboret, E. Murphy, T. Harrison, H. Rogers, S. Aikins, W. T. Armstrong, E. W. Lyons, J. W. Aldudge, G. W. Marshall, J. T. Harwood, J. Borris, W. Jones, D. C. Clark, G. Vessey, M. Mills, W. Kindell, L. Bianitt, C. H. Johnson, J. Henry, and twenty-five others.

Mr. J. Edward Sims, a writer on the *Press-Post,* of Columbus, paid a visit not long since to Chattanooga, Tenn., and while there met Judge Cowart, famous for having been a member of the court of Hamilton County nearly ever since he was old enough. The Judge insists that he was but twelve years of age when he came to Camp Chase. It was on account of his youth, no doubt, that he fared so well. Learning that Mr. Sims was from Columbus, Judge Cowart remarked that he knew something about Columbus, or a place near there. He then told of his imprisonment at Camp Chase and of the only act that he was ever sorry for while in prison there.

"I was not in prison long," said the Judge, "until I fell into the good graces of a Union lieutenant, who treated me with great kindness. I was permitted many liberties, and was allowed to go across the road to the Four-Mile House to get water. One day a raw recruit who did not know about the freedom accorded me was on guard, and, seeing me go out of the camp, began to curse me and threatened to shoot. Fearing that he might fulfill his threats, I hastened back, but swore vengeance. I laid in a good stock of bowlders unperceived by the guards and waited for the raw recruit. In a short time he was on duty again, but this time on the wall, overlooking the prison. Being permitted to go out at will, by the orders of the lieutenant, I found an advantageous point for my stone battery. The first fire was sufficient to put the guard out of duty. The stone struck him in the face, and he reeled and fell from the parapet. He was unconscious for some time. It is unnecessary to say that I beat a hasty retreat. I was not discovered. For several days quite a hunt was made; but being an innocent-appearing lad, I was never suspected." Not even to his brother, who was in prison at the same time, did young Cowart tell the story of the assault until they were exchanged and were entering Richmond. The Judge assured Mr. Sims that his treatment by the lieutenant was all that could be desired. He was not only accorded unusual liberties, but his brother was well treated.

In the fall of 1863 there was talk of removing the prison to some locality more healthful. If it was unhealthy for the prisoners, it was equally so for the soldiers of the North, although their greater liberty was altogether in their favor. The *Ohio State Journal* of September 1, 1863, says: "Whatever credit is due for the idea of removing Camp Chase from its present filthy location attaches to General Mason. At his instance the survey and examination had been made and the estimate of cost sent to Washington." Nothing came of the effort, as is well known, for the last Confederate prisoner to leave Columbus for his Southern home went from Camp Chase Prison.

A story of conspiracy was published in the Ohio papers of November 2, 1863, that caused much excitement:

It appears that for some time past the United States military and civil authorities have been engaged in ferreting out the existence of a secret organization of the most treasonable nature. There have been in circulation various rumors relative to the treasonable design of certain persons who, it seems, were members of this organization; but nothing definite was known upon the subject except to a few officials, who have been diligent in pursuit of evidence to fasten the guilt upon the parties concerned; and this having been secured and other things being in readiness, the blow was struck yesterday morning. State School Commissioner C. W. H. Cathcart, Nathan Cressup, who was a cutter in Child's clothing establishment, a man who gave his name as Slade, and Dr. Lazelle, a Rebel surgeon on parole, were all arrested yesterday morning, and are now in charge of the proper authorities for safe-keeping. They are all charged with aiding and abetting the rebellion by furnishing means and information to the enemy, and have been taken on a special train to Cincinnati. Slade is supposed to be a spy in the Rebel service, and has been arrested before on a similar charge; and when he was taken yesterday he boasted that he would get away, as he had done on previous occasions. He was in irons and was closely watched. Lazelle's arrest was made by the provost guard on the ground that he had broken his parole in addition to his complicity with the other parties. Three more men have doubtless been arrested ere this, as the officers were in search of them last evening. In addition, seventeen men were also taken yesterday in Cincinnati on the same charge, and other arrests were to be made in several places.

Another report was as follows:

An extraordinary case of treason has recently come to light, implicating several persons in this city, Columbus, Covington, and Newport in a conspiracy to release the Rebel prisoners at Camp Chase and overthrow the State government.

The conspiracy was brought to light by United States detectives, who were supposed by the parties to be spies from the Rebel army and were treated with full confidence. The plot as declared to the detectives was that an attack would be made on Camp Chase, the prisoners (three thousand five hundred in number) released, and the arsenal at Columbus seized. It was also planned to take possession of the penitentiary, release John Morgan and other officers confined there, and then to commence a Rebel campaign in Ohio.

United States Marshal Sands and Provost Marshal Piany arrested the persons implicated in the plot: Charles W. H. Cathcart, of Columbus, School Commissioner; Mr. Cressup, of Columbus, and formerly a sutler in the Eighteenth Regulars, who were to lead the attack on Camp Chase; James D. Patton, of Covington, a regular agent of the Rebel government, who frequently furnished money to detectives under the impression that they were spies, and, according to agreement, met Carthcart and others at Camp Chase and assisted in maturing the plans for the attack; Ruth McDonald, of Covington, who acted as mail carrier through the Rebel lines, and whose house was headquarters of the Rebels; Samuel P. Thomas, a merchant tailor, of Cincinnati, his wife, and Catharine Parmenter, of Cincinnati, from whom information was obtained that an organization exists in Illinois, waiting for the outbreak in Ohio to produce similar results in that State. Other particulars are known to the authorities, but not yet made public.

The arrested parties were kept in prison a short time and admitted to bail. While the report of the detectives was sensational and caused no little excitement in the State, there was nothing done in the matter and all were finally released.

In 1865 there was a commission appointed by Governor Brough, of Ohio, to consider and allow claims for damages to citizens on account of the Morgan raid. The amount allowed came to $576,225. The sum asked for was $678,915. It was claimed that Morgan damaged the people of Ohio to the amount of $493,372. The other damage came from United States and the militia forces that followed the Morgan command.

The peace Democrats of Southern Ohio and Indiana welcomed General Morgan gladly in most cases, and did not fail to tell him that they were his true friends. The General, ever polite and gallant, smiled upon them, but did not hesitate to take their horses. The most rampant hater of secession did not fare worse than did these men who told their friendship. Some of the General's men, more diplomatic than their leader, usually replied that if they were as friendly as they claimed they should willingly furnish a few horses. When the commission was appointed to pass upon the claims for damages, these men were promptly on hand with an itemized bill of the damages inflicted by the enemy.

There appeared in the Northern papers of July 8, 1864, an item in which three of General Morgan's men figured. The dispatch stated that a United States steamer took to New York thirty-one prisoners captured on board the prize steamer Thistle, a vessel captured while attempting to run the blockade at Wilmington, N. C. The prisoners made claim that they were British subjects, and twenty-eight of them were discharged by Marshal Murray under instructions from the War Department relating to foreign subjects violating the blockade. The remaining three, whose names were James Crowders, Charles Drake, and J. D. Allison, were discovered to be Kentuckians, formerly prisoners at Camp Chase, who had escaped and made their way to Canada. They proceeded by way of Halifax to Nassau, and from there they sailed for Wilmington, N. C. These facts were elicited by the closest examination, for the prisoners possessed great shrewdness.

and ability. They were taken to Fort Lafayette, from where it was considered more difficult to escape than from Camp Chase.

On May 18, 1865, the Columbus papers told about the departure of hundreds of Confederate prisoners for their homes. Up to that time 538 were exchanged, or rather given transportation, after taking the oath of allegiance. From the 1st of May to the 18th 1,870 prisoners had been discharged, and there were left about 3,400. All of this number were anxiously awaiting their turns to go, with the exception of fourteen who refused to take the oath of allegiance. On June 20 there were less than fifty Confederate prisoners remaining in Camp Chase. All the others had returned to their homes in the South.

When the last Southern soldier had left Camp Chase, there arrived forty-five men from Little Rock, Ark., bound for the Ohio penitentiary. The prisoners had been sentenced by court-martial for various offenses, none of which were political. They were charged with larceny, burglary, and assault with intent to kill. There were one Confederate captain, forty-two enlisted men, two citizens, and the guerrilla, Cyrus Chappel, who had been sentenced to be hanged, but whose sentence was commuted to ten years' imprisonment in the penitentiary.

CHAPTER XIII.

After Forty-Two Years.

The Intercepted Letters Found in the Ohio State House by State Librarian Galbreath—Some of the Letters Photographed—Some Letters from Down South—List of Letters Not Used in This Volume—History of Mrs. Clark, by Her Son, Frank P. Clark.

When the work of preparing the history of Camp Chase was almost completed, Mr. C. B. Galbreath, State Librarian, was kind enough to send the following letter to the author:

Columbus, Ohio, August 30, 1904.

Dear Colonel Knauss.

I am pleased to learn that you are having prepared a history of the Confederate prisons of Ohio. Permit me to invite your attention to a collection of manuscript letters in the State Library that may be of service to you.

When the material of the library was classified and rearranged, these letters were discovered in a place where they had evidently lain unmolested for years in dust and obscurity. Upon examination, most of them were found to have been written by Confederate prisoners at Camp Chase. They were transferred to our manuscript department, where they will be permanently preserved.

I do not know how the letters originally came into the possession of the library. I have read only a few of them. In the hope that among them may be found something of interest to the numerous readers of your forthcoming volume, I take pleasure in offering you for reference use this manuscript collection.

Very truly yours,

State Librarian.

That there are those living to-day who wrote some of these letters is presumed. The sons and daughters of many others are doubtless living; and surely a letter so long buried in the mystery that surrounds these would be of rare interest. How they came to be put away in a sort of lumber room in the State House at Columbus, no one knows. One thing is certain: they were never kept from the South by orders of Governor Tod, who was a most humane man and who extended every courtesy to the prisoners possible. It is unwritten history in Ohio that he was defeated for nomination for a second term because of his humanity—not simply to the Southern prisoners, but to the boy in the ranks who by bravery earned promotion. Many rich and influential families appealed in vain to Governor Tod to give commissions to their sons at the expense of the brave boys who had risked their lives on the battlefields.

Interesting as these are, only a portion of them can be used. As will be observed, the letters not published were gone over and addresses given when it was possible to do so. This is done that any survivor of the prison not mentioned by letter, and whose name appears in the list of unpublished letters, can write for a copy of same by giving the number of the letter.

It is fitting, therefore, that the letters found after so many years be herein introduced. The first is from the gallant officer, so kindly alluded to by Colonel Barbier, Thomas J. Carruthers, Lieutenant of Heavy Artillery:

CAMP CHASE, PRISON No. 3,
COLUMBUS, OHIO, April 20, 1862.

Rev. John K. Harrison.

MY DEAR FRIEND: You may be surprised at hearing from me away up here, but the fortunes of war are varied. I am at least a prisoner of war—was surrendered at Island No. 10, of which surrender you have doubtless heard. I was sick, but am now much better. I was making my escape with seven or eight of our company to a farmhouse. The whole command was surrendered the same night.

I do not know what became of brother and the balance of the company. I would like much to hear from him. He may be here, as there are more of the Island No. 10 prisoners in the other prisons—there being three separate prisons, numbered 1, 2, and 3. We had a terrible time of it on the island. I know you must have stirring times about Jackson. We get the papers in here every day. We fare very well—are well cared for, have plenty to eat and good houses to stay in. This prison contains three acres, inclosed with a high plank wall, on which the sentinels walk.   There are about eight hundred prisoners here.   We are not permitted to go outside; we can get anything we want, though.   The people are kind and accommodating.   Tell our friends we are not suffering.   I should like to write you a long letter, but the rules forbid.   Mrs. Clark, a sister of the Moons, of Memphis, will take this across the lines to Richmond.

God bless you, my Christian friend!

Your friend,   Thos. J. Carruthers, *Lieutenant.*

In some of the letters severe criticisms upon the course pursued by General Mackall, the commander of Island No. 10, in regard to the surrender were made, and in others his course was defended.   Lieut. J. T. Menefee, of the First Alabama Infantry, wrote:

Camp Chase, April 20, 1862.

Dear Father:

As you are aware, I am a prisoner of war.   We endured much and suffered much, and I have been sick, quite sick; given up to die with cramp colic; but am still living, thank God!   I hope to be entirely well in a few days.   Captain Rush and Lieutenant Listrunk are here with me.

The company was sent to Chicago.   We were not allowed to tell them good-by.   This was attributable to hurry, and not inhumanity, on the part of our enemies.   The separation occurred at New Madrid.   We accomplished everything General Beauregard expected, and that was to hold in check a large column of the enemy.   This we did for eight weeks.   We are here without clothing except that upon our backs, and also without money to buy what we need.

They feed us well, but sick men want something else besides what we draw.   If there is any chance to get us gold, I wish you, B. Rush, and B. Campbell, who is Listrunk's friend, would arrange with Hon. D. Clopton to do so.   I send you herewith authority to draw sufficient to buy, say, fifty dollars in gold for me.

Kiss my little boy and see that he is well trained.   God bless the poor little motherless and now almost fatherless fellow!

Your son,   J. T. Menefee.

Camp Chase, April 21, 1862.

Hon. David Clopton, Richmond, Va.

I hereby authorize and empower you to make out my pay account from the 31st of December, '61, to the 1st of May, '62, and in my name draw the same from the Confederate States of America.

This I hope you will do, as I need the money. Your kindness in this will add to the obligations I am always under.
Respectfully,
J. T. MENEFEE, *First Lieutenant First Ala. Regt.*
Attest: C. C. KNOWLES, *Lieutenant;* J. W. RUSH, *Captain.*

Capt. Jackson, of the First Alabama, has a few words to say about the battle at Fort Donelson to the Hon. David Clopton, a Senator or Representative at Richmond:

Hon. David Clopton.   CAMP CHASE, April 22, 1862.

SIR: I was surrendered with ninety-six men, all from Alabama, and we are now confined in prison for the want of generalship upon our part. I am sorry to say that we were badly outgeneraled at Fort Donelson. We have comfortable quarters and good rations, and we are very kindly treated. We all are in good health. I want you to write to my father, William Jackson, and tell him that I am well. Write to Erin, Ga., Pike County; also G. W. Jackson, the same address. And I want you to send me some money.
When I was taken prisoner I had but little money; and now I have not one dollar; and if you will send me some, call upon William Jackson, Erin, Tallapoosa County, Ala., eighteen miles north of Dadeville, at Newsite; or you can hold my wages in the army, which is now $500. I am sure we could get the money that way. This lady (Mrs. Clark) is doing all she can for our comfort. I wish you to do all you can to have us exchanged. My home is at Newsite, Tallapoosa. Examine the records at Richmond and you will find my company upon the records.
I do not know whether you will ever get this, but I think Mrs. Clark will carry it to Richmond; but you may be at home.
Truly yours,   J. P. JACKSON, *Captain.*

Mr. William Jackson.   CAMP CHASE, April 22, 1862.

MY DEAR FATHER: There is a kind lady by the name of Mrs. Clark going to Richmond from here, and I hope you may get my letter. I am sorry to say to you, father, that I am a prisoner of war, but proud that I am well and hearty and weigh more than you ever saw me. The disadvantage that I labor under is my clothes are all too small for me. We have good quarters and good rations and very kind treatment.
I would like if you would go to Alabama and look after my family; and if they will go, I want you to move them to Georgia, as I can't tell when I will get home, but when I do get there I will have money to pay for all they consume. I think it best for my family to move to Georgia.

After three days' hard fighting at Donelson, we were compelled to surrender. I had only one man killed in my company. Our loss was great, and I never want to see another battlefield. It was fearful to me to look over the field and see the blood run from my fellow-man. I felt the wind of many a bullet, but fortunately escaped unhurt. We were in the heat of the battle, and my company bore the colors. I would write more, but I do not want to trouble Governor Tod to read so much, as he is kind enough to let us write. He is very much of a gentleman and very kind to us. May God bless you and family!

J. P. JACKSON, *Captain.*

DEAR WIFE: This is the first chance I have had to write you, and I don't know whether this will go through. I am well and hearty, so well that my clothes are getting too small for me. I think I shall weigh two hundred by the time I get home. The health of my company is good. We have plenty of good rations here, and are well treated. I want you to attend to my business the best you can until I get home. I can't tell anything about when that may be. Rear our children for God and our country; and if I never see you any more, tell them to think well of their father.

I think it would be the best thing to sell all my effects except the land and go to Georgia and live there until I get home. Do just as you think best. Kiss the children for me.

J. P. JACKSON, *Captain.*

Prisoner of War.

CAMP CHASE, COLUMBUS, OHIO.

General Curnes.

DEAR COUSIN: Knowing the uncertainty of the country mails in Dixieland, I address you, hoping you may communicate to my father's family the following intelligence: that I am a prisoner of war at Camp Chase, Columbus, Ohio; surrendered at Fort Donelson. All the officers of our regiment are with me. The privates were sent to Springfield, Ill. All were well at the last account. Basnet Cracey is with them, and well. We enjoy prison life better than I expected; our only uneasiness is in regard to our friends at home. I have written several letters home, but have received no assurance that any of them reached their destination.

I want for nothing here and am enjoying excellent health. Have a prospect, through the influence of Kentucky friends, of a parole of honor, but I may not succeed. Please transmit the above to my father, and write me.

Yours,

JOHN G. HALL.

The following letter to a prisoner at Camp Chase is of interest, but the name of the prisoner is unknown, as the letter simply uses his Christian name. The envelope by some means was lost. The Dr. Hoge mentioned in the letter was an eminent divine, a man known far and near for his learning as well as his Christian graces. He was at that time pastor of the First Presbyterian Church of Columbus. His death occurred in 1864:

DOBBS FERRY, N. Y., July 25, 1862.

DEAR ROBERT: Some three weeks ago we heard that you had been wounded and taken prisoner at Shiloh. I wrote immediately to Chicago and to Louisville, but could hear nothing from you. This morning, in a letter by Wilson Bruce, I found that you are at Columbus, Ohio.

I hope you were not seriously wounded and are now recovering. You should have written to us at once. To-day I write Dr. Hoge, of Columbus, to see you and do what he can to make you comfortable. Write, if possible, by return mail and let us know particularly how you are and if you are in need of anything we can supply. If you are capable of being moved and could be liberated on parole, come here, and we will gladly do all we can to make you well.

We heard from Mobile, through Mr. Bargett, about a month ago. He and Mrs. Bargett left Mobile about the 13th of May to run the blockade. They were captured by a United States vessel and brought to New York. They were most kindly treated by the United States officers and were at once liberated. When the Bargetts left Mobile your father and mother were quite well. They do not know much about the children. All the women and children who could get away were sent from the city to the country. Your Aunt Sarah will close this note.

Yours truly,   W. MEIKLE.

DEAR ROBBY: We were so sorry to hear you were wounded. Our great desire is to get you to our home to nurse you, if you can possibly be moved. We will send you the money to bring you on, if you can come.

I thought of going to see General Scott, if he could do anything for you; you know he was an old friend of your grandfather's. I do hope, Robby, you will keep up a good heart; your mother's prayers, which are many, will surely be answered, and God will take care of you. I have but a few moments to send this to the post office.

Your affectionate   AUNT SARAH.

Few letters of the many found in the lumber room at the Ohio Statehouse contain more genuine pathos than the one written by Lieut. P. L. Dotson to his wife in April, 1862. There is not a man in the North who may read this letter but will wish that the Lieutenant returned safely to this good wife, Mary, and "Little Bob."

The swiftly flying years have left age marks on little Bob, if he be living, and it would afford no little pleasure to those who made this late reading of his father's letter possible if he should find it in this volume.

From Lieut. P. L. Dotson, Company D, Twentieth Regiment, Mississippi Volunteers, Prisoner of War, to Mary W. Dotson, Brooksville, Miss.:

DEAR WIFE: I take this opportunity to write to you. This leaves me well, and I hope it may find you well also. O, I want to see you so much! I have thought that I wanted to see you before, but I did not know anything about it. I hope I will see you and my sweet little Bob one of these days. Here the days seem as long as months, but if I were with you all would be right.

I feel happy sometimes when I think I have done my duty; but when I look around on my condition, and know that I am so far from you and little Bob my heart sinks. It is not so hard to be a prisoner, after all, for we get plenty to eat and are treated very well. O, I hope it will work out right, whether for our good or not. I think I will end my days with you, whom I prize dearer than my life. O, Mary, it sends a thrill of happiness to my soul to think I will be with you by and by! Be of good cheer; there is a better day coming. Although I am in prison, I have much fun. We play marbles and the boys fiddle and do anything to keep our spirits up, or do anything amusing, and so don't be uneasy. I think I will get home in July, and then I will stay with you for some time. I have been in camp and in a fight that lasted nearly a week, and now I am in Camp Chase; and when I get out of this, I will return, I hope, to stay with you. I always found in my Mary a kind and good wife; and O, if I could be with you to-day and go to church with you! It can't be happiness to you, sweet one, to go there and not see your own dear boy sitting in his own easy way close by you and little Bob.

I trust this war will soon stop. I hope, Mary, I shall see you again; but it may be possible that I shall never hold my dear one in my arms again. I pray to the Being on high to protect you and little Bob.

Mary, I have volumes to tell you, dear one, of the battlefield, but I can't tell it here, and you must be brave and stand it out.

Tell Bob to be a good little boy and mind his ma, and that his pa is thinking of him and his ma all the time. O, I never think of anything else! I will close by saying: Teach him to love his pa and ma. Farewell; may God be with you and protect you! Kiss Bob for me. P. L. DOTSON.

In Chapter XI. the *Journal* mentions the name of Lieutenant Dotson as having arrived March 1, 1862, with a number of others.

CAMP CHASE, April 20, 1862.

MY DEAR MERRITT: You have doubtless heard of the surrender of our forces at Island No. 10, which included the First Alabama. We all regretted this much, but we were surrendered without knowledge or consent. Our boys stood up to the enemy like men and brave soldiers. We were drawn up in line of battle in sight of the enemy several times, and not one of them, I am glad to say, flinched in the least, but, on the contrary, were perfectly cool and determined. I was very proud of them, indeed, and love each one of them as a dear friend.

After our surrender we were separated, the officers being sent here and the men to Chicago or Springfield. It was hard for me to part with them, and they seemed to feel it much; but such is war. We are very well treated here, but are closely confined. We are anxious to get South. Some of the boys, I believe, made their escape. Lieutenants Hall and Tuttle are here, and are well.
Your friend, J. F. WHITEFIELD.
To Lieut. M. C. Pratt, Prattsville, Ala.

CAMP CHASE PRISON, April 21, 1862.

DEAR BELOVED WIFE: It is by the blessing of God that I am permitted to drop you a few lines to let you know that I am in reasonable health at this time, hoping these few lines may find you enjoying the same blessings when they come to hand. I have nothing of interest to write you, but many things to tell you, if we ever meet again, which I hope will be the case, and under better circumstances than the present. I can say that I was sadly disappointed in my treatment; it has been far better than I expected. So far it is very good; and there is but one thing I fear, and that is disease. We have some cases of smallpox in prison at this time. I hope that I may escape it.

I hope that we may be permitted to spend some happy days together soon. I cannot tell at this time. If you ever see me, you will find me the very same. For the present I close by signing myself your loving husband until death.
With love, D. R. FLETCHER.

Camp Chase Ohio
April 20th 1862,

Dear Uncle

As another opportunity presents itself I will again write you a few lines. We are all still at camp chase near Columbus all are very well indeed enjoying excellant health after getting accustomed to the climate and particularly the strong limestone water in this region of country, I drink it now with impunity, while in the first place I could not touch a drop of it unless mixed with an acid of some kind Capt. Guy is also writing to his father requesting him if possible to send him some funds You had better act with him and send me some too true we get a plenty of meat flour and meal and potatoes and other things from the U S Government but be sure that we would like to have some to buy butter lard and eggs, and particularly books of some sort to amuse us in our confinement We hear from the company about once a week They are at chicago, all well and treated kindly by the Federals both officers and soldiers) With regard to our treatment and condition I can speak of it in no other language than that of praise and commendation They have acted towards as soldiers and as gentlemen. I would like very much to be down south this beautiful weather it is still quite cool up here we have had several spring days. Well I must close you must write to me if you can I will write every time I see a slight chance

Your affect Nephew John Guenant
2d Lieut of Artillery
Floyds Brigade)

/62

Camp Chase near Columbus Ohio April 20th

My Dear Mother

An opportunity having offered its self by which I can get a letter through the lines I willingly embrace it to drop you a few lines As doubtless you are aware I am a prisoner of war Camp Chase We arrived here from Ft. Donelson on the 1st March. On arriving we were put in a prison of about 3 acres surrounded by a fence fifteen feet high. within the enclosure are comfortable houses large enough to entertain twelve or fifteen persons which constitute a mess The houses are comfortably built & streets regularly laid off & named by us such as Lee St Buckner &c. Our rations are issued to us of the same quantity & quality as they issue their own soldiers, perhaps a little better; with the rations & what delicacies we buy we live in fine style My mess are all Virginian mostly from the lower portions of the State. most of them having friends in the north get man eye enough to do us very well I wrote to Uncle Alfred Brown but have not heard from him why I cannot say perhaps I was mistaken in his Office If you can get a letter through the lines let me know his Office. The authorities here are very kind indeed & try to make us comfortable. I am limited as to how much I write I am in fine health now but was quite unwell for some time after I was taken With love to all I am as ever Your affson

Wm A. Colman

CAMP CHASE, COLUMBUS, OHIO, April 21, 1862.
W. S. Greary.

DEAR SIR: I write to let you know where and how I am. I am a prisoner of war; was taken February 14. I was forwarded from Bowling Green to Louisville, but was kept several days with the army, to be exchanged; and as there was no proposition made, I was sent forward from Louisville and on to this place. I have been treated with the greatest kindness while at Bowling Green. I was on parole and was quite a show to the Federals, for I was the first Rebel some of the officers had ever seen. When I was in my room, there was always a crowd of officers. When our prisoners are sick they are sent to the hospitals and are there well cared for, besides being visited by man's guardian angels—women.

Give my regards to the boys; also to Hiram.

Respectfully,   S. W. GASSARVAY.

To W. S. Greary, Corinth, Miss.

CAMP CHASE, PRISON NO. 3, COLUMBUS, OHIO.

MY DEAR WIFE: I expect you are in a good deal of trouble about me. I want you to give yourself as little bother about me as possible, for we are treated as kindly as prisoners deserve. We have good shanties, furnished with good cook stoves, and have plenty of good, wholesome food to eat. The only thing that is bad is liberty. We can't go home or anywhere else farther than our prison bounds.

I want you to do the best you can until I come home; I can't tell when that will be. E. H. Stewart is with me; let his wife know that he is well. J. G. Hall was left at Madrid Bend, and we have heard nothing from him since the privates were sent to Chicago. All the officers of the Eleventh Arkansas Regiment are here and a great many from Tennessee, Mississippi, Alabama, and Kentucky. I do not know the number. Write to me.

Yours ever until death,   J. M. SANDERS.

To Mrs. J. M. Sanders, Rockfort, Ark.

CAMP CHASE, April 21.

MY DEAR WIFE: If you received my letter from Island No. 10, you are not surprised to learn that I am a prisoner of war. We have comfortable quarters, plenty of everything to eat, and are kindly treated. My health is very good. I bear my lot with fortitude, and my only trouble is on your account. Be of good cheer, my dear wife. Write short letters and nothing contraband, or they will not be permitted to come. May God bless and protect you and my dear children!

Your faithful husband,   A. J. EVANS.

To Mrs. Augusta Evans, Okolona, Chickasaw Co., Miss.

CAMP CHASE PRISON, MESS 3, April 21, 1862.

Hon. Landon C. Haynes, U. S. Senator, Richmond.

DEAR SIR: I am a prisoner of war in Camp Chase. I am a first lieutenant in the Fiftieth Tennessee Regiment, surrendered at Fort Donelson. I am feeble in health, and am very anxious to be exchanged.

By the bearer of this I have written to Colonel Wigfall, United States Senator from Texas, asking his influence in carrying out a plan for my exchange. I imagine the most expeditious way to effect an exchange is to select an officer of my rank, who is a prisoner in the South, and release him on parole to visit Washington and have me released, or, in case he failed in that, to return to his status in prison. Knowing that the Confederate government has such a prisoner, by the name of Lieutenant Riley, of the Forty-Seventh New York, I have selected him as a suitable man to have exchanged for me.

I feel the more confidence in asking your influence from the fact that you are well acquainted with my brother-in-law, Frank E. Williams, of Rush, Tex., formerly of East Tennessee; and also from a fact (which, perhaps, you are not aware of) that I was the first man to suggest through the public prints your name as a suitable man for Confederate Senator. Can I hope that you will cooperate with General Wigfall in procuring my release?

Hoping through your influence to soon be beneath the skies of Dixie, I remain, my dear sir, very respectfully yours,

JOHN WARD.

FORT WARREN, BOSTON HARBOR,
May 31, 1862.

Mr. Valentine Wiss.

MY DEAR SIR: Sometime ago I asked Colonel Gantt where his men were sent. He could not tell me, but presumed Chicago. I wrote you anyway, and directed it there, and, having received no reply, concluded that the letter never reached you. I have made various inquiries, but could never hear a word from Wiss. Why is it that you and Dr. Green could not write to me? If you don't, I will take all the sewing from you I can and do other little underhanded tricks, and of course my influence will seriously damage the bugler's future chances. In view of these threats, I think you will readily see it will be greatly to your interest to write. Tell Jerry if he doesn't write I will do all I can when I go home to injure his very flattering prospects on Haley's Creek.

From accounts, you have all heard from old Hickman oftener than we did. Be sure to write me on receipt of this. All are well here.

Your friend,   JOHN F. GRAY.

CAMP CHASE, COLUMBUS, OHIO,
April 21, 1862.

DEAR SISTER: I was taken prisoner at Island No. 10 the 8th instant. We remained there one night and left on boat for Cairo; from that place to this by rail. My health is good. We have better quarters and better treatment than a great many in your section of the country would suppose. We live in plank houses, and have the same amount of provisions and clothing that Federal soldiers do. We have free access to about six acres of land.

Yours,   J. M. WALL.

To Mrs. Evalina Jones, Tickfaw Station, Livingston Parish, La.

CAMP CHASE PRISON, April 20, 1862.

MY DEAR SISTER: As Mrs. Moon has a permit to visit Virginia, she has kindly offered to take letters along with her. My health has been very good since I have been a prisoner. I have been confined in rather a small prison, but now we have a larger one and I have more fresh air. I am engaged in making rings of buttons. I set them with pearl sets, which I sell and get money to buy different things with. I can't tell you when I will be home, but trust in God I will see you sometime. Give my regards to all inquiring friends.

I remain, your loving brother,   W. H. MILLER.

Miss E. Miller, Luray, Va.

CAMP CHASE, April 22, 1862.

MY PRECIOUS WIFE: To relieve your anxiety, if possible, I shall try to give you as accurate an account of my past as the space will permit and tell you how I am situated at present. While at Madrid and Lsland No. 10 we suffered severely day and night for eight weeks, or nearly so. Rain, snow, sleet, ditching, marching, watching—in a single word, soldiering—used us up. For ten days we all thought our doom was sealed either to surrender or be slaughtered at any hour. We were surrendered on the 8th. My health had become good, and I was present at the surrender, commanding my men to stack arms with a sad heart. The men were separated from us the same day, and I have not seen them since. They were sent either to Chicago or Springfield. The officers of the line and the staff were all sent here and the field officers to Fort Warren.

Now, my dear, I want you to be cheerful, for my health is good, except a cold, which I hope soon to be rid of, and the treatment we all receive is very courteous and kind. Indeed, so clever are they that I am much astonished. To be a prisoner of war is not such a very bad thing, were it not for the absence from loved ones and duty. We are in good houses, cook on stoves, and have plenty of wood, water, and wholesome food.

When you hear of barbarity, cruelty, and the like, just say it is all false. I have not seen the least bit of it, and don't believe it is practiced anywhere.

My roommates are Lieutenants Menefee and Listrunk, with ten others, officers of the First Alabama Regiment. Captain Lacke, Captain Sullins, of Tuskegee, Lieutenants Andrews and Riley, of Pike County, Lieutenant Gilland and Captain Ramsey, of Wilcox, are among them. I found my old schoolmate, Dick Hall, of Autaugo, who is here, and Lieutenant Knowles, of Macon County. I met here a cousin whom I had never seen before—Captain Mooney, of Arkansas. You see how strange are the fortunes of war.

We are like brothers and enjoy ourselves as well as we can, but are restive, of course, when we think of home. Everything I had was lost except the clothes upon my body at the time, and I have not a cent of current money. If Ben can make arrangements to send me some, I will be very much obliged. Indeed, I will.

We are all as poor as church mice. If the friends of all our men should send money, some good men could be selected who would be allowed to bring it to us.

From James Deeler to Sarah A. C. Deeler, Kosciusko, Miss.

CAMP CHASE, OHIO, April 25, 1862.

DEAR WIFE AND LITTLE DAUGHTER: I write to tell you that I am getting along tolerably well since I was captured at Fort Donelson. Sally, I do want to see you and little Mary very much. The time seems long since I last saw you. I do hope and trust this difficulty will soon be settled, for I am weary of it. The officers and the privates are separated, and I have not seen any of the company since the 25th of February. I got a letter from Gus sometime ago, and they were all tolerably well. Some of the boys are dead. A. D. Roberts has been sick, but is getting better. I do hope I will get to see you before long.

Your affectionate husband until death.

DEAR FATHER, MOTHER, AND SISTERS: I inclose my letter to you, father, and I want you to take care of what I have, and take good care of Sally and little Mary until I come home. Father, try to get me exchanged, for no man wants to stay in prison. We are well cared for here; the confinement is what I object to most. We have not room enough to exercise, but we are very well treated. I am lighter in weight than ever you saw me since I grew up.

Your son, JAMES DEELER.

From James Deeler to Sarah A. C. Deeler, Kosciusko, Miss.

Prison No 3 Camp Chase O
Near Columbus Ohio
April 21 1862

Dear Parents

I have been de-
sirous of writing to you for
some time & now avail
myself of the first opportunity offered since I was
taken prisoner at Fort Donelson   I heard from you
through Jno Walker & Moses
Craddock who were taken
at Island No 10.

My health is remarkably
good and I am very pleas-
antly situated taking into
consideration that I am
a prisoner . I trust this
will find you both well —

Your affectionate Son

James Griffen.

Camp Chase Prison
Columbus Ohio

Dear Pa— April 24th

It snowed here this morning
consequently it is partly cold today
I have been tolerably sick I was
in the hospital six weeks but by
the goodness of God I was spared
Mrs Dobson nursed me like a
brother. I am going to Sandusky
tomorrow or next day. We will have
better quarters and a healthy situation
Pa I want to write a long letter
but as that is prohibited I will write
that I am well now and doing
very well under the circumstances
Jimmie Cottrell is dead— Died at
Chicago about the middle of March
My love to all, God bless you Your son
JSP
J S Levy

I sent you 120$ by Mr Ross from F.D

CAMP CHASE, COLUMBUS, OHIO,

April 20, 1862.

DEAR JANE: I have written you fully all the particulars in regard to our surrender at Island 10 on the 8th instant. Fifty-three of my company were included in the surrender, a list of which I herewith inclose. Have it published in the *Herald* [The list of names mentioned appears in the back of this history.—AUTHOR.], that all our friends may see it. All the officers were separated from their companies at New Madrid. My boy was well when I left him. He will be sent to Chicago or Springfield, Ill. You must not take this misfortune of mine too much to heart; many others are in the same condition. Besides, I am happy to say that we have nothing to complain of in regard to the treatment.

We are quartered in houses, with everything furnished us that we could ask for. Were it not for the fact that we are prisoners of war and confined to the camp, we would feel quite easy. I make myself satisfied, and bear my imprisonment with as much patience as possible under the circumstances. All I fear at all is sickness. I hope and pray that we may be exchanged before the sickly season of the year. My health at present is very good, and all the mess, composed of Captains Moss and Mather, are well. The greatest inconvenience I find is having no money that I can use. Confederate bonds are not used at all. I think I shall be home soon. Should any one come from Arkansas to bring us money, be sure to send me some gold. My sword is still at the Washer House, Memphis. My trunk was left on a boat in the hands of Mr. McDonald. I presume he will send Conden to get my sword and trunk. Keep them until I am released. I suggest that you remain at father's until I get back; but do as you think best. Kiss the children for me and tell them where I am. I will have plenty of money to meet any arrangement you make. Remember me to all our friends and relations. When you write me, direct your letter to Capt. L. Logan, Prisoner of War, Camp Chase, via Fortress Monroe. I send a stamp to pay postage this side of the line.

Yours forever,   J. L. LOGAN.

List of Captain Logan's Company surrendered at Island No. 10 April 8, 1863: J. L. Logan, Captain; F. T. Scott, E. C. Lockhart, l. K. Whitfield, G. W. Elleatt, I. T. Webb, W. F. Mack, E. H. McLaughtin, J. W. Grauger, E. C. Alford, J. E. Basten, J. W. Bussell, H. L. Brazil, Peter Connelly, C. A. Conine, G. W. Cathey, J. A. Cogan, H. C. Davis, W. H. Water, J. A. Emerson, D. L. Davis, E. S. Greeney, E. A. Wane, E. B. Whitfield, E. C. Haddox, J. B. Halison, I. Wardin, W. Jackson, J. .H. Lang.

J. E Side, L. O. Meyers, W. M. Mitchell, J. M. Malone, A. J. Mims, J. A. Price, A. H. Patton, R. R. Shelton, John Jones, Joe Schaeffer, T. I. Sullivant, J. Sloan, R. J. Tumer, J. F. Todd, J. I. Todd. G. W. Taylor, A. M. Webb.

CAMP CHASE, April 28, 1862.

MY DEAR PARENTS: I wrote you the other day; but as Mrs. Moon [Note: The Mrs. Moon mentioned was Mrs. Clark, whose family name was Moon.—AUTHOR.] has kindly offered to take letters from prisoners to Virginia, I have taken the opportunity, hoping you may hear from me again. I have written you so often, and not hearing from you, that it is almost enough to discourage one from writing; but, according to the old adage, "no news is good news." I will hope for the best. Mrs. Moon is a native of Virginia, and has a permit to visit there; on what business, I cannot say. There are some ladies here that are very kind to us. Mrs. Moon, wife of a preacher, and Mrs. Thurman have visited the hospital that contains our sick and given comfort to our prisoners.

There were sixteen who came when I did, and there are only four now. One of them, poor fellow, I am afraid, will never be well again; he has consumption. He was captured with a man named John Bruly, of Arkansas. The little boy that was with us we left at Bearly. Perhaps they will make a pet of him. Of the sixteen, four died and the rest have been sent home. They were all citizens except five, and one of them died. I haven't much to say except for you to remember me in your prayers, and, next to ourselves, to remember our country; and may God bless you!

Yours forever,   J. HENNEY.

CAMP CHASE, April 18, 1862.
Miss E. H. Fussell.

DEAR COUSIN: I write to let you know that I am still in the land of the living. I am enjoying fine health here. If I could just hear from home! Since the 15th of December I have not heard one word. I have written several letters, but it must be that they never got them. The mail facilities are very bad in this country now.

Cousin, if you get any chance, please write to me. Tell ma I am in better health than ever I was in my life. Give my best respects to all inquiring friends, and accept for yourself the assurance that I am, as ever, your devoted cousin,   W. W. HUGHES.

To Miss E. Fussell, Columbia, Tenn.

CAMP CHASE, COLUMBUS, OHIO,

April 15, 1862.

MY DEAR FATHER: The last time I wrote to sister I told her that in a few days we would be slaughtered or captured. My expectations are fully realized. On the 8th we were surrendered and on the 13th placed in Prison No. 3, Camp Chase. I lost everything except the clothing on my body at the time of the surrender. The Feds have treated us very kindly, and I think will supply our wardrobes with at least a change of garments. They have been doing this.

My money is worthless here, but I am very healthy and my spirits cheerful, as they should be. We have plenty of good food and comfortable cabins; nothing to complain of except our confinement. This is a matter of course. Tell Ollie not to grieve. I know her heart is bowed down with sorrow and she at times is very sad. She cannot come to me, or I would make application for it. Tell her to stay wherever she wishes. I have no idea how long we will remain here or be confined as prisoners. If you can do anything to get me out, I wish you would do so.

The officer in charge of us is Colonel Moody, a preacher. Perhaps you know him. I wish to form his acquaintance, if he will permit. We will have preaching on Sunday. I will preach myself, if they cannot be served better. My heart is right, my faith strong. My love to all.

Yours,   W. RUSH.

P. S.—April 19. I am suffering with a cold, but not much. If you can make any arrangements to have me some money sent, I will be a thousand times obliged, for really I have nothing. Only officers are here; the privates all were sent to Chicago or to Springfield, Ill. There are about eighteen hundred of us here. All well treated and in pretty good spirits. I wish we could get out and go home.

May God bless you and mother and all! My dear wife and children are in my thoughts all the time. God be merciful to them! I enjoy thinking of you here. Pray for me.

Yours,   W. RUSH.

CAMP CHASE, OHIO, April 23, 1862.

Colonel Trigg.

SIR: Having learned the object of your visit to this prison and the terms on which you think we prisoners of war can be released, I desire to say that, as Tennessee is my home, I am willing to return my loyalty to the State of Tennessee, and further I am not willing to do. These are the terms I am willing to abide by.

Respectfully,   WILLIAM W. BRICKEEN.

CAMP CHASE, April 20, 1862.

DEAR BROTHER AND SISTER: I am well at the present time and just getting over the effects of my wound. I was sent from Clarksville March 20, thence to Cincinnati; stayed in the hospital there until the 18th of April and then brought to this place. There are about five acres inside the walls of this prison, and we are pretty comfortably fixed here, and yet I do not like it at all. I shall have to put up with it anyhow.

I have received a letter from Sandford's folks. They are all well but Irene, and she is poorly. I send my love to you all and all who may inquire.

From your affectionate brother,   J. P. YATES.

Hope for better days. Kiss the children for me.

[The letter did not give the regiment or the rank of the writer. It was addressed to D. A. Yates, Esq., New Orleans, La.]

CAMP CHASE, COLUMBUS, OHIO,

April 21, 1862.

DEAR WIFE: You have heard before this that our regiment, with others, was surrendered on the 8th of April as prisoners of war by General Mackall. The circumstances I can't give you. Suffice it to say, we were completely surrounded by overwhelming numbers and forced to succumb. The officers were brought here and the privates sent to Chicago and Springfield, Ill.

I have not seen Jim Niles since I left home. We have an abundance of everything and are kindly treated. I am not nearly so exposed as when in camp. May God Almighty shield and protect you from all harm and aid and comfort you in this dark hour! I would write more, but I am limited. Kiss my dear boys and train them to love and remember their pa. God bless you and the children!

Yours ever,   W. SMITH.

To Mrs. W. E. Smith, Oaktuppa, Ala.

CAMP CHASE, COLUMBUS, OHIO,

April 22, 1862.

Mr. J. C. Durham.

DEAR COUSIN: I drop you a few lines, but I don't know whether they will reach you or not. This leaves me in good health. I will write to my wife to-day, and will direct it to West Point; and if she is not there, I hope you will forward it to her. I am in prison four miles west of Columbus, Ohio.

I cannot tell you when I will see you, but I hope I will sometime. I can't write much. Our food is very good, better than I expected. O, but we think this life is a hard one, and we hope for better days.   J. Z. DURHAM.

Mr. J. C. Durham, West Point, Ga.

Camp Chase Ohio April 25th 1862

Mrs Lyara P Parmele
Winona   Tell Jas to Write
Carroll Co   Sanduskie
Mife   Johnson's Island
        Dear Wife   Michigan
                        I have no news to
write only that I am a Prisoner of War at Camp Chase
as you will See from the Caption and in fine health
and well Can o fes a Plenty of Provisions and all
that Prisoners Can ask for except liberty all of
the 4th Mife Rgt Officers and Privates are well and
in good health W C Thompson Malcomb Stafford and
Benj E Curtis have died Wife be of good Cheer
who Kiss all the Babies and tell them Pa is well
and think of them every day tell all my Relations
and friends howdy tell Jas to Stay at home
and take Care of our Family
                I am your Affec Husband
write me of you can   W J Parmele
and direct as above to
Prison   no 2 mess 13

                        I omitted to say that W F Webb
and Tommy Ratliff were Killed on the Battle Field. I
and our Regiment are being Sent to Sanduskie Johnsons Island
in Lake Michigan so direct all of your letters.

CAMP CHASE, April 21, 1862.

DEAR MOTHER: My health is tolerably good at this time, but I have been very sick since I came here first, which was after Fort Donelson was taken. I guess I have got to stay here, for I see no chance of getting anywhere else. I hope the time will soon come when I may go home, but you need not look for me until you see me coming. We are treated much better than I expected. We have plenty to eat and good cabins to stay in. I send this by Mrs. Clark, who will take it to Richmond.

Yours until death, URIAH GARDNER.

To Mrs. Mary Gardner, Jackson, West Tennessee.

CAMP CHASE, COLUMBUS, OHIO,
March 20, 1862.

DEAR MOLLIE: You will doubtless be surprised to learn that I am in this region and in the confines of a prison. We were surrendered on the 8th instant at Island No. 10 by General Mackall, and not even a colonel had any intimation of it until it was announced that we were surrendered as prisoners of war.

I am happy to say, however, that we are well treated, and I hope we will be exchanged soon. I now have the painful necessity of informing you of the death of William D. Johnson, who died on the 16th instant of pneumonia and measles. I hope that you are all well at home, and that I may soon be permitted to visit you. I would write often, but it is very uncertain as to your receiving my letters.

My respects to the friends and my love to you and the baby.

Your husband, R. H. RILEY.

CAMP CHASE, COLUMBUS, OHIO,
March 16, 1862.

DEAR BROTHER: I take pleasure in writing you a few lines to inform you that I am well at the present, and I hope that you and my dear family are well also. The health of the men here is not very good at this time. Captain Read and Lieutenant East died yesterday. Dave, I want you to see J. F. Gresham and get him to draw my money and pay it to you, and you can dispose of it as you see proper.

We are very well treated here by the enemy. I would like to see you all very much. I want you to write to G. A. Inders and have my trunk sent home. I am in hope I will be released soon and sent home. You will read this to my family and tell them to weep not for me, for I am game. The same Hand that led me through dark scenes will lead me home.

I remain your brother, W. P. PARDIER.

[No envelope inclosed this letter.]

Mention is made in the introduction of this chapter that only
a portion of the letters found would be used. After the letter
from W. Meikle, of Dobbs Ferry, New York, was in type a few
more letters were found, and one of them gave the information
desired about "Robby." The following letter from St. Catharines, Canada, mentioning Mr. Meikle, shows that he was Mr.
Robert Beers, supposed to be in prison at Camp Chase, but the
envelope contains a notation of the fact that Mr. Beers was not
at Camp Chase, and was signed by Tiffany, an officer having
charge of Confederate mail.

Mr. Robert Beers.   ST. CATHARINES, June 30, 1862.

MY DEAR FRIEND: I write a few lines and will wait to see
whether you get them before I write much to you. I have had
some intimation that you were at Camp Chase, and so I direct
there.

Myself and family are here in Canada. I wish we could see
you, for your mother's sake, as well as your own. She was well,
as usual. So were your father and other friends. They know
that you were wounded and that you were in the hospital when
it fell into the hands of the Union troops, so that they judge you
are a prisoner. Still, they are very anxious lest your wound
might prove fatal. Your poor mother, however, bears all with
fortitude. I have heard from Eddie Treat, and have notified Mr.
St. John, who is in New York, of his whereabouts, and he has
sent Eddie money.

We were at Mr. Meikle's house and stayed all night. I told
them all I knew of you at that time, and Mr. Meikle immediately
set about searching by correspondence for you. As soon as I
heard you were at Camp Chase I sent him word. You must let
him and me both know how you are and what you need to make
you comfortable.

I have written to a minister of my acquaintance in Columbus,
and requested him as a special favor to give you some attention.
Tell Mr. Plum that his mother has been quite sick, but is again
well, and that his sister is also well. They were both very anxious
about him, as they had heard he was wounded.

I was compelled to stop preaching for a while on account of illness, so I started for Europe via Havana. Our vessel was captured
and we were brought to New York, where we were at liberty
to go where we wished. We came here, and I may not go to
Europe. We have to return to Mobile in a few months, so that
I may resume my labors.

There were fifty-eight additions to our Church last year. Be
of good cheer. God bless you and your companions!

Your affectionate friend and pastor,   J. W. BURGETT.

CAMP CHASE, COLUMBUS, OHIO,
April 20, 1862.

DEAREST MOTHER: God has willed it that I be far from all my near relations and dear friends, but it is his desire. I will bear it cheerfully, thinking of the poor men here suffering. I have only God to thank that I am well and strong, and I do thank him with all my heart. I often think of your affection and kind and gentle care. Since my confinement I have been somewhat blue, but now, thanks be to God, I am over it. Tell pa to use all his influence to have me again restored to you. Give my love to him and all the family, and embrace them, one and all, for me.

Write to me often, as that will be one of my greatest consolations. You can easily do so on a flag of truce. I send this by a noble Southern lady, who has done all in her power to relieve our suffering as much as she can.

Your son, JOHN Z. GUTHRIE.

Mrs. John Z. Guthrie, care of W. O. Greenlaw, Esq., Memphis, Tenn.

CAMP CHASE, April 21, 1862.

David Bradley.

DEAR SIR: I desire to inform you that I am a prisoner of war at Camp Chase, Ohio. We are in tolerably good health. I would like to see you all very much, but I can't get home just now. I wrote several letters to you all, but have received no answers, and I want to hear very much. Tell John I would like to hear from him. Tell Aunt Sarah howdy, also, and say that I am all right.

Show this letter to all who desire to see it, and tell Ad I want to see him too. Tell old Mrs. Davis that I heard from Frank a short time ago. Tell Capt. D. P. Curry to have us four exchanged. I have been here since last September, and am getting tired of staying in this place. He can have us exchanged if he will. Henry Whitman is here, and John McCutchen and Hugh McTuanns.

When you write don't put in anything contraband, for our letters are all opened before we get them. Tell old Mr. Ebberd that I wrote to Ben Ventrick, but have not heard from him. I must close by saying: God be with you all. It is the sincere prayer of your nephew, JOHN W. THOMPSON,
Rock Creek Guards, Twenty-Fifth Va. Regt.

"When this you see, remember me,
Though many miles apart we be."

Tell all the girls howdy for me.

To Mr. David Bradley, Goshen Bridge, Rockbridge Co., Va.

CAMP CHASE, April 15, 1862.

MY DEAR FRIEND ALLISON: We were captured December 5, 1861, and taken to Calhoun, where we stayed three weeks, and while there my mother and several of my fellow-townsmen came to see me. We were kept there longer than necessary, expecting every day to be exchanged; but no offer being made by the South, we were sent to Louisville and there lodged in the military prison, where we had comfortable quarters and were kindly treated. Friends and relations were allowed to visit us twice a week, and they came in crowds, bringing. clothes, tobacco, and everything we needed. I made the acquaintance of several fine young ladies while at Louisville.

We left Louisville March 21 and arrived here the next morning, where we are safely housed in an inclosure, with four rows of comfortable cabins extending from one end of the prison to the other. We draw ample rations and cook for ourselves, each cabin being supplied wth a cooking stove and all necessary utensils; so you see we are as well situated as prisoners could expect, my company being Capt. Charles R. Biller and Lieutenants Wickleffe and Hanis. We have been waiting through all the long months of our imprisonment for an exchange, but alas! we have looked in vain. Our desponding hearts have been many times cheered by the rumor of a speedy exchange, but as many times sorely disappointed. Jim Watthal is well.

Your friend,   J. B. HALL.
To Allison G. Hall; no address.

CAMP CHASE, PRISON No. 3, MESS 2,

April 20, 1862.

DEAR BROTHER: I am in good health. There are fifteen in a mess. All well with the exception of Capt. J. Smith, of Morgan County. I have had the mumps. I was vaccinated, and it has taken good effect. We have had since the first of this month four cases of smallpox. There is one case in this prison at this time, but none have died as yet with the disease. There were several deaths since the 1st of March. Dr. Houston is the only one of my acquaintances here. I get letters from the other boys at Camp Douglas. They all have been sick; two have died—A. J. Braden, on the 18th of March, and Green Harber, on the 5th of this month. The boys say they are all very well treated, but anxious to get home. Robert Clarke and Wren both are doing pretty well. All of us are guarding against smallpox. I have made several requests for clothing. It looks favorable for me now.

I remain,   P. PORTER, *Prisoner of War.*
Gallatin, Ky.

CAMP CHASE, NEAR COLUMBUS, OHIO,
April 18, 1862.

DEAR CAPTAIN: Our second campaign has been a very unfortunate one, and the First Alabama is now in durance—prisoners of war. Our accommodations and fare are far better than any of us expected. The privates have been sent to Springfield or Chicago. We officers, including Major Know, are rusticating at this place. I have written to my parents, but have received no reply.

When we abandoned Island No. 10 we lost all our clothing and comforts. We are now realizing the truths of the expression: In a strange land, without money, "duds," and almost minus friends. We neither fear pickpockets, shoplifters, nor are we in dread of "false alarms." My space is limited and ideas cramped; so I will conclude.

Your sincere friend,   S. B. MOORE.

My address is: Lieut. S. B. Moore, Camp Chase, Prison No. 3, Columbus, Ohio.

CAMP CHASE PRISON,
COLUMBUS, OHIO, April 20, 1862.

MY DEAR BETTIE: Nine weeks have elapsed to-day since I, with my regiment, was surrendered at Fort Donelson. I have as yet received no news from home, but I hope you have at least received some of my letters written since my capture. A kind lady of this State, Mrs. Clark, has obtained permission to visit Richmond, and very kindly offers to carry our letters beyond the lines and mail them. There is at least a possibility of this reaching you. I hope, however, ere this that some one of the fugitives from out the regiment who escaped has informed you of my safety. My health thus far has been unusually good, and bids fair, through the regularity of all my habits, to continue so. How much longer I am to remain a prisoner depends upon so many contingencies that it is impossible to conjecture. Major Brown was paroled several days since to Richmond, to effect, if possible, his exchange for me. Whether he has been successful, I have not learned. Immediately after our surrender we were taken to Chicago, and there the officers were separated from the men, the men remaining there and the officers brought to this place.

On last Thursday the other officers of my regiment, with one exception, were taken to a prison on an island in Lake Erie, where they report they are more comfortably quartered than here. Lieutenants Siddile, Jeff, Monroe, and Stoddard are there. Some two days since, Captain George was removed from here.

Your brother,   F. B. KEYES.

To Miss Anna Keyes.

CAMP CHASE, April 20, 1862.

MY DEAREST WIFE: I have written to you several times since I have been in prison at this place; but, owing to the difficulty of my letters passing the Federal lines, I send this by a lady who will leave for Richmond in a day or two. My health has improved. I was confined in the hospital for some time after my arrival here, but, with the help of God, I now feel quite well. I am in a cabin that at least keeps me dry. We draw plenty of rations of flour, meal, bacon, beef, sugar, coffee, tea, candles, soap, vinegar, salt, potatoes, and hominy. In addition to this, we buy butter, eggs, and molasses, or anything else we prefer. We are now paying twenty cents a pound for butter and seven cents a dozen for eggs. We still have Giles to cook for us. In a word, we want nothing but liberty to be doing better than soldiers in the field possibly can.

We have bought useful books and pass the time reading, jumping, foot-racing, etc. Indeed, I have but one thing to disturb me, and that is your welfare. If I were assured of that, I should be content. I find my Bible, that you were thoughtful enough to put up for me, of great use and comfort.

The officers in charge of this prison have been generally kind to us. There are about six hundred prisoners here now, mostly officers. Poore and Menly are here. Poore was shot through the hip with a Minie ball, but has entirely recovered. John Morris and —— Pleasants have been released on parole through United States Attorney General Bates. They both live near the courthouse; and if you see them, you can get all the particulars.

The officers and men are all indignant at the surrender at Fort Donelson. Do the best you can, and sell everything on the farm if you cannot collect the money due me. My love to Bessie and Billy. Kiss Dig for me.

Affectionately yours,   JOHN TALLEY.

To Mrs. Dollie A Talley, Bula, Va.

CAMP CHASE, April 24, 1862.

DEAR PA: It snowed here this morning, and it is pretty cold to-day. I have been tolerably sick. I was in the hospital six weeks; but, by the goodness of God, I was spared. Pleas Dodson waited on me like a brother. I am going to Sandusky to-morrow or the next day. We will have better quarters and a healthier situation. Pa, I want to write a long letter, but I am limited. I will write that I am well now and doing well under the present circumstances. Jimmy Cotheral is dead; died in Chicago about the middle of March. Love to all.

Your son,   J. A. COX.

P. S.—I send you $1.50 by Mr. Ross, from F. D.

CAMP CHASE, April 20, 1862.

MY DEAR MOTHER: An opportunity having offered itself by which I can get a letter through the line, I will embrace it to drop you a few lines. As doubtless you are aware, I am a prisoner of war at Camp Chase. We arrived here from Fort Donelson on the 4th of March. On arrival we were put in a prison of about three acres, surrounded by a fence fifteen feet high. Within the inclosure are enough houses to entertain twelve or fifteen persons, who constitute a mess.

The houses are comfortably built, and the streets are regularly laid off. Rations are given to us just the same as to their own soldiers, perhaps a little better. With rations and what delicacies we buy, we live in fine style.

My mess are all Virginians, mostly from the lower part of the State. Most of them, having friends in the North, get money enough to do very well. I wrote to Uncle Albert Brown, but have not heard from him. Why, I cannot say. Perhaps I was mistaken in his address. If you can get a letter through the line, let me know his office.

The authorities are very kind, and try to make us comfortable. I am limited as to how much I write. I am in fine health now, but was quite unwell after I was captured.

With love to all, I am yours, WILLIAM O. COLEMAN.

CAMP CHASE, April 25, 1862.

Mrs. Lydia Parmelee, Winona, Miss.

DEAR WIFE: I have no news to write you, only that I am a prisoner of war at Camp Chase, as you will see from the caption, and that I am in fine health and well cared for. Have plenty to eat; all the prisoners can ask for but liberty. All the Fourth Mississippi Regiment officers and privates are well and in good health. W. O. Thomson, M. Stafford, and R. E. Curtis have died.

Wife, be of good cheer; kiss all the babies and tell them pa is well and, thinks of them every day. Tell all my relations and friends "howdy." Tell James to stay at home and take care of the family.

I am your affectionate husband, W. J. PARMELEE.

Write me if you can, and direct, as above, to Prison No. 2,. Mess No. 13.

I omitted to say that W. F. Webb and Tommy Ratliff were killed on the battlefield; and I and our regiment are being sent to Sandusky, Johnson Island, in Lake Erie; so direct all your letters there.

Tell James to write.

Sandusky, Johnson's Island, Ohio.

CAMP CHASE, April 21, 1862.

R. W. Price, Esq.

MY DEAR FRIEND: I, for my first time, have an opportunity of writing you since becoming a citizen of Ohio. Last February I removed from Bowling Green, Ky., to Fort Donelson, Tenn., arriving there on the 10th, and on the 15th something like a fight occurred, accounts of which you have seen. The number of the enemy is unknown; that of ours, 13,890; our killed, 209; wounded, 965.

Sunday morning, February 16, the whole Confederate force were sold to General Grant by a man named Gideon Pillow. He sold us, skulked off to Nashville before daylight, and left his men to suffer the consequences. As the result I am here with a portion of our regiment, as a prisoner of war; but I am proud to inform you that my health is good, and we live just as well as we wish, each mess having a nice little house, with a good cooking stove in it. Part of our regiment is at Indianapolis and a portion at Fort Warren and some of us here. The health of the prisoners is generally good. Captain Reed and Lieutenant Rast are dead. Captains Sharp and Demo are both here, as lively as ever. I would like very much to be at home and know who of our friends suffered at the battle of Shiloh. We are all hoping to get home soon, but God only knows when that time will come. If you can get any money for my wife, do so. I am allowed to write only one page, so I must close. Send this to my wife at Burnsville.

Believe me forever your friend,   GEO. W. SMITH.

Written to R. W. Price, Eastport, Tishomingo County, Miss.

The letter from George W. Smith to R. W. Price mentions the death of Captain Reed and Lieutenant Rast, but there is no record of their burial at Columbus, either in the Camp Chase Cemetery or the earlier one, where a number were laid to rest in what was called the City Cemetery. The only name found among the list of the dead mentioned in any of the letters was Lieut. John F. Allen, of the First Alabama.

CAMP CHASE, April 20, 1862.

MY DEAR WIFE: I take this opportunity of writing to you. I am well and doing very well. After we left Somerset, we were taken to Louisville, Ky., and stayed there four or five weeks, and then brought to this place, which is near Columbus, Ohio. I am well treated and comfortably situated. Tell father and mother where I am, and not to be uneasy about me, for I am well and perfectly safe. I don't know when I shall be at home, but shall come as soon as I can.

You must keep a good heart and not be troubled about me any more. Kiss our dear little ones for me, and do the best you can for them. You need not answer this; don't think it would reach me. Good-by, dear wife.

Yours ever, I. J. LOWE, *Twenty-Ninth Tenn. Vol.*

From a prisoner of war to Mrs. Martha A. Lowe, Midway Depot, Greene County, Tenn.

CAMP CHASE, COLUMBUS, OHIO,

April 21, 1862.

AFFECTIONATE COMPANION AND LITTLE CHILDREN AND MOTHER: I drop you these lines to let you know that I am in tolerably good health, and hope this will find you all well. I am enjoying myself as well as the nature of the case will permit.

We have plenty to eat and ground enough to exercise. We are all well treated by the Federal officers and men. L. B. Martin and our men are at Camp Douglas. I got a letter from there three days ago stating that B. had been sick weeks, but was thought to be mending. John Martin is dead; he died on March 1. W. C. Brandon and James Logan died at St. Louis about March 10. We left Captain Davis at St. Louis sick. I heard a few days ago that he would join us in a few days.

John Evans and myself are all that are here from our company. I have no knowledge of when I will get home; but if not before, we will have a chance at the end of the war. So do the best you can, and I will do the same.

I am all right. SEBERN PHILLIPS.

P. S. Phillips.

CAMP CHASE, PRISON NO. 3,

NEAR COLUMBUS, OHIO.

DEAR PARENTS: I have been desirous of writing you some time, and now avail myself of the first opportunity offered me since arriving here. I was taken prisoner at Fort Donelson. I heard through John Walker from Moss Craddock. They were taken at Island No. 10.

My health is remarkably good, and I am very pleasantly situated, taking into consideration that I am a prisoner of war. I trust this will find you both well.

Your son, JAMES GRIFFIN.

STATE OF TENNESSEE, HICKMAN CO.,
May 1, 1862.

DEAR HUSBAND: I write you a few lines to find out whether you are dead or alive. I want you to take good care of yourself, and do not be uneasy about me; I will do the best I can.

I am trying to have a crop made. I wish I could send you some money and clothes. I am waiting with patience for you to come home, thinking about the time when we will meet. I'd rather you were there than to be here fighting against the Union. The prisoner who was pressed when you were is in Mississippi.

I wanted our Union to stand, for I lived happily then and see no pleasure now. I want you to write to me. Direct your letters to Nashville, for I can get them there. I send my love and best respect to you and all the Hickman boys. If Wilson Overley is dead, please some of you write to me, and all about his sickness. I will say no more   BANCKEY OVERLEY.

To Wilson Overley.

COLUMBIA, TENN., May 4, 1862.

DEAR GEORGE: I have just written a letter to my brother, Eugene, and concluded to inclose a short one to you. Mr. Pease had service to-day, the first time for weeks; delivered a good sermon and read a portion of the morning service. There is quite a change in the people since you left a few days since. Three prominent gentlemen of Columbia presented a Union flag to the troops here. It was presented by Messrs. Chesly Benum, Charles Crawford, and Jerome Wilson. The latter, you remember, married Miss Hailey. The flag is now waving over the courthouse.

Colonel Branch and your Uncle Jerome left a day or so since for Arkansas. Pa has been in Mississippi ever since the fall of Fort Donelson, having left mother and myself here alone. We are completely surrounded by tents, but have not been molested. We have nothing to complain of, but much to be thankful for. The Provost Marshal, Captain Green, came out to see our sick soldiers of Colonel's cavalry; treated us very kindly, requesting us to keep him until his health was restored; when he took the oath of honor, got a pass and left. We were very grateful for his kindness, as he might have made it a very distressing visit to us.

I see your ma often; she is quite well and cheerful; gave me a very valuable part of your property, "Rip." He was so firm in his affections for his home I could not get him home with me. Jimmy Johnson died of consumption a few days since. William Witral's remains were brought home. Mr. Lee is married to Miss Branch, of Nashville. No one from this place was killed in the battle at Shiloh, but one man in the First Tennessee Regiment was killed—F. Cox, the paroled prisoner from this place, who returned. Eddy Saunders is well and safe. I understand your Uncle Gis's place has not been disturbed. It is a pity his family did not remain at home. I saw a young lady in an open carriage; she was so completely veiled I could not see her countenance, therefore could not judge if her heart was imprisoned. Major Price is walking the streets, looking, as usual, quite consequential, taking many things on himself which would be much more becoming to leave undone. Mr. J. H. Thomas has returned home with permission from Governor Johnson to remain unmolested.

I am sorry I have not more to write that will interest you. Let me hear from you soon. Mother joins me in much love to you.

Yours affectionately,   M. R. LYKE.

This letter was without envelope or further address than what appears in the communication.

WEST POINT, Ky., May 26, 1862.

Brother Rogers.

DEAR SIR: I arrived in Louisville yesterday morning just one hour after you left, with an order from General Duffield for your release. When I first heard of your arrest and learned of the cause, I had no doubt but what you would have a trial and be acquitted, and thought but little of it until Saturday night about nine o'clock, when I heard of your sentence to Camp Chase.

Sunday morning I went to work to get up evidence to secure your release, and started to Louisville about ten o'clock Monday morning with the testimony. I found General Duffield at Dr. George Syms's, and when he read it promptly made out an order for your release; but, as before stated, I was one hour too late in getting to Louisville.

General Duffield told me last night he would have you brought back to Louisville, which I think he will do. I learn since, however, that there is some doubt as to his jurisdiction. Yet he stated to me, as well as in the order for your release, that you had been wrongfully imprisoned. You may expect to hear from me again soon. All your Union friends responded readily with me in the effort to secure your release. We are all well.

Yours truly,   D. C. FUSEY.

OWENTON, May 30, 1862.

MY DEAR HUSBAND: I received your kind letter; and knowing you are as anxious to hear from home as I was from you, I hasten to answer it. I should have written before, only I expected you home every day, being assured by the Union men of Owenton that you would be released, and not dreaming that you had gone farther from me. When, O when! will I see you? It appears like two months, instead of two weeks, had gone. I was so glad to hear you were well. The children are all well. Minnie says tell her papa she wants him to come home. Frank was asleep when you left, and slept until next morning. When he awoke and found you had gone, the tears rolled down his cheeks, which made me feel more than ever I had lost my best friend on earth—but only for a little while, I hope. It will surely be the happiest day of my life when we meet again. God grant it may not be long! You were uneasy when you left for fear the children would catch the sore throat from Mrs. Foster, but they have had no sign of it as yet. Mollie Foster died the same evening you left, and they carried her to Grenup on Sunday, and none of the family have as yet returned, owing to several of the other children having taken the same disease. Minnie and Willie have been to school every day. Minnie is delighted. I had to make her go the first day, but she is up and ready long before Willie. Mr. Snale has been here and looked over your executions, and says he will see them returned and all fixed up right. I have not seen Mr. Murdoff but once—a few minutes. Your notes and papers of all kinds I will take good care of. Daisy was here yesterday, and I sent your horse to father's by her. Father has been here once and stayed all night. He wanted me to go home with him, but I thought I had better stay at home and keep the children in school every day and attend to my garden, which looks very well. My cabbage plants that I set out before the first rain are looking very well, and I will have peas in a few days. If you were only here, everything would look bright and beautiful. Everybody around me has been as kind and good to me since you left as they could be. Baby is here now, laughing and trying his best to talk. Ben, you must send a name for him, and write me what to do and how to manage to get along, for I don't know where to begin. I will do the best I can for the children, and still hope it will not be long before I see you. If you need money or anything else, let me know, and I will find a way to get it to you. It is not necessary for me to write anything of your friends' families, as I believe they are all writing by this mail. Your friends all send their kind regards to you. Ben, I wish I could find a way to get you out of that dangerous place. Your friends say they have done everything they could for you, for which I thank them from my heart, but if they could only have brought you back with them! Ben, take good care of yourself and don't forget your   MATTIE.

May 30, 1862.

MY DEAR FATHER: I have just returned from Owenton, and left ma and all the family as well as you could expect under the circumstances. Ma suffers more in mind about you than if you were already dead, as she would know that you were beyond suffering; but now she doesn't know how much you will suffer, and she can't do anything for you. This is the time to try men's souls. We have found many friends good and kind in places where we least expected them. There is not a man in ———— who will not do all in his power to have you all released. Some of the Union men will go to Washington if they cannot accomplish it without it. You must try to be cheerful and hopeful; and don't give up, for it operates against your health.

The women dread your getting sick. Tell your fellow-prisoners their families are hoping for the best. Trust in God, and he will never forsake you.

Willie will stay with ma, which necessity, I hope, will not be long. Ma will write you soon, but she feels that she cannot do so for a few days, and that is why I have written first, feeling that that is my privilege, as I am your eldest, your firstborn.

Your loving   JANE.

[Address not given.]

LIMESTONE COUNTY, ALA., June 10, 1862.

MY DEAR HUSBAND: I take the present opportunity of writing you a few lines to let you know that we are all well and doing very well, and I hope that when this reaches you you will be enjoying the same blessing.

Dear Jim, I am anxious to hear from you. I heard that you were wounded and taken prisoner at Corinth, Miss. Please write to me and let me know whether I can come and see you, for I do want to do so. When you write let me know whether you know anything about my brother Andrew and Hart Manley or not.

Direct your letter to Athens, Limestone County, Ala. Pa's family are all well. I bring my letter to a close by sending my love to you and saying, Write soon to your wife. The little children grow very fast and want to see you.

Martha L. Chapman to James H. Chapman, Breckinridge's Brigade, Colonel Hale's Regiment, Captain Gard's Company.

If any person who reads this letter knows of Mr. Chapman, I will be thankful for information.

The cemetery records show that J. L. Chapman (not J. H.) died in August, 1865, and was buried in Grave 1332.

A portion of a long letter written by Mrs. Elizabeth A. Harris is given because of its homelike gossip and news. The letter was without envelope or address and no town is mentioned that gives a clue to where it was from. The mention of Louisville indicates that it is not far from there. The hemp mentioned suggests the vicinity of Lexington, Ky. The husband was not at Camp Chase at the time, or the message would doubtless have found him.

Sunday Morning, June 29, 1862.

My Dear Husband: We received yours of the 20th and were glad to hear from you, and so gratified to learn that you had been in good health and that you had received the box we sent. The old Bourbon was sent by your old friend, William Guiton, and the wine by B. Patterson, except one bottle, which was Susan's nice grape wine. We did not know it was contrary to the rules of your prison, or we would not have sent it. I thought you would need it if you got sick. No one put anything in the box but Jennie and myself to eat, except Mr. Patterson, who put in a few things. Mrs. Cardwell sent Jimmie a box the first of last month, which he has probably received before this.

Your friends think there is a prospect for you to get out and come home. If not, we will send you another box. Mr. Cook has just returned from Louisville, and says he had a long talk with J. Bogle, who felt certain you would be released very soon.

Fred told me to say that the crops are looking very well. His hemp is first-rate and the corn growing finely. He has plowed the big field three times. A part of the corn at Theodore Davis's is waist-high. The corn in the big field on the far side of the branch does not look so well. He has been cutting the small grain for three or four days, and has most of Davis's wheat cut. He cuts it with a cradle; he could not get a machine.

Sunday Night.—I did not finish my letter this morning. I have had company all day. Mr. Levi Walters came out to see me to-day. Mr. Cook, Mr. Sam Miller, Mrs. Grant, and Nannie Cook came up this evening and stayed until after supper. George Tomkins and wife and Mrs. A. Warden were here awhile to-day; also Mrs. Taylor. Saw Jimmie yesterday. He thought he would get home certain this week. If you do not, I shall be sadly disappointed. Do not hesitate a moment in taking the oath, or do anything they request that would not be dishonorable. You do not know how bad I want you here. The anxiety and uneasiness about you have nearly worn me out. We have a fine crop of rasp-berries and have a great many vegetables of every kind. The children wish every day that papa was here to eat raspberries. I do hope you will be home this week.

Your affectionate wife,   Elizabeth Harris.

On April 21, 1862, Lieutenant Menefee wrote to Mrs. John F. Allen (address not given) that her husband, Lieutenant Allen, had been ill with typhoid fever, but was recovering. "Your next letter will be from him," the Lieutenant wrote, "as he is now getting along nicely."

The letter was a brief one; and had it gone upon its way, it would have cheered a lonely, aching heart in far-off Alabama. The cheering letter was written on the 21st of April, and the record shows that he was buried on May 24.

The foregoing letters were loaned by Mr. Galbraith, that copies might be made, in the latter part of July, 1904. From that time until October diligent effort was made to locate the Mrs. Clark mentioned.

Through the kind assistance of Mrs. M. V. Randolph, of Richmond, Va., Miss Virginia Moon, a sister of Mrs. Clark, of Memphis, was found, who related so much of the history of her sister in those days as she recalled, and gave the address of Rev. Frank Pinckney Clark, of Front Royal, Va., son of Mrs. Charlotte Moon Clark; and this letter given below tells as nearly as ever will be known, perhaps, the story of the letters never delivered:

I was only a child of eight years when the Civil War began, so my recollections are vague, as are often the remembrances of boyhood. But I was afterwards told of many of the events of those days and the effect they had upon our after life.

At that time my father, Judge James Clark, lived at Hamilton, Ohio, where he began the practice of his profession after his graduation from the law school at Cincinnati. He soon became prominent in the legal world and was appointed Judge of the Court of Common Pleas by the Governor of Ohio about the year 1852.

He was afterwards elected judge by the people of his judicial district at least twice, and then retired from the bench to practice law.

In politics he was a friend of Judge Thurman and Messrs. Vallandigham and Voorhees and others, and took an active part in the campaign of Stephen A. Douglas.

My mother's father, Robert S. Moon, went from Virginia to Oxford, Butler County, Ohio, back in the thirties. He was a firm believer in the teachings of Thomas Jefferson, both belonging to the same county—Albemarle—in Virginia. Among other of his political ideas was that of the ultimate emancipation of slaves *by their owners.* He took his own to Ohio and then to Indiana and freed them, going security for their future good behavior;

MRS. CHARLOTTE MOON CLARK.

and I have been told that he had to pay quite a large sum for the misconduct of some of them.

It was at Oxford my father met my mother. He was a student at Miami University, and she was attending a young ladies' school taught by Dr. Scott, whose daughter, the late Mrs. Benjamin Harrison, was one of my mother's schoolmates.

My parents were married in 1849, and the interval until 1860 was passed quietly in Hamilton. My mother's three brothers were in the Confederate Army, two of them being Virginians by birth.

After the fall of Fort Donelson my mother heard that one of her brothers was at Camp Chase. She at once went to Columbus, and Governor Tod gave her permission to go through the Camp to find her brother, although there was no record of his being there. He was not there; but she found many friends and acquaintances who were in the prison camp. At once my mother began a crusade to make these prisoners as comfortable as possible; even succeeded in getting Governor Tod to parole some of them in the city of Columbus, where they were able to secure comfortable quarters. In this connection, I have been told of a reception given the paroled prisoners at Judge Thurman's house, and that when the Judge got home he found his house full of men in Confederate uniforms, with only one bluecoated gentleman present, an officer named Hunter, who had been exceedingly kind to the prisoners and was very popular with them.

My mother undertook to inform the relatives of some of the prisoners of their health, condition, needs, etc., and both wrote herself and carried some of their letters to friends in Kentucky. This brought about a sudden catastrophe for two clergymen who were at our house when my mother returned from one of these trips to Kentucky, where she had given letters to one of General Morgan's brothers, and where she came near being caught and arrested by one Colonel Metcalf. These ministers wrote home to their wives how Mrs. Clark had evaded every attempt to stop her and made her way into the forbidden neighborhood of the Morgans. Unfortunately, these ministers were arrested in Cincinnati and searched.

The same night a telegram from Mr. John Bond, of Cincinnati, warned my mother, and she left on the midnight Northern express for Niagara, taking me with her. We crossed the suspension bridge only a short time before a telegram to arrest my mother arrived on the New York side.

This will probably account for the package of letters being delayed so many years in Columbus. If they were written while my mother was getting ready for that Kentucky trip, and kept for her return to Columbus, she never heard anything of them,

for soon afterwards she returned to Ohio to make some final arrangements to go South. She was threatened with arrest by
General Rosecrans; but General Burnside, then in Cincinnati,
arrested my mother, aunt, and grandmother, and after detaining
them a short time, sent them South. I understand that General
Burnside, who was an old friend, took them thus under his protection to save them from prison.

My mother remained in the South until after the war was over,
when my father settled in New York to practice law and my
mother began a literary career, which brought increased luster
upon her name both in this country and abroad. In the autumn
of 1895 she left this life for the greater, at my home, the rectory
of St. George's Protestant Episcopal Church, West Philadelphia, Pa.

In "The Modern Hagar" my mother gave a graphic account
of the 1856 convention held in Cincinnati, which Mr. Charles
Anderson, brother of Gen. Robert Anderson, esteemed one of
the best pieces of writing with which he was acquainted. My
mother's full name was Mrs. Charlotte Moon Clark, and her
nom de plume was Charles M. Clay, she being a descendant of
the Clays on her mother's side, and of the Moons and one of
the first colonial governors' of Virginia, Thomas Digges, on her
father's side.

Besides corresponding for Southern and Philadelphia journals
when abroad in the seventies, she did much journalistic work at
home, after her return to New York, and wrote the following
novels: "Baby Rue," published by Roberts Brothers, Boston,
"The Modern Hagar," published by the same house, and "How
She Came into Her Kingdom," published by Jansen, McClurg
& Company, Chicago. By such critics as George Cary Eggleston
"The Modern Hagar" was esteemed as a great book.

Very respectfully yours,   FRANK PINCKNEY CLARK.

Front Royal, Va.

Mr. Clark's letter has been used, believing the story of his
mother's work for the South more interesting, as related by himself, than any story that might be written with the letter as
foundation.

The letters and the story of how they were so long hidden
from sight we have given so far as it can be learned.

The following is a list of letters not previously mentioned:

8. April 21, from John S. Stewart, Camp Chase, to wife, Sarah Stewart.
   No address.

25. April 20, from James A. Cox, 14th Miss., to Mrs. Addie Cox, Siloam,
   Miss.

43. April 21, from Lieut. Keyes, 20th Miss. Vols., to Hon. O. R. Singleton, House of Representatives, Richmond, Va.

88. April 21, from Lieut. John R. Farrabee, Camp Chase, to Joseph
Maples, Memphis, Tenn.

89. April 20, from Lieut. W. Osbourne, to Mr. M. Osbourne, Little Rock,
Ark.

117. April 14, from Aunt C. C. H. to her nephew. No envelope or address.

118. April 20, from W. A. H. Shackelford, Camp Chase, to F. Shackelford.
No address.

119. April 20, from R. M. Walker, to Mrs. S. S. Walker, Palestine,
Ark.

120. April 30, from H. M. Hallan, Camp Chase, to Jerry Hallan, Banks-
ton, Miss.

121. April 30, from Henry H. Hart, Colesborough, to William Harned
or Adkin Harned, Camp Chase.

123. March 24, from Nathan D. Cross, Nashville, to Connolly T. Figg.
No address.

124. April 20, from Charlotte Norman, Hopewell, Ohio, to A. Norman,
supposed to be in Camp Chase.

125. April 20, from C. C. Knowls, Camp Chase, to William Nunn, Auburn,
Ala.

126. April 21, from A. S. Levy, Camp Chase, to Miss Ella Levy, 196 Main
Street, Memphis.

127. April 20, from Lieut. J. H. Sanford, Camp Chase, to Asa Sanford,
Dadeville, Va.

128. April 20, from Lieut. Theodore Smith, Camp Chase, to Miss Theodore Smith, Frenchville, Va.

129. April 19, from J. S. Carruthers, Camp Chase, to T. W. Carruthers,
Mason's Depot, Tenn.

130. April 30, from M. S. Neely, Camp Chase, to Mrs. Julia Neely, Den-
mark, West Tenn.

132. April 19, from Clabourne Watkins, Camp Chase, to George W.
Watkins, Little Rock, Ark.

133. April 21, from T. H. Shackelford, Camp Chase, to Miss Virginia
Shackelford, Okolona, Miss.

134. April 21, from W. T. Rogers, Camp Chase, to Mrs. L. W. Malone.
No address.

135. April 29, from T. T. Cagar, Danville, Ky., to "Dear Doctor," Camp
Chase.

137. April 21, from G. D. Cross, Mount Gilead, Ohio, to A. H. Cross,
Camp Chase.

139. April 20, from James H. Wilkins and Bettie Wilkins, of Bowling
Green, to David Rhea, Camp Chase.

140. June 8, from Thomas York, Tennessee, to A. York, Camp Chase.

141. March 1, from W. H. Hanlon, Loachapoka, Ala., to his father (no
name), supposed to be in Camp Chase.

142. April 17, from F. M. Smith, Cincinnati, Ohio, to his brother, Camp
Chase.

143. April 20, from A. D. Black, Camp Chase, to Mrs. C. M. Black, Dorcheat, Ark.
145. April 19, from R. M. Clark, to James Clark, Moulton, Ala.
146. April 22, from J. C. Durham, Camp Chase, to Iscia Durham, Milltown, Ala.
147. April 20, from John Hudson, Camp Chase, to Noah Hudson, Westville, Ala.
148. April 21, from James F. Cook, Camp Chase, to Capt. Ridley, Corinth, Miss.
149. April 20, from Lieut. Furney Clark to Mr. Austin Clark, Han Ridge, Coffee County, Ala.
150. April 21, from Sam P. Jukes to Mrs. Susan Hagood, Van Buren, Ark.
151. April 21, from W. M. Smith, Camp Chase, to Kate. No address.
152. May 20, from E. A. Britz, Utica, to his brother, Camp Chase.
153. April 20, from G. A. Owings, Camp Chase, to J. R. Owings, Pond Springs, Ga.
154. April 9, from B. H. Bridgefortt, Camp Chase, to his brother. No address.
155. April 20, from George Cox, Camp Chase, to his father. No address.
156. April 20, from R. J. Moore, Camp Chase, to S. R. Moore, Bay Springs, Miss.
157. April 20, from P. J. Yates, Camp Chase, to his sister. No address.
158. June 13, from Sam D. Crockett, Bridgeport, to J. R. Middleton, Camp Chase.
159. April 20, from J. Woodhall, Camp Chase, to I. H. Woodhall and wife, father and mother, Chattanooga, Tenn.
160. June 29, from J. W. Cardwell, Harrodsburg, Ky., to Nim, Camp Chase.
161. July 1, from J. T. Harris, Harrodsburg, Ky., to his father, Camp Chase.
162. May 8, from G. W. Hart, Johnson's Island, to Lieut. G. P. Chilcutt, Camp Chase.
162. May 8, from P. A. Morgan, Johnson's Island, to G. P. Chilcutt, Camp Chase.
163. July 8, from E. Paschal, Johnson's Island, to Lieut. G. P. Chilcutt, Camp Chase.
163. April, from A. G. Hammach, Camp Chase, to his brother. No address.
164. April 19, from W. S. Pardue, Camp Chase, to L. J. Pardue. No address.
165. June 10, from Owen Breckennah, Payne's Depot, Ky., to Dear Billy, Camp Chase.
166. April 21, from M. S. Miller, Camp Chase, to Mrs. Nana Miller. No address.
167. April 19, from J. S. Thomas, Camp Chase, to his father. No address.
168. April 20, from Lieut. W. P. P. Wrem, Camp Chase, to his father. No address.

169. April 20, from Harden Long, Camp Chase, to C. M. Long, Bridgeport, Ala.

170. April 21, from R. H. Woolen, Camp Chase, to C. H. Adkins, Polersville, Tenn.

171. April 20, from A. Moffin, Camp Chase, to Miss M. J. Maffin, Covington, West Tenn.

—. April 20, from M. G. Gallaway, Camp Chase, to his brother. No address.

173. April 19, from J. B. Hall, Camp Chase, to Allison G. Hall. No address.

174. April 19, from J. M. Reese, Camp Chase, to his mother. No address.

175. August 24, from M. L. Stockton, Camp Butler, to G. W. Stockton, Camp Chase.

176. April 21, from Capt. Thomas M. Atkins, Camp Chase, to Hon. C. A. Henny, Confederate States Senator, Richmond, Va.

177. May 31, from J. F. Gray, Fort Warren, Boston, to Valentine Wise, Camp Chase.

178. April 20, from G. T. Willis, Camp Chase, to Miss G. A. Willis, Chattanooga, Tenn.

179. April 21, from W. D. Leay, Camp Chase, to William P. Leay, Richmond, Va.

180. April 20, from J. K. Whitfield, Camp Chase, to Mrs. J. K. Whitfield, Camden, Ark.

181. April 19, from Capt. W. D. Twitley, Camp Chase, to his wife, Athens, Ala.

182. April 20, from R. A. Silvidge, Camp Chase, to his wife, Falcon, Ark.

183. April 21, from C. C. Knowles, Camp Chase, to his wife, Loachapoka, Ala.

184. April 21, from Lieut. J. T. Durham, Camp Chase, to Mrs. Anna J. Durham, West Point, Ga.

185. April 21, from Lieut. F. T. Scott, Camp Chase, to his mother, Mrs. E. T. Scott, Gainesville, Ala.

186. April 21, from L. H. Kemp, Camp Chase, to A. H. Kinchelor and others of Co. D, 5th Ky. Regt., C. S. A., First Kentucky Brigade.

187. April 20, from Lieut. C. Tuttle, Camp Chase, to F. B. Officer, Esq., Mobile, Ala.

188. April 20, from John Lilly, Camp Chase, to Mr. John Woodman, Red Sulphur Springs, Va.

189. April 21, from Capt. W. B. Locke, Camp Chase, to Mr. Jessie Locke, Perote, Pike County, Ala.

190. April 20, from D. A. McKenzie, Camp Chase, to Mr. William Johnson, Morton, Miss.

191. April 20, from Lieut. L. J. Laird, Camp Chase, to his uncle, E. M. Kulds, Eufaula, Ala.

192. April 21, from F. A. Ragsdale, Camp Chase, to W. J. Brooks or J. W. Markham, No. 10 Shelby, Memphis, Tenn.

193. April 20, from J. H. Christian, to Mr. J. T. Christian, Tanngville, Tallapoosa County, Ala.

194. April 22, from William Lauirs, 12th Ga. Regt., Camp Chase, to Mrs. Mary Lauirs, Buena Vista, Ga.

195. April 21, from Samuel M. Moses, Camp Chase, to Charles Moses, Black Creek, Augusta County, Va.

196. April 20, from W. S. Smith, Camp Chase, to his mother, Mrs. Ann Pows, Black Creek, Choctaw County, Ala.

—. April 21, from John Custer, Camp Chase, to Mrs. M. A. Custer, Marion County, Ala.

198. April 22, from Z. M. Hall, Camp Chase, to his sister, Mrs. S. S. Griffin, Butler, Ala.

199. April 20, from Lieut. W. R. Felton, 1st Ala. Regt., Camp Chase, to his sister, Mrs. J. L. Strend, Richmond, Va.

200. April 20, from H. Y. Shine to his father, J. F. Shine, Goodman, Miss.

201. April 20, from R. H. Woolen to Joseph N. Moss, McNutt, Miss.

202. April 21, from Lieut. Jeff Thompson to Mrs. Jeff J. Thompson, Greensburg, La.

203. April 21, from Thomas F. Kneeland, Camp Chase, to Ben May, Esq., Bank of West Tennessee, Grenada, Miss.

204. April 21, from J. T. Whitfield, Camp Chase, to Lieut. M. C. Pratt, Prattsville, Ala.

205. April 20, from J. T. Williams, Camp Chase, to W. C. Williams, Memphis, Tenn.

206. April 21, from C. C. Moore, Camp Chase, to Mrs. Louise Moore. Houston, Miss.

—. April 21, from Thomas Filly, Camp Chase, to Private Jasper Anderson, Co. B, 5th Ky. Vols., Breckinridge Brigade.

208. April 21, from T. T. Foster, Camp Chase, to T. Boyd Foster, Stevenson, Ala.

209. April 21, from J. M. Jackson, Camp Chase, 42d Tenn., to Dr. W. B. Garrison, Guntersville, Ala.

210. April 20, from J. C. Hubbord, 40th Regt. Prov., to W. R. Marshall, DeWitte, Ark.

211. April 21, from F. M. Whittaker, Camp Chase, to Jessie Whittaker, Monticello, Ark.

212. April 20, from W. R. Seludge, Camp Chase, to T. T. Carlock, Fallon, Ark.

213. April 19, from Camp D. W. Ramsey, 1st Ala., Camp Chase, to Rev. A. C. Ramsey, Allenton, Ala.

214. April 19, from T. J. McGehan to Hon. Thomas H. Foster, Richmond, Va.

215. April 21, from Theodore Kelsey or Thomas F. Knulland to Ben May, Memphis, Tenn.

216. April 21, from Lieut. E. A. Poe, 11th Ark., Camp Chase, to Mrs. Martha J. Poe, Belfast, Ark.

217. April 20, from J. Stoughton Carruthers, Adjt. 51st Tenn. Vols., to Mrs. B. Fannie Carruthers, Mason Depot, West Tenn.

218. April 19, from Lieut. Henderson, 1st Ala. Regt., Camp Chase, to John Henderson, Talledega, Va.

219. April 20, from R. Gailland, Camp Chase, to Hon. Thomas H. Watts, Richmond, Va.
220. April 21, from Charles B. Carters, Camp Chase, to Mrs. Eliza Carters, Waynesboro, Va.
221. April 21, from Charles B. Carruthers, Lieut. Heavy Artillery, Camp Chase, to Rev. John R. Harrison, Jackson, Tenn.
222. April 21, from Lieut. Felton, Camp Chase, to Noah Felton, Loachapoka, Ala.
223. April 20, from Capt. J. P. Jackson to G. W. Jackson, Erin, Ga.
224. April 20, from J. F. Whitfield, Camp Chase, to his wife, Mrs. J. F. Whitfield, Montgomery, Ala.
225. April 21, from Lieut. C. C. Knowles to W. W. Drake, Auburn, Ala.
226. April 19, from S. L. Knox, Camp Chase, to his father, Dr. J. C. Knox, Talladega, Ala.
227. April 20, from Mrs. W. D. Riblett, Millfall, Va., to Michael Riblett, Camp Chase.
228. April 21, from Lieut. J. Z. Wall, Camp Chase, to Mrs. Pauline R. Sittoon, Ponchatoula, La.
229. April 20, from Charles B. Carter, Camp Chase, to James Carter, Meheny River, Va.
230. April 20, from J. M. Jackson, Camp Chase, to Dr. John Ball, Richmond, Va.

CHAPTER XIV.

JOHNSON'S ISLAND.

A Prison Comfortable in Summer, but Cold in Winter—The First Prisoners to Arrive at Sandusky—The Town Turns Out to See Them—A Sad-Faced Lad—Making a Rope of the Flag—The Chaplain's Consoling Words—Letters from Johnson's Island—The Number of Prisoners upon the Island Each Month in 1862, 1863, 1864.

THERE certainly could not have been a more pleasant spot chosen for a military prison than Johnson's Island, at least in the summer. Put-in-Bay and Cedar Point are now popular summer resorts, both within a few miles of Johnson's Island. The island was evidently fixed upon for prison purposes because of its safety for a large number of energetic and intelligent men who had an abundance of time to devise ways and means of escape. Men could tunnel out of the prison in the summer, but there was the lake, and the shore was three miles away. Prisoners sometimes undertook to escape in winter; but if accomplished, it was ever a desperate undertaking.

An account from the *Confederate Veteran* of July, 1900, is so liberal and fair that it is here reproduced with no little satisfaction. The article in the *Veteran* is vouched for by Lieutenant Cunningham, of Louisiana, who was at Johnson's Island sixteen months. Lieutenant Cunningham says:

I am satisfied that, as compared with the enlisted men at Point Lookout, Elmira, Rock Island, Camps Morton, Chase, and Douglas, the officers merely tasted purgatory; the men went beyond that.

The *Veteran* says:

Johnson's Island is situated at the mouth of Sandusky Bay, overlooking Lake Erie, and is about a mile long and a mile and a half wide. It was an ideal spot for a prison post. The grounds were inclosed with a fence twelve feet high, with a platform top, upon which sentinels moved night and day. To the north Lake Erie stretches away for fifty miles; on the east, across three miles of water, lies Sandusky; while west and south of the island are broad stretches of Sandusky Bay.

JOHNSON'S ISLAND (NEAR SANDUSKY, OHIO) IN WAR TIMES.

The island was used almost exclusively as a prison for officers, the total number confined there from first to last aggregating over fifteen thousand. The first prisoners were taken there in April, 1862, and in September, 1865, the last of them were sent to Fort Lafayette, when Johnson's Island was abandoned as a prison post.

The men confined on Johnson's Island represented the chivalry of the South. They were largely professional men and planters, among them being many who were prominent in science, literature, and art.

These men were treated during the period of their imprisonment as befitted men in their station of life, so far as circumstances would permit, of course. They were lodged in comfortable houses, provided with suitable clothing, and their tables were furnished with an abundance of the substantials and many of the luxuries. They were subjected to no petty tyranny; but, on the contrary, were granted privileges enjoyed by prisoners at no other military prison in the North, an exception being made in their case, because, as a class, they were considered superior to ordinary prisoners, and were put upon their honor in many instances when it would have been hazardous to have trusted men with less scrupulous regard for their words.

While this was true as to 1862, and perhaps 1863, in 1864 the cords were drawn and unnecessary cruelties were practiced. It is doubtless true that Johnson's Island was one of the best. Had prisoners, North or South, been guarded by veterans who had fought, the stories of cruelty would have been different. As a regiment, the Eighty-Eighth Ohio, at Camp Chase, was never outside the boundary of the State. Many of these men—not all, perhaps—enlisted to stay at home and do guard duty. The veterans from the front, returning home for reenlistment, disliked this regiment much more than they did any regiment of "Johnnies." The treatment of prisoners, as a general thing, in 1864 and 1865 was a great, dark blot, an imperishable stain, upon American civilization.

While Johnson's Island is within three miles of Sandusky, the county seat of Erie County, the island belongs to Ottawa County. In Ohio's war history the story of Johnson's Island is the story of Sandusky. The establishing of a prison on Johnson's Island was brought about through the energy and exertions of a few of the leading business men of Sandusky. These gentlemen saw that such a station would be of great value to trade in that

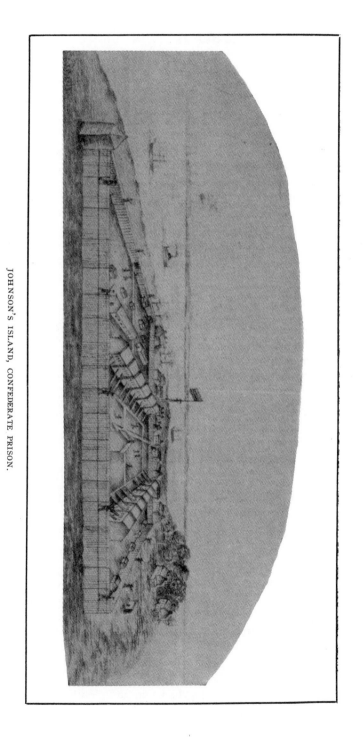

JOHNSON'S ISLAND, CONFEDERATE PRISON.

city, and that the officers' quarters would be in and about the town rather than on the Island.

The War Department sent an officer to look over various sites for a prison, and he was inclined to favor Detroit, and went to Sandusky with but little thought of locating the prison there. The business men, however, accorded him a warm reception, and made such offers of substantial aid to the government that he could not do otherwise than select the Island.

Greater interest and importance was given this prison through the exploits of John Yates Beall, who made a fruitless attempt to rescue the prisoners of the Island.

The first prisoners to arrive there were curiosities to the inhabitants. As soon as the news spread that there were two hundred Southerners coming—men who had fought and were considered dangerous mortals—and that these soldier prisoners wearing gray uniforms were to sojourn for a time on the beautiful island over in the bay, excitement ran high.

The Sandusky *Register* said:

The great agony is over, and some of our people—in fact, a good many of them—have seen Rebels. For the benefit of such as could not get out last evening, we will give a minute description of them. In the first place, they have the build of men— ordinary men. They would not have visited our city with just such an escort as they had yesterday, from choice. They were clad variously. We learn they were all officers, and some of them had the carriage and bearing of gentlemen. Some had the don't-care-a-dime swagger, some were sullen, and others jocose. One lad we saw leaning against the stay irons to the smokestack, after they were on board the Queen, looking musingly into the water with something of sadness on his face.

The war had so blinded the writer of the above that he could not see in imagination a far-away Southern home, where the flowers were blooming and the birds singing. The editor could not see the tears that would come to a mother's eyes, even though she sought to be brave, as she felt it to be her duty. Perhaps the lad, who was an officer, saw as he looked into the water a face so fair and sweet that there was not another like it in all the world. Perhaps he saw in the depths of soulful eyes the look they wore when he marched away. The editor, though not heartless, could not see the "wrinkled front of war" as it loomed up darkly between that far-away home in the South and the sad-faced boy on the boat. "Some were mischievous," the paper continued. "Captain Orr had hoisted the national flag, and one of the prisoners wadded up one corner, spat upon it, and wound it around the flagstaff. The Captain spoke to him in a friendly way, which so changed his mind that he untied the flag and did not trouble it more."

On April 28, as a train bearing a number of Confederate prisoners was nearing Sandusky, a daring man, whose name was not given, made a leap from the train and took to the woods. The train was stopped and a search made, but the guards could not find him. The sequel to this story was told June 30. The prisoner remained hidden until the 30th, when he went to Green Springs, Ohio, and entered the South-bound train. The conductor proved to be the one in charge of the train from which he escaped, and recognized him. When the train arrived at Kenton, the police were notified and the Confederate was taken to the Island.

On the 29th of August four Confederate prisoners were released on taking the oath of allegiance. They announced their intention of entering the Union army. Three of them said they were from the North and had been impressed into the Confederate service. The *Register,* commenting upon the case, remarked: "It is singular that impressed men were made officers." They were released, however, and gave their names as follows: S. B. Moore, impressed in Alabama; H. C. Wringer, Lancaster, Pa., impressed in Arkansas; W. H. Rupert, Pekin, Ill., impressed at Memphis; and J. W. Swanson, from Tennessee.

Whitelaw Reid, in his historic work, "Ohio in the War," gives the following as the number of prisoners at the post during the different months: 1862, average for April, 444; May, 1,074; June, 1,105; July, 1,149; August, 14,524; exchanged during the month of September, 1,123. Average for September, 595; aggregate October 31, 893; aggregate November 30, 295; December 31, 209.

Mr. Reid further adds in this work:

It should be remembered that a cartel for a general exchange of prisoners of war had long been expected, and was finally agreed upon July 22, 1862. Under that cartel and special arrangement exchanges went on until July, 1863, and a continuance was expected. This expectation, with the belief of general loyalty in the North and the want of help in Canada, had its legiti-

RUINS OF OLD FORT, JOHNSON'S ISLAND.

PRISON GROUNDS, JOHNSON'S ISLAND, 1904.

JOHNSON'S ISLAND, 1904.

CONFEDERATE CEMETERY, JOHNSON'S ISLAND, 1904.

mate influence on the prisoners, and undoubtedly prevented efforts at outbreak and resistance until late in the fall of 1863.

The stoppage of exchanges, followed by the assembling of considerable forces from the Confederate army and navy in Canada, and the machinations of disloyal organizations in Ohio, Indiana, and elsewhere, known to intend a rescue of these prisoners, with attendant devastations on the lake towns and commerce, showed these posts (Johnson's Island and Sandusky) to be unsafe without considerable reënforcements. Six companies of the Twelfth Ohio Cavalry, with the Twenty-Fourth Battery (six guns) and two detachments of the First Ohio Heavy Artillery (with seven heavy guns), were sent to the Island early in November, 1863, followed promptly by the Forty-Ninth and Fiftieth Regiments of the National Guard and a Pennsylvania battery. These National Guard commands remained only a short time; the other troops remained all winter.

The First Brigade, Third Division, Sixth Army Corps, including five regiments, attended by two brigadier generals from the Army of the Potomac, reached Sandusky on January 13, 1864. Four of these regiments, with General Shaler in command, were stationed on the Island. The other regiment, with Gen. H. D. Terry commanding the whole, was at Sandusky. They all remained until April 14, 1864, when three regiments, under General Shaler, returned to the Army of the Potomac, Sixth Corps.

It is learned officially that there were on January 31, 1863, 2,603 prisoners on the Island; February, 2,206; March, 2,192; April, 2,088; May, 2,134; June, 2,309; July, 2,441; August, 2,556; September, 2,663; October, 2,621; November, 2,747; December, 3,209; while the numbers at the end of each month for the year 1864 were: January, 2,603; February, 2,206; March, 2,192; April, 2,088; May, 2,134; June, 2,309; July, 2,441; August, 2,556; September, 2,662; October, 2,621; November, 2,747; December, 3,209.

Except about one hundred, they were officers of the Confederate army and navy, of all grades from second lieutenant to major general.

The following letters from Johnson's Island were found among the Camp Chase letters at the Ohio Statehouse:

SANDUSKY, OHIO, April 25, 1862.

MY DEAR MAMMA: An opportunity for sending letters through to Richmond has at last presented itself; consequently, I write to inform you that I am in good health. I arrived here yesterday evening, having been quartered at Camp Chase, near Columbus, up to this time, and regretted very much to leave there. We were kindly treated and well provided for in every necessary way by the authorities, headed by Governor Tod. Only myself and Lieutenant Anderson came from our mess yesterday, but I learn all the prisoners now here are to come in a few days. The object in removing us is our health during the summer and fall; but I believe I would rather have risked that for the consideration of other advantages, etc.

I am now in a mess with Alex Trotter and three strangers. Say to Willie that Trotter is in fine health.

I never suffered more in my life than for six weeks after our surrender, principally from cold. I am now suffering in mind for want of news from home. You can have an idea of the solicitude which I feel for my friends, and also my country's interest. You must all write me long letters, addressed to this place.

I shall hope to hear from you all by Mrs. Clark, if she remains in Richmond long enough to get your letters; and if not, it is possible to get them through by flag of truce via Norfolk.

My best love to all my friends, particularly the feminine portion of them. It seems I would give the world for an hour of liberty at home now, yet I entertain bright hopes for the future, more so than I have ever done. My love to all the family.

Your son,   WALTER A. ASHBY.

P. S.—I have not touched on matters relating to the war—our struggle at Fort Donelson—fearing that it would not be allowed, and in consequence of which my letter might be stopped. Tell Mrs. Everett that John M. E., John Garborough, William McQueen, and George Estis were all well last week.   WALTER.

SANDUSKY, OHIO, April 25, 1862.

DEAR UNCLE: There being such a slight probability of this ever reaching you, I shall make this a mere note. I am well and as comfortably situated as could be expected. Give yourself no uneasiness, and be assured I will be provided for—if not comfortably, at least well. Mr. Cornell is with me. McGowan is at Camp Chase. I just received a letter from Eggleston, who says the deaths from our county in the Fourteenth at Chicago are W. J. Woodward and T. B. Evans, Shubuta County; Ed Wellington and W. G. Strangham, Enterprise County; John T. Hardie.

You can let their friends know of their fate.

With love to all, your devoted nephew,   ALEX TROTTER.

To Gen. W. B. Trotter, Quitman, Miss.

These were the only letters from Sandusky, Ohio, in the box of letters found in the Statehouse.

CHAPTER XV.

STORIES OF THE PRISON IN SANDUSKY BAY.

Prison Rules at Johnson's Island—The Grapevine Telegraph—The Opinion of Whitelaw Reid—The Execution of Corbin and McGraw—A Pathetic Letter—A Deserter Shot—Campbell, the Spy—Wanted Back in Prison—Adventure of Capt. Gubbins—How Lieut. Bowles was Killed—A Brave Kentuckian Calmly Meets His Fate.

THE government report shows a total of 7,357 prisoners at one time or another at Johnson's Island, and there are 260 graves. The record shows that only two were killed for disobeying rules.

REGULATIONS OF THE UNITED STATES MILITARY PRISON AT JOHNSON'S ISLAND.

HEADQUARTERS HOFFMAN'S BATTALION, DEPARTMENT OF PRISONERS OF WAR, NEAR SANDUSKY, OHIO, March 1, 1862.

ORDER No. 1.—It is designed to treat prisoners of war with all the kindness compatible with their condition, and as few orders as possible will be issued respecting them, and their own comfort will be chiefly secured by prompt and implicit obedience.

ORDER No. 2.—The quarters have been erected at great expense by the government for the comfort of prisoners of war; so the utmost caution should be used against fire, as in case of their destruction the prisoners will be subjected to much exposure and suffering for want of comfortable quarters, as others will not be erected and rude shelters only provided.

ORDER No. 3.—All prisoners are required to parade in their rooms and answer to their names half an hour after reveille, and at retreat.

ORDER No. 4.—Meals will be taken at breakfast drum, dinner drum, and half an hour before retreat.

ORDER No. 5.—Quarters must be thoroughly policed by 10 o'clock in the morning.

ORDER No. 6.—All prisoners will be required to remain in their own quarters after retreat, except when they have occasion to visit the sinks; lights will be extinguished at taps, and no fires will be allowed after that time.

ORDER No. 7.—Quarrels and disorders of every kind are strictly prohibited.

ORDER No. 8.—Prisoners occupying officers' quarters in Blocks 1, 2, 3, and 4 will not be permitted to visit the soldiers' quarters in Blocks 5, 6, 7, and 8, nor go upon the grounds in their vicinity, nor beyond the line of stakes between the officers and soldiers' quarters, nor will the soldiers be allowed to go upon the ground in the vicinity of the officers' quarters, or beyond the line of stakes between the officers' and soldiers' quarters.

ORDER No. 9.—No prisoners will be allowed to loiter between the buildings or by the north and west fences, and they will be permitted north of the buildings only when passing to and from the sinks; nor will they approach the fences anywhere else nearer than thirty feet, as the line is marked out by the stakes.

ORDER No. 10.—Guards and sentinels will be required to fire upon all who violate the above orders. Prisoners will, therefore, bear them carefully in mind, and be governed by them. To forget under such circumstances is inexcusable, and may prove fatal.

By order of William S. Pierson.

B. W. WELLS, *Lieutenant and Post Adjutant.*

In speaking of that great news agency in all prisons, "the grapevine telegraph line," Colonel Barbiere says in his "Scraps from Prison Mess:"

The grapevine of Johnson's Island is one of the most remarkable things on the island. It is under the control of men whose reputation for creating expedients are of camp-wide notoriety. They build up the most wonderful stories of speedy exchange, of paroles, of great victories by the Confederate armies, utter annihilation of Federal hosts, and the taking of thousands of prisoners. It has an agent in each mess, whose arrival with the latest news is received with strained eyeballs and palpitating hearts, every word of which is eagerly swallowed, because the wish is father to the thought; and hope is the strongest element in our nature, lasting beyond the grave.

I think the grapevine line was a powerful agent in assisting to develop the slumbering element that burst upon the country with the inauguration of war. Legislatures were influenced by its action. The grapevine line did much in bringing this bloody and fraternal strife upon the country. There are true men who know this to be a fact.

The sutler, Joe, is the Sandusky agent of this line, and is quite a character in his way.

Captain Riley is the chief, but Joe is the "Friday" of the establishment. Joe winks at you and says, "It is all right," smuggles in a drop of the "crather," and charges you double price.

Joe is a clever fellow and, for a sutler, is as honest as a sutler can well be. He has been kind and obliging to us, and has our hearts' remembrance.

Speaking of affairs at Johnson's Island in 1864, the Hon. Whitelaw Reid, in his "Ohio in the War," says:

Here were officers enough for an army and navy of eighty thousand men. They were within a short distance of the Canada main, and still nearer to a Canada island. The prevailing sympathy in Canada was largely in favor of the Rebels, and their every facility and encouragement, short of direct participation in our war, was extended to the large Rebel force from its army and navy maintained in Canada to effect a rescue of these officers.

If by such efforts war could be brought on between the United States and England, a great point would be gained by the South. No other depot of prisoners was on the frontier or exposed like this. During the season of navigation it could be reached from Canada in a few hours' night run, and during the winter season men and teams could conveniently cross the lake from island to island, not over five miles of ice intervening in any place.

During the season of ice the location of the depot of prisoners practically ceased to be an island. The capture of that depot, or the rescue of the prisoners confined there, would not only be of immense advantage to the Rebel cause and give them great eclat, but would be a deep humiliation to our government and people, and would almost certainly be attended by attacks upon our lake commerce and devastation of our lake towns.

The officers confined on the Island had a large range of friends and acquaintances in the loyal States. For them the Rebel emissaries traveling in those States, and in the secret orders known as "Knights of the Golden Circle" and "Sons of Liberty," had an especial sympathy, and were anxious to aid them by means of rescue, or with places of refuge or concealment. They had the means of knowing each other.

These facts, with the difficulty about exchanges, stimulated machinations for rescue, front and rear, and kept the prisoners constantly on the *qui vive* for any desperate adventure until after the fall of Petersburg.

During the month of May, 1863, a number of sympathizers with the Southern cause were brought to Johnson's Island to serve sentences at hard labor. One of these was named Thomas Sullivan, who had attempted to enlist a company of men for the war. He was ostensibly recruiting for the Union army, but subsequent events showed that he hoped to get his men South. He was court-martialed in Cincinnati and sent to Sandusky in irons, but no further mention is made concerning him in the newspapers of that day.

On May 4 of the same year six prisoners reached Sandusky and were immediately hurried over to the Island. One of them was sentenced to hang May 8, and the two others to be shot May 15. The two sentenced to be shot on the 15th were William F. Corbin and F. C. McGraw, and were charged with being Confederate spies. The Commander at Johnson's Island was ordered to see that the sentence be duly executed upon that date.

EXECUTION OF CORBIN AND McGRAW ON JOHNSON'S ISLAND— PRELIMINARY ARRANGEMENTS—GOING TO THE PLACE OF EXECUTION—IMPRESSIVE SCENE PRECEDING THE LAST ACT—ADMIRABLE PERFORMANCE OF THE PAINFUL DRAMA BY THE MILITARY!

The foregoing were the most prominent headlines in the Sandusky *Register* of Saturday morning, May 16, 1863. Nearly two columns were devoted to the narration of the sad scene, a portion of which is used:

Yesterday afternoon the sentence passed upon William Corbin and F. G. McGraw, convicted by court-martial assembled at Cincinnati on a charge of recruiting for the Confederate army within the lines of the United States forces, and of carrying mails and information to the Confederates, was executed on Johnson's Island depot of prisoners of war, near Sandusky. The execution was strictly military, none being allowed on the Island except the soldiers, officers of the government, and reporters for the press. In the morning the Island was picketed by Lieutenant Wells, and the prisoners in the yard restricted to close quarters about the buildings occupied by them.

At 1 P.M. the battalion formed, under command of Capt. T. H. Linnell, and marched by flank from the parade to the south side of the Island, fronting the bay, and formed in line of battle. At twenty minutes past one the prisoners were securely bound and, under guard of the execution party, accompanied by their escort and the chaplain, left the prison for the place of execution.

The prisoners rode in a two-horse wagon, seated upon one of the coffins, their spiritual adviser, Rev. R. McCune, chaplain of the Post, sitting between them, and the band playing the "Dead March." As soon as they reached the place of execution they were taken from the wagon and seated in their coffins in front of the battalion. The battalion immediately formed a hollow square, the execution party, under command of Lieutenant Hollenback, acting provost marshal, occupying a position immediately in front of the center, facing the prisoners, their escort and chaplain attending them, while Major Pierson and staff occupied a position to the right.

Adjutant Bailey then read the finding of the court-martial, when Rev. R. McCune stepped forward beside the condemned men and said:

"I am desired by these unfortunate men to return their thanks to the commander of this Post, and to all the officers and men with whom they have had intercourse, for the kindness and sympathy they have received since their arrival here. I am also charged by them to say to all in attendance that they die forgiving all their enemies and accusers and in love and charity with all men, believing in the gospel of Jesus Christ, and that they have been thus far consoled and sustained by its truths, and that, trusting in the mercy of God, they have hope of eternal life."

The Chaplain then, in an earnest, impassioned, and fervent manner, invoked the Throne of Grace for the unfortunate men. The prisoners were blindfolded, the provost marshal gave the necessary commands to the execution party, and McGraw and Corbin paid the penalty of their acts.

The firing was instantaneous, so that the sixteen muskets seemed to make but one report. Both men fell back upon their coffins and died without a struggle. The bodies were taken to Kentucky for burial, General Burnside having given orders that they be turned over to a friend who had been devoted to them— Mr. Cal DeMoss, of Flag Spring, Ky.

All the proceedings attending this execution were peculiarly solemn and impressive. Both prisoners appeared perfectly composed and collected, and met their fate like men. For several days they had given up all hope of pardon or reprieve. They manifested a great deal of gratitude for the kindness shown them by the chaplain of the Post, who had been unremitting in his attentions.

The day before he was shot Corbin received a beautiful and pathetic letter from Rev. Robert Graham, a minister of the Disciples or Christian Church, of Eighth Street, Cincinnati, which is here given:

"CINCINNATI, May 13, 1863.

"*Mr. W. F. Corbin.*

DEAR AND AFFLICTED BROTHER: At the request of your sorrowing sister, and moved by my interest in you, I will commune with you, in all probability for the last time on earth. It is with deep sympathy in your affliction and that of your dear mother and sister that I endeavor to do this.

"To contemplate death at any time is solemn and well calculated to awe the human soul; but in a case like this we feel all our pity awakened and our sympathy called forth. I would I had the power to describe the feelings of your family and friends, in view of your approaching end. I am charged by your sister to assure you that neither she nor your mother can attach ignominy to your memory. Though you die a violent death, and are so required by the laws of the country, they can make allowance for the influence under which you acted, which others who know you not cannot make. Your sister and Mr. DeMoss got here the day you were removed from this city. I told your sister the substance of what you said to me during our interview. It was a cordial to her wounded spirit to be assured that you would meet your end prepared for the solemn change through the mercy of God in Christ, and that you will attain the crown of eternal life.

"Mr. Patterson, Brother Bishop (formerly mayor of this city, afterwards governor of Ohio), Mr. DeMoss, your devoted friend, and myself had an interview with General Burnside and presented a petition in your behalf signed by some of the most influential citizens of your country. The General treated us very kindly and heard all we had to say. He assured us it would be one of the happiest acts of his life to recommend you and Brother McGraw to the clemency of the President, if he could do so consistently with his views of duty in the responsible position he now fills. We were all deeply impressed with General Burnside's goodness of heart and his sincerity. He kindly offered to send the petition to the President. We had a certified copy taken and gave the original to the General to send to Washington. Mr. DeMoss and your sister went immediately to Washington and used every power and influence possible with the President to get your sentence commuted. They returned day before yesterday. Before this reaches you some of your friends will have seen you and told you all. I will only add, while on this point, that all praise is due your devoted friend, Mr. DeMoss, for his untiring labors for your pardon. Had you been his own brother, he could not have done more.

"I need not say that your sister has been most devoted to you. Let these reflections cheer you in this dark hour.

"Your grave shall be wet with tears, and fervent prayers shall go up to our God that your faith fail not.

"Read this letter to Brother McGraw. Though written to you, it is for him also. Farewell, brethren. May the God of all mercy and grace, who alone can know our hearts, and before whom we shall shortly appear, comfort, console, and support you, and at last receive both of you into his everlasting rest!

"Again farewell; in tears, but in hope and love, farewell!

ROBERT GRAHAM."

On the 15th of June, 1863, a private of the Sixtieth Indiana Infantry, named Reuben Stout, was taken to Johnson's Island. He was heavily ironed and a death sentence hung over him for desertion and murder. He was to be shot on the 26th instant, but before that date arrived orders came to defer the execution thirty days. Finally, the day was fixed upon when he should expiate his crime—October 23, 1863. Before he was shot he told the story of his disgrace and wrongdoing; and as it was of more than ordinary interest, it will be briefly narrated:

Stout had been induced to enlist by an enrolling officer in what he supposed was a cavalry company; at least, the promise had been made that he should go in cavalry. He was made a member of Company E, Sixtieth Indiana Infantry, however, and with this change he was much dissatisfied. After some months he was given a furlough, and while home took sick, and while ill he was urged not to go back at all. Not only did his relatives urge this, but a number of disloyal Democrats promised to aid him if he would join the "Knights of the Golden Circle." It was at Delphi, Ind., while hiding at the home of his father-in-law, that he joined this disloyal organization.

He attended many meetings, he said, and took an oath not to support the government, but to resist the draft, if one was made, and to do all in his power to aid the South.

Afther staying four months with his father-in-law, he found it necessary for his safety to go to the home of his brother, some distance from Delphi. Stout was married, and his wife accompanied him on his visit to his brother. It was then that the tragedy occurred that led to his execution. On the evening in question Stout was upstairs, while his wife and his brother's family were sitting talking in the family room, when a sharp rap came which startled all of them. The brother of Stout went to the door, and as soon as it was open two men quickly entered. After a brief conversation upon general subjects, one of the men, who gave his name as Huffman, asked if Simon Stout were there. The brother said he knew no such man. Huffman, pointing at the deserter's wife, said that he was, and that it was his wife sitting there.

"You are the wife of that cowardly, Copperhead deserter, aren't you?" he asked.

"No," replied the wife timidly; but her looks belied her words.

The other man, named McAffee, asked for a candle, as they proposed to search the house. McAffee had made his request politely, when Huffman angrily said: "Don't ask any favors of these miserable Copperheads. The deserter is here, and we will get him if we have to shoot him."

Stout, who was at the head of the stairs, listening to the conversation, had his pistol in hand. Huffman secured a light and was about to go upstairs, when Stout, who was concealed by the darkness, ordered him to leave the house.

"We have come for you and will take you, dead or alive!" answered Huffman, as he held the candle up that he might see the man he was hunting. Stout fired, and Huffman fell, exclaiming: "O God, I'm killed!"

Stout then rushed from the building as McAffee was bending over the body of the dying man. The deserter ran to the house of a neighbor, who was one of the "Knights of the Golden Circle," and he was expected to warn other members of the order and unite in saving him—by force, if necessary. The man was either afraid or did not act promptly enough, for Stout was captured by a posse before morning.

.   .   .   .

Sometime during the month of August, 1863, eighty-one Confederate officers were sent from Alton, Ill., to Johnson's Island, and were in charge of a number of men from the Thirty-First Iowa, known as the "Gray-Beard Brigade." A Sandusky paper, in speaking of the arrival of the prisoners, said:

This regiment is one of the curiosities of the war, as it is composed entirely of old or middle-aged men. The average age of the entire regiment is fifty-seven years. One man is eighty-one years of age and has twenty-one children—fifteen sons in the Union army. This is a world-beater—a father and fifteen sons in the army at the same time! We learn that most of these men are in good circumstances, some of them being wealthy. Many of thm wore long, gray beards, making their name, "Gray-Beard Brigade," most appropriate. . . .

In the issue of the Sandusky *Register* of April 29, 1863, the announcement was made that Thomas A. Campbell, of the Confederate Army, had been captured within the Union lines, and that a military court had found him guilty of being a spy and sentenced him to be hanged by the neck until dead. General

Burnside ordered him brought to Johnson's Island, and that the commander of the Post see that the sentence be duly executed at noon of the 1st day of May. On April 30 the announcement was made that the execution would be deferred until May 8, between the hours of 12 M. and 3 P.M. On May 4 the paper said that Campbell had sgnified his willingness to inform on other spies, and would not, therefore, meet the penalty of death.

May 7 the following appeared:

According to the programme, the spy, Campbell, has only one day between him and the gallows. We understand that no word has been received from Washington setting aside the death penalty.

Two days later the same paper said that the execution was postponed until the 22d of the month. May 21, 1862, the announcement was made that Campbell would die Friday, May 29.

On May 26 the execution of Campbell was indefinitely postponed, and no further mention was made in the papers about the case; and it is therefore presumed that he remained a prisoner until the close of the war.

On the night of January 5, 1864, two men dressed in Federal overcoats stopped at the home of a man by the name of Lilas, who lived near the Seven-Mile House, seven miles from Sandusky. They asked to stay all night, and were accorded permission to stay. They were careful not to remove their overcoats, even though urged to do so. They said they were from Chicago and had business in that part of the country. They spoke about having traveled quite a distance that day in the cold, and early begged to be permitted to retire.

A son of Mr. Lilas was at home at that time, he being a member of the Eighth Ohio Regiment, and the young man conceived the idea that the men were not what they pretended, and went to the Seven-Mile House and reported his suspicions. This was on the morning of the 6th, and at the time young Lilas left, the men were at the home of his father. Three men—Isaac McKisson, H. A. Lyman, and James McKisson—decided to accompany Lilas and take the men into custody until it was determined who they were. The strangers had left in the meantime; but the pursuing party soon overtook them, they being in sleighs and the travelers afoot. When invited to ride they made no protest, and ere long faced the provost marshal at Sandusky. To this official they reiterated their former statement about being from Chicago, where they had lived for some time. When asked about the army overcoats, they said they purchased them in Chicago. They were required to unbutton their overcoats, when beneath the blue the gray appeared. They said they had purchased these gray suits at Chicago also. The provost marshal was inclined to doubt these statements, and placed the men in the hands of the sheriff of Sandusky.

They had not long been in jail until the provost official received a note, saying:

I am desirous of being sent to Johnson's Island and confined there again as a prisoner of war. My name is J. Crawford Johnson, and my rank is that of lieutenant colonel, C. S. A. Also, Capt. D. Burton Coulter, C. S. A., wishes to be sent to that place. We were sent here this day by your order, under the names of J. Crawford and David Barton.

I am your obedient servant,

J. C. JOHNSON, *Lieut. Col., C. S. A.*

It is needless to say their request was granted. They did not, however, give any information in regard to their escape, or how they came by the United States overcoats.

On the evening of January 2, 1864, Captain Gubbins made an unsuccessful attempt to leave Johnson's Island. He made a dash for liberty; had a day of freedom—cold, unsatisfactory freedom. It seems he had provided himself with a board having cleats upon it, a board of sufficient length to reach to the top of the stockade. He waited until the guards patrolling near the point from which he wished to escape were receding from each other, made a dash, and cleared the inclosure. After getting outside, he encountered one of the outer line of pickets and apparently surrendered. Watching his opportunity, however, he knocked the guard down and broke for the ice. It was quite a severe blow, and when the guard gathered himself together the Confederate captain was swiftly hurrying over the frozen lake. During his flight he lost his cap, but he did not attempt to secure it; he was bent on getting to the peninsula, which he reached in safety. Where he spent the night is not known; but he called at the home of Mr. Henry Miller, about four miles from Port Clinton, early Sunday morning. He told Mr. Miller who he was, and inquired the way to Sandusky, and also as to the likelihood of being arrested if he reached there. Mr. Miller made no effort to arrest him, being alone; but later managed to get a message to his sons, living near, and when they appeared demanded the surrender of the Confederate officer. The Captain surrendered gracefully, and was returned to the Island.

One of the rare tragedies of Johnson's Island occurred about 1 o'clock A.M. December 14, 1864. During those days prison fare was less abundant and prison courtesies fewer than in 1862-63, and men took more desperate chances to get away. The following were the headlines to an article of considerable length in the Sandusky *Register* on the morning of December 14, 1864:

ESCAPE OF PRISONERS FROM JOHNSON'S ISLAND—THEY IMPROVISE SCALING LADDERS—TWENTY-FIVE OF THEM MAKE A RUSH UPON THE GUARD LINE—FOUR OF THE PRISONERS SCALE THE FENCE—THE GUARDS FIRE PROMPTLY—BRING DOWN ONE AND KILL LIEUT. JOHN B. BOWLES, SON OF THE PRESIDENT OF THE BANK OF LOUISVILLE, KY.—SIXTEEN OF THEM RETURN—BEATING THE LONG ROLL—DILIGENT SEARCH MADE FOR THE FUGUTIVES—THEY ARE RECAPTURED—CITIZENS ON THE ISLAND AND PENINSULA ON THE ALERT.

About one o'clock yesterday morning, by a preconceived arrangement, a rush was made by twenty-four prisoners upon the center of the guard line, on the northwest side of the prison. The prisoners had improvised eight scaling ladders by attaching cleats to boards. These boards were light and easily carried and just the thing for scaling the high prison fence. The rush occasioned the cry, "Turn Out the Guard!" accompanied by a rattling fire from the guard line; but the rush was so impetuous, and by so many different prisoners, that, in spite of the guard, four men out of the twenty-four scaled the fence, passed the guard, escaped from the Island, crossed the north channel, and went over upon the peninsula. Of the others who did not get through, one received a shot, cutting away his coat at the waist, narrowly escaping a death wound, was knocked down and captured. Another, Lieut. John B. Bowles, son of the president of the Louisville Bank, was shot twice through the body and killed. The other eighteen found the work too hot, and retreated to their barracks. The rush upon the guard was followed by the signal gun and long roll sounded. The long roll had sounded but once before, and that was when, in September, 1864, a tornado swept one-third of the fence away. At that time, when the tornado raged, the prisoners were content to remain in their quarters, where they could only pray or wish that the howling storm might not destroy their shelter.

It was impossible to tell how many had escaped or what had become of all of them. To make sure of any who might be lurking on the Island, awaiting better opportunities to elude observation, three companies of the Sixth Regiment, Veteran Reserve Corps, were ordered out to patrol the Island and make a thorough search.

At the same time detachments of the One Hundred and Twenty-Eighth Regiment were ordered off in pursuit of the escaped prisoners who had passed the picket on the northwest side of the Island, receiving a fire from them at long range. The fleeing prisoners made the best time possible. The morning roll call showed that but four had left the prison.

The four men who escaped crossed over the ice to the peninsula, hoping to hide there successfully until they could get away to Canada.

There is a large vineyard near the point on the peninsula, owned by a Mr. Wright, who, when he heard the cannon-firing and the rattle of musketry, arose, dressed hurriedly, grasped his gun, and started for the fray. Presently he saw three men approaching him—men who were winded, but who were making violent efforts to make good time on the ice. He saw by their dress they were Confederates, and called to them: "Stop, or I'll put holes through you!" The prisoners halted and were returned to the stockade. The fourth prisoner was recaptured sometime during the following day. There was considerable excitement at Sandusky on account of the cannon-firing. It was afterwards learned that it was done to break the ice and prevent further attempts at escape.

The body of Lieutenant Bowles, at the request of his father, was prepared for burial and forwarded to Louisville.

On the afternoon of September 2, 1864, there occurred an occasion of no little moment, even in wartime. A young man, not yet twenty, handsome and manly, a soldier who did not flinch or cringe or beg for life, when told that a military commission said that he must die, and by hanging, received the intelligence with great calmness and prepared for the end.

This young man was John G. Nickell, of Kentucky, who had enlisted in the Confederate army at the age of eighteen. Later he became a partisan ranger and killed one or two men.

At a quarter before one the troops, under the command of Col. Charles W. Hill, were formed into column and marched to the field west of the prison, where the gallows was erected. The prisoner, accompanied by the chaplain, rode in a wagon guarded by twelve men and accompanied by the burial party, preceded by martial music playing the "Dead March." On the arrival of the condemned the regiment was formed into a hollow square around the scaffold and he was seated on the coffin. The proceedings of the military court were read by Adjutant Hayes, after which the chaplain read a paper signed by the prisoner a few moments before leaving for the place of execution, stating that he was born in Kentucky September 26, 1843. In twenty-four days he would have been twenty-one years of age. He had enlisted in the Confederate service at the age of eighteen years. The prisoner expressed thanks for the kindly treatment by officers and men during the short time he was on the Island. He also made a statement in regard to the crime with which he was charged, and asked that it be not printed, which request was observed by the representatives of the Sandusky papers present at the execution. Prayer was offered by the chaplain, and then the prisoner was told to arise.

He stood up promptly, with head erect, but without bravado. His quiet, brave demeanor impressed his enemies—enemies without enmity at that solemn moment. The rope was speedily adjusted, the cap drawn over his eyes, the spring touched, and the tragedy was at an end. Brave and handsome was this young Kentuckian at noon of that September day. Soon afterwards the stalwart form was lifeless.

There were six specifications against him, all of which the commission found him guilty of; and to all he pleaded "not guilty," except the first. They charged: "The unlawful taking up of arms as a guerrilla and military insurgent; the unlawful killing of Logan Wilson, in Morgan County, Ky., February 3, 1863; the killing of John D. Nichols and Preston Pettit, of Kentucky."

A grave was prepared on the Island, and he was interred therein; but his name does not appear in the list of dead on Johnson's Island published in this book.

CHAPTER XVI.

THE GREAT CONSPIRACY.

Plan to Liberate the Prisoners on Johnson's Island—Beall Captures the Philo Parsons and the Island Queen—Capt. Cole Fails to Capture the Gunboat Michigan, Guarding Sandusky Bay—The Conspirators to Spike the Guns of the Land Batteries—In Face of Danger They Weakened—Capture of Cole—How Beall Got Away with the Philo Parsons—The Effort to Get Canada Involved in War with the United States—Great Excitement at Sandusky—Warning of the Toronto (Canada) *Globe*—The Trials of Beall and Burleigh—Southern Version of the Plot.

THE most important episode in the history of Johnson's Island was the plot to free the prisoners, capture Sandusky, destroy it and such other lake cities as could be reached, and escape either through Canada, or, if reënforced by Southern sympathizers in sufficient numbers, march through Ohio and reach the South by way of Kentucky. The plot came near involving this country in a controversy with England—possibly the primary object of the conspirators; but, fortunately for the North, and Canada as well, the plot failed.

The Sandusky *Register* of Wednesday morning, September 21, 1864, printed a story, under startling headlines, that alarmed the people of Ohio and made most Union citizens look askance at their Democratic neighbors. From mouth to mouth the story went that the "Knights of the Golden Circle" were to have taken an important part in a general uprising, but for some unknown cause failed to do so.

For the last six weeks Colonel Hill, commander of the forces at Johnson's Island, says the *Register,* has been daily receiving warnings to the effect that a Copperhead-Canadian-Rebel refugee raid was maturing to surprise the forces and release the Confederate prisoners confined on the Island. The plans of Colonel Hill to frustrate their designs were too well conceived and deeply laid to admit of a surprise. During the afternoon of day before yesterday Colonel Hill received a dispatch from Detroit to the effect that a portion of the conspirators would arrive in this city on the afternoon trains. After notifying Captain Carter, commander of the Michigan, of the dispatch, he immediately ordered a posse of men aboard the Princess, to proceed to this city and take charge of the trains on their arrival.

Aboard the Sandusky, Dayton, and Cincinnati train were a large number of men, most of whom left the train before its arrival at the depot and proceeded to scatter about the city. The larger portion were finally overhauled and found to be laborers and mechanics rendezvousing at this point to proceed to Nashville, where they were to be employed by the government.

The passengers on the Mansfield train were placed under arrest long before they reached this city; but notwithstanding, a crowd of men eluded the vigilance of the conductor and escaped at a station some four miles from the city.

A suspicious character, C. H. Cole, who has been boarding at the West House for a considerable time, was then arrested by Captain Steiner, provost marshal of the district. Since his arrival in this city Cole has been lavish in his expenditures, feasting and drinking with several of the military officials. Frequent suppers were given, at which no expense was spared, and all bills were settled with gold.

After his arrest a search revealed a number of letters and documents giving the particulars of the plot to capture the steamers, sink the Michigan, free the prisoners on the Island, and destroy Sandusky. The whole scheme was to have been put in operation yesterday. Revelations made by Cole led to the arrest of Abraham Strain, John H. Williams, Dr. E. Stanley, John M. Brown, and a Jew named Rosenthal, all residents and prominent Copperheads of this city. The Sandusky conspirators were to go to the camp of the Cleveland Artillery, spike the guns and use other means to make resistance useless. A party of Rebels were to take passage on the Philo Parsons at Detroit and capture her on the way down, with such other steamers as could be seized. The Michigan was lying at anchor off Johnson's Island, and the purpose was to steal quietly down on her with the Philo Parsons, then suddenly run into her amidships, cutting her down and sinking her.

The Confederate prisoners were then to rise and, with the assistance of their Canadian reënforcements and the local Copperheads, overpower the guard, make their escape, commit all the damage possible, and either open a campaign in Ohio, with the help of the "Sons of Liberty," or else escape to Canada.

After the return of the Michigan an accomplice of Cole's named John Robinson was arrested, and, with Cole, is confined on board the Michigan, whilst the Sandusky conspirators are confined on Johnson's Island. Cole is a young man, rather below the medium size, and from his financial transactions was strongly suspected of being engaged in the interests of the rebellion soon after his arrival, and closely watched.

During his stay in this city he became noted as a drunken loafer, and was only countenanced in accordance with the money spent. He was a fierce McClellan man.

The steamer Island Queen left Kelley's Island about 6 P. M. yesterday with about thirty-five members of Company K, One Hundred and Thirtieth Regiment, Ohio National Guard, for Toledo, to be mustered out of the service, together with a lot of passengers. They put in at Middle Bass Island to wood. The steamer Philo Parsons was lying across the end of the dock, when the lines of the Queen were unsuspectingly fastened alongside of the Parsons.

She was then boarded by about thirty Confederates, who had captured the Parsons, and, with revolvers and hatchets in hand; drove the passengers and crew of the Island Queen into the hold of the Parsons, not even excepting Captain Orr, who was afterwards called up and, it is supposed, made to pilot the Parsons. The engineer of the Parsons was shot at while engaged at his post at the engine, and was afterwards seen bleeding. How severely he was wounded, or what became of him, is not known. As a matter of course, all were surprised and could do nothing but surrender, which they did with the best grace they could command. Some of the passengers, not obeying the orders of the raiders as quickly as they desired, were roughly used, the raiders hitting them on the heads with hatchets and revolvers.

After throwing some thirty cords of wood aboard the Parsons, the passengers were ordered from her hold, some of whom were paroled, while others were not molested except being examined for arms. The soldiers of the One Hundred and Thirtieth Regiment were afterwards called out and more closely scrutinized, but the pirates were in too big a hurry to do their work thoroughly.

About half past five A.M. the gunboat Michigan hove in sight of Kelley's Island, where were a number of passengers who had been released by the raiders. The islanders, not knowing whether she was in possession of her own officers and crew or the raiders, were not a little alarmed; but soon their fears were dispelled, as the form of the jolly old commander, Captain Carter, was observed upon her deck.

The Michigan then proceeded to search for the captured boats, steering for Middle Bass Island. When about halfway between the two islands she met a sailboat having on board Mr. Ashley, clerk of the steamer Philo Parsons, and a number of other captives, headed for Sandusky. These gentlemen informed the commander of the Michigan that the Parsons had been seen about two o'clock in the morning steaming in the direction of Malden. The gunboat then proceeded on her cruise in the direction of Middle Bass Island, where she was heartily cheered by the remaining captives on shore. She then started for the mouth of the Detroit River, where, falling in with vessels and tugs, she was informed that the Parsons had not been seen in that vicinity. The Michigan then put about and steamed down the lake, inquiring of vessels for the missing steamer, without effect. She then steamed for Middle Bass again, and shortly after leaving there discovered the Island Queen on Chucanola Reef. The vessel was sunk in seven feet of water.

The Island Queen is a small sidewheel steamer, running between Sandusky and the Islands, and is owned by the Messrs. Kelley, of Kelley's Island, and commanded by Captain Orr, of this city.

The Philo Parsons is a steamer of similar build, perhaps a third larger than the Queen, and for the past season has been running between this port and Detroit. The Parsons is commanded by Captain Atwood. The destruction of these vessels is a severe blow to the residents of the islands, as they almost solely depended upon them for transportation of their freight and passengers to and from the islands.

Captain Orr gave the following account of the capture of his boat:

"The Philo Parsons left Detroit at 8:30 Monday morning, with a number of passengers on board. One of the men said to the clerk that he had some friends at Windsor, Canada, whom they wished to have taken on. Five came on board at this place. At Malden, Canada, they took on more men, who brought with them an old trunk tied with ropes. From there they went to Kelley's Island, where several more got on. About a mile after leaving Kelley's Island the men opened the old trunk and took out arms, which they concealed under the long-tailed coats, and then stationed themselves in squads at the commanding parts of the vessel. At a signal a squad went to the pilothouse, and holding pistols at the head of the wheelman, told him that if he did not direct the boat as they wished they would blow his brains out. The wheelman did as they ordered—there was nothing else to do—and they steamed down the lake, in full view of Sandusky, for a short time.

"They then turned up the lake and stopped at Middle Bass Island. Here she ran alongside of the Island Queen, made fast, got out a gangplank, and began unloading freight.

"About this time six or seven of the pirates got on board the Island Queen from the Parsons's aft, and perhaps twenty got on forward, and presently notified all on board that they were prisoners. There was quite a crowd at the wharf, and the crowd was augmented by the passengers the raiders had ordered off the boat. Presently they fired several shots indiscriminately into the crowd. Mr. Lorenzo Miller, of Put-in-Bay, was seriously injured.

"After this they went to the engine room and ordered the engineer to come out; but he not being quite so prompt as they wished, they fired upon him, one of the balls taking effect in his right cheek. He was the only one of the boat seriously injured by the shots. They then put most of us into the hold of the Island Queen. A short time afterwards they sent for me to come out on deck, and asked me if many strangers came into Sandusky that afternoon. They wanted to know if there was any excitement in the city, and if it was known that the steamer they were in possession of was coming. Then they took me into the cabin, where the ladies were, together with several men. The ladies and children were given permission to go ashore, after exacting a promise that they would not give any information of what they knew to any one for twenty-four hours.

"Pale with fear, the ladies promised, and were permitted to go ashore at Middle Bass.

"They then ordered the soldiers who came on board at Kelley's Island to come upon the deck, and made them swear they would not take up arms against the Confederacy until legally exchanged, after which they were permitted to go. The citizens were forced to take an oath not to divulge what they knew until twenty-four hours had elapsed. They were then permitted to go ashore. Having cleared the vessel, they got the stern line out, lashed the boats together, got under way, and stood out for Sandusky. When between Kelley's Island and Put-in-Bay, they inquired of one of their men who had been sent into the hold if he had scuttled the Island Queen. He said that he had knocked off the head of a pipe so as to let in a stream of water four inches in diameter. They then lowered the yawl and took it in tow of the Island Queen, leaving the Parsons to her fate.

"While under way they talked of taking the Michigan, but doubted their ability to do it. One or two of the men objected to 'going into a slaughterhouse,' as they put it. When opposite Kelley's Island they forced me to go into the fire hold, and while there they consulted and waited, apparently, for signals.

"Then discretion overcame their valor, as they put off up the lake and steamed up into the Detroit River, while I, with nine others, was put off at Fighting Island, some seven miles from Detroit. They asked me who I was going to vote for, and I told them Lincoln. They then asked what McClellan's chances were, and I told them very small indeed. They replied: 'I reckon they are rather slim.' "

The clerk of the Philo Parsons gave the following version of that boat's capture:

"The steamer Philo Parsons left Detroit on the morning of September 19, at 8 A.M., with about forty passengers. Immediately after leaving Detroit a young man, whom I had frequently seen before, came to me, and, calling me by name, said there were four passengers who wanted to take the boat at Sandwich, a small town on the Canadian side of the river, some three miles below Detroit. I reported the same to Captain Atwood, and he stopped and took them on. They said when they came on board that they were taking a little pleasure trip, and intended to stop at Kelley's Island. All the baggage they had was a small hand satchel.

"At Malden, twenty miles down the river, on the Canadian side, where the boat stops regularly, about twenty more came on board and took passage for Sandusky. As it has been quite common of late to take on that number of passengers nearly every trip at this point, no attention was paid to them.

"The majority of those who took the boat at Malden were from Ohio, who, getting starved out in Canada, were returning home. I at once set this party down as a lot of the same kind. A large, old-fashioned trunk with ropes constituted the baggage of the party. Everything went off quietly during the day. The boat stopped at a number of the islands, taking on quite a number of passengers. Captain Atwood stepped off the boat at North Bass Island, where he resides.

"Shortly after leaving Kelley's Island, and between the island and Sandusky, I was standing in front of my office, when four of the party came up to me and, drawing revolvers, leveled them at me and said that if I offered any resistance I was a dead man. At the same time the old black trunk flew open, and in less time than it takes to tell it the whole gang of about thirty-five were armed to the teeth with revolvers, hatchets, etc. I then told them that they apparently had the strongest party, and guessed I should have to surrender. They then stationed two men to watch me, the remainder rushing into the cabin threatening to shoot any one offering resistance. There was a large number of ladies aboard, who were badly frightened.

"The boat was then headed down the lake for about an hour, and then turned and run to Middle Bass Island. While lying there the steamer Island Queen came slowly alongside and was instantly seized. Quite a number of shots were fired and quite a number struck with hatchets, but I think no one was killed. The passengers of both boats were put on shore, and a portion of the baggage.

"After taking what money I had, they requested me to go ashore. They permitted me to take my private property, but my books and papers, belonging to the boat, they kept. The boats were then started out in the lake, the Parsons towing the Queen a short distance into the lake, and then letting her go adrift. After putting off the passengers at Middle Bass, the Philo Parsons headed for Sandusky, and was gone about four hours. She afterwards returned under a full head of steam, and after passing Middle Bass headed for Malden and steered in that direction as long as we could see her.

"The crews of both boats were retained and made to do the bidding of the parties in possession. The captain of the gang informed me he would place myself and passengers where we could give no information until morning, and before that time their work would be completed. He said it was their intention to run to the mouth of Sandusky Bay; and if they received the proper signals, they would run in, attack the United States steamer Michigan, lying off Johnson's Island, and then release their friends imprisoned at that place.

W. O. ASHLEY."

The name of Cole is mentioned in the *Register's* account of the exciting event, but the name of the daring man who, in reality, made the only successful movement in the entire affair is not mentioned. At that time, too, they did not know who Cole was, but that develops later. The man who captured the Philo Parsons was a Virginian named John Yates Beall, sometimes mentioned as Bell, and who was subsequently arrested and tried in Canada, as was another raider by the name of Burleigh.

The history of Erie County, Ohio, gives an account of the incident which follows:

The plan of rescue that led to the open attempt on the 19th of September was conceived by John Yates Beall. He was to conduct the operation from the Canadian side, while Major Cole was intrusted with the work of gaining the confidence of the officers at Sandusky, and particularly the officers of the gunboat Michigan, that lay in the waters of Sandusky Bay, in the immediate vicinity of the prison. The Michigan was the only government boat then acting in defense of the island, and, with an ample crew of marines and her eighteen guns, could repel any attack that might be made—especially when acting in conjunction with the guard force of infantry and artillery on the island and Sandusky.

The first step, therefore, in accomplishing the main undertaking was to obtain control of the gunboat, and this was the part of the programme assigned to Cole. He is well remembered by many of the present residents of Sandusky as an active, energetic fellow, possessing education beyond the average; a fine conversationalist and a royal entertainer. He made prodigal use of his money, with which commodity he appeared to be abundantly supplied. He dined and wined the officers of the Michigan, and sought to ingratiate himself wholly in their favor. But in the chivalrous acts of this daring young fellow he rather overdid the matter, and Yankee cunning proved more than a match for his arts. When he thought he had the officers just about where he wanted them, the picture reversed, and the officers had Cole where they wanted him, and he fell a prisoner into their hands.

Cole arranged a wine party at the time that affairs were expected to culminate, and the liquor was heavily drugged; but the officers never partook of his bounty, and instead of their falling victims to his plans he himself fell into theirs.

The Sandusky *Register* has this to say of the after effects of the raid:

The plans of Beall were equally well formed, but, through the failure of Cole, were also futile so far as carrying out the main effort was concerned. Beall, with a few rough characters, took passage on the steamer Philo Parsons as that boat was making her passage between Detroit, the Islands, and Sandusky. At Malden twenty other men also came on board.

After passing from the landing place at Kelley's Island the men approached the clerk of the boat, who, in the absence of the captain, seems to have been in command, and, with revolvers pointed at him, demanded a surrender. Without much resistance the steamer passed into the charge of the piratical crew, and was turned back toward Middle Bass Island, where a landing was made.

About this time the Island Queen reached the dock at Middle Bass, but no sooner had she touched then she was boarded and captured; not, however, without stout resistance from her commanding officer and the engineer, both of whom were overpowered, the latter being shot in the face. On board the Island Queen was a party of about one hundred discharged soldiers returning home; but, being without arms, they were powerless in the face of a score or more of heavily loaded revolvers in the hands of determined, desperate men.

The Queen was scuttled and sent adrift, after which the prow of the Parsons was turned toward Sandusky Bay. After cruising about for a long time, anxiously watching for the signal from the land supposed to have been successfuly organized by Cole, Beall wanted to make the attempt at rescue without the assistance of Cole's coöperating force; but knowing the power of the Michigan's guns, and fearful of the result, Beall's desperate crew weakened and declined to take the chances.

Disheartened and discouraged, the daring leader reluctantly put about and made for Canada, where the steamer was abandoned and her former crew released from temporary imprisonment. This was the only open attempt made to effect the escape of the officers confined on Johnson's Island, and it proved a failure. What would have been the result had Cole's effort been successful is wholly a matter of speculation. Several prominent citizens of Sandusky were arrested, charged with complicity in the attempt. They were temporarily confined on the Island, but were afterwards released.

Beall seems to have been less fortunate. He was captured near Suspension Bridge, N. Y., and taken to New York City and confined on Governor's Island. He was charged before a military court with the seizure of the steamer Philo Parsons, also the Island Queen, and of being a spy in the Confederate service.

He was also charged with attempting to wreck an express train between Buffalo and Dunkirk, for the purpose of robbery. He was found guilty and sentenced to be hanged. The day of the execution was fixed for February 18, 1865, but President Lincoln granted him a respite of six days, that his mother might see him once more.

Prior to the attempt to release the prisoners on Johnson's Island, Beall was a captain of a company of Virginians under Gen. Stonewall Jackson. He possessed at the time of the breaking out of the war a valuable plantation, and was a young man of large means and great promise.

The *Confederate Veteran,* in the issue of July, 1900, has this to say upon the event:

Jacob Thompson, formerly Secretary of the Interior under Buchanan, Maj. C. H. Cole, of the Fifth Tennessee Confederate Regiment, Maj. Thomas C. Hinds, of Bowling Green, Ky., and several others hatched a conspiracy for the liberation of all the Confederate prisoners in the North.

Their object was to capture the man-of-war Michigan, which was at that time on Lake Erie, seize the Philo Parsons—which was done—and release the twenty-five thousand Confederates, of whom four thousand were at Johnson's Island, eight thousand at Camp Douglas, nine thousand at Camp Chase, and four thousand at Camp Morton, Indianapolis. Then, with the aid of ten thousand Confederate and Southern sympathizers who visited in the North, and who had gathered at various points to aid in the consummation of the plot, they hoped to strike a fatal blow at the Union at a time when, according to the calculations of the conspirators, General Early was to lay siege to Washington, and thus make it impossible for the Federal government to send troops to the points to be attacked.

A part of the programme was carried out. Major Cole, who had been deputized to capture the Philo Parsons, did so, and sailed away with her. But the conspiracy to seize the Michigan and liberate the Confederates failed, and Cole and his men were captured. Their betrayer was Colonel Johnson, of Kentucky, a prisoner on Johnson's Island, who, seized with remorse for the act, committed suicide shortly afterwards.

The *Veteran* is evidently in error as to the part Cole played. Cole was a prisoner at the time Beall was cruising about Sandusky Bay, waiting for a signal from Cole that he was in possession of the Michigan.

The statement that the plot was betrayed by Colonel Johnson is something the Northern writers seemed to know nothing about, as no mention is made of it in any of the stories of the time or in the reports of the Federal officers. Nor has it been mentioned in subsequent Northern accounts of the episode. The *Veteran* further says:

Cole was tried and sentenced to be shot, the execution to take place on Johnson's Island; but influential friends interceded for him, and his sentence was commuted to life imprisonment. He was taken to Fort Lafayette in 1865, remaining there one year; was then pardoned, and is now living on a ranch in Texas. Thus ended one of the most gigantic conspiracies of the war for the overthrow of the North.

In following the subsequent history of the great conspiracy many remarkable statements concerning the capture of the Philo Parsons were found. The Buffalo *Commercial Advertiser* of November 27, 1864, says:

The examination of G. B. Burleigh, alias Captain Beall, the Lake Erie pirate, was commenced before Recorder Duggan, at Toronto, Wednesday. Mr. R. A. Harrison appeared for the Crown, and Mr. M. C. Cameron defended the prisoner. The only witness examined was a young woman named Gertrude Titus, of Detroit, who was a passenger on the Philo Parsons at the time of her seizure by the armed men.

She fully identified the prisoner, and testified that he was the most conspicuous and active of those who seized the Parsons and perpetrated the outrages on board. Mr. Cameron contended that no case had been made out, or at least the prisoner could not be claimed, as his case did not come under the Ashburton treaty. The Queen's proclamation recognized the Confederates as belligerents, and therefore it was no act of piracy or robbery for any body of men to act as these men had. They were right, according to the laws of nations, in liberating the prisoners at Johnson's Island if they had the power to do so.

The Sandusky *Register,* in an editorial on December 6, 1864, says:

G. B. Burleigh, who was charged with being in recent acts of piracy on Lake Erie, and was on trial for the same at Toronto, was discharged and immediately arrested on a charge of robbery, preferred by W. O. Ashley, clerk of the Philo Parsons, and awaits trial for that offense. ⸱

On the following day the same paper contained the following:

Evidence is still accumulating to prove that the Canadian Rebels had formed an extensive plot, not only to release the prisoners on Johnson's Island, but to prey upon and destroy the commerce of the lakes. The Detroit *Tribune,* in giving the particulars of the arrest of Burleigh, one of the pirates concerned in the seizure of the Philo Parsons and Island Queen, says:

"As soon as Burleigh's friends became aware of his arrest, they sued out a writ of habeas corpus before the Court of Queen's Bench, which was made returnable on Tuesday at twelve o'clock. As he had previously been committed by an alderman of the city, who had no authority in the premises, his discharge from arrest was a foregone conclusion. Mr. Brown, Assistant United States District Attorney, arrived in Toronto about ten o'clock on Tuesday, and upon learning the turn matters were likely to take, at once had a warrant taken out before the recorder and placed in the hands of an officer.

"Before this could be accomplished, Burleigh had been discharged. Fortunately, or unfortunately, as the case may be, his Rebel friends, who were present in large numbers, stood ready to congratulate him on his release, and thus detained him for probably half an hour. This circumstance worked in Mr. Brown's favor, and the regular warrant was served on the Rebel chief ere the echoes of his friends' cheers had died away.

"Instantly signs of disturbance were manifested by the crowd. The game was pronounced a Yankee trick, but Burleigh's counsel prevailed upon him to quietly submit to the course of the law, and he was taken back to jail, followed by a large concourse of long-visaged Rebels. The Yankee trick did the job. The examination that followed has been fully reported.

"Burleigh is a young man about twenty-four years of age, of thickset, athletic build, apparently of Scotch origin, and boasts of having been an officer in the navy. He was not the leader of the pirates, but held a secondary command to Bell. He was, however, the most officious, malignant, and insulting of the gang; and if his wishes had been law, he would have been satisfied with nothing less than the destruction of the Philo Parsons and everything that came in his way. Indeed, Bell was once forced to put him under arrest for insubordination. His friends have retained for him the best criminal lawyer in Canada, and he will undoubtedly make a desperate fight. They are very confident of his final release, and it is not at all improbable that amid the technicalities of British law, and with the sympathies of the Canadian people, not to say of the Canadian judges, in his favor, he may manage to escape.

"The case cannot finally be heard upon its merits until more witnesses are procured. It was once hoped that he might be brought to Windsor for examination, but there seems to be no law authorizing the transfer.

"When first arrested, Burleigh told the officer that he wished to God his arrest had been postponed one week, as he had an important job on hand. During a conversation with him he indirectly revealed the fact that he had been engaged in purchasing an armament for the propellor Georgian, which steamer recently passed this city on her way to Collingwood. The armament was to have been put on at or near Port Sarnia, but the vigilance of our government officers in making the arrest doubtless frustrated the movement. It may, however, give the key to the combined Rebel plot, and will doubtless be acted on as such."

There was yet another story of the Canadian conspiracy, and this was issued by a Dr. Ayer in pamphlet form. As the story is without doubt long since out of print, the review of the sketch in the editorial columns of the Sandusky *Register* of May 8, 1865, together with the editorial comment, is here presented:

We have received from the author, I. Winslow Ayer, M.D., a pamphlet bearing the title of "The Great Northwestern Conspiracy." It takes in the entire plot to burn the Northern cities, release the prisoners from Johnson's Island, Camp Douglas, and other places, as well as the piracy of the lakes and the trial of the conspirators.

After speaking generally of the Rebels in Canada, and the manner of their support, the author proceeds to relate the history of what has been known as the "Lake Erie Conspiracy" and the Philo Parsons raid.

He says that it is given just as he received it from the lips of two Confederate officers who were engaged in the affair, and who commanded detachments on board the Philo Parsons. Although familiar with the transaction, there are some things relating to the affair that are new to us, and some that are devoid of truth, and which do great injustice to certain parties spoken of.

The plot was matured, if not originated, at the Chicago Democratic Convention, at which point they were to release the prisoners at Camp Douglas, and at the same time of the assault on Camp Douglas a simultaneous effort was to be made to capture the United States war steamer Michigan, carrying eighteen guns, and at that time anchored in Sandusky Bay. The prisoners of these camps being released, and the steamer Michigan in their hands, they expected to inaugurate an army that would terrify the Northern people and really overturn the government at Washington.

With the steamer Michigan they expected to destroy the commerce of the lakes, effectually closing their ports, and laying all the large towns and cities under contribution, exacting large sums of money through fear of bombardment. Here we shall make a few quotations from the book, using its exact language:

"The plan of the conspirators to get possession of the Michigan was by bribery and surprise.

"Mr. Thompson, in his efforts to seize the vessel, secured the services of a man named Cole, of Sandusky, Ohio, who had been a citizen of Virginia, and who still retained his sympathies for the rebellion and took an active part in aiding it whenever he had an opportunity; and a woman, said to have been his paramour, who carried dispatches backward and forward between the parties. This man Cole seems to have been the most wily conspirator of them all, and played his infamous part with most adroit shrewdness. The defeat of the whole scheme was not owing to any blunder of his, but rather the blunder of those who employed and furnished him the means.

"Having been well supplied with money by Mr. Thompson, and no limit put to his expenses, he began his work with a will. He seems to have begun by getting generally well acquainted with the affairs of the vessel, by feasting the officers and now and then lending them money, or accommodating them in some other way, until he had won the confidence of all those in command of the steamer, as well as those in charge of Johnson's Island. After a time he found out those who were most vulnerable on the money question, and those whom he did not dare approach upon the subject. Of the latter class, there is one mentioned in particular by the Rebels, whose suspicions they did not dare to arouse, and which they made every attempt to lull. This was an officer named Eddy, from Massachusetts. He then bribed the chief engineer, who they said had agreed for twenty thousand dollars in gold to get the machinery out of order and otherwise aid in the vessel's capture, and one or two others.

"Of the remainder of the officers of the Michigan, they thought their well-known Democratic faith and sympathy with the rebellion would prevent them from seeing or knowing too much until too late to avoid the disaster. Of these last the conspirators did not seem to entertain the least fear, some of them being Southern men by birth, and at most but passive in their fidelity to the government. As the writer has stated before, the attempt on the steamer Michigan was to be simultaneous with that at Chicago, and while the Rebels and their friends were assembling in Chicago they were also gathering in Sandusky City for the capture of the Michigan. The actual number of conspirators in Sandusky at that time was not known to the writer, nor the details of their plans; but let it suffice to say that they were there armed and ready.

"When the time for action arrived, however, the engineer and his accomplices were not to be found; and after waiting for nearly two days the Rebel portion of the conspirators, with the exception of Captain Beall, returned to Canada. On their return they said that the prisoners whom they had bribed were afraid to carry out their infamous and hazardous part of the contract.

"The Rebels were in great fear lest something had happened that would put an end forever to their hopes in regard to the steamer, but in a few days after this the nonappearance of the engineer and friends was duly explained, and the alarm caused by it quieted. And another time was set for the attempt.

"The day being set once more, preparations were again made to capture the vessel, and this time occurred what was called the 'Lake Erie piracy.' Nearly everything connected with this event was so disgraceful to the United States service that, although the government hastened to remove all the reprehensible officers and retain those who deserved well of their country, yet seem to have endeavored to keep some of the facts connected with it from being made public.

"About one week before the time for the second attempt arrived, Captain Beall returned from Sandusky to Windsor, Canada, and announced that all was ready for the capture, and immediately telegraphed to Jacob Thompson, who was at the Queen's Hotel, in Toronto. Thompson at once answered that he would come to Windsor that night, and desired not to be recognized. That evening he arrived at Windsor, and, without apparently being known, got into a carriage waiting and was taken to the residence of Colonel Steele, where he was expected. During this week all the men who were to participate in the affair were notified, and this time the services of some of the men who had been to Chicago during the convention were called into requisition. The Confederate officers could be seen running about here and there to the different boarding houses where the men were stopping, carrying ominous-looking carpet-bags, distributing from them pistols, ammunition, and other things deemed necessary for the undertaking, which was to be made on the night of the following Monday.

"Most active in these efforts to incite these men to deeds of desperation were Colonel Steele and Jake Thompson, or, when he used his assumed name, Colonel Carson.

"Cole was to give a champagne supper on board the Michigan that evening to the officers, and was to be there himself with a party of Confederates, who had also become well acquainted with the officers, and who were invited, at the request of Cole, to join in the festivities of the occasion. It was intended for the Philo Parsons to reach hailing distance of the Michigan about eleven or twelve o'clock that night, in order that by this time as many of the crew as possible, through the champagne, would be incapable of rendering any assistance. When the Parsons was hailed by the watch on board the steamer, Cole and his associates were at once to take possession of a gun, which would sweep the whole decks and prevent that portion of the crew who were not rendered incapable by drink from attempting any effectual resistance to the conspirators boarding her from the Parsons.

"Once in possession of this vessel of war, the prisoners on the island were to be immediately released, landed at Sandusky, when the 'Sons of Liberty' and other secret societies were to seize the opportunity of rising up and asserting their peculiar doctrines, under protection of this powerful man-of-war. The same general plan was to be pursued at Cleveland and other places along the coast, where their secret societies were in full blast.

"The conspirators expected to exact enormous tribute of the loyal portions of these communities to save their property from the dangers of bombardment. This expected-tribute of ten millions of dollars—to be divided equally among them—from the border cities was the greatest inducement held out to their associates by the Rebel leaders before leaving Canada, in order to excite their cupidity and zeal and to influence their minds to such a pitch that they would render a strict obedience to their officers, and hesitate at no act of violence."

The whole of the programme was carried out, even to the chartering of the little Scotia. But on arriving at Kelley's Island, and receiving no message from Cole, the conspirators were in a dilemma. The suspicions of the passengers had become aroused, and a remark which fell from a passenger, that he would have them all arrested at Sandusky, created great consternation among the conspirators. They at once resolved to take possession of the boat, go back to Put-in-Bay, get a supply of wood, and put off the passengers—all of which was accomplished. After dark that night they ran down into Sandusky Bay; but, failing to see the signals agreed upon, and after waiting a short time, again returned to the open lake, convinced by this time that something had happened to their friends at Sandusky.

Captain Beall, seeing his project had failed, determined to cruise on the lake as long as possible, burning and destroying all he could. His men feared the consequences, and insisted upon going back to Canada. Beall said that if it had not been for the mutinous scoundrels composing his crew he could have run the lakes for two weeks, burning and destroying all the vessels he met with, before the Yankees could have made him land.

The first attempt spoken of, and the band of desperate men who were among us for some days, is news to all the loyal portion of this city, and that they were feasted and toasted by any portion of our loyal Union inhabitants, of whom most of our business men are made up, we do not believe for a moment. We have no doubt that Captain Beall and his conspirators were here, and probably feasted and toasted, but not by our prominent citizens and business men.

The editorial was as follows:

When the people of the Confederate States inaugurated their rebellion against the Union, they counted to a certainty upon the alliance of Great Britain. All the testimony we have confirms this fact. It was no use arguing with them; no use trying to persuade them that England would not join in the mêlée. They had but one answer: "Cotton is king." There were no "ifs" about it; she must go to war; she had no other resources. Bitterly disappointed have they been, we all know. With the prospect that the Confederacy will soon be numbered amongst the things that were, they are ready to adopt any means, however desperate, at all likely to better their situation. In this condition the hopes they once indulged in revive again. They counted on the alliance of England; can they not force it? The prize is worth a struggle, much sacrifice, even obloquy and shame.

"Necessity knows no law;" they must get some aid or perish. These considerations have doubtless caused the Confederate Goverment to instigate and to authorize the raids made from Canada upon the United States. The captors of the Chesapeake pleaded their commission. The plunderers of St. Albans made the same excuse. The man Burleigh, accused of robbery on board the Philo Parsons, follows suit. Munitions of war, too, have been purchased in this province, and at least one attempt made to export them, evidently for the purpose of supplying Rebel marauders with means of offense.

Doubtless, too, had these men been arrested, they would have pleaded Richmond-given authority. Upon these facts, then, if they stood alone, should we not be warranted in saying that the government was seeking to involve Britain and the United States in war?

But they do not stand alone. Yesterday the telegraph stated that a raid was apprehended on Detroit. Perhaps most readers passed it over as a mere invention. Such, we are sorry to say, is not the case. We do not know that Detroit is more menaced than any other lake port; but that a plot is on foot to make an attack on our neighbors of larger proportion than has hitherto been attempted, there is little doubt. Information has been received by our government to the effect that a regiment of Confederate soldiers have been detailed to find their way to Canada as best they may. Temporarily disbanded, they are to reach here by ones and twos; but they will know where and how to unite, and if the chance be given them they will strike a blow somewhere on the frontier.

Fortunately, having received timely warning, our government will make their task more difficult than they perhaps apprehend; but still the amount of success which has attended previous attempts is sufficient to show that their project is far from being impracticable. It is abundantly time that we were thoroughly upon our guard. The American people—and no one can be surprised at it—are much exercised at the depredations already committed.

They are armed and prepared. If an attack be made on any lake city, the probability is that the people will follow the marauders across the frontier, and the consequences that will ensue it is easy to conceive. The wish of the South for war between England and the North would, it is feared, be realized speedily. It is not to be expected that, under such circumstances, the pursuing force would conduct itself with the calmness of a judge on the bench. Wrongs would be committed on our fellow-subjects. Resistance would certainly be made, mutual recrimination and bitter feelings would arise, both parties would refuse redress, and war would follow. At any rate, we defy any one to imagine circumstances better calculated to bring about such a consummation.

It is currently reported, too, in the larger cities that these Southerners count upon the aid of the Fenians, both here and in the States. What truth there is in this we do not profess to know; but, at any rate, the object of both parties is identical. The Fenians see in war between the Republic and Great Britain a chance for what they call the "regeneration of Ireland." In

other words, they think they would be able to convert the "Gem
of the Sea" into a huge Donnybrook fair. The Southerner sees
in such a war an assurance of the independence of his own
country.

Their interests being identical, there is no reason why they
should not coalesce. We do not know that people generally are
aware of the length to which the law of nations allows a country
to go for the purpose of self-preservation. If these raids continue, we shall not only render it probable that Canada may be
invaded by United States troops, but we shall actually give the
United States a right so to do. It is to no purpose, we may
allege, that we have done all we can to stop the raids. Should
they be made, the fact will be proof either that we had not done
all we might or that we are incapable of preserving our neutral-
ity—either way giving the United States a very good plea to
justify pursuit of their foes into our territory.—*Toronto Globe.*

CHAPTER XVII.

A Thrilling Escape.

Prisoners Plan to Escape—Maj. Winston, of North Carolina, Maj. Stokes, of Virginia, Capt. McConnell, of Kentucky, and Capts. Robinson, Davis, and Stokes, of Virginia, Scale the Wall—The Thermometer Thirty-Three Degrees below Zero and the Wind Blowing a Gale—Capt. Stokes Recaptured—Making a Raid on a Farmer's Stable—A Troubled Dutchman—No Sleep for Sixty Hours—Going through Toledo, Ohio—Breaking through the Ice—Safe under the British Flag.

THERE was told in the *Southern Magazine* for October, 1872, the story of a daring escape from Johnson's Island that, from its intense interest and the long time since it was first related, is here reproduced. The author was permitted to get this story through the courtesy of Capt. James Dinkins, of New Orleans. The story, corroborated by the Sandusky *Register* of January 5, 1864, announced an escape of a few Confederate prisoners, and that the men would soon be caught, as they could be easily run down during the intensely cold weather that prevailed.

There were a few beautiful days during the latter part of December, 1863, but on the 30th it began to rain and was warm. On the 31st a gale quickly veered from south to west, and then to the north. It rained, sleeted, and snowed all within an hour or two. Then it grew too cold to snow; but the bitter north wind continued, and on the 1st day of January, 1864, the thermometer in Ohio ranged from twenty-five to thirty-five degrees below zero.

A guard at Camp Dennison, Ohio, was found frozen, and then the guards were relieved. In Tennessee men froze to death. How the guards endured such a night on Johnson's Island, with that terrible north wind howling down the lake, is inconceivable. The prisoners in the shanties or barracks, with blankets, nearly froze to death.

It was on this awful night that six desperate men scaled the fence and crossed over to the mainland. The story by one of the survivors is as follows:

Various efforts to bribe or persuade the sentinels were made, and some promised success; but not a prisoner had ever made his escape in this way. On one occasion, indeed, a gallant brigadier and four or five other officers did bribe a sentinel to let them over the walls; but after they had handed over the gold watch and stipulated sum of money a line of armed soldiers rose up around them and marched them back to prison, too poor to attempt bribing again. A great variety of plans to escape was suggested and attempted. Probably the one most assiduously followed was that of tunneling, or "gophering," out. Five or six men would form a party to escape. After selecting a "block" as near to the wall as possible, they went to work under the floors, digging with case or pocket knives, and any other instrument that came to hand. As but one man could work at a time, this took many days. Several parties escaped from the prison, but were invariably captured on the Island, as they had no means of crossing the water.

Such was the vigilance of the garrison and the nature of the difficulties to be overcome that every attempt at escape had failed up to January 1, 1864, except in the case of one young officer (from Baltimore, I think he was), who, with others, was sent into the hold of the island steamer after straw for bunks, and instead of returning went to the bottom of the straw, and that night, when the boat was lying at the wharf at Sandusky City, he cautiously crept forth and, unperceived, went away.

New Year's day, 1864, was extremely cold, as stated, and that night the mercury fell to thirty degrees below zero. As the cold north winds beat with cruel violence against the thin weatherboarding, the shivering prisoners, whose blood was unused to such rigorous climate, felt peculiarly sad. "If we could only get out of prison, we could leave the island on the ice; but it is too cold to live through the night in the open air." So thought many of the prisoners; but Major Stokes and Captains Stokes, Robinson, and Davis, of Virginia, Captain McConnell, of Kentucky, and Major Winston, of North Carolina, determined to risk a desperate attempt that night. They came to the conclusion that the boldest was the best way to get out of prison—viz., by scaling the wall. So a rude ladder was extemporized by tying with clotheslines the legs of a bench across a board at intervals of about three feet, to answer for steps. Of course this was all done after dark to prevent suspicion. Our means of escape ready, we made such preparations as we could to protect ourselves against the cold weather. Our chums were exceedingly kind in furnishing all the citizens' clothing they had. The next thing was, who should go first. The lot fell to Major Winston.

"The time has come; an affectionate good-by, kind friends," said Captain Davis and Major Winston, and promptly left the room, each placing himself flat on the frozen ground at his end of the ladder. Thus they dragged the ladder up the sewer to the corner of the building, thence across toward the "dead line." "Hold, Davis, lie low. Don't breathe; the new relief is coming," said some one. They double-quick on the wall and relieve the sentinel just above us, and double-quick on, the new sentinel walking slowly to and fro on his beat. With great caution we crawl on over the "dead line;" reaching the wall, we stand our ladder against it. Davis holds while Winston mounts. Davis screams in whispers and jerks at the feet of Winston, who, fearing they were discovered, stooped down and asked, "What is the matter?" "Get off my thumb!" The ladder proved to be about four feet too short. It was no place to be making a noise climbing over, for the sentinel would be sure to detect it. However, Major Winston succeeded in pulling himself over on the parapet as silently as possible; and after looking to see if he was seen by either sentinel on his right or left, he let himself down, first on a brace that supported the wall and then on a large stump, to the ground. Evading this line of sentinels (for there was one on the wall and one on the ground on the outside), he sat behind a large oak some fifteen steps from the wall. Captain Davis soon joined him; then came Captain Robinson; next came Captain McConnell, who very nearly lighted on the head of the man on the ground, but fortunately was not discovered. Finally this sentinel on the ground saw Captain Stokes, but not until he had reached the ground, and took him to be a Federal soldier returning from a henroost expedition, and so failed to fire on him when he refused to halt. I forgot to mention that Captain Stokes, failing to get a sufficiency of clothing, declined to leave. So our party was all out, and to prevent discovery Captain White very kindly took the ladder back to the dining room. Captain Stokes never got with the balance of the party, but ran acros the island and, after great exposure and suffering, crossed the ice to the Ohio shore and remained for several days in the neighborhood, when he was betrayed and taken back to prison and committed to a dungeon for refusing to tell who had escaped with him. His feet and hands were badly frosted; several of his fingers he lost. When the sentinel ordered Stokes to halt, the other four behind the tree ran across the island and, finding the ice firm, ventured on it. It was about one mile to Ottawa County, Ohio. About half-way across we found a large air hole, and in our heedless hurry came near being ingulfed; but fortunately that night a thin snow whitened the ice, while the water appeared black. After an exciting run, slipping, sliding, and tumbling, we reached the shore almost breathless. It was half-past ten o'clock, and we could hear the soldiers on the distant walls calling out the numbers of their posts and "All's well!" The officer of the day examined the wall with a lamp to see whether any Rebels had dared to saw or cut out, doubtless deeming it impossible to elude the vigilance of the sentinels on the wall.

A short rest and we started on our long journey, over fences and through fields, toward the west. We observed lights in all the houses we passed, which gave us some uneasiness, as it might be a system of signals to show that our escape had been discovered. We concluded, however, that in this cold climate it might be necessary to have fires all night. We had mapped out our course, and when we got to the Port Clinton road we took it. We found it much warmer in the woods. Two hours before day, foot-sore, chilled, and weary, we sought shelter in a straw stack, but it had been wet and frozen. We went to a farmer's stable, and, groping in the dark, found bridles and two large, fat horses. This last condition was quite a consideration to men who expected to ride rapidly and bareback. While the honest man slept and slumbered, each of his spirited animals bore away two Rebels. On they sped over the level country, passing farmhouses and woods. When many miles had fled behind us, just as streaks in the east ushered in another gray, cold morning, Captain McConnell stopped his horse and complained that he was freezing. Major Winston, who rode behind him, said, "I hope not." After going a little farther, McConnell repeated, "I am freezing," and fell from his horse, groaning like a dying man. Winston tried by chafing to revive him, but to no effect, as he had on too much clothing. We tied the bridles over the horses' necks and turned their heads homeward; from their eyes to the head was white with frozen breath. They were in a trot the last we saw of them. Poor McConnell was straightened up and pushed along until his frozen hinges got in working order again. Awhile before sunup we knocked at a door to warm and, if possible, breakfast. Mine host asked us in, and soon had the sheet-iron roaring. We passed ourselves off as land speculators walking over the country prospecting, but our jaded looks, and especially the dilapidated condition of our apparel, excited his curiosity. He "guessed" how we were doing this, and that and the other thing and a thousand things about which we were disposed not to be communicative. After such fatigue and exposure to cold, we would go to sleep in spite of ourselves. We gratified our friend's curiosity by reliefs, as soldiers say. Bread, strong coffee, and fat bacon were soon prepared and dispatched. We left the little man standing in the door wondering why land speculators should be too mean to pay for breakfast. Don't, kind reader, indulge the same reflection, for, understand, three little gold dollars were to defray the expense of four men three thousand miles.

For fear of being overtaken, we shunned the highways. Painful feelings stole over our minds when we reflected on balls and chains and dungeons, and possibly death, in case those irate guards should ever lay eyes on us again. Moreover, though horse-stealing may be punished by a long term in the Ohio penitentiary, yet the order of "Judge Lynch" is much more summary. Especially would this be the case with prowling Rebels; nor, we may presume, would our jurors be very inquisitive as to whether we had stolen the horse or a ride. The frost told badly on our ears, fingers, feet, and noses, though the skin did not peel off till we reached Canada. We heard large oaks bursting about in the woods, I suppose from the moisture in the trees crystallizing.

In the evening of January 2 we stopped at an Irishman's for rest. His person constituted his family, and he was not disturbed at our tumbling and snoring around his hearth and on the bed. Awhile before sundown we wended our way to a troubled looking Dutchman's. We exhausted ourselves in endeavoring to talk his countence smooth, so we might venture to ask for supper, but apparently to no effect. Finally we asked: "Well, sir, can we get supper?" He replied, "I'll ask my woman," and addressed a question in his knotty idiom to her, who was ironing at the other side of the room. We had observed that her face seemed to be the counterpart of her lord's—his was troubled, hers the troubler. This parody on the gentler sex growled in tones of distant thunder, "Nix!" The poor husband cowed back to the fire, and informed us that it was not possible to get supper that night. We often afterwards thought of the poor Dutchman in the woods. We left him to the tender companionship of his wife, and pursued our footpath through woods, over marshy country. At ten o'clock we stopped to warm in a village. The people were stirring about, dropping in and going out; we spurred our drooping spirits to appear lively, too. We were not land speculators this time, but wood choppers going to the pineries in Michigan. Our appearance bore out our calling. After sitting and talking awhile, a soldier came in and joined the conversation. We thought our time had come, but tried to betray no uneasiness; but we expected every moment to see a squad of soldiers file in. To our great relief, the soldier proved to be on a furlough. The cold weather was the general topic. We carelessly observed that those Rebs of Johnson's Island must be enjoying the cool lake breeze. From their comments we concluded that they had heard nothing of our escape. We journeyed on, and a little after midnight Captain McConnell stopped at a house to get some soda for the heartburn. Several hours he continued to grow worse; before sunrise he gave out and begged to be left at the next house. We placed him on the doorstep and gave him one-fourth of our money, and with much sorrow parted, requesting him not to knock at the door till we were out of sight. Since the war we learn that he recovered in a day or so, and went to the next depot and traded off his watch for a ticket for Detroit. While on the cars he saw a man eying him suspiciously, and determined to leave the train when it stopped again. As he did so the detective patted him on the shoulder and said, "Let's go back to Johnson's Island." Of course he had to comply.

Our party, now reduced to three, stopped for breakfast at a house half a mile beyond the next village. We had traveled twenty-four hours on one breakfast, and would not be hard to satisfy; but the prospect did look a little discouraging when we saw that the landlord and lady and nine children all slept and ate in one room, "with no visible means of support." However, the brisk woman raised the lid of a box in the corner, and was not long in setting before us corn bread, fat bacon, and gravy. We divided our mites with him—I forget in what proportion, but he seemed satisfied. We followed the railroad all that day, January 3.

Near night we called at a hut where lived an old Irishman and his little grandson. To a request, the old man replied that he could not accommodate us that night with either bed or bread. A view of his surroundings had almost brought us to the same conclusion; but we were so tired and hungry, and, moreover, it appeared to be a safe retreat, so we asked almost against hope for entertainment. At every settlement shelter was sought. The houses were generally occupied by Germans, who from their bad English we thought had been but a short time in this country. They seemed easily frightened. We knocked at the door, where light and human voices gave some hope that rest might at least be found. They became silent. After listening awhile at the pounding on the door, an inmate ventured to inquire, "Vocht dat?" To our importunity for lodging they sternly replied, "Nix." Some way farther on we sat beside the road to rest in the deep forest. The old oaks, whose giant arms must have defied the storms of centuries, groaned in the cold night winds. We sat and shivered and thought of the loved ones far away in the Sunny South. Extreme exhaustion and feverishness caused shapeless images to flit through our minds. The glands in our groins had swollen nearly to the size of a hen's egg. We had been in motion almost continuously forty-eight hours, and except an hour the first evening, our eyes had not closed in sleep for sixty hours. Toward midnight one of our party asked admittance to a house larger than common on the road. To our great relief, the door was opened and we were invited to the fire. A few questions convinced us that we were in the hands of a "down-Easter." He seemed to suspect something; asked where we were from. "New Bedford, Mass.," replied Captain Robinson. "Ah! that's my old home," and he began by naming different residents of that old place to try Captain R. But the Captain, who had been many years in the whaling service, and of course had at least visited New Bedford, was posted. He soon lighted us upstairs to bed. All three huddled together. We retired quite uneasy, for might not this man have heard by telegraph of our escape, and early next morning cause our arrest? After a few hours' sleep we slipped into our clothes and, passing down through his room, gave him to understand that it would be quite agreeable to share his hospitality longer, but we must reach Toledo in time for the up train. We knew he was then not prepared to follow us, and would make arrangements to overhaul us at the depot if he attempted anything. We crossed the river into Toledo about daylight, and were in time to join the early workmen going to their places of labor.

After leaving the city we abandoned the railroad and bore away to the lake shore road. Some long-legged boys were skating down the old canal; the ease, the grace, and the rapidity of their movements appeared to be caused by the wind. We remarked to each other that if we could adopt that mode of travel as skillfully as those boys we would not fear pursuit. At noon our treasurer, Captain Davis, purchased some cheese and crackers at a country store, the first food we had eaten, I think, for thirty hours.

That night, January 4, we passed through Monroe, during a snowstorm, and met people coming from church. We had walked a long day's journey, but it was ten o'clock before we could find a hospitable roof. This was a French-Canadian, who had moved to Michigan a short time previously. We tumbled all three together on a pallet and were very soon asleep; had no supper, and left early next morning before breakfast. After going about a mile Captain Robinson discovered that he had left his pocketbook, probably on the pallet. It contained papers which showed that he was an officer in the Confederate army. Major Winston went back to the house and the good woman handed him the pocketbook, apparently unopened. Davis and Winston had left all their papers in prison, and were provoked that Robinson had not done the same.

We led people to believe that Detroit was our home. We met an officer going to a depot which we had just passed, and we continued the Detroit road until he was out of sight; we then turned to the right, fifteen miles from that city, and made for

Trenton, a village on the Detroit River near its entrance into Lake Erie. About noon we stopped at a house for something to eat; the person we saw was a woman, who invited us in to seats. I must stop to remark that we all observed to each other that she wore the sweetest expression we had almost ever seen. She was not pretty, nearly middle-aged, and rather pale; but she had evidently gone through enough of this world's trials in some form to mellow her soul. Her conversation evinced the same. She gave us a piece of light bread half as large as a man's head and a good portion of butter. We sat on a log on the roadside and enjoyed our lunch very much, as we had not eaten anything since the cheese and bread twenty-four hours before.

Two miles from Trenton we stepped into an old man's house, ostensibly to warm, but really to make inquiries concerning the crossing of the river. The old gentleman said eighty winters had passed his head, but he had never seen such a cold snap before. We changed our brogue to the nasal twang of New England; but not effectually, as he nearly threw us off our guard by asking, "Are you not from the South?" Captain Davis quickly gave some Eastern town as our home. He replied: "You talk like Southerners." After eliciting what information we could without raising suspicion, we resumed our weary journey. We were delighted to find on the snow a half biscuit, dropped, as we supposed, by children from Trenton school. This was divided, as our appetites were quite keen. We soon picked up, in this way, quite a little sack. Just at dark we entered Trenton, passed down a street, and jumped on the ice. A man watering his horse through the ice seemed astonished at our haste, but said nothing. The ice at first seemed smooth as glass. Captain Robinson was so stunned by a fall that he scarcely recovered that night. We took it to be one mile across to Fighting Island, and two miles across the channel of the river. Briers and marshes made our progress on the island quite slow. We passed one or two dwellings, but were not disposed to stop, as we felt that our troubles were almost ended.

On the ice again, and now for Canada! After going about a mile the ice became exceedingly troublesome. A storm a day or two before had broken and blown it about in waves. We clambered over the broken blocks, slipping and sliding at every pull. Major Winston felt the ice giving away and remarked that we were nearing an air hole, and as he turned one foot broke through. Captain Robinson endeavored to get back, but both feet broke through, and he barely saved himself by leaning over on firm ice. Davis and Winston kneeled over and pulled him out; almost instantly his trousers were frozen stiff. This treacherous hole had well-nigh cut short our earthly pilgrimage.

Had we gone under, the current would have washed us under the firm ice. The dark water in these places had before marked such contrast with the snow.

Our situation was a critical one in the extreme. We would not return to the United States side and be captured; a step farther was fate; to remain in the sweeping northern wind equally fatal. Our only chance was to feel our way around this dangerous place. To avoid turning back in our confusion, Davis placed himself about ten feet in advance of the others, and under their direction made toward the north star. Poor Captain Robinson was so worn out and stunned by his fall that he threw his arm over Winston's shoulder, who bore him on. When we felt that we could not dispense with our beacon, clouds suddenly shut out every star. Just then a light immediately before us in Canada rekindled our hopes. Davis said: "If we ever get there, I will kiss the ground." Near the shore another airhole obstructed our way. We concluded, after going up and down the beach trying for firm ice till we grew desperate, to run across one at a time; and if one broke in, the others could save him. The ice did not let us in, but cracked. We were safe!

A few steps drew us to the door of a pleasant woman, a Mrs. Warrior, half French and half Indian. She was glad to see us, gave us some pies—all she had cooked—and laid a pallet for us before the fire and near a large stove, both of which were kept roaring all night. The reader can somewhat appreciate our feelings of relief when he recollects that this was ten o'clock of the 5th of January, four days and four nights to an hour since we left the prison. In these four days and four nights we had eaten two regular meals and three snacks, counting the biscuit in the snow. Above all, we were safe under the protection of the British flag.

We rose the next morning stiff but refreshed. Young Warrior and our party walked on the beach before breakfast. Captain Davis, pointing in the direction of our previous night's path over the broken ice, remarked: "That was a bad place for people to cross." Warrior remarked: "People never cross there." When we beheld the broken ice and contemplated the ship channel slightly covered with treacherous spray, we shuddered. I suppose that any soldier who spent four years in active service can refer to scenes of thrilling interest, but I am ready to declare that this night's trials on the ice were the severest of my experience. In the battle we are generally in action; there is enthusiasm and sometimes exhilaration. But now the warmth of our very nature was chilled. No sight or sound cheered us, dark clouds obscured the stars, and all was deathlike stillness save the whisking of the freezing winds among the sharply broken ice.

At breakfast we were informed that some refugee Kentuckians resided near Malden, one mile down the river. Captain Robinson's and Davis's feet being sore from frost, Major Winston visited these people to get some information from them. They occupied a large brick building, and were three or four in number, strong, hale-looking young men, and apparently men of wealth, but the meanest Union and Confederate soldiers they met on the fields of Chickamauga or Gettysburg were too good to speak to the craven spirits who were forward in proclaiming their love of a country whose liberties they were too cowardly to defend. They were gloomy birds, croaking over the prospects for Confederate people in Canada, and remarked that they would have remained on Johnson's Island. Maj. Winston indignantly returned to his companions. The good widow had two horses hitched to a sleigh to take us to Windsor, thirteen miles up the river, without charge; and well so, for we had nothing with which to remunerate her. The trip was delightful to wearied pedestrians, gliding over the snow, and a good portion of the way on the river itself. We found Mr. Hiron, to whose hotel we had been recommended, a fat, chuffy Englishman, his appearance bearing marks of good living and his countenance of a good man. We honestly told him of our situation; the Federal armies between us and our homes; we had no money, and the prospects of getting any very gloomy; but we assured him, under the circumstances, that if he could take us for some days we would work (laborers there earning good wages) and repay him if we failed in getting means otherwise. He seemed to be touched with our story, and made us welcome to his house during our pleasure. We were much surprised and pleased to find the Hon. C. L. Vallandigham, then in exile, stopping at the same house. He invited us to his room several times, and drank toasts to our distressed South. He said that he hoped the war might soon end and peace make us all happy again, etc. One of our party went a little farther and proposed "General Lee and the success of the Southern arms." He shook his head and put down his glass, saying, "No, no! in that event the Union is gone forever," and in the strains of the most touching eloquence gave his trials in his struggling for the Union as our fathers left it to us. He wanted fraternal feelings restored, but said that war was not calculated to do it. He was afraid of the means; the same sword that conquers the South might subjugate the North as well. "For this cause," he exclaimed, "I am here to-day, an exile from home, family, country." That man a traitor?

Major Winston wrote to a merchant in New York requesting a check for two hundred dollars. He promptly replied that he did not know or care to know how he got to Canada; he was

only too glad to serve a kinsman of his old friend in North
Carolina, with whom, in former days, he had large dealings.
Major Winston received the check in a few days, and went five
hundred miles, to Montreal, to solicit means among other friends,
refugees and Canadian sympathizers in that city, to bring the rest
of our party that far on their way to the South. He arrived at
the Donegaba House, in Montreal, a little before day, and registered from North Carolina, retired to sleep, but before breakfast received several visitors, and preparations for sending for
his comrades were soon made, and they, together with some of
General Morgan's scattered command, arrived next morning.
We remained in the city about ten days, and probably in all that
time did not dine or take tea at our hotel more than twice, being
invited out. People were exceedingly kind. When the time for
our departure came, ladies and gentlemen went with us to the
depot and gave us a purse of thirteen hundred and fifty dollars
in gold. On our way down the St. Lawrence we stopped over a
day at Point Levi, opposite Quebec, to visit the fortifications of
Quebec. They appeared indeed to be the Gibraltar of America.
We went one hundred and ninety miles farther down the river,
to Riviere du Loup, all the way from Montreal by rail, as the
river was frozen. At the Riviere du Loup we started on a
long journey around Maine, through New Brunswick and Nova
Scotia, to Halifax—five hundred miles. This part of our trip
we traveled on sleighs. We went by Little Grand Falls down the
St. John River, many miles on the ice, to St. John's City. In
our eagerness to get home we remained in Halifax only long
enough to witness the opening of Parliament, and to be honored
with a dinner at the rooms of some club. We took passage on
Her Majesty's mail steamer the Alpha to St. George's, Bermuda.
As we sailed out of the port the face of the earth was white
with the thick covering of snow. A few days and nights, and
we were winding our way among the hills and the cliffs into the
harbor of St. George's. Here early spring greeted us in all her
loveliness; children were picnicking on the greensward, and
lambs and calves nibbling about on the grassy hills.

In a day or two the North Carolina blockade runner, the
Advance, was signaled. Here she comes bounding over the bil-
lows, bearing aloft the beautiful banner of the South—the white
flag of peace, if we could; but if not, the fiery cross in the corner
was for a sign that we were not afraid of war. The steamer
made a short stay, and then we were on our journey again. We
saw many ships and steamers, but we were quite shy of them
until we could see that they were not armed. Indeed, there was
but one feeling that detracted from the pleasure of this trip: we
felt that we had stolen something. But, fortunately, we did not

fall in with any of the ironclads till we got in the network of the blockaders; and it was dark then—just before day. Our good and faithful steamer glided slowly among them, tacking this way and that. At one time she stopped and backed out of an encounter with a grim old warship, apparently asleep, not many waves ahead. Just as the day began to dawn the captain said, "Let her slide!" She moved on up the bay at the rate of ten knots. We were safe. Not yet! We strike on a sand bar within the easy range of a blockading squadron. Every effort to get off was unavailing. We signaled distress to Fort Fisher. News was flashed to Wilmington that the Advance must be captured or sunk when it grew a little lighter. The lifeboat began to drop into the water, carrying the escaped prisoners to shore. Just then the steamer floated off and, going around the sand bar, made for Fort Fisher. Now we are safe.

The three points, as speakers say, of my narrative were scaling the walls, crossing the Detroit River, and running the blockade at Wilmington; but the greatest of the three was the crossing of the river.

CHAPTER XVIII.

Plain Living at Johnson's Island.

The Story of Lieutenant Cunningham—Eighteen Months a Prisoner at Johnson's Island—An Interesting Story Cleverly Told—The Lights and Shades of Prison Life—Pierson's Ten Commandments—Nothing in the Lord's Prayer to Cover the Emergency—Getting Home at Last—A Hugging Match.

THE following story is told by Lieutenant Cunningham, and appeared in the *Century Magazine:*

In giving my experience as a prisoner of war for eighteen months, sixteen of which were spent in the military prison on Johnson's Island, in Lake Erie, I shall confine myself strictly to an individual experience, or to such events as came under my immediate observation. As I kept no diary during my imprisonment, I must necessarily trust entirely to my memory, giving such facts as are indelibly impressed there and which are susceptible of proof. When the least doubt as to the correctness of a statement has arisen in my mind, I have omitted it entirely. I shall endeavor to tell my story fairly and truthfully, without comment or criticism, assisted by the feeling that a quarter of a century has removed all vestige of bitterness.

I enlisted from St. Helena Parish, La., in a company commanded by Capt. James H. Wingfield, which on its arrival in New Orleans was assigned to the Fourth Louisiana Regiment, commanded by Col. Henry W. Allen, afterwards brigadier general and later Governor of Louisiana. He died self-exiled in the City of Mexico. During the first year of service our regiment was distributed along the Mississippi Sound, and we despaired of active participation, fearing that the war would close before we could contribute our share toward a successful result; but this idea was dispelled at Shiloh. There were several firmly rooted ideas rudely shaken up before we got through.

From Shiloh to Vicksburg, thence with Breckinridge to Baton Rouge, it was in May, 1863, that I found myself a lieutenant in the Ninth Louisiana Battalion, doing duty in the trenches at Port Hudson, Miss.

For nearly two months we successfully resisted all efforts of the Federal troops to effect an entrance. But the end was near.

Short rations and constant and fatiguing duty in the trenches were doing their work, and the fall of Vicksburg simply hastened the inevitable. We were constantly on duty, and our food was neither savory nor plentiful. And right here I wish to be placed on record by stating that the patient mule as an eatable is a pronounced failure and no addition to an army bill of fare.

I think that it was on the morning of July 7 that an unusual commotion in the enemy's camp excited our curiosity and sharpened our vigilance. Shouting, yelling, band-playing, and the wildest hurrahs showed that good news had come to them, which, if true, meant the reverse to us. It was good news—too good to keep—and we soon learned that Vicksburg had fallen. There was not a man in the camp that did not realize the meaning of this, and we were anxious to know what surrender meant for us.

When the white flags went up on the works, the space between the lines was soon filled by the men from both armies, and "Yanks" and "Rebs" fraternized in so friendly and amicable a spirit that it required some little effort to realize that these men had only the day previous been shooting at one another on purpose.

They now became our hosts, and invitations to supper were freely extended by the "boys in blue" and as freely accepted by the "boys in rags." I do not think that a single invitation was declined. I did full justice to the first square meal that had fallen to my lot in many days. They were invited into our lines, with many courteous inquiries as to why they had not come over sooner, with the equally courteous reply that they had started to do so on several occasions.

In a day or two the Union forces took formal possession of the place; and as, drawn up in line, we faced each other, the difference in the personal appearance of the men was strongly marked and most decidedly in favor of the "Yanks." As our men were not dressed with any degree of uniformity, they presented none of the pomp of war in their appearance, no two being dressed exactly alike, and strongly suggesting the nursery-rhyme beggars that caused the dogs to bark, "for some were in rags and some in tags;" but the velvet gowns were conspicuous by their absence. In common with many others who followed the fortunes of the Confederacy, it has been my fate at times to find my wardrobe in a most unsatisfactory condition; so much so that on several occasions, prompted by my innate modesty, I have backed up against some friendly fence or wall whenever a lady came in sight.

The terms of surrender paroled the noncommissioned officers and the privates. The officers were allowed to retain their side arms, and were to be held as prisoners of war. This was a gloomy outlook, but we were much relieved by the assurance that an early exchange was only a degree or so removed from a certainty—not too early, you know, but early. We philosophically accepted the situation, which, as there was no other course left open, was much the best thing to do under the circumstances. Besides, we felt that we had well earned a short vacation and were entitled to some rest and recreation after our arduous labors.

During the latter part of the siege I was in the habit of visiting the hospital, where some members of my company lay wounded or sick, and carried with me some of the corn beer brewed in the camp and much relished by the convalescents. On a cot near one of these lay a young Union soldier badly wounded in the hip. He was a mere boy and much too young to follow the fortunes of an army. I became interested in the little fellow. He soon drew his rations of beer with the rest, and we became fast friends. Standing on the transport which was to convey us to New Orleans, a Federal officer mentioned that a Union soldier wished to see me in the cabin. Going to him, I found my little hospital friend; and, at his request, I assisted in removing him from a stretcher to a berth. Asking me to sit with him awhile, he told me that in all probability we would be sent North, and should I at any time find myself free, either by escape or by parole, by all means to make my way to his home and be assured of any help he or his could give me. He gave me his address, and at the time I thought but little of the matter. But many times before I reached Dixie this slighted invitation weighed as heavily as a crime, for the opportunity came later on and I let it pass.

On our arrival in New Orleans we were assigned quarters in different parts of the city, the larger portion, myself among the number, being quartered in the customhouse building, where our treatment, rations, and bestowal were all that could be desired. We shook off the mud of the trenches with the clothes that held it, and, thanks to our friends in the city, were well clad, and dainty food was the order of the day. If such was to be the existence of a prisoner of war, it seemed strange that whole armies did not allow themselves to be captured. Visitors were admitted to the reception room, and, giving the name of the officer they wished to see, he was immediately sent for. No restrictions nor limit seemed to be placed on the number or value of the presents given us, and even the confinement was broken by frequent leaves of absence from the building. Visits were paid in the city, though we never remained out all night unless "chaperoned" by some Federal officer; and it was pleasant association with some of these that opened our eyes to the fact that, when not engaged in trying to kill you, a "Yank" was a first-rate fellow. You see, we knew so little of each other before the war. So pleasant were our surroundings, and so changed our mode of life, as compared with the discomforts of camp and trench, that we rather hoped that the exchange might be delayed yet a little longer and leave us in our fools' paradise. I do not think our wishes carried any weight in the matter; but we had our will—the exchange was delayed.

We had been occupants of the customhouse about two months when we were informed that we were to be sent North for exchange. By this time most of us were in full citizens' regalia, and uniforms were the exception. Side arms were disposed of—few carrying them North—being distributed as souvenirs or left for safe-keeping, and in some instances given as presents to Federal officers. Preparations were made for departure, adieus exchanged, and in some cases simply *au revoir,* as we expected to return by way of New Orleans; and one day about the middle of September some three hundred well-dressed Confederates took passage on the steamship Evening Star, bound for New York City, as different outwardly from the "Rebs" who left Port Hudson as the butterfly from the grub. Many, many times in the near future how we missed the grub days and wished them back again!

Nothing of importance occurred on the voyage save a seven days' fight with seasickness.

We found waiting on our arrival two lines of guards extending from the gangway, and after an hour or two I started ashore, certainly not expecting that I would not be allowed to pass beyond the limits, with no other desire than to be on shore once more. I most certainly did not dream of escape. As I passed quietly along, dressed in civilian garb, I was roughtly ordered by a voice shod in a rich Milesian brogue to "Get out of that," the owner of the voice stepping aside at the same time to allow me to pass. I could scarcely think the man in earnest, and looked at him to see if he meant it, and was fully convinced of his sincerity by the manner in which he emphasized his request with his bayonet. Passing to the rear, I got out of that; and walking into the streets of New York, I found myself a free man. But now that I was free, of what use was my freedom? I was entirely without friends, not even an acquaintance, in a strange city. I was too well dressed to play the rôle of beggar without exciting suspicion, all the more that my absence would be noted.

My funds were painfuly limited, so much so that my last dollar deserted me at Sandusky. I had not the least idea of what the future had in store for me, and could judge nothing save by the past, which carried with it only pleasant recollections. The invitation of my little hospital friend was duly considered and dismissed. We were brought here to be exchanged. In a few weeks I would be once more in Dixie. Why escape at all?

I hurried back, and had to explain that I belonged on board of the steamer before I was allowed to pass. On rejoining my companions I mentioned the incident, and two of them tried the experiment. One reached home in safety, as I afterwards learned. The fate of the other I do not know. During the long, weary months of confinement that followed, I had ample leisure to curse my mistake, and, though hungry, cold, and sick, I cannot remember the time when I had not vitality enough left to improve the opportunity. Even at this late date, when thinking it over, I feel that I am fairly entitled to share the reputation of "Thompson's colt." After a few days on Governor's Island, we were informed as to our final destination; this, we were given to understand, was merely preliminary to an exchange. We were to be sent to Johnson's Island, Lake Erie.

Our route lay over the Erie Railroad, and we made the trip on parole. The guards placed at each door of our coach were not for our comfort only, as we were objects of marked curiosity during the trip, and would have been overrun with visitors had not admittance been refused. At the different stations we mingled freely with the people on the platform; and found them, with few exceptions, courteous but inquisitive. We were, no doubt, a disappointing lot. There was nothing in our apparel to mark the Rebel soldier, and as we mingled with the crowd surprise was freely expressed that we were not as their fancy painted us, though just what shape that fancy took I never learned.

The ladies, as was the case both North and South, were intensely patriotic, and read us severe and no doubt salutary lectures on the evil of our ways, which were submissively and courteously received and duly pondered.

There was one question that you could safely wager would be asked by five out of ten, and that was: "Do you honestly think you are right?" This conundrum was offered to me so often that where time allowed, being in President Lincoln's country, I answered in President Lincoln's style by stating that it "reminded me," and told them of the couple who took their bridal trip on an ocean steamer, with the usual result. As the husband would return from sundry trips to the rail of the vessel his young wife would inquire: "Reginald, darling, are you sick?" To which he at last replied: "Good heavens! Rebecca, do you think I am doing this for fun?"

Sandusky reached, just across the bay we caught the first glimpse of our future quarters, the military prison on Johnson's Island. Up to this time we had been kindly treated in many respects—far better than we had hoped for or expected. Our intercourse with the Union soldiers so far had been confined to men who had served in the field, and was uniformly of a pleasant nature. I am sure that the men both North and South will bear me out in the assertion that as soon as your enemy captured you he became your friend, as far as consistent with his duty.

We were soon to learn the distinction between front and rear. In order to know how to treat prisoners, you should have a hand in capturing them.

Leaving the ferry, which brought us across the bay, we walked into the office, where we were registered and searched, all money being surrendered and receipted for. Its equivalent in the prison was represented by sutler's checks, a form of currency answering all purposes until, owing to the restrictions imposed upon us, it ceased to be of service.

All formalities completed, the big gates swung open to admit us, and, greeted on all sides with cries of "Fresh fish! Fresh fish!" we entered and joined our comrades—"not lost, but gone before." And so sometime in October, 1863, the writer took what at that time he supposed to be but temporary quarters in a Northern prison. His stay was prolonged far beyond what he expected, and it is the story of a sixteen months' forced visit that he tells as best he can without embellishment, assuring the reader that, while some few may have fared better, his experience is that of the majority and does not represent the worst.

Curiosity has never prompted me to revisit the Island, and I have been told that there now remains nothing by which it could be recognized by its former occupants. [Note.—Lieutenant Cunningham here gave a description of the prison on Johnson's Island, which is left out, as it has been described previously in this volume.—Editor.]

It was the severity of the winters that told so heavily on us. Many were from the extreme South, and some had never seen a fall of snow. Coming from New Orleans, and wearing such clothes as were adapted to its climate in the month of September, the first day of January, 1864, was a revelation.

On that day the thermometer marked twenty-five degrees below zero, and the writer was not more warmly clad than when now on a summer's night in that same city he writes these lines. So intense was the cold that the sentries were taken from the walls, and the ice king kept watch and ward for Uncle Sam. The big gate could have been left open and few of the prisoners would have taken the chance of escape, in view of almost certain death. The entire winters were bitter cold, and from our exposed position I am satisfied that the cold was much more intense than on the mainland.

Occasional gales would now and then sweep across the Island, testing the strength of our buildings, and it was during one of these that two officers took refuge in a dry well as affording the greatest protection against the storm. One of these, on being asked by the other to offer up a prayer for their preservation, replied that he was acquainted only with the Lord's Prayer, and there was nothing in that to cover the emergency.

The bay around Johnson's Island was guarded by the United States steamer Michigan, which, when the season permitted, lay within a few hundred yards of the shore. Other steamers, loaded with excursionists, would occasionally run close in, prompted by curiosity, and taunt us by their shouts and jeers. Their favorite pastime was, or seemed to be, the singing of patriotic songs, which was admissible, and I could find no reasonable cause of complaint as to the sopranos and contraltos; but when basso-profundos and baritones musically expressed their intention to "rally 'round the flag," I thought of thousands of Northern men already engaged in that occupation far to the front, who, if not so vocalistic, were at least equally patriotic.

I was assigned to Block 11, Room 3, and was advised at once to study "Pierson's Ten Commandments." The first eight of this decalogue, with the exception of No. 6, referred to matters of police and fatigue duty only, but the rest were of a different character and were well worth committing to memory in order to avoid serious accidents. [The prison rules mentioned by Lieutenant Cunningham as "Pierson's Ten Commandments" are given elsewhere.—EDITOR.]

Thirty feet from the fence was the "dead line" referred to in Order No. 9. On the north side the sinks were situated, in the rear of the buildings, about ten feet from the fence, and consequently they lay twenty feet within the dead line. It was on this side of the inclosure that Capt. J. D. Meadows, of the First Alabama Regiment, was shot by the guard on Post 13 and severely wounded.

I have read articles in which the terrible dead line was held up and denounced as brutal and inhuman, but I doubt if there existed an inclosed military prison North or South that did not possess this distinctive feature. Its use was to prevent prisoners crowding against the fence, and I do not remember that we regarded it in any other light than a very necessary precaution. We knew that the sentinel was required to shoot without warning the prisoner who crossed that line, and we felt that most of them were willing to do so; hence, if we violated Order No. 9, we were liable to be killed under Order No. 10. The matter rested entirely with ourselves.

We had to bear evils of a far more serious nature, over which we had no control, and such trifles as dead lines worried us but little. The time I was at Johnson's Island there were about twenty-five hundred in confinement, and the quarters were well crowded. The sleeping arrangements consisted of bunks in tiers of three, each furnished with the usual army bedtick stuffed with straw, and far superior to the earth and ditch which had been our beds for months previous to our capture. The crowded condition of the prison necessitated that two men should occupy each bunk, which had the redeeming feature in winter that the occupants were sheltered by two blankets instead of one.

It was an evil genius that selected my bunk, for it lay just under the roof, and sometimes the snow, finding its way in, would cover me like a wet blanket. I have a vivid recollection of the result in the form of an attack of lumbago that sent my forehead to my knees and put it beyond my power to assume the position of a soldier for many days. With the thermometer well down in the tube, scantiest of bedclothing, and no fire, you can well imagine what portion of "tired nature's sweet restorer" fell to our lot. Under the circumstances, it is not strange that pulmonary and rheumatic complaints should have prevailed to a great extent. I know of one man who is now, after the lapse of twenty-five years, chained to his chair, hopelessly crippled—a souvenir of his imprisonment.

Rations and wood were brought in daily, and to each mess were delivered an ax and a bucksaw. These were collected and taken out each night; and should any mess fail to return them, no wood was brought in until the missing tools were given up. This happened once during my stay; but private enterprise, looking to the escape of a few, had to give way to the public weal, and the ax and saw showed up. Details from the mess were made each day for police and fatigue duty; and the most fatiguing duty, as I remember it, was sawing wood—not that there was so much to saw, but the most of us were not used to it. Shortly after reveille a noncommissioned officer and guard entered the room and we were mustered for roll call. Sometimes the guard would bring us the newspaper, giving double-leaded information, ofttimes revised and corrected in subsequent issues.

After roll call we were free to kill the monotony of confinement as best we could, all parts of the inclosure being for our use except the north side and beyond the dead line. "Retreat" sent us to our quarters, and, knowing the penalty, we were strict observers of this rule. It was for an alleged violation of this rule that Lieutenant Gibson, of the Eleventh Arkansas, lost his life. He was visiting some friends in a neighboring block and, hearing "retreat" sounded, started to his room and was about to enter, when the sentinel ordered him back to his quarters. He endeavored to explain that he was then going into his room, but the explanation was evidently unsatisfactory. The sentinel fired and killed him.

The only antidote to the terrible ennui of prison life was occupation, and very few were without employment of some kind. In fact, during the latter part of our stay it was an infallible sign of surrender when the men became listless and no longer cared for the things which had heretofore been either their work or their recreation. Workbenches sprang up in every available spot; rings were made of gutta-percha buttons; rulers and oyster shells were transformed into charms, rings, and breastpins, equal in artistic design and execution to the best specimens of professional handiwork. In one instance, with nothing better than the wood pile on which to draw for material, one of the men fashioned a violin; while a four-bladed penknife, complete in all its parts, attested the skill of one of my messmates. Articles manufactured by the prisoners were in demand and found a ready sale, the medium of traffic being the prison officials, who sold them on the out side, returning the proceeds to the manufacturer, who was enabled to better his condition until such time as money lost its purchasing power. I do not remember that a visitor was ever allowed inside the prison walls; but I do recall that a wife once obtained permission to visit the Island, and, standing on the outside of the "pen," was allowed to look at her husband as he stood on the landing of the stairs of Block 2. I do not think that the termination of the war would have been delayed five seconds had they taken him under guard to the wife or allowed her to enter the prison.

Books and newspapers were admitted, after due examination, and with many of us formed our sole refuge. Classes were opened and studies resumed or new ones begun. A first-class minstrel band, known as the "Rebellonians," gave entertainments from time to time and played to crowded houses. All the popular airs of the day were conscripted and the words rewritten to express our peculiar views of the situation. The dramatic element had its innings, and I think that Peeler's "Battle of Gettysburg" had the unprecedented run of three weeks, at one performance per week. We never succeeded in putting on a first-class ballad. These performances took place in the afternoon; for, as before stated, the guards had very pronounced views as to our being absent from quarters after retreat.

All letters to and from the prisoners were opened and examined by our jailers, and if found in order were stamped with "Examined" and the initials of the man who had read the letter and passed it. Our correspondence was limited only as to the number per diem, space, expression of political sentiment, and ability to pay postage. With these exceptions, there were no restrictions. We were allowed to write on one side of a half sheet of paper, and our correspondents were subjected to the same rules.

I have received notifications that letters addressed to me were held because they violated this rule, and have been instructed to inform the writers accordingly. To be placed on the black list meant stoppage of our mail; and, in order to realize the severity of the punishment, you must put yourself in the position of a prisoner with letters as your only communication with the outside world. It must have been from this cause that I acquired a terse, jerky style that has clung to me ever since. Sentimentally, "cleanliness is indeed next to godliness;" practically, it is conducive to health and comfort, and we tried to enforce its unwritten laws. When a "fresh fish" was assigned to our room, he was initiated by being required to take a bath and to boil his clothes, long experience in army matters having proved that this was the only way of getting rid of that energetic little pest known as the *Pediculus vestimenti.* It was one of the species crawling on a lady's bonnet string that suggested an ode to the poet Burns.

As our clothing gradually grew worse soap and water seemed to lose their powers, and we resorted to dyeing such garments as needed renovation, using for that purpose a liquid dye. You simply emptied the vial into a pot of boiling water, immersed the garment to be operated on, and *voila!* One of my mess was a Lieutenant Blank, who knew some things very well; and he, wishing to improve the appearance of an old flannel shirt, sought out the hospital steward, who sold the liquid, and put the question: "What is it you fellows dye with here?"

The steward, supposing that he had some inquisitive statistician on his hands, answered that they died of different things, but thought that pneumonia had the call just then. "Well," said Blank, "give me a two-bit bottle." Of course the story leaked out, and the lieutenant ran the gantlet. Some mornings afterwards Blank mounted a chair and made a speech. In crude but unmistakable words, and with a depth of meaning in their utterance, he announced that the next man who said "pneumonia" in his hearing would have him to whip. Most of us, knowing the difficulty of the undertaking, were so much on our guard that we did not dare to cough or to give in any way the least suggestion of pulmonary complaint, lest we should have cause to regret our indiscretion.

Retreat found us in our quarters, and at 10 P.M. taps extinguished our lights. I have heard that for a violation of this rule the guards would often fire into the block. Believing this to be true, I can vouch for its having happened at least once during my stay. It was during the evening that we gathered around the stove or the long table and discussed matters of interest (the war and the absorbing question of exchange), swapped yarns (some of the number being exceptionally good *raconteurs*), or listened while some "Truthful James" taxed our credulity to the verge of courtesy.

And here, lest I forget it, I desire to apologize in behalf of our stove. I have known it, when doing its best, to fail to melt the frost on the window panes, less than eight feet away.

"Taps" sent us to our bunks, except such night owls as grouped together and conversed in undertones. Sometimes a voice would start in song, another and another would join, and though neither voices nor execution were of a high order, the wet eyelids of many a homesick "Reb" would pay tribute to "Home, Sweet Home" or "Only Waiting." It was at night, alone with our thoughts, that we carried our heaviest load, when fancy bridged the distance that separated us from the homes that had been silent to us for many months.

I do not know how nostalgia ranks as a separate and specific disease, but I do know that it handicaps a man terribly in his struggle for life. Later on, during my convalescence in the hospital, one of my command lay near me, and I could hear him murmur to himself, "I shall never see home again;" and, steadily sinking, Lieutenant Starns turned his face to the wall and died.

During the earlier portion of our stay we constantly looked forward to exchange, and it was this hope that served in a measure to mitigate the ills of our prison life. The "grapevine" spoke to us of little else.

The main feature of this prison telegraph was its complete unreliability. As I remember, it was never correct, even by accident; but it sang songs of exchange and release, and, while feeling the notes to be false, we yet liked the music and hoped it true.

It was toward the fall of 1864 that I began to give up all hope of exchange, and could see no prospect of release save the close of the war or death. I looked the matter squarely in the face, and could see no rational reason why the North should either desire or consent to an exchange. The Southern army, unable to recruit its losses, was being depleted; for every man killed, wounded, or missing made a permanent vacancy. With grim humor it was said that our conscript officers had been ordered to take every man not over two weeks dead. Why, then, should the North make the mistake of recruiting the Southern army with fifty thousand veteran soldiers, and they with experience enough of prison life to justify extra exertions in avoiding a second visit? I could then see no reason for it; and though I have since read much concerning the reasons for a nonexchange, I am satisfied that the above is about the correct solution of the problem.

Were I to write only the experience of the first four months of our imprisonment, I could have little to say in the way of complaint aside from the ills which necessarily attend confinement and form a part of every prisoner's lot. It was not heaven, but as yet it did not represent the other extreme.

Our treatment by the officers of Hoffman's Battalion was, as

far as I know, courteous enough; and as to the enlisted men who
guarded us, my principal objection, aside from their propensity to
shoot, lay in the fact that most of them could not address us as
"Rebels" without qualifying the term with the adjective "damned."

Our food was abundant, owing to our ability to purchase from
the Post sutler and the hucksters who came into the prison daily,
besides which many were in receipt of supplies from friends and
relatives in the North, and hence were entirely independent of
the prison rations and fed on dainties not found on the prison
menu. The men looked well and strong, and in marked contrast
with their appearance later on. Just when the change took place
I do not remember, but it came suddenly. I connect it in some
way with the spring of 1864. We bade a final adieu to sutler and
purveyors of every kind, and realized that a limited ration would
hereafter be our only supply, that we must content ourselves as
best we could with such quantity as the government saw fit to
give.

Money could buy nothing in the way of food; and, speaking
for myself, I reached at last that stage when, were it in my power,
I would have bartered gold for bread ounce for ounce. We were
forbidden to write for food, and it was only by strategy that, if
written, such letters reached their destination.

It sometimes happened that the Post surgeon would allow such
packages as reached the Island to be delivered to their owners.
He evidently had a professional dislike to sickness and suffering.

The vital question with us was the victuals question. As to the
daily ration, I remember that it consisted of a loaf of bread and a
small piece of fresh meat. Its actual weight I do not remember,
if I ever knew. I do know that it was not sufficient to satisfy
the cravings of hunger, and left us each day with a little less life
and strength with which to fight the battle of the day to follow.

I heard that our surgeons (Confederate) furnished a protest, in
which they asserted that the quantity of food furnished each
man was not more than sufficient to sustain life. Coffee was unknown, and I remember on several occasions, far apart, receiving
two potatoes and an onion. If these were given medicinally, the
dose was homeopathic, and it was certainly scurvy treatment.

As the months passed on a marked change was noticeable in the
appearance of the men. They became depressed and listless, and
unsuspected traits of disposition cropped to the surface. The
parade ground was dotted with gaunt, cadaverous men, with a
far-away look in their eyes, and with hunger and privation showing in every line of their emaciated bodies. It was believed by
many of us that this mode of treatment was enforced as a re-
taliatory measure; and this belief certainly received strong support when, looking across the bay, we saw a city whose waste
alone would have supplied our wants.

I have seen a hungry "Reb" plunge his hand into the swill barrel of some mess and, letting the water drain through his fingers, greedily devour what chance had given him, if anything. Speaking for myself—and well aware of what I state—I assert that for months I was not free from the cravings of hunger. One-half of my loaf and the meat portion of my ration were eaten for dinner. I supped on the remaining piece of bread and breakfasted with "Duke Humphrey." I sometimes dreamed of food, but cannot remember in my dreams ever to have eaten it, becoming, as it were, a sort of "Johnson's Island Tantalus."

When we arrived on the Island the rats were so numerous that they were common sights on the parade ground. Later on they disappeared. Many of the prisoners ate them. If asked if I myself have ever eaten one, I answer no, because to cook a rat properly (like Mrs. Glasse's hare) you must first catch him. I have sat half frozen in our mess kitchen armed with a stick spiked with a nail, but was never fortunate enough to secure the game. A dog would have served the purpose better, but the chances were that some hungry "Reb" would have eaten the dog.

One of the Northern illustrated papers published a picture of one of the Belle Isle prisoners which certainly showed an extreme state of emaciation. Some of the mess suggested that I compete with him, kindly offering to back the Confederate entry.

I think they would have won their bets; for, though regretting that I must acknowledge the fact, I am confident that I was the worse-looking specimen of the two. I had entered the prison weighing over one hundred and forty pounds, and then weighed less than one hundred. To a demonstrator of anatomy I would have been invaluable as a living osteological text-book. The prolonged confinement had told severely on us, and the men could not but yield to its depressing influence. There was but little to vary the dreary monotony that made each day the repetition of the day before and the type of the day to follow. This alone would have been sufficient; but when scant food and cold were thrown into the scale, it is little wonder that both mind and body should yield under the constant strain. Many of us were far into the second winter of our confinement, and with all hope of release gone, we had nothing left to wait for but the end, whatever that end might be; and it was weary waiting.

It was generally known among us that some mitigation of our condition would be afforded such as took the oath of allegiance; and as this meant increased food and better clothing, some few availed themselves of the offer. But one case came under my notice—that of a member of the mess. He, I presume, could not help it, as it was with him simply a question of endurance, and he gave it up. It was said of him that he froze up early in the first of

November and did not thaw out until the following June. The prospect of a repetition was too much for him.

It is small wonder, then, that many found their way into the prison hospital (then managed by Confederate physicians, prisoners like ourselves), and thence to the prison graveyard. Thanks to the generosity of a Louisiana officer (Col. J. O. Nixon, I think), who furnished the lumber, headboards were placed at the graves of our dead; and as very many of these were carved in our room, I have some personal knowledge as to their being numerous, though I cannot speak with certainty as to the actual number of deaths or the percentage of mortality. I would here state incidentally that the only occasion on which I passed beyond the limits of the inclosure was when, with two or three others, I assisted in placing these boards in the graveyard. I met and conversed with a couple of ladies, the first with whom I had spoken for more than a year. Our appearance aroused their womanly sympathy and, being Rebel prisoners, we excited their feminine curiosity. I waited, and at last it came: "Do you think you are right?" Seated on a grave, I told of Reginald and Rebecca for the last time, the application all the more apropos for the extra year of imprisonment and what it brought.

It was early in January, 1865, that the writer fortunately found himself occupying a cot in the hospital and slowly recovering from an attack of fever. I use the term "fortunately" advisedly, since convalescence brought with it comforts in the way of food to which we had long since been strangers.

Like Little Dorrit's protégée, Maggy, I have pleasant recollections of the hospital. Not "such d'licious broth and wine," perhaps, nor yet "chicking," but I renewed my acquaintance with the almost forgotten taste of coffee; and while a slice of fat pork would scarcely rank now as a sick room dainty, the surroundings were different, and I regretted the improvement that sent me back to the old life.

Sickness proved a blessing in disguise, for orders came that the sick should parade for inspection, the worst cases to be sent South on parole. Many succeeded in passing muster, and one day in February the big gate swung open and a number of us took up our line of march across the frozen bay—homeward bound—and bade a final adieu to a spot unmarked by a single pleasant recollection.

We left Sandusky knowing nothing, caring nothing, of our route, so long as our course pointed toward "Dixie." The passenger coaches which brought some of us sixteen months before were replaced by box cars, which we warmed by packing the floors with earth, on which we built a fire; which afforded a minimum of heat with a maximum of smoke. It was at Grafton, W. Va., that we sidetracked long enough to enable us to sit regularly at table and indulge in the novelty of a first-class meal. It was *table d'hote,* and I fear the landlord realized but scant profit at so much a stomach and they such chronic cases of vacuum.

One of our men stated that he felt the first mouthful of food swallowed by him strike on the sole of his foot; but as this statement has its foundation on an anatomical impossibility, I give it no credence.

It was here or at some neighboring station that we met a batch of Federal soldiers returning from the South. We learned that they were from Andersonville, and, as usual, we mingled together, comparing notes and indulging in the usual chaff which was generally a feature of such meetings. As we separated they expressed their intention of again visiting us, and in turn were solicited to bring their guns with them. This practice of poking fun, in spite of its frequency, was rarely carried beyond the bounds of good temper.

In this connection I would mention an incident which occurred on the Island, in which the "Reb" came out second-best.

A regiment of hundred days' men was in camp outside the "pen," and when Morgan was on one of his raids this regiment was sent out to meet him. As they marched by, one of their number sang out: "Boys, we're going to bring John Morgan to keep you company!" In due time they returned. They had met Morgan and had exchanged their accouterments for a parole. As they went by, one of our number shouted: "Boys, where's your guns?" And quickly came back the retort: "Morgan's got them; where's yours?" No reply was made to this. Under the circumstances there was none to make, and the rest of us wished the fellow had kept quiet.

A slow, fatiguing, and uncomfortable trip brought us, via the outskirts of Baltimore, to Fort Henry, and thence to Point Lookout, where we were turned loose in that "pen." Thinking that we had exhausted the capacity of prison life for harm, we were little prepared for the sight which met our eyes as we entered this place; but, seeing these unfortunates, we felt that we stood in the presence of men who had touched depths of suffering that we had not reached. All along the route we were fearful lest some evil chance should turn us back again to the old life; but that fear became secondary to the dread lest we should call a permanent halt at this point, and we drew a long breath of relief when we marched out of the place.

There was little need to ask questions. It was entirely unnecessary to mine for information—the nuggets of misery lay scattered on the surface and told the pitiful story without assistance from human tongue. Since that time I have conversed and compared notes with men who had a story of imprisonment to tell, and I am satisfied that, as compared with the enlisted men at

Point Lookout, Elmira, Rock Island, Camps Morton, Chase, and Douglas, the officers at Johnson's Island merely tasted purgatory; the men went beyond that.

A few hours too many, and we were checked and counted and loaded on the steamer that was to carry us to City Point, the last stage of our journey, and for that reason the most satisfactory portion of our trip.

As we came alongside the vessel a voice hailed us with, "Have you fellows ever had the smallpox?" and then gave the cheering information that there was plenty of it aboard. He was correct in his statement; but in view of what had already fallen to our share, I think we looked upon smallpox as one of the lesser evils and scarcely gave the matter a thought. It remembered me, however.

We were placed in the lower hold of the vessel, the space between decks being occupied by the sick, and it required skillful maneuvering to mount by the ladders up the hatchway and avoid the filth that trickled down. The contrast between this steamer and the Evening Star was much more marked than the distance between the passenger coach and the box car; but our journey was so near an end that a few extra discomforts scarcely added to the already heavy load which was to drop from our shoulders in a few days.

After the "James River," City Point, the flag of truce, the usual formalities, and the march to Richmond, the late inmate of Block 11, Mess 3, drew his forced accumulations of pay and registered at the Spottswood Hotel, paying sixty dollars per diem— not an exorbitant price when we consider that at the time a cord of wood on the lower Mississippi might without much exaggeration have been said to be the equivalent of a cord of Confederate money.

Still the pay of a modest lieutenant would not justify a prolonged, stay at these figures; and, finding myself seriously ill, without in the least suspecting the cause, I left by rail, going as far as Charlotte, N. C., where that mode of transportation came to an abrupt termination.

Blazing with fever and dazed from its effects, in company with several others who were bound for the extreme South, I took the tedious walk which slowly carried me through the State of South Carolina; and it was when nearing Milledgeville, Ga., that I thought for the first time that the eruption which had made its appearance on my body was in some manner connected with the smallpox on the steamer, and all doubts, if any existed, were dispelled when, on reaching Montgomery, Ala., I was ordered to the pesthouse.

It was in April, 1865, that General Wilson captured the place; but, thanks to the pesthouse, backed by a parole, I was unmolested, and once more started for home.   I was indeed a veritable tramp—walking or having an occasional lift on a wagon and wholly dependent for food on the bounty of such as lived on my line of march, often scanty, for the South had been raided until it seemed as though all had been swept away.   It was when nearing Jackson, Miss., that I learned of Appomattox, and that our service had been in vain; that the voluntary contribution of death and suffering had been given to a "Lost Cause."   We were all prisoners of war.

Two years to the month had passed since I was locked up in Port Hudson, and during that period I had heard actually nothing from my home.   I opened the gate and, walking up the lane that led to the house, could see the female portion of the family sitting on the gallery, none missing.   In fact, there was a little niece that had put in an appearance since my departure.   Soldiers were too common a sight to excite curiosity; but a half look of recognition swept over their faces, and as they rose from their seats to get a better view I dropped my valise and sang out: "Come on; it's me!"   I know I should have said, "It is I," but I didn't.

Then followed a rush and a hugging match, in which the odds were four to one against me.

This happened over twenty-five years ago, and I am not exchanged yet.

CHAPTER XIX.

PERSONAL STORIES OF CAMP CHASE.

Diary of Capt. A. S. McNeil—Nine Months a Prisoner at Camp Chase—
An Unbiased Story of Prison Life—Going Home at Last—Story of R.
H. Strother in Prison at the Same Time as Captain McNeil—Shooting
at Prisoners—The Narrative of Lieutenant Mitchell—He Tells of Lieu-
tenant Grasty's Escape—How Captain Herbert Came to Camp Chase—
A Pleasant Deputy Sheriff—The Effects of Overeating.

THE goodly town of Bristol lies in Tennessee and Virginia.
One of the well-known business men of the place is Capt. A. S.
McNeil, who in 1864 was a prisoner at Camp Chase. The Captain was a member of the Forty-Fifth Virginia Regiment. This
regiment was at Cloyd's farm, near Dublin, Va., on May 9, 1864,
where it met a heavy force of Federals in an engagement, and
Captain McNeil was made a prisoner, as were sixty-one of his
regiment. In all, two hundred and seventy-five prisoners made
a long and weary march of ten days, during which time twenty
made their escape.

The Captain placed at the disposal of the author the diary kept
during his imprisonment at Camp Chase, with a brief account of
the trip to the prison.

They boarded a boat at Charleston on the 22d, and on the 23d
arrived at Gallipolis. From there they went up the Ohio River
to Wheeling. At this point the diary says: "We Rebels attracted
a great deal of attention, and the wharf was lined with women,
children. and old men, looking, probably, to see if some of their
friends were among the prisoners."

From Wheeling they went down the river a few miles to Bellaire, where they went aboard a train for Columbus.

Captain McNeil describes the appearance of the prison, which
need not be repeated. The term used, both North and South, for
a new prisoner was "fresh fish," and the diary says:

We "fresh fish" were put on Giddings Street. This prison contains some three acres, inclosed inside a plank wall, with sixty-
four houses in it and twenty men to a house. My residence is

Giddings Street, Mess 57, west end of prison, near the wall. Gave our money to Lieutenant Sankey, who gave receipts for same. I found, to my surprise, that many prisoners were called "razorbacks," men who were anxious to take the oath of allegiance; but it seems that the privilege had played out, and I was glad of it.

Quoting from the diary, he states:

A man who will fight two, three, or four years and then leave his country is not to be depended upon. We have a house sergeant and one street sergeant to superintend the street and draw the rations, make details, etc. I was appointed street sergeant, and soon grew familiar with my duties. The position is one that keeps me very busy, but one which helps pass the time away very well. I have one hundred and twenty-one on this street to look after and to draw rations, wood, and blankets for. When I draw these rations, etc., I divide the same with the house sergeants, and they give them to the men or arrange it to suit themselves. We are getting sugar, coffee, vinegar, beef, bacon, rice, hominy, one loaf of bread or ration of corn meal, and soap.

May 27.—Only have one dollar in gold, twenty-five cents in silver, and seventy-five cents in greenbacks. Think I will try and learn to make rings, as we can buy buttons from the sutler, also files and sandpaper.

May 28.—Roll call and a call for men who wish to take the oath, or "swallow the puppy," as the boys call it. There are men here who applied to take the oath six months ago. This surprised me, but out of such a number of men one might expect some "razorbacks." Some men have been here thirteen months and are still "bully" for Jeff.

May 29.—Nice day; the sun seems to rise when it ought to set. The days are very warm and the nights cool—drew fifty blankets to-day. Everything seems to go on very well, more so than one not in prison would think. Everything has to move like clockwork, and orders are very strict. Two Irishmen to-day, belonging to Mess 57, closed their door and fought for half an hour— neither one badly hurt.

I do not know what I will do when I get out of clothes and tobacco. Money is very scarce and worth more than I ever realized before. No papers are allowed to come in the prison, but plenty of reports of various kinds are circulated.

In 1862 the prisoners bought papers whenever they desired of the sutler.

May 31.—A lieutenant and a lady appeared on the parapet and walked around the prison. It seemed to amuse them to look at us Rebs and view our awful condition. Some of our men were bare—doing their washing, etc. They have a splendid band here, which plays every evening at sunset at the east end of the prison.

Thursday, June 2.—Rained a nice shower, street muddy. Had a visit from an Alabama friend. Four "razorbacks" went out. A "razorback" came into my mess, cursing Jeff Davis and the government generally. Halterman, of the Sixty-Second Virginia, and I politely put him out of the shanty.

Friday, the 3d.—Drew rations—no sugar, no coffee, no candles; rations shorter than ever before.

Saturday, 4th.—A report is current that the "razorbacks" are to be moved out of this prison.

Sunday, 5th.—Cleaned the street and had inspection. There was another fight in Mess 57, between two Irishmen. Rooney cut the other one badly in several places with a knife. The Confederate surgeon dressed the wounds.

Thursday, 9th.—There is a call for volunteers to go into the gunboat service; good many joining; they get $500 bounty.

Wednesday, 15th.—Myself, J. Crockett, two men from Louisiana, and two Irishmen began to dig a hole to escape; four men scaled the wall and got out, but were caught and brought back.

Saturday, 18th.—Report of an exchange; "razorbacks" reported our tunnel, and we had to fill it up. We had but ten feet to dig until we would have been outside the wall. Another tunnel was nearly completed from Mess 60, but the traitors reported it.

About this time (July 15) the prison was enlarged, and the Captain and his mess moved into the new place bag and baggage. In this prison there were about five acres. Instead of barracks, however, there were tents. There was not a house. There were some seventeen hundred men in the prison at this time. Captain McNeil was quite ill for several days. Soon after this a call came to the prisoners to volunteer to build quarters. They were offered full rations and good clothing.

July 2.—Rained all night; nice day follows. I am on the top of a new building, looking out into the world once more; have a splendid view; country very level. I am spending some of the happiest moments of my prison life; see a woman, who looks charming to a poor prisoner shut out from the world and society.

Sunday, July 3.—Very warm. One hundred and eighteen new prisoners bring good news.

Monday, July 4.—There is a roar of artillery at Columbus. A great celebration is going on there to-day. I am busy making rings. When at 9 o'clock wagons came in with wood, some forty Rebs charged the gate. The guards on the parapet began to fire on the men; fire continues all around the parapet. I jumped up and ran out of my tent; I saw a sentinel with his gun up; he fired; I ran up to the gate. All of us were ordered to return to our quarters, or were told that they would fire on us. As firing continues and is heard in the distance, there is great excitement, and no rations are to be issued to those who charged the gate for two days. One man was wounded and found lying close by the gate.

Tuesday, July 5.—Beautiful morning. Excitement continues. No news. O God, deliver us from this awful place!

Thursday, July 7.—For the first time in this prison, we had roll call. We are ordered to remain on the north side of the ditch runnng through the center of the prison, east and west. Cloyd, from Wilson County, Tenn., was shot through the leg for trying to cross. He says he did not hear the order. His leg was amputated. His father was shot on the 4th instant, and his arm amputated.

Saturday, July 9.—Have been a prisoner two months to-day. The time seems as long as six months. We turned over our blankets and cooking vessels, and drew an equal amount. I kept two extra blankets.

July 13.—Getting better. Two men shot to-day—one in the breast, the other in the thigh. Leg amputated. They were shot for throwing out a cup of water against orders. Both men were wounded by one ball.

Wednesday, July 20.—Working hard making rings. Sell them readily for fifty cents each. Moving into our new houses. They are one hundred feet long by eighteen wide, and contain one hundred and ninety-six men—terribly crowded.

Friday, July 29.—An order is issued prohibiting the sale of a great many things. There are two very good eating saloons here. We can send out and buy anything we wish to eat.

August 1.—Cloudy. Five hundred fresh prisoners from Johnston's army arrived to-day. They were all in fine spirits.

Saturday, August 6.—Nice day. Two hundred prisoners came to-day. Grant was terribly defeated at Petersburg.

August 10.—Will be exchanged soon. Got a letter from Uncle John D. Vincil, who sent me ten dollars; also his photograph. Met a cousin from Alabama. Still working hard making rings.

Friday, August 12.—Four hundred new prisoners came to-day, several from my native country. Heard from home. Glad to see them all in good spirits.

September 2.—Sentinels very talkative—all for McClellan.

September 5.—No eatables allowed to come in here only on approval of the doctor. Hard times will be with us now. I am walking five times around the wall every evening. I feel much better by taking exercise.

Friday, August 9.—Smallpox raging.

Many of the entries in this diary during this time related to reports from the front, about the armies and what they were doing. In the meantime one hundred prisoners were taken out for exchange. On October 4 there were sixteen cases of small-pox in the prison. Out of one hundred and ninety-six cases, thirteen died. On October 8 it snowed, and there was only one stove to each house.

November 1.—Rations were better than for some time.

November 8.—This is the great day in the North—the election for President. God grant that something may be done to close this unhappy war!

Thursday, 10th.—McClellan seven hundred ahead in Columbus, large majority in Cincinnati. Rations very short.

Wednesday, 16th.—Abe elected. Went out and drew a pair of pants and shirt; gave us splendid Confederate gray.

Monday, 21st.—I put on my new gray suit and gaiters yesterday; felt like a man once more. Report is that we will get full rations once more.

Thursday, Dec. 1.—Talk of exchange. I get as much engraving as I can do. Men go out every day by taking the oath. Rations are very short. This is enough to try any man's pluck—get up hungry, stay hungry all day, and go to bed the same way. They promised us straw to sleep upon. The promise was all we got.

Sunday, 18th.—The report is out that we are going to get better rations. This pleases the boys, for we are half starved. Rations are sold to us at half price.

Wednesday, 21st.—We had an election of officers to receive Confederate supplies. Colonel Hawkins, Captain Smith, and Colonel Jose, of Arkansas, got the most votes.

Thursday, 22d.—Colonel Hawkins is making a speech, and says we will soon get plenty to eat. All in fine spirits, a smile on every man's face.

Sunday, 25th.—Christmas day. Raining a little. Prison awful muddy. Have had a splendid dinner for the first time. We have one week's rations of beans and hominy. My mess has saved a spoonful of meal out of each man's rations for a month past, so we have four pints of meal and our day's rations. I think I never enjoyed a Christmas dinner as I did this one today. We had as much as we could eat for the first time for many long days.

Monday, 26th.—Mud four inches deep all over the prison; an awful place.

Saturday, 31st.—Colonel Mulford goes to Richmond to arrange for exchange. We are all in hopes he will succeed.

1865. Sunday, January 7.—Snowed all night; eight inches

deep; drifted in places four and five feet deep. Drew molasses for the first time since being a prisoner. Rations short again.

Tuesday, 17th.—Looks like all of Hood's army was coming here.

Thursday, 26th.—There are upward of five thousand men in this prison now. Thirty-four men died in the last twenty-four hours.

Sunday, 5th.—At 9 o'clock Lieutenant Sankey and several officers appeared on the parapet and, to our great surprise, said that all who wanted to go out on exchange come forward. There was yelling and cheering, and soon we became a solid mass of Rebels. Order was restored, and Lieutenant Sankey addressed the crowd. "Gentlemen," he said, "the Colonel commanding this Post has received orders to make rolls for exchange in lots of five hundred from Missouri, Tennessee, Louisiana, Arkansas, and Kentucky; then the other States in rotation. All others from States not named will retire; the others remain." It is impossible to find language to express my feelings when I heard the officer say "exchange." God speed the day when I shall be permitted to bid a final farewell to my long home in Camp Chase! The first five hundred will leave Wednesday, and five hundred every other day. Hope that there is no humbug this time.

Monday, 6th.—Still calling and making out rolls. Papers confirm the exchange. Men still dying at a fearful rate.

Tuesday, 7th.—A good many men are refusing to be exchanged. Five hundred out of the first eight hundred signed the roll. They would rather be paroled. I don't see into that.

Wednesday, 8th, has come and the first squad has not gone. Some two hundred have refused to go. Lieutenant Sankey says they will have to go if they don't get enough to exchange for their men.

Sunday, 12th.—First five hundred have gone. This begins to look like exchange sure enough.

Monday, 13th.—I have been called and all who came with me.

Tuesday, 14th.—We signed the parole and are now ready to go.

Thursday, 6th.—Had good rations of flour and beef. Squad ordered to be ready to leave for "Dixie" in the morning.

Saturday, 18th.—We are drawing fourteen ounces of flour per day. Very good.

Sunday, 19th.—W. H. Gose, of Tazewell, died last week.

[NOTE.—In the list of Confederate dead of Camp Chase the name of W. H. Gose, Sixteenth Virginia Cavalry, will be found. He died February 10, 1865, and was buried in Grave 1144, as shown in the plat.—EDITOR.]

Monday, 20th.—The sutler is selling apples, potatoes, onions, cabbage, parsnips, and turnips. He cannot or does not supply the demand. Every one crowds to the sutler's, so that it is almost impossible to get anything.

Saturday, 25th.—Third squad called. Lacked four names of reaching mine. Sadly disappointed. They have taken several of my mess, also my old friend and fellow-ringmaker. We have been working together now nine months. They call the roll alphabetically—got down to L. One more letter is mine.

February 28.—I am doubtful if I can sleep much to-night, so anxious am I to go.

Wednesday, March 1.—Report is that the exchange is played out. Many long faces to-day.

Thursday, 2d.—Raining. Fourth squad called out. I was fifth name called. One hundred of the Eighty-Eighth Ohio to guard us. Mud very deep. Arrived at Columbus at sundown. Got aboard box cars pretty well filled with straw.

There is much omitted from Captain McNeil's diary. He anticipates its complete publication some day.

Mr. R. H. Strother wrote a story of Camp Chase to the *Confederate Veteran.* The narrative, an interesting one, is as follows:

I regret very much that I am unable to give you a detailed history of my stay in prison at Camp Chase. I can recall events better than dates. It has been a long time ago. I failed to keep a diary, and many things connected with my life in Camp Chase have passed from my memory. I am satisfied that a true history of prison life at Camp Chase would not be believed by a large number of people in the Northern States; but whether they believe it or not, those who were there and passed through the terrible sufferings imposed upon them know from sad experience that what they say is true.

I enlisted in the Confederate army September 10, 1862, and left my home in Trimble County, Ky. I became a member of Company E, Fourth Kentucky Cavalry. Our command, up to the time of my capture, operated in Kentucky, Southern Virginia, and Eastern Tennessee.

I was captured in the Rheatown fight, in Tennessee, about October 13, 1863, and taken first, after capture, to Greeneville, Tenn., then to Knoxville, where I remained until the first of November. Then, with about one hundred and fifty other prisoners, I was sent to Nicholasville, Ky., afoot; thence by railroad to Covington, where I, with one or two others, being sick, was left in the hospital. I remained there until about the middle of December, 1863. I was then sent to Camp Chase. On the way stopped in Columbus and remained there three or four days in the barracks, then on to Camp Chase. On my arrival at the prison I was put in the hospital, in old Prison No. 2. In a short time I was able to be on my feet again. I was then assigned to duty in the hospital, where I remained for a short while, and was then sent to one of the barracks in the prison. . . .

When taps sounded at eight o'clock at night, all fire and light had to be extinguished; then the prisoners retired to their bunks to sleep, if they could. Imagine a man sleeping sweetly and comfortably whose bed was a hard plank, and whose covering was one blanket, with the thermometer registering fifteen and twenty degrees below zero. On the 31st of December, 1863, snow fell to the depth of several inches. That night the weather turned extremely cold, and New Year's day was known the country over as "the cold New Year's."

On the morning of January 1, 1864, an officer with guards came into the prison, and ordered the prisoners from their barracks, one mess at a time, under the pretext of searching for concealed arms. We had to form in line in front of our barrack and stand in the snow shoetop-deep, the coldest day I ever saw, for nearly an hour. Quite a number had their feet frozen and frosted, and I, for one, suffer from it to this day. The sequel proved that, instead of searching for weapons, they were searching for extra blankets; and where there were found to be more blankets than men in a mess the extra blankets were taken away. I shall never forget the sufferings of that winter. In the spring following the prisoners, to change the monotony, concluded to organize a State government. We had in our prison then many distinguished men from the different Southern States.

As well as I remember, Col. W. S. Hawkins, of Tennessee, Maj. Sanders, of Virginia, Gen. Robert Vance, of North Carolina, and Col. Carter, of Tennessee, were the opposing candidates for Governor and Lieutenant Governor. On the day set for the election the prisoners got permission from the officers in command to allow them to meet *en masse* and hear the different candidates present their claims. Quite a number of the Federal officers and a large number of ladies appeared on the parapet and listened, seemingly with great interest, to the speeches, as the candidates were orators of note. After the speaking the ballot was taken, and Hawkins and Carter were declared elected, and installed as Governor and Lieutenant Governor. Members were elected to the State Senate and Legislature; courts were established, from police court to the Supreme Court; a standing army organized, with Maj. Lamar Fontaine as commander-in-chief. A daily paper was established, entitled, *The Rebel Sixty-Four Pounder; or, The Camp Chase Ventilator,* and had for its editors and correspondents talented and able men. There were but three or four copies of the paper put out each day. They were posted on bulletin boards in different parts of the prison. It was amusing to see the boys gather around these bulletin boards to read the morning news. We all enjoyed the novelty of our government, for it served to keep our minds from our surroundings; but our government lasted only a short time. I don't know why, unless those in authority saw we were deriving some pleasure and amusement from it, and concluded we were not suffering sufficiently; so they forbade the prisoners collecting in groups of more than two or three persons. Then, as we could no longer enjoy the privileges of our government, we had to submit to that of Uncle Sam.

During the spring and summer of 1864 quite a number were transferred from Prison No. 2 to Prison No. 3, about a half mile north. Here we underwent the same treatment and the same monotony as Prison No. 2. During this season, Prisons Nos. 1 and 2 were remodeled, and a new prison built at the west end of Prison No. 2. They were all in a row, with a partition fence between them fourteen feet high, on which was a parapet for the guards who, in patroling their beats, could see what was going on in each prison, as well as the guards on the outer walls. After the walls were placed around the new prison, and before the barracks were completed, the prisoners from old Prison No. 3 were removed to new Prison No. 3, a great many having to occupy tents until the barracks were completed. The barracks in the new were superior to those in the old prison. [They have been described elsewhere.—AUTHOR.]

The prisoners had to do all the nursing of sick. Doctors were provided by the government. They made their rounds in the morning. The death rate was at times very high. In February, 1864, if I mistake not, it was 600. At times we were treated humanely; at others barbarously. Whether it was the fault of the government or the officers in command, I am unable to say. We were not allowed to have over one dollar at a time by the prison regulations; and if a prisoner succeeded in concealing his money when searched on entering prison, he could not use it if it was in bills or coins of a larger denomination than a dollar, for the sutler was ordered to confiscate all bills of a larger denomination when you went to purchase from him.

At times the prisoners could buy eatables from the sutler; at other times he was allowed to sell only paper, envelopes, stamps, tobacco, and articles such as were needed in our wardrobe to cleanse ourselves. Occasionally we were allowed to receive boxes of provisions and clothing from our friends.

In our correspondence we were limited for a long time to writing one letter per week and only one page of note paper. But I often sent six or eight and some of them four pages of foolscap, and they were not examined; but I will not give my friend away. He may yet be living, and I would not like for him to be called a traitor in his old days. He was true to his country, but humane to prisoners, and I shall cherish the memory of that man through life.

I have not mentioned the dark side of prison life in Camp Chase. I wish that I had never witnessed it. I should like to think better of my fellow-man. When, without cause, you see men shot down by your side, it is awful.

One day while I was conversing with a young man from Tennessee, standing near the center of the prison, I heard the report of a gun. The young man with whom I was talking reeled and fell, shot by one of the guards; and why, we never knew. He was shot through the leg, between the knee and thigh. The bone was shivered and he lost his leg. He is still living. On another occasion a young man went to one of the wells and, after drinking, turned to leave, when he was shot. The ball passed through his arm between the shoulder and elbow, then through his side and out through his arm again between the elbow and wrist. The same ball passed on through a tent, wounding a man who was sitting in the tent reading his Bible. He had his left hand resting on his left leg. The ball cut off his little finger and passed through his leg, which had to be amputated. This was without any provocation.

On another occasion one of the prisoners was killed at night while sitting by the stove. It was against the prison regulations for fire to be kept burning in stoves after 8 P.M. On the night mentioned the prisoner was sick and nearly frozen, it being very cold, when he made a fire in the stove and was quietly sitting by it. The sentinel, seeing the smoke from the stovepipe, got the proper range, fired, and killed the poor fellow. Many were the shots fired into barracks at night, sometimes wounding some one. Many were the attempts made to escape, but few were successful. Tunnel after tunnel was made, but before reaching the outside was discovered. There were spies in the prison who reported.

On one occasion in our barracks we discovered one of the spies. That night after taps he was taken from his bunk, a blanket wrapped around his head, and he was plunged into a barrel of water that stood at the corner of the building; but before he had been in the barrel long enough to drown, another spy that we had not found out reported to the guard and he was rescued. But it was the last seen of the gentleman in that prison.

I could give many other instances of cruelty practiced on the prisoners, but I forbear.

I left Camp Chase in the spring of 1865 and came to my Kentucky home, where I have resided since; but the cause for which we fought is still dear to me—the principles of a true republic.

In a letter to Col. Knauss he wrote:

I know of you from what I have read concerning the interest you have taken in the graves of the Confederates at Camp Chase, and have wished that I could be present sometime on Decoration Day. Your friends in the South are legion. May God bless and prosper you! is the wish of your unknown friend.

LIEUT. D. T. MITCHELL.

D. T. Mitchell, a planter and merchant living at Highlandale, Miss., has prepared for this volume the following interesting little story of his escape from Camp Chase Prison:

In June, 1864, we had a severe fight at Mt. Sterling, Ky., in which our loss was very heavy. Lieut. Samuel G. Grasty, of Danville, Va., and myself were wounded and left on the field, being carried to the hospital in town and kept for some two months. We were moved then to Lexington and there kept in the hospital a few days, then to Louisville a few days; and our wounds still improving, we were taken to Camp Chase, Ohio, landing there sometime in August. About that time they were sending all the officers to Johnson's Island, and immediately on leaving Mt. Sterling Grasty proposed to get the officer in charge to change the roll and put us down as sergeants, to which I readily agreed; and we had to plead with them very hard to get them to do it, by telling them that the mistake occurred by our acting as lieutenants in the absence of the regular lieutenants, and they got to calling us lieutenants.

His (Lieutenant Grasty's) object in the matter was then to keep from going to Johnson's Island, for if they sent us to any inland prison, we would have a better chance to make our escape, as the exchange of prisoners had been discontinued. and the idea of staying in prison indefinitely was horrid. That winter of 1864-65, when it was so cold the Federal authorities did not have so many guards upon the parapets, Grasty watched all one morning, and, as he thought the time had come for him to try the hazardous undertaking, he came into the barrack and said he was going to make the effort. Not one of us but thought that he would be captured or more probably killed. I had some good citizens' clothes sent to me from my friends in Kentucky, and we dressed him up pretty well, and a Federal blue coat and pants over them, and I wrote him a pass myself, and it read about thus:

"HEADQUARTERS, CAMP CHASE, OHIO.

"All guards will pass Corporal ———.

"LIEUTENANT SANKEY, *Officer of the Guard.*"

I have forgotten the name I substituted for that of Grasty; but I remember that there was a Lieutenant Sankey who made his appearance on the parapet very often and sometimes threw us our letters, and we all knew him well.

After we had finished dressing him, the great object was a little greenback money, in case he should get through.

As it happened, I carried some in there with me. I had it under the lapel of my vest. It had been given to me by friends while in the Louisville (Ky.) hospital, and on entering Camp Chase I pulled out a two-dollar bill, handed it to the officer, and told him that was all I had. He rubbed his hands over my clothes a little, and said: "That fellow has been in the hospital; he hasn't got anything. Let him in." I then had forty dollars secreted on my person. I then gave Grasty the last ten dollars I had. The clothes and money all ready, then it was for two brave men to go to the parapet with him and lift him up high enough so he could reach the parapet with his hands, pull up, and jump to the ground, and go walking along the same as a guard, corporal, officer, or any other soldier. The chance Grasty wanted was just as a guard turned to walk the other way on his beat. He and his two men then jumped to the parapet, and up they hoisted him. He went right along following the guard. A man by the name of Penn, from Tennessee, was one of the mess who helped him up; the other I have forgotten. The reason I was not the other man was because I had not entirely recovered from my spell of sickness. It was so bitter cold that the guard had the cape of his overcoat entirely over his head, so that he never saw or noticed Grasty, and neither did any one else. I learned afterwards that they found the Federal blue coat and pants where he pulled them off and threw them away. He wrote several letters to me, and dated them Quebec, Canada; but they were always mailed in New York, where I knew he had friends. This was the second time he made his escape.

This is as brief as I can make it, and exactly as it occurred, though many little incidents are omitted. I was brevetted Second Lieutenant, Company H, Fourth Kentucky Cavalry, C. S. A. Born and reared in Henry County, Ky. Was then in my twenty-fourth year of age; now in my sixty-fourth, this September, 1904.

D. T. MITCHELL.

The following is told by Capt. W. H. Herbert, at present Deputy Mayor of Sandusky, Ohio, prominent in business and a prominent Elk. The Southerner who may make a pilgrimage to Johnson's Island will find a good friend in Captain Herbert. He was not confined upon the Island at any time, as his narrative will show. A copy of a special order assigning the Captain (then Lieutenant) to the command of a number of exchanged prisoners is here given, he having kept it through all the years:

HEADQUARTERS EX-PRISONERS, JACKSON, MISS.,
December 9, 1862.

SPECIAL ORDER NO. 50.

Lieut. W. H. Herbert.

Company A, Eighty-Ninth Virginia Regiment, is hereby ordered to take charge of two commissioned, four noncommissioned officers, and forty-two (42) privates and proceed without delay and report them for duty at Lieut. Gen. T. J. Jackson's headquarters, they having been duly exchanged.

Quartermaster will furnish necessary transportation.

By order   BRIG. GEN. D. RUGGLES,
A. A. and Inspector General.

In speaking of the time he was at Camp Chase, in 1862, Lieutenant Herbert says:

Forty-two years have elapsed since then, and the boys who were with me are either all old men now or have passed over to "the home beyond the tide." I have dwelt at length on our trip from Wheeling to Camp Chase, for the reason that it is one of the pleasant events in my war experience, and have only the kindest remembrances for those who entertained us so royally.

The latter part of October, 1862, J. Biddle Leopard and I were captured on the Bloomery Gap Road, four miles northwest of Pughtown and about fifteen miles from Winchester, Va., by a raiding party, consisting of a portion of the First New York Cavalry, under command of Major Bailey. On the same raid three others were rounded up—viz., Bob Heironimus, Jake Heironimus, and Mr. Linthicum. We were taken to Paw Paw Station, on the Baltimore and Ohio Railroad, thence to Cumberland, Md., and Wheeling, W. Va. There we were joined by a Mr. Brandreth, of Mississippi, Jim Daily, of Cumberland, Md., C. C. Martin, of Virginia, and four others whose names I have forgotten. We remained in Wheeling prison several days, leaving there one evening, the first part of November, under a guard of seven for Camp Chase, Ohio.

On reaching Newark a gentleman coming into the car took a seat just in front of me. On the way to Columbus we fell into conversation, when I told him I was a Confederate prisoner. He was surprised and wanted to know how many there were of us. I gave him the number—twelve prisoners and seven guards. Then he said: "When we get to Columbus I would like to do something for you boys. If we find a restaurant open, I'll set up supper for the party." I referred him to the officer in charge, who, upon being informed that the guard was to be included in the supper, gave his consent.

We landed in Columbus about 11:30 at night, marched up High Street, looking for a restaurant. Luckily we found one on the corner of High Street, opposite the Statehouse, that was still open. It was in the basement, entrance down steps on the street leading out to Camp Chase. Here we had a supper fit for the gods. Our host, who proved himself a royal entertainer, was then deputy sheriff of Franklin County.

There was a bar in connection with the restaurant, and while supper was being prepared "John Barleycorn" flowed freely to those who wished to imbibe. We all seemed that way inclined, some more so than others. Several Union officers who had been captured and released on parole came in, and when they found we were Confederate prisoners they were exceedingly kind.

They requested the proprietor to give us the best of everything the house had to offer.

About that time General McClellan had been relieved from the command of the Army of the Potomac and General Burnside appointed to the place. These officers were strong McClellan men, and were loud in their opposition to the change.

After we all had had our supper we took *one* farewell drink "from the same canteen" before starting on the tramp to Camp Chase. The most of the party were groggy and wabbled along as best they could. As we emerged from the west end of the covered bridge we found that one of the prisoners and one of the guards were past locomotion; they were simply paralyzed. The officer in charge had them carried to the roadside at the end of the bridge wall and left them lying there, the balance taking up the line of tramp to the prison, which was reached in due time. When the roll of prisoners was called and one found missing, the officer said he was left by the roadside, *too sick* to travel, and that he had left a guard with him.

As day was breaking we marched through the gate to our quarters in Prison 2, Mess No. 12. About nine o'clock the same morning a cart came driving in with our absent brother. What became of the guard, I never learned. A Major Zinn was then in command of the prison.

The prison was a long barracks built of rough boards, one story high, running lengthwise of the inclosure, divided off into apartments, each containing twelve bunks, six on a side, three men to the bunk, thirty-six comprising the mess.

A high board fence surrounded the inclosure, at the top of which was a walk used by the guard, and at intervals were small shelters used in inclement weather. The roll of the prisoners was called very morning and evening by the officer from the top of this fence, and all letters were distributed from there also. One of the sad incidents that occurred was the killing of a citizen-prisoner from Kentucky and the wounding of a citizen-prisoner from Virginia by the guard one night after taps had sounded. In each mess was a small cook stove, which sat in the middle of the floor with mouth toward the door. When taps were sounded the guard would call: "Lights out!" On this occasion the light kept flickering from the stove mouth, which could be seen through the cracks between the boards. He called out again, "Lights out!" then he fired his gun into the mess where he saw the light, killing one man and wounding another.

One of the funny incidents that occurred while I was there was that a woman was permitted to come inside to do washing for the prisoners. She would have her tubs just inside the dead line near the fence. Some soldiers were fond of their toddy, and generally got it by hook or crook; so they worked on the tender sympathies of this washerwoman, and she would bring in a bottle now and then concealed under her dress, and when the opportunity offered they got it. One morning she came in with a quart in one of those old-style flat glass bottles, with General Jackson's head on one side and an ear of corn on the other. The bottle was not quite full. She began her washing. The guard on duty kept close watch, so that the party for whom the whisky was intended could not get it at once. She kept on rubbing the clothes. The motion agitated the whisky, creating a gas in the bottle, and there was an explosion like unto the report of a mountain Howitzer. The guard turned out, and, when the cause of the explosion was solved, the old lady was escorted through the gate to the outside. She never returned while I was there. After this occurrence the sutler would furnish spirits on the sly, labeled "Butter," at two dollars the quart.

About two hundred of us left Camp Chase the latter part of November, 1862, with three days' rations, via Dayton and Cincinnati, for Cairo, Ill. Here we were joined by boys from Johnson's Island and Louisville—about eleven hundred in all. At Cairo we took steamboats, convoyed by ironclads, and passed down the river to Vicksburg, where we landed on December 9, the last exchange of prisoners at Vicksburg, as General Grant began operations there shortly after. At Jackson, Miss., the boys were apportioned off to their different commands, each command placed in charge of an officer, who was furnished transportation in kind and ordered to report with them to their headquarters.

We of Stonewall Jackson's Corps, forty-nine all told, reached his headquarters, near Fredericksburg, Va., December 26, and got what was left of the Christmas turkey, having traveled at least three thousand miles to reach headquarters, when, by going to Old Point Comfort when captured, we could have gotten there in one hundred and fifty; but such are the ways of war—"long way 'round."

The Mr. Brandreth mentioned above, from Mississippi, was originally from Springfield, Ohio, having migrated in the fifties to Canton, Miss., where he had a drug store when the war opened. Samuel Shellebarger, who represented the Springfield (Ohio) District in Congress in 1862, was married to Brandreth's sister. The Jim Dailey mentioned was a brother of Miss Dailey, of Cumberland, Md., who married General Crook, the Indian fighter, just after the war closed. Jim Dailey was with McNeal when Generals Crook and Kelley were captured, in February, 1865, at Cumberland, Md.

CHAPTER XX.

Johnson's Island Stories, New and Old.

Incidents of the Island Prison First Told in the *Confederate Veteran*—
Pen Pictures of the Place in 1864.

In the concluding chapter on Johnson's Island mention is made and quotation given from an article printed in the *Veteran* which seems to have raised a commotion in some parts of the South. There could have been nothing truer than this article, if it had been confined to the year 1862 and the greater part of 1863. The letters given in this volume from Camp Chase in 1862 tell the story plainly. There is no doubt that in 1864 the situation was different in many respects. It would not pay any one at this time to try to fix the blame. One would probably have the same opinion when the unprofitable argument ceased. Parts of these letters are quoted for their historic interest, but many of the comments which are ridiculous are left out.

During the earlier days of the prison at Johnson's Island the Sandusky *Register* complained that the imprisonment of the Southern officers was rendered farcical, outside of the fact that they were deprived of their liberty. Their Northern friends shipped them clothing, fruits, game, wine, and all kinds of provisions.

This was finally stopped by confiscating the provisions and liquors and giving the same to the guards. When the terrible stories of Andersonville were first circulated in the North, great quantities of provisions and clothing were sent there from the North, but never reached their destination.

Lieut. T. B. Jackson, of Norfolk, Va., in the *Veteran*, says:

I was carried from David's Island Hospital, New York, in the latter part of September, 1863, being left wounded on the Gettysburg field in Pickett's charge July 3, 1863, with some two hundred wounded officers. I reached Johnson's Island about the 1st of October, and had scarcely enough clothing to cover me. All that I received from October, 1863, until March 22, 1865, when paroled and sent South, was such as came from Southern sympathizers.

My case was an exception as to the receipt of clothing; for of the forty officers in Room 4 of Block 10 not more than five received a stitch of any description during the sixteen months they were in the prison, and those not handy with the needle were more or less ragged.

There were some in the prison who had friends in the North, and from them received clothing and occasionally a box of provisions, but these were rare cases.

Capt. J. H. George contributed an article to the October (1900) *Veteran,* which follows:

I was among the first prisoners that were confined at Johnson's Island. I was captured at Fort Donelson, imprisoned at Camp Chase, and from there was transferred to Johnson's Island, where I remained to the 1st of September, 1862; hence I was an eyewitness to much that took place on the Island during that time. Your correspondent states that we were provided with suitable clothing; while if there was a garment furnished to any of the prisoners, I did not see or hear of it. Those who were fortunate enough to have money bought clothing, but those who had none did without. This writer states that our tables were furnished with an abundance of substantials and many luxuries.

All luxuries that I knew of were paid for by those who happened to have money, and always at double prices. Not a pound of flour did we get only as we bought it from the sutler at five dollars per barrel, when it was selling at Sandusky City at two and a half to three dollars per barrel. We were prohibited from buying from any one except the sutler, who was placed there by the commander of the prison. Colonel Pierson had leased the privileges of sutler from the government, and the luxuries furnished by him were hard-tack, poor beef, with bacon and coffee once a week.

In this same issue Lieut. E. D. Patterson, then of the Ninth Alabama, now President of the Bank of Savannah, says:

No one who passed through the year 1864 in prison has forgotten, or ever will forget, the awful suffering from cold and hunger experienced there. During the summer and fall of that year the newspapers of the North were publishing blood-curdling details of the treatment of prisoners at Andersonville, and our rations were reduced to an amount that was barely sufficient to sustain life. Boxes of edibles sent by friends on the outside were declared contraband.

I used to think if those clamoring so loudly for retaliation could look in upon prison life and see men staggering about, weak and hollow-eyed from hunger, searching in vain in the slop barrels for scraps and eating rats to keep soul and body together, they would have been satisfied.

I was a prisoner on Johnson's Island for about twenty-two months, and helped to nurse and bury many of those who sleep their last, long sleep upon the Island, and I have no doubt that the lives of several of them could have been saved if they had been furnished with proper medicines and nourishing food.

The *Veteran* for March, 1891, has a letter from A. W. Side-bottom, Chattanooga, Tenn., from which a few extracts are used:

Like Comrade Patterson, I think nothing is to be gained by recalling the wrongs done to prisoners to either side; but, if we do speak of them, let us have the truth. At this late date I am not disposed to do any one the least injustice without a proper hearing. Telling the truth never does that. Therefore, I would suggest that your July correspondent, over his signature, tell us who he is, what command he belonged to, and at what time he was a prisoner on Johnson's Island, and how long he was confined there.

The finer feelings of the people, North and South, were not so blunted in 1861-62 as they were later on. Prisoners were no doubt better treated, and some Confederates might have met with unexpected kind treatment by the North, and your correspondent may have been one of that number.

As to what we were given per day to eat, and how much of it, it is immaterial now; but I could have eaten at one time all I drew for two days. I have seen men eat at one sitting all they drew for three days, and take the chances of finding bones, catching rats, etc., to tide over until rations were issued again.

Most of us used tobacco in some shape, but were not allowed to buy it; but, thanks to a Bluecoat who slipped me in half a plug or so at a time in exchange for finger rings, a few of us enjoyed that luxury as long as it lasted. Not a penny's worth of anything was sold at the sutler's shop as long as I was there, nor were we allowed to receive anything from home, friends, or any one else.

Early in 1865, in answer to complaints from the inside as to what we were given to eat and the small quantity of it, from a stairway inside the prison overlooking quite a crowd of us, Colonel Hill, commander of the Post, said he knew our complaints were just, that we were not being given enough to eat, but he was powerless to do more than he was then doing. I believed then he spoke the truth, and believe so yet.

In preparing this history no attempt has been made to shield any official who was unnecessarily unkind. Was it possible to learn the name of any guard who shot at an unarmed prisoner, he would be named; but it would have been better had these letters never been read. They are here because it would not do to have it said that an attempt had been made to keep such pictures from the public. One would gladly forget such things. Most people who know the author believe that he prefers to remember the noble rather than the ignoble; but he is presenting the story of these prisons for Northern readers as well as Southern, and he seeks to tell the truth.

That circumstances color one's views of situations was never better illustrated than by the story of Maj. James A. Wilson, of Colonel Cluke's regiment of Kentucky cavalry. Colonel Cluke died at Johnson's Island, but not of starvation or exposure. The Colonel was well-to-do and had money and every luxury that money could buy in those days, and yet death came, just as it enters the home of rich and poor alike to-day.

CHAPTER XXI.

A Confederate Spy in Ohio.

Promoted from First Duty Sergeant to Major—Scouting in the Mountains—A Narrow Escape—Recruiting for the Confederate Army in Ohio—Meeting the Knights of the Golden Circle—Makes Columbus His Headquarters for a Time—Visits Camp Chase—A Peep into the Prison—Getting Confederate Recruits through the Lines—The Story of Major Marlowe.

A. J. Marlowe now lives in the city of Columbus, Ohio. For four years he followed the fortunes of the Confederacy, a portion of which time he was engaged in the perilous duties of a spy. While this chapter is not strictly of the "Story of Camp Chase," it is kindred to the subject.

In a brick cottage, 750 West Broad Street, the spy had his headquarters. It is a one-story building and stands to-day looking much as it did forty years ago. Every prisoner on his way to Camp Chase, during the time that Marlowe was in Columbus, passed by his door, while the spy, peering from the blinds, watched the march of his Southern comrades to Camp Chase.

This, however, is anticipating the story which the Major was requested to relate for the readers of this volume.

Major Marlowe's remarkable story is as follows:

I enlisted early in the war in Company C, Second Virginia Infantry, and was made first duty sergeant, which position I held until the 23d day of May, 1863, when I was promoted to the rank of major and transferred to the Nineteenth Virginia Cavalry. Even at that time I had taken part in thirty-two engagements, some of which were severe battles. A portion of this time was spent as courier, carrying orders from one general to another, and through these duties I became acquainted with most of the leading generals in the Army of Northern Virginia.

I served under Gen. Stonewall Jackson until his death, after which I was under Longstreet, with Gen. William L. Jackson my brigade commander. I had delivered messages to Gen. R. E. Lee, the Hills, Early, Breckinridge, and others. I received my commission from Gen. William L. Jackson, and by him was sent through the lines as scout and spy.

While the soldier who has participated in a number of battles knows what danger is, he is in the midst of excitement, with his comrades about him, and forgets the danger to a great extent; but the new duty to which I was assigned made me realize perils that I had not yet known. I knew that death was the doom of the convicted spy. The orders were issued, however, and I at

MAJ. A. J. MARLOWE, CONFEDERATE SPY.

once bade the boys good-by and started away on my new line of duty.

My first night was sleepless, for I was busy with my plans. No general ever went over the details of a battle more carefully than I did over mine. There was one subject ever uppermost in my mind—the saving of my life while doing good service for the Confederate cause.

My camp was near a place called Cloverdale, and morning finally came. Of course I had slept some, but it was a restless, disturbed slumber, and I was not sorry when the early dawn bade me stir about.

I made my way the first day to Warm Springs, Bath County, Va., and put up for the night at Maise's Hotel. I gained some information from the landlord, who claimed to be a neutral man. He was neutral, as far as doing anything for either side was concerned.

He told me where the Union army had been encamped, and how they had left a considerable amount of army stores—clothing, blankets, etc. I found the stores and proceeded to help myself, for there were none of the Federal soldiers nearer than nine miles. I selected a sergeant's uniform and as many blankets as I needed, and was then ready to proceed on my way.

I intended going by Hot Springs, but was informed of the presence of the enemy in that direction, so I retraced my way a few miles and took the mountain road to the Pocahontas Valley and stopped for the night. I got my breakfast at a farmhouse and had my haversack filled also, for they were true Confederates.

They gave me information about the Federals, and the safest route for me to travel. I rode across the mountain and was not molested all day. About nine o'clock at night I arrived at Mrs. Hinkle's, who resided on a farm at the top of Upine Mountain. Mr. Hinkle had been killed by the Union soldiers early in the war, and the widow conducted a large stock farm. Mrs. Hinkle made me very welcome, and I stayed a couple of days and rested. I kept concealed most of the time, for the Federal cavalry were liable to visit the place any hour. Sure enough, they came, two companies of them, and stayed about two hours. I was hidden in an orchard, some one hundred and fifty yards away. The soldiers gave Mrs. Hinkle some advice about not assisting the Confederates, and that if she did, what might happen. From my place in the orchard I could only look on and wonder when they would leave. They rode away finally, taking two pigs and about thirty chickens.

I decided to leave my horse with Mrs. Hinkle and travel on foot, so that I need not follow the highways. My pocket compass was now needed. I wanted to travel in a northwesterly direction, so I took my bearings, changed the gray uniform for the blue, loaded a sixteen-shooter and two seven-shooting revolvers.

I traveled all day, and about sundown came in sight of a large cabin on the side of the mountain. I stopped for a while and looked the place over and finally decided to go in. When I got to the house I met with a cold reception. I heard some one say: "He is a d—— Yank!" It seemed a bit rough, coming from a woman; but it was not hard to forgive her, for she was my friend, if I could only explain the blue clothes.

As I approached the door two women appeared. The look of

disdain upon their faces as their eyes ranged over the uniform told how cordially they hated the "Yankees." They did not invite me in, but I invited myself.

"You ladies don't seem to like the Yankees very well?" I said.

"I reckon you might know what we think of you. The looks of your back going down the road there would be pleasing," said one of the women.

"I don't believe you know a Yank' when you see one; and

HEADQUARTERS OF A CONFEDERATE SPY ON WEST BROAD STREET, COLUMBUS, OHIO.

there is no use in us fighting, anyway," said I. "I am a Rebel scout and spy."

They did not believe me at first; but I convinced them, and then we were friends. They made me welcome, and I arranged to stay all night. Supper was not ready until a late hour, for we had much to talk about, and they took the time to get me a good supper.

At last, as we were about to go to the table, the door was thrown open, and in walked nine well-armed men. They were a sturdy, dangerous-looking lot. I reached for my revolver promptly, and one of the women, noticing my movement, cried: "This man is a Rebel soldier!" "He don't look good to me in those blue rags," said the leader of the rangers, or guerrillas, for such they were; but he smiled good-naturedly when I was introduced as a Confederate spy. We all ate supper together, and they told of their exploits in the mountains as bushwhackers.

The Union home guards made life unpleasant for men in sympathy with the South; and from the stories these men told, they did as much against any one suspected of being for the Union. I urged them to join the Confederate army, as they could do more good there, and I succeeded in enlisting seven out of the nine. They agreed that they would go South with me when I returned; and they did, but the number had increased to seventeen.

It was not a bad place to stay, and I remained two nights and a day. The women helped me to secure a guide who knew every mile of that territory, and, as I was not familiar with that portion of Virginia, his services were very acceptable. I learned the whereabouts of the United States forces, and enlisted twenty-one men. I then returned with these to the home of the women, where the seven men I had enlisted were to meet me.

As has been said, they were there with ten additional recruits. I now had thirty-eight men armed with rifles and shotguns, and, after camping for a day or two, started South by the way of Mrs. Hinkle's, where I had left my horse. When we reached the headquarters of Elk River we ran into a squad of Union home guards, and with these we had a sharp skirmish. They wounded two of my men, and we wounded four of them, killed one, and took eleven prisoners. We reached Mrs. Hinkle's the second night, and left for Newmarket the next day at noon. We went by the way of Piedmont, at which place we met a body of Confederate scouts and turned over our prisoners. I then went to Newmarket and turned my men over to General Early. This ended my first trip.

. . . .

On the 12th day of October, 1864, I left the army at Mount Sidney, with orders to go through the lines and get all the information possible regarding the movements of the Federal army, and to enlist all the men I could get. I went by the way of Buffalo and Panther Gaps, and met with no incident worthy of note.

At Lewisburg I found my old regiment and had a visit with them and a talk with Gen. W. L. Jackson, who did not think well of my proposed trip.

I was to go to the Kanawha Valley, and there were more Federal soldiers in the valley than there had been for two years preceding, and the Union scouts were also thick in that part of the country. This was General Jackson's view of the situation; and if he had had the authority, he would have countermanded my orders. He advised me to keep away from Charleston; but as that was one of the points I wished to make, I did not obey his orders. The night of the 18th I stayed with a Mr. Baird, a mountaineer and hunter. He was taciturn, and it was hard to get any information from him. To any question I asked he would simply answer "Yes" or "No." Finally I got him started telling hunting stories. I had found the key to his tongue, and he told many interesting adventures as a hunter on the wild and rugged mountains.

After a few bear stories I went after him again about people. I told him frankly I wanted the news from Charleston. He said he would go and find out how many soldiers were there and let me know when I came back. We started the next day. I accompanied him for a time. We stayed all night in a deserted cabin on Gauley Mountain. He went on toward Charleston, while I crossed the mountain and went to the home of T. Sanders, on Elk Mountain.

Sanders was a noted Southern sympathizer. He gave me a list of the names of the Union men whose homes I would pass on my way to the head waters of Pond Creek.

Here I put on the blue uniform again, and had gone but a few miles when I ran across three Union soldiers, who wanted to know who I was. I told them I lived on Pond Creek. They then asked me about a number of persons supposed to live on the creek, but of course I did not know any of them. I was not to be caught that way, however. They wanted to know to what regiment I belonged, and I told them the Eleventh West Virginia Regiment. They asked me where my regiment was encamped, and I told them we did not have time to go into camp, as we were kept scouting all the time in the Gauley Mountains. I was not sorry to part with them, and traveled the rest of the day unmolested.

I found the houses Mr. Sanders mentioned, and stayed all night with a Union man and talked over the war with him. Of course we agreed on war questions; and when I told him how we made the Johnnies get up and dig out he was greatly pleased, and we had a royal good time. Some of the neighbors were invited in, and we had a big supper. The breakfast was a good one also; and when I left, the lady of the house filled my haversack with biscuits, butter, etc., that made an excellent dinner. I found out considerable about the home guards and what they did with people suspected of being Rebels. They made the women cook big meals for them; and if they found any men, made them prisoners and took them to Camp Chase.

I reached Bellville, on the Ohio River, on the 21st, and was then within seven miles of my home—the home I had not seen since the war began. I stayed all night with Mr. Pennypacker, and learned there were many in the community who were in sympathy with the South, and that there were numbers in Southern Ohio who were waiting a chance to go South. I learned considerable also about the Knights of the Golden Circle, an organization in sympathy with the Confederacy. I had never met any of these men before, but had heard of them, and very soon was to make myself a member of the order. I decided I would go to Columbus, Ohio, and find out what I could about Camp Chase, and whether it was true that they were sending citizens there.

On the 22d I left Bellville, crossed the Ohio River and went to see a farmer, Mr. Bell, and found him one of the strongest Southern sympathizers I had ever met. I stayed overnight with him, and together we went to a neighboring town, where I bought a suit of citizens' clothing, and sent my blue suit back with Mr. Bell. I then went to Lancaster, and stopped at a private boarding house. I overheard some conversation that led me to know that there was a Knight of the Golden Circle organization in the town or near by, and, after some discreet inquiries, was led to the place of meeting. I was persuaded to remain over until the next day and attend the meeting.

The meeting place was in a large barn about a half mile from town. I was permitted to go inside the barn, but the meeting was held in the other end of the building from that in which I was placed.

The meeting had not been in session long when two men came to me, asking quite a number of questions. They then left and returned to the meeting, and another man came to escort me into the presence of the Circle—the Rebel Circle, as the Unionists called them. I was surprised when I saw the number of men present. There must have been upward of one hundred. I was questioned many times, and was then asked to join the order. In a moment I saw it was the very thing for me. A Confederate spy was safer inside the Knights of the Golden Circle than out of it.

When I had become one of them, I told them frankly who I was and what my business was in Ohio; and I told them further that I expected their support, as they had pledged, and as their pledge gave me the right to ask. Then I got the grip and password. When the meeting was about to adjourn, a man from Tupper's Plains called for order and made a few remarks that appealed to me personally. He asked me how well I was off financially. I replied that I had no money to spare. He then moved that a collection be taken up, which was done at once. It was a collection that would have delighted the heart of many a country preacher.

In about three minutes I was about fifty-nine dollars richer. I took the name of the secretary and his address, that I might get more when needed. I have the name and address yet, but it will do no good to name these people. They befriended me when I needed their friendship. Had even *one* of them betrayed me, I should have been hanged in a week's time. The citizens of Columbus to-day easily forget that I, a citizen, was a spy in their midst, but they would not so readily forgive a Northern man who was a traitor to the cause of the Union.

I stayed overnight with one of the men, and on the morning of the 24th hired a man to take me to Slabtown, where I had been directed to the house of a friend in my new order, who could give me information regarding the general sentiment of the people of Southern Ohio. I remained all night with the man, and got in close touch with him when he learned who I was. I made arrangements with him to send any men who wished to enlist in the Confederate army to Eagle and Vinton Furnaces, and I would meet them there and take them through the lines. He was to let the Knights at Lancaster know, so that all who wished to enlist should go to Vinton Furnace and ask for any kind of work they could get until I came. I went to Rushville and stayed overnight, and from there I went to Newark by way of Jacktown. I had the names of some parties I wished to see in Newark, who were members of the Golden Circle, but they were not at home.

I spent two days in Newark, the 27th and 28th of October, 1864, and the greater part of the time I put in at the office of the United States recruiting officer. The officer's name was Drake, and I got acquainted with him and received some good offers to go in the Union army. The draft was on them, and they were paying anywhere from three hundred dollars to thirteen hundred dollars for substitutes. I was looking for men myself, so naturally could not enlist. I was not paying any bounties, either.

I then decided to go to Columbus, thirty-three miles distant from Newark. The morning train would get me in at ten o'clock, and so I went, stopped at the hotel, took in the city, and on the morning of the 30th went to Camp Chase.

I went to headquarters and inquired for the commandant, and a man with the rank of colonel made his appearance, demanding to know what I wanted. I told him I wanted to see the Rebel prisoners. "Why?" he asked sharply.

"I have never seen a Rebel," said I, "and I want to see one." I told him that I was in Columbus for the first time, which was the truth, and that I had heard so much about the Rebels that I really wanted to see one, which was also true.

The Colonel got back at me all right, though. "Why don't you enlist and go in the army?" he asked. "If you will enlist and go South, you will see more Rebels than we can show you here." I knew he was telling the truth. He then asked me where I lived. I told him, "Away up in Michigan," and the only reason that I was not in the army, I was my mother's only support.

The Colonel finally said I might see the prisoners if I came back at two o'clock. Previous to going to Camp Chase I had engaged a room at 750 West Broad Street, at which place I took my meals, and I went to the room and waited for two o'clock.

The officers waiting around headquarters had some fun with the green man from Michigan. The rules of the prison forbade visitors upon the grounds; but in company with an officer a few visitors were at times permitted upon the parapet. Even the guards were not allowed to converse with prisoners. It was only for a few moments at best that I was allowed to gaze upon the faces of my Southern comrades, and there was nothing I could do for them.

The Colonel asked me what I thought of the prisoners, and I told him I thought they looked pretty tough. He said to me: "Young man, those men may not look well, but they are brave men, no doubt, and it is not a sign that they were cowards that they are prisoners of war."

I then went to my room, got my supper, put on a paper collar, and left for the depot. I took the night train for Bellaire and got there at daylight on the 1st of November. I went to Wheeling, four miles distant, stayed overnight, and went on a trip to Pittsburg. I was afraid to go around without any excuse, especially to military camps. I bought one hundred copies of a paper called the Washington *Herald* and took them with me to an artillery camp that I visited at Pittsburg. I talked with the men and sold or gave away my papers. I left Pittsburg on the evening of the same day I arrived, and on my way South met another spy. He was captured the next day, and as he attempted to make his escape from the guard he was killed.

While at Wheeling I got a pass to go to the island in the Ohio River where were confined a number of Southern prisoners. I found a few regular Confederate soldiers, but the most of them were citizens who had refused to take the oath of allegiance.

I remained in Wheeling a couple of days and then took a boat to Marietta, then up the Muskingum to Zanesville, arriving there on the 8th of November. I left there on the 10th with three recruits, gotten through the aid of the Knights of the Golden Circle. We left on horseback and rode to Newark. From there we went by way of Rushville to Lancaster. From the Lancaster Knights I received fifty-four dollars. On the 12th the party went to Eagle Furnace and there got eleven men. Here, after a conference, the men divided into little groups and left for Vinton Furnace.

By the 15th we were all there and looking for work. All told the same story of having heard that the Eagle Furnace was about to shut down and we had come there for work. They could give us no work at Vinton, as we well knew; so the boys left in couples, all going to the Ohio River. Our place of meeting was a point near Pond Creek. I got nine men at Vinton, making twenty-three in all. I need not follow every detail of the trip. We got out of Ohio, crossed the mountains, and I landed my men finally at Staunton, Va. I saw the men enlist in the Twentieth Virginia. I made a report of my trip to General Early.

After my trip through Ohio I spent some time scouting in the Shenandoah Valley. I left Woodstock for a trip to the mountains in West Virginia, and spent a little time with some of Rosser's Cavalry at Mount Jackson, and rode with them to Piedmont. Here we met some of the enemy, who opened fire upon us, killing two men who, with myself, were a part of the advance guard. I distinctly heard the command given to fire, but before they could reload we were upon them and they were prisoners. Captain Hahurst, who had command of a company of independent scouts, had given his men orders to take no prisoners, and when this became known to the men in my charge they became almost uncontrollable. They would have made a quick end of this scout had I not been there.

They were disposed not to obey me until I told them I would report them to their commander. In looking over the names of the prisoners I discovered that two of them had been members of my old company, who had deserted. I did not bring this against them, knowing what their fate would have been.

I wish to explain what kind of men these were and how little the loss would have been had summary measures been taken. In what was known as the Ligrate Valley, in easy range of which we were at that time, were a band of men whose numbers were estimated to run from three to five hundred, who were deserters from both Northern and Southern armies. They banded themselves together for plunder, and it made no difference which command they saw fit to attack, provided it was not too large. Their chief occupation was capturing wagon trains. They had by some means secured a cannon and gave it the name of the "Swamp Dragon," and it soon became unsafe for small scouting parties to pass through that part of the country.

After burying our two men who had been killed, we had dinner, the prisoners and our men eating together in a free and easy manner. Some of the prisoners and some of my men found that they were related. After dinner we traveled toward Buchanan, but when night came on we had gone farther than we had orders to go. We went into camp in a wood near a farmhouse, near by a fine spring. My men, not on guard, slept with their arms in their hands, but the night was quiet and peaceful.

When the sun rose on the morning of November 23, 1864, its rays fell on fields and woods white with frost. There was much to do and we were early astir. As the ranking officer of the little expedition, I told Captain Smith, then in charge of the force, to turn Captain Hahurst over as a prisoner of war and to return to his command by way of Meadow Bluffs.

I then started on a trip to the Ohio River. I was told at the farmhouse, near which we camped, that it was about twenty miles to Buchanan, and that there were quite a number of Federal soldiers encamped there. While I questioned the farmer and his wife closely, they would not tell me whether or not they were in sympathy with the South. I had on my blue uniform, and it may be that this had something to do with it. I bought of them enough bread and meat to last me for a tramp of three days, and they looked at me pretty closely when I took a roll of greenbacks from my pocket to pay them. "It is easy to tell what side you are on," said the woman. "Yes," I replied, "but would you rather have Confederate money?" "It makes no difference," said the woman.

I had been paid off at Woodstock, and so had quite a little sum of Confederate money. I walked all that day, and about five o'clock stopped at a house some three miles from Buchanan.

The house was occupied by an old gentleman and his wife. I told them I was hungry and asked if I could get supper. The old lady said that if I could put up with what they had I could get something to eat. I replied that "beggars should not be choosers;" and with that they laughed and made me welcome. At the supper table I brought up the subject of the army, and the lady said: "You soldiers must see pretty tough times." "Well, we do," I replied; "but may I ask if you have any friends in either army?"

The woman started to reply, when the old gentleman gave her to understand that he preferred that she should not discuss that subject.

"You need not fear to tell me," I replied. "All you may say to me will be regarded as strictly confidential. Most people in this part of the country have friends in one army or the other. You are old people, and no one will cause you harm if you tell them the truth."

"I have two sons in the army," said the old man.

"And on which side are they?" I asked.

"One is on your side and the other is a Confederate," he said.

"Do either one of the boys ever come home?" I asked.

"The one in the Rebel army has gotten here only once or twice," said the old gentleman.

"How about the Union soldier?"

"He comes often," they said.

Then I asked them plainly which side they were in sympathy with, and again the old lady was cautioned as she was about to reply.

"Don't be afraid of me," I said. "You have a right to your opinion, even if we might not agree. I simply ask you these questions for personal reasons."

Then she said: "Pa and me both think the South is right, but maybe that is because we were brought up there."

I had noticed in the course of the conversation that they frequently mentioned the son in the Confederate army and rarely alluded to the other, and this led me to the conclusion that they were all right.

"Look here," I said, "I want to tell you something, and what I tell you is to be a secret."

They both looked at me curiously. When they had promised, I said: "I am a Confederate soldier—no matter about this uniform —and I am here to find out how many Federal soldiers are camped in town and all such information as I can get."

They told me then that there were three regiments at Buckingham, and the regiment their son belonged to had gone to Parkersburg. They told me, upon inquiry, that it was the Sixty-Third Ohio that their son belonged to. I asked them where the pickets were, and they told me. I then asked the old gentleman if he knew the country well.

"I have lived here eighteen years," he answered, "and I have tramped these mountains until I know every path for twenty miles."

"I want you to guide me around the pickets," I said.

He hesitated. "If you will go with me to-night, I will give you twenty dollars." I then asked the old lady if she would be afraid to stay alone.

"I have often stayed alone," she replied. I then gave her one dollar for meat and bread, which I added to my goodly supply. I gave the old gentleman twenty dollars as soon as we were ready to go. The lady of the house said "God bless you!" as we strode out into the darkness. The night was intensely dark, for there were neither moon nor stars to be seen. We stumbled over logs or ran into bushes and briers or fell over piles of stones. We dared not have a light, for fear of calling the attention of the men we wished to avoid. By and by the old man discovered that, notwithstanding he knew every path in twenty miles, he had lost his bearings. We simply rambled around and sometimes sat down to think over the situation; but at last daylight came, and we discovered that we were on top of the hill overlooking the Union camp, where we could see here and there a camp fire.

The old gentleman asked me what we should do, and I told him the best thing to do was to do nothing. There was nothing else to do just then except to eat. The guide had a flask of apple-jack and I had plenty of rations, so we ate an early breakfast.

We found near by a thicket of grapevines about an old rail fence, and here we rested until the old gentleman got the lay of the land. I suggested that he go to town, make some small purchases, and while there go to headquarters and secure a pass and go home. This idea pleased him, and I watched him until he had safely passed the pickets. At one time four men from the camp came near where I lay concealed. They played cards for a while and then went back to camp. With my field glass I could see all that was going on in camp. I took quite a comfortable nap during the afternoon, preparing for a night tramp over the mountains.

At sunset it clouded up and by eight o'clock it was raining. I never traveled a darker night and could not see my hand before me. Finally I determined to light a match and look at my pocket compass; but a compass is of little use to a man lost in the woods on a dark night. I stumbled on awhile longer and came to a small stream of water, and I lighted a match again to see in which direction the water was running. I had an idea of the general direction of the Ohio River; and if this stream flowed into the Ohio, I should follow it. When I looked, the water was running in just the opposite direction from what I thought it should. I climbed to the top of a hill and sat down to think it over and perhaps stay until morning and chance a daylight trip. I had been seated but a short time when I heard some one approaching. There were several of them; I could tell by their footsteps.

I waited breathlessly their approach, with my finger on the trigger of the repeating rifle. Presently they stopped and one man said: "I believe we are near the Yankee pickets." What a relief! I spoke to them in a low tone: "Are you lost, boys?"

There was no reply. A few moments of deathlike silence followed, and I spoke again, bringing my gun to my eye.

"I've got you cornered, boys. You had better answer me," I said.

"Who are you?" one asked.

"I am a Johnny," I replied.

"How many are there of you?"

"Just myself," I answered. They joined me at once, and there were nine of them. They proved to be from Jenkins's Brigade, and each had a thirty-day furlough and were slipping through the Federal lines for a visit home. They had not been home since the war commenced, and naturally would take some dangerous risks to get there.

We waited until daylight and climbed to the top of a high hill, from which I could see the town through my field glass. We could see where the pickets or Union outpost was some distance below us, so we sat awhile and discussed our situation. Finally I said I would go to a house some distance away and get such information as we needed. They ridiculed the idea; but, to show them I was in earnest, I left my gun and two revolvers with them and went to the house.

I spoke to the lady of the house and asked if I could get breakfast for ten men. She said she was getting breakfast for us now. I told her I thought not. I saw a number of soldiers, perhaps a half dozen, sitting inside the house, and they were listening to our conversation. As I turned to go one of the men asked me what command I belonged to.

"Company D, Sixty-Third Ohio," I answered.

"Where is your regiment?" he asked.

"It is encamped near Parkersburg," was my reply.

"What are you doing out here?" he questioned.

"We are here after that horse thief, Bill Gundey, and were close onto him last night. You need not be surprised to see my men in Rebel uniforms," I said, "for it is a great help in some places around here."

"Where are the rest of your men?" he asked.

"Up on the hill there; and I'm going after them. You will see a nice bunch of Rebs when they come."

I was soon in the midst of the men, and told them the situation and what questions to answer about the Sixty-Third Ohio, etc. I told them that if the Yankees undertook to give us any trouble we could clean them out, but that it was best to stick to our story of the Sixty-Third.

Breakfast was ready when we got there, and the Union sergeant and I took seats side by side, and the men in gray sat facing our men in blue.

We laughed and joked and told stories of battles. We remained about an hour, and just as we were leaving there came along about eighty Union cavalry. As soon as they got sight of the men with the gray uniforms they halted.

"Where did you get those fellows?" asked the Yankee captain.

I told him what we were doing—hunting the horse thief—and it was best that some go in Rebel uniform. He wanted to know how we were going to get back to Parkersburg, and I told him that at Teacher's Mills we expected to meet another lot of our scouts, and that if we did not catch Gundey we would go to Parkersburg by way of Stillwell. They then rode away and left us. We left the pickets all in fine humor, and they wished us good luck and we did the same, and we traveled all day unmolested upon the public road.

We reached the Mills all right and stayed there until after breakfast, when the boys left me and scattered in every direction to their homes. I determined to go to my home, which I had not seen for nearly four years. I got home safely and changed my clothing. I stayed there several days. I left one revolver and my sixteen-shooter, as it would not do to go through Ohio armed to the teeth. I crossed the Ohio River and went to Cedarville, then to Cooleyville and on to Tupper's Plains.

At the village of Dexter I found a camp of the Knights of the Golden Circle, and enlisted some forty men to go South in May. I went to Jacktown, thence to Newark, and from there to Columbus. I wanted to once more see the prisoners, if possible.

I left Newark for Columbus by train and arrived in time to see about six hundred prisoners march up High Street. I went to the usual place, 750 West Broad Street. I was permitted to visit the prisoners again. The lady of the house where I stopped gave me a lecture on patriotism. She thought an able-bodied young man should go into the army. I told her some one had to stay at home and look after the women and children.

I remained in Columbus until the 26th of February, 1865, when I concluded to go to Newark. I had promised the Knights of the Golden Circle to be there on the 14th day of March, at about two o'clock, on the public square. Instead, I arrived on February 26, put up at a boarding house run by a Mrs. Smith, near whose house was a recruiting station. I spent a portion of my time about the recruiting station and got acquainted with a Colonel Jones. He wanted me to go into the army, saying I could get as much as thirteen hundred dollars if I went in the place of a certain man.

Of course I could not take the big pay. Wishing to stay about Newark until the time agreed upon when I was to meet the Knights of the Golden Circle, I secured work at the depot for about three weeks. On the 14th of March I went to the public square; and seeing a man apparently looking for some one, I gave him the secret sign of the order, which he answered and came toward me, giving me the grip and the word of recognition. After some conversation of a general nature, he asked if I had the note. I told him that I did not have it with me.

"If you had the note, I could pay you," he said.

"How would it do if I gave you a receipt and I destroy it when I go home?" I asked.

"That will do," said he.

I wrote the receipt and paused, waiting for him to name the amount.

"It is fifty-seven dollars and the interest."

"Never mind the interest," said I, "for the note is not yet due."

There were people standing about and passing to and fro near us, and the conversation was intended to lead any one that might be listening to think the note a genuine business transaction. I had never met the man before, but he was a good member of the Golden Circle.

I spent a short time in Newark, and often ran over to Columbus to get the news from the front. I occasionally went out of town to attend a meeting of the Circle. I felt that the time had come for me to go South, and I left Newark the last week in April. I went to Bellaire and from there to Parkersburg by boat. From this point I went up the Little Kanawha to Kanawha Station, and from there traveled through the mountains afoot. A portion of the trip two men accompanied me; but after three days in the Gauley Mountains they left me, and I was alone untli I came to White Sulphur Springs, where I put up at the hotel for a couple of days. There were Union soldiers here, and I went to the headquarters and got a pass to go to Lewisburg. I arrived there safely, and inquired of the soldiers if it would be safe to go to Oakland Station, about twenty miles south. They told me that point was held by Union troops, and that a wagon train was going that way and might give me a ride. To the man in charge I showed my pass, and he kindly gave me permission to ride in one of the wagons.

When we had traveled about ten miles of the way a volley of musketry was fired at the train from the deep woods near the road, killing the horses of the two front teams. I leaped from the wagon and took shelter behind a big oak tree. The guards with the train fired on the force in the woods from under the wagons. It was a party of Mosby's men, sixteen of them, and the men in charge of the wagon train were all made prisoners. They were taken some ten miles south and paroled. I left the Mosby men at the same time the Union soldiers were paroled, and pushed on.

I arrived at Wytheville without further adventure. Here I met a portion of my old regiment, and they had with them some two hundred stragglers from all commands. They informed me that General Lee had surrendered and they were on their way to join Johnston in North Carolina. I took command of the men and moved on. I met General Forrest in Southwestern Virginia and was attached to his command. He gave me orders to go east and scout in the direction of Lynchburg and to let him hear from me daily. The second day I reported, but the third day I could get no word to him. I proceeded on in the direction ordered, keeping a close watch for the troops under General Grant, for we wished to join Johnston. I divided my men in squads to travel upon certain roads and meet at certain designated places. One day as we were riding leisurely along we saw some persons bathing in a pool or pond near the road. We saw the blue uniforms, and I ordered the men to charge on them. We captured two negro soldiers who had been sent out to gather up the wagons and army equipments that were scattered through the country.

My men, seeing these negro soldiers and feeling enraged that the cause they had fought for four long years was lost, shouted: "Kill the d—— niggers!" I had all that I could do to save their lives. I told my men that the negroes were United States soldiers and must be treated as such.

I wish to digress from the story of that time to say that one of these same colored men whose life I saved lives in Columbus and is my barber. He keeps a shop on West Broad Street, in sight of where my headquarters were whenever I was in Columbus during those days. His name is James W. Byrd, and he has not forgotten the time nor circumstance.

We went on with our two prisoners to the place where we were to meet the rest of the scouts, who had been waiting for us. They had captured seven Union soldiers and their horses as well. We scouted about this part of the country several days, and found ourselves in possession of twenty-seven prisoners. I decided to leave this base of operations, find some command to which I could turn the prisoners over, and get additional instructions.

I went through Southwestern Virginia and over into North Carolina, where I met about five hundred Confederate soldiers going home. They told me that Johnston had surrendered some seven days before that time. As soon as I was convinced that all was over, I gave command for the men to move into a field, and there I told them the news. I turned to the prisoners and told them they were free and to go at once. Then I turned to my men and told them that the war was over and that we were soldiers no longer. I then took each man by the hand and thanked him for the heroic work that he had done for four long years. All that was left for us to do was to go home and begin life over again.

I then thought of my own position. I had been a scout and spy, and I felt, some way, that I would be safer in Ohio until all was settled; for one could not know then what would be done with a spy, even if the soldiers in the ranks were going home. It was a long way from the border of North Carolina to the Ohio River, but I had a good horse, and many a long, weary mile did I ride. I finally reached the Ohio River, and at a small town sold my fine horse for eighty dollars in greenbacks. This horse was one I got from the wagon master of the train that had been captured by Mosby's men on my way South. I bought a suit of clothes, boxed my gray suit and sent it home, and the next morning took a boat for Wheeling. From there I went by train to Newark and remained there while the paroling of the prisoners at Camp Chase was going on. I spent much of my time at the headquarters of Colonel Brown at Newark, and at times I did work of different kinds. I saw in the Columbus papers that they were paroling the prisoners at Camp Chase, and among the number a few officers that had not been forwarded to Johnson's Island. One morning I was in the office of the Colonel and read aloud to him the article, but he seemed to pay no attention to it, but kept on writing. Presently I asked: "Colonel, what are you going to do with me. I was one of those Johnnies, as you call them."

He did not reply at first, still continuing with his writing. When he had finished, he said that I would have to prove it.

"Let me have your knife," I said. He handed me the knife. I began to rip the lining of the top of my boot. I drew from the boot the paper that told who and what I was.

When he had read it I saw a frown gather, and he asked: "Why did you not tell me long ago?"

"The war was not over long ago, Colonel; and if I had told you then, I should not have been living now," I replied.

"I don't know what to do with you, unless I hang you," he said; but there was a sort of twinkle in his eyes.

"You can put me under arrest and telegraph to Columbus and see what they want to do with me."

Then he told me to consider myself under arrest and report once a day. This lasted for about a week, and one morning the Colonel called me in. "Well, I have received word from Columbus," he said.

I bowed, waiting for him to finish.

"All spies caught within our lines when the war closed are to be hanged," he said.

Notwithstanding the seriousness of his words and his attempt to look very solemn, I could see a smile lurking on his face, and was not alarmed, as I said: "But you did not capture me. I came here and told you about it. But if you are anxious to hang me, get at it, for I'm in something of a hurry this morning."

He laughed and replied that he had orders to parole me. I asked him the nature of the parole, and he read it to me, the substance being that I was not again to take up arms against the government of the United States, etc.

He then called his clerk and told him to look after things. To me he said, "We will make a day of this;" and we did, but not in getting drunk. Neither drank a drop of intoxicating liquors; but O how we did eat! We celebrated the end of the war that way.

I went back home to Virginia, and some years ago I moved to Ohio, and my home for the past ten years has been in Columbus, and I live in less than three squares from the little house at 750 West Broad, where my headquarters had been located.

In the latter portion of Major Marlowe's story he mentions the capture of two colored soldiers and that one of them, named Byrd, was a barber on West Broad Street, whom he had patronized for some years. When Major Marlowe's story was being prepared for this volume, the attention of the author was called to the statement, and he immediately had Byrd interviewed as to his recollections concerning his capture. When he was asked if he knew a gentleman by the name of Marlowe, he said he had known him several years, and that he had been a patron of his place for some time before he knew that they had met in the South. He was asked to relate his recollection of the particulars, and he said:

I lived in North Carolina before the war and was a fireman on the North Carolina Central Railway, under an engineer who was a down-East Yankee. After a while I learned that the Confederate government meant to get all of us free colored men (I had never been a slave) in the service of the South (I think we were to work on fortifications and such like), and I told the Yankee engineer that I was going to turn up missing mighty soon. He told me where to go and how to get there, and it was the Quakers who helped me. I got through all right to the Yankee lines and enlisted in the First United States Colored Cavalry, Company A, commanded by Capt. Charles W. Dye.

After the fall of Petersburg a battalion was sent south and west of there (if I remember the direction aright) to bring in abandoned cannon, ammunition, etc. While on this trip I went to a nice pond or pool to bathe and wash my clothes. Well, while we were busy cleaning up, another man of my company and myself, we were surprised to find ourselves surrounded by a squad of some sixty men in gray. They looked like a guerrilla band, and I was pretty certain they were when two or three big, tall fellows cried out: "Shoot them! They are nothing but d—— niggers, anyway!" I thought it was about sundown for me, when a man rode in front of them and said: "These men are United States soldiers and must be treated as soldiers."

While some of them kept on swearing that they would kill us, he just quietly told them that they wouldn't do any such thing, that he was their superior officer and they should obey him.

They took us along with them for several days; and when at last they learned the war was over, the gentleman in charge said to us that we could go when we wished, as they had nothing more to do with us.

I thought that a negro who had fought in the army would not get much show in the South; and, not knowing what became of my regiment, I started for Ohio, where I had some relatives. I traveled on foot some six weeks, and at last found myself at Gallipolis, Ohio.

I knew the war was over and there was no use for soldiers any more, so I did not look up my regiment; in fact, I did not know how to go about it.

I finally came to Columbus, and worked here for years at my business, that of a barber. One day a colored man who had been a soldier asked me if I got a pension. I told him I did not, and that when the war was over I was a prisoner in the hands of the guerrillas, and was telling him all about it, when I noticed Mr. Marlowe, who had been shaved, listening to us talk. When the colored man went out, the Major commenced asking me a lot of questions, all of which I could answer. Pretty soon I asked him who he was that seemed to know all about the time I was captured.

"Do you remember the man who rode a nice horse—the shoulders or collar of the horse was white?"

"Yes, sir, I mind him," I said. "It was that man saved me from dying right sudden. I mind that."

"Well, I was that man," said he. Then he told me that he had often wondered where he had seen me before he came to my shop, and I told him I had wondered, too. It was sort of strange that the man who saved my life should be living here and me living here too. He comes very often and gets shaved, and he is one man from the Southern army that I'm mighty glad to see come.

CHAPTER XXII.

GETTING TOGETHER.

Some True Stories That Illustrate What Friends Americans Can Be, though Enemies Once—The Man Who Shot Me—Telling the Story of the Battle—The Captured Silverware—Drinking from the Little Cup in After Years—Plowing with the Yankees' Horses—A Little Rebel Bootblack—Hunting a New Home—A Northern Office Holder—Governor Campbell's Last Pardon.

CHAPTER IV. contains an address delivered by Gen. W. D. Hamilton, who was colonel of the Ninth Ohio Cavalry.

Some years after the war he went to Alabama looking after business matters there, and this business called him to Florence and Athens, Ala., at which places his regiment had been stationed. Those who read the General's speech will recall its lofty patriotism and its broad and generous charity. Having had part in the decoration services, and having lived for a time in Alabama, it occurred to the author that some reminiscences of this personal friend would be of interest to our readers generally.

In speaking of the incident of the silverware the General said:

In April, 1864, I was ordered by General Sherman to Florence, Ala., with two regiments of cavalry to feed on and destroy the corn and other supplies of the Tennessee Valley in that locality, on which General Forrest depended when going into Tennessee. I encamped on Cypress Creek, two miles from the city, and sent out teams to collect food for men and horses.

One evening I found that one of the companies was using a large amount of silverware at supper, and learned, upon inquiry, that it had been brought in by the detail that had been collecting supplies.

The sergeant in charge said the silverware had been found in a cave covered over with corn. It was found on the plantation of W. H. Key, on the river seven miles below my camp. I had the silverware brought to my tent, and the next morning sent it back to the family with a note telling the circumstances. I informed them also that if they had any other valuables hidden to take the same to their home, as nothing of that kind would be disturbed. A little later Mr. Key called upon me at the camp to thank me for the return of his property. I was invited to dine with them, which invitation I accepted.

While at the table Mr. Key was called out by the appearance of a squad of soldiers with wagons, who came to get supplies of corn, meat, etc. He asked what command they belonged to, and was informed that they were from the Ninth Ohio Cavalry.

"The colonel of your regiment is at dinner with me," said Mr. Key. "Had you better not see him?"

"It is not worth while," replied the sergeant. "We are simply obeying orders."

Mr. Key informed me of the situation, asking what he should do. As I had been ordered by General Sherman to collect supplies, I could do nothing but say to the gentleman that I was powerless to prevent the men obeying my orders, and that I thought the men would act fairly with him. He produced the keys to the smokehouse and the corncrib, and the men took a portion of the smoked meats, leaving him a fair amount for family use.

"I am placed in a most humiliating position, Mr. Key," said I. "Sitting at your table as your guest, my men come and take your provisions; and I must make no effort to stay them because of my orders. It is indeed humiliating, but it is one of the unfortunate circumstances of war."

My men, however, had treated him with courtesy and politeness, saying, as I had, that it was an enforced duty; and Mr. Key did not find fault. He realized that it was the duty of soldiers to obey orders.

Twenty-five years from that time I was in that locality again, and Mr. Key and his wife were still living; and when he learned I was in the neighborhood, he called and invited me to dine with him again. It so happened that it was the twenty-fifth anniversary of my first dinner with him. At that first dinner there was a shy little girl about four years of age, who came slowly into the room where I sat. She had been told there was a Yankee there, and her eyes were wide and fear seemed to dwell in their depths, notwithstanding the presence of her parents. It was not long, however, until she sat upon my lap and I was telling her stories.

In the twenty-five years that elapsed between dinners at the plantation of Mr. Key the little girl had grown to womanhood and had married and had gone with her husband to Florida; but on this occasion of my visit she was at home, and when dinner was announced took me by the arm, and when seated at the table said: "This little silver cup was my first birthday present, and it was with the silver under the corn in the cave where your men found it. You sent it back to me, and now I want you to drink out of it for my sake." I did drink out of her little cup—I cannot remember what—but it was like Bobby Burns's "Cup o' kindness, for Auld Lang Syne."

.   .   .   .

General Hamilton related another story of Florence, Ala., that happened a few days after the return of the silverware to Mr. Key. A Mr. Patton, living some miles distant from camp, was without teams to cultivate a crop of corn. Both armies had drawn upon him for horses and there were but two left, and some of the Ninth Cavalry had taken the one horse that was fit for anything. The help had gone. Once there had been many slaves on the plantation, but these had disappeared and the planter was doing the best he could himself.

When the one horse of any value was taken he went to the headquarters of Colonel Hamilton and told how he was situated, saying: "My negroes have all gone, leaving none but the children and old folks—they who took care of us when we were children and who are too old to do much work. At the best I am not much of a plowman, but was doing the best I could to put in a crop of corn, when your men came, Colonel, and broke up my team. I do not come with any complaint, as I know the laws of war; but to satisfy my wife I have come to see you."

"Your wife was right, Mr. Patton, and I may be able to do something for you; at least, we will see what can be done. My men were acting under my orders," said Colonel Hamilton. "I have to keep my men mounted, but I have some horses whose backs have become so injured by the saddle that I cannot use them. Come, we will look over them and see what we can do for you."

The Colonel was well satisfied that the horse his men left was a poor specimen, and he proposed to give Mr. Patton all the benefit of the trade that circumstances would permit.

It is not inappropriate at this point to say that the Ninth Ohio Cavalry a few months before had been well mounted; but they had traveled a long way, from Louisville to Nashville, and from Nashville to Athens and then to Florence. Many of the horses were sadly galled and unfit for service. Colonel Hamilton picked out a team and then gave him an extra horse, in case it was needed, and Mr. Patton cultivated his crop.

In the fall of 1866 Mr. Patton was elected Governor of Alabama, and Colonel Hamilton had occasion to go to Montgomery two days after he was inaugurated. He thought he would call upon the Governor, and presented his card. The official door-keeper took the card, saying to the Colonel that the retiring Governor and the newly inaugurated one were very busy and could not be seen. Colonel Hamilton, after leaving his card, turned away to look over the Statehouse and its grounds. Presently the official who had his card came hurrying to him, stating that Governor Patton wished to see him at once. There were present the retiring Military Governor, Parsons, and his staff; and Patton, meeting Hamilton in the middle of the great room, called Ex-Governor Parsons and his staff about him and said: "I want to introduce you to a Yankee; and I take pleasure in saying to you in his presence, and to him in your presence, that he and the Ninth Ohio Cavalry did more to reconcile the people of North Alabama to our defeat than he has any knowledge of, for he taught us that, after all, there were gentlemen in the North."

There have crept into this story of the prisons and cemeteries of Ohio, from time to time, little incidents that were foreign to the story proper; but the reader will grasp the idea the author seeks to present—viz., the universal brotherhood of Americans.

A Democratic Governor of Ohio was James E. Campbell, who retired from office as William McKinley succeeded to it. His last official pardon given a prisoner was one for a Union veteran, and the person who sought the pardon was a man who, when a lad, was known as "Johnny, the little Rebel bootblack."

The Secretary of the Board of Managers of the Ohio Peni-tentiary during the Campbell administration was Mr. James Newman, who related the story of his boyhood:

My home was in Mobile, and there were only my mother and myself. My father had been dead since my babyhood, and I was the man of the house. I was not yet twelve years of age, when one day the cannon thundered all about Mobile, and the men in gray marched away and strange men in blue came instead.

I had been selling papers and blacking boots or doing any-thing I could to make a living; and when these strangers came, I wondered what I should do. I first ventured into the camp of an Indiana regiment with a little bundle of papers and my blacking kit. They were rough but kindly men, these Hoosiers, and it was not long until I was on good terms with them.

I was getting along quite well, and was proud of the fact that

I could make mother fairly comfortable, when one night she suddenly grew worse, and I was frightened when she turned her
white face toward me and whispered: "Jimmie, Jimmie, I'm going. Be a good boy!"

The Indiana men saw traces of tears on my cheeks when I
went to the camp the next morning. At first they joked me
about some one giving me a whipping; but when I did not answer them, and when they saw me trying to swallow a lump that
would continue to rise in my throat, one of the men put his
arm about me and said: "What is the matter to-day, Johnny?"

I told him then of the mother that was lying dead in our poor
little home.

"You've been working to keep that sick mother for a good
while, haven't you, Johnny?"

I nodded assent. I could not say much.

"Well, run on home," said he, "and come back in a couple of
hours. Have you got a place to bury her?" he asked as I was
hastening away.

"Yes," I replied. "Some society in the city will see to that."

"All right," he answered. "Tell them, Johnny, that we are
going to get the coffin."

And they did—those great, rugged, fearless, fighting veterans
of the Hoosier State; they bought the finest coffin that could be
gotten in Mobile.

"Johnny's maw," said one lank, tow-headed private, "Johnny's
maw isn't goin' to be put away in no unpainted coffin; there's
goin' to be some trimmin's on this one, ef we hev to stand the
sutler off." The sutler got a goodly portion of Lige Davis's pay;
but poor, weak Lige meant all right.

When it was all over I went to camp and lived with them, and
they made me a little blue suit out of a Federal uniform and proposed that when they went home I should go with them, and they
would see that I should have a home and a chance to go to
school. I went with them and had a home with one Jim, a member of the regiment, who seemed to think well of me. His wife
was a mother to me during the short time I lived with them. Jim
took home with him an unfortunate habit that got him in trouble
more than once in the army. When sober, Jim was a kind man;
when he took to drinking, he was a demon. The poor wife had
hoped that he would return to her free from the grip of the
monster.

It was less than a month after he returned that he went to the
county seat and came home the wild beast. I got out of bed to
put his horse away, and then he proposed to beat me. I eluded
him and hid until he was asleep. That night I packed my few
belongings and in the morning I said good-by to the poor woman,

whom I knew would have been better off with Jim asleep on some battlefield.

I have often thought there is many a Jim that is only a poor old drunkard hanging on to life that might have been a dead hero had the leaden messenger only have come; but I'm preaching a sermon now instead of telling my story, so I'll go on.

I had heard of a man by the name of McFarland, who was good to homeless boys, and inquired the way to his house. The snow lay deep in fields and wood, and I trudged on and learned that McFarland was in his woods hauling logs. When I drew near, I saw he was struggling with a big log that was too much for him. I grasped a handspike lying near, and in a moment the log was on the sled. He looked at me a moment and asked: "Who are you?"

I told him who I was and what I wanted. He stood whistling softly to himself a few moments, and cried to the horses: "Get up!"

When we got out of the woods he turned one way and I another. I felt the lump rising again that was there when mother died, but I did not say a word.

Presently I heard him shout: "Where the devil are you going?"

"To hunt a home," I called back.

"I thought you wanted to live with me?"

"You didn't tell me"— I began.

"Don't stand there in the snow jawing about it. Come on!"

I helped him to put the horses away, and then we went to the house, where supper was waiting. And O such a supper! In fancy I catch the odor from the kitchen often, and I'm hungry in a moment.

"Mother," said he, "this is a little Johnny Reb that the Sixty-Ninth brought home from Mobile. Do you suppose we can find a place for him?"

"We have always a place for a good boy," she answered gently.

I lived with them eight years, going to school in winter and working on the farm in summer. I became a school-teacher and later came to Ohio and bought out a Democratic newspaper in Piqua; and, as you know, I am Secretary to the Board of Managers of the Ohio Penitentiary, and all I have on earth I owe to those Indiana soldiers.

Such was the story Newman told the newspaper man, and later the newspaper man had a story for him.

There came to the Ohio Penitentiary one day in summer a man whose name was given as Samuel Miller. The reporter met him and was impressed with the rugged, honest face of the man; and when he had learned the story of his supposed crime, he was impressed with the old man's innocence. It was a real estate deal and a few political enemies that made it possible for this man, who had fought for his country in the Mexican War and the war of the sixties, to be a convict.

It was a legal outrage, and the reporter set about helping the old man. The strange thing about it was that he did not go at once to Newman, but he forgot the story of the newsboy for the time being, but later, recalling it, he went to the clerk of the Board and said there was an Indiana soldier in the penitentiary who was innocent. The pretended crime was committed in Greenville, Darke County, Ohio, although the accused lived in Indiana. Finally Newman took the matter up; but only a day or two were left, as Governor Campbell was to leave the office and he (Newman) would soon be supplanted.

The old soldier convict was sent for. When he came into the presence of the Secretary, he stood with bared head.

"You are Number —— ?"

"Yes, sir," answered the old man.

"Your name is Miller?"

"Yes, sir; Samuel Miller."

"You were an Indiana soldier, I am told."

"Yes, sir."

"What regiment?" asked Newman.

"I was captain of Company B, Sixty-Ninth Indiana."

"What?" asked Newman, excitedly.

The prisoner repeated the statement.

"Did you ever hear of 'Johnny' Newman? The boys called him Johnny."

"The little Rebel bootblack?" inquired the prisoner.

"Yes, the little Rebel bootblack."

"I knew the boy well. Some one of the regiment took him home with him; but I wouldn't know him, it's been so long."

"It's been a long time, has it not?"

"A long time, yes." And the prisoner looked away with misty eyes.

"Captain Sam Miller," spoke the Secretary sharply to hide the break in his voice, "Captain, I am that little Rebel bootblack, and I'm going to get you out of this place."

"Are you little Johnny? Are you—are you really? And the old man was shivering as with the ague.

Then the Secretary put his arms around the old man, who was sobbing pitifully. "Go back and take it easy," he was saying. "I'm going to see Governor Campbell right now."

The Governor was alone, and Newman said: "I've come for a favor that I must have."

"I haven't an office left, Newman. McKinley will have them all to-morrow."

"I don't want an office; I want something better." And then he told the Governor the story.

The Governor sat a moment musing, a far-away look in his eyes, and said: "Tell the old man that you will hand him his pardon in the morning."

CHAPTER XXIII.

The End at Last.

A Hero or a Dunce—The Story of a Spy—He Was Captured at Newark, Ohio—Sentenced to Be Hung—How It Ended—One Hundred Dollars Reward Offered for a Prisoner—Dangers of the Ice Bridge—The Death of Lincoln—Colonel Hill Announced It—His Letter to the Sandusky *Sentinel*—The Money of the Prisoners in Bank—A Pathetic Poem—Going Home at Last—A Visit to Johnson's Island in 1904— The End.

THE Sandusky *Register,* the only source of information concerning the events at Johnson's Island, told a seemingly incredible story. It was on January 13, 1865. The paper stated that on the preceding day there arrived in Sandusky a pleasant-appearing, honest-faced, intelligent young man, who inquired for the provost marshal. He was directed to that functionary, who listened in surprise to the young man's story. He informed the official that he was Lieutenant McClung, of the First Tennessee Artillery. He was captured by General Stoneman December 14, 1864, and paroled by the General to report in Knoxville, which he did. At this point General Carter paroled him. He was allowed to go wherever he wished in the city, and this parole was good for forty-eight hours. He was then sent to Louisville under guard. How long he remained there, or under whose charge, the volunteer prisoner did not state. He had been informed, however, that his destination was Johnson's Island.

He had remained in Louisville as long as he felt it his duty to stay, when he was expected at that former summer resort on Lake Erie; and without waiting for Uncle Sam to provide him with passes on the railroads, and to arrange for his board and lodging, he set out one morning from Louisville and reached Sandusky January 12, by way of Cleveland.

He had traveled by easy stages, and no one in the North had an idea that he was a Confederate officer traveling leisurely to prison. The astonished provost marshal, not to be outdone by a "Johnny," had the gentleman from Alabama remain in the city until after dinner, as the menu at the West House was somewhat superior to that in the "Bull Pen."

Lieutenant McClung did not ask for an escort to the island, nor did he need it; but Provost Marshal Jenny thought he should at least have a guard of honor, and thus the young man went to the island.

This story sounds somewhat "fishy" after forty years have elapsed to think it over, but it was told in all seriousness by a paper which at that time preferred to consider a Confederate in the light of heavy man or villain instead of leading man or hero in the national tragedy then being played. If Lieutenant McClung is yet living, the author suggests his writing to the *Confederate Veteran.*

From Newark, Ohio, a dispatch went out to the country saying that Lieutenant Davis, of the Confederate army, had been arrested at that place. He was on the South-bound train. He had lately been in Canada, and was making for the South via Washington.

At Newark he was to change cars, take the Central Ohio to Wheeling, and the Baltimore and Ohio from there to Washington. As he stepped from the train the provost marshal of Newark placed him under arrest. The superintendent of the Sandusky, Mansfield, and Newark Railway was on the train, and being told who the man was, had sent a dispatch from Mt. Vernon, Ohio, requesting his arrest.

The arrest which ended his career as a spy was brought about through a memory of his face by two men who had been in Andersonville Prison. Among the thousands in that dreadful stockade were Archibald Parker, a young fellow of some eighteen years of age, who belonged to the Sixteenth Illinois Cavalry, and Frank Beverstock, of Lexington, Ohio, a well-known business man of that village, who had gone into the army. Both of these men had been taken prisoner, and both had been in Andersonville during a period that Lieutenant Davis was there as one of the officials.

At Monroeville young Parker caught sight of the man whom he had seen frequently down in Georgia, and he immediately boarded the train and took a seat near the Southerner, with a view to having him arrested at some point where there were United States officials.

The train on its way South passed through Lexington, the home of Beverstock, who boarded the train there on his way to Columbus. Lieutenant Davis was indifferently watching the landscape and the villages through which they passed, little dreaming that there was any one in Ohio that would know him, and that there sat near him a young man who seldom took his eyes from him. Beverstock entered the car and, walking down the aisle looking for a convenient seat, dropped into that beside Davis. They entered into conversation in a casual manner, as travelers do, and presently Beverstock was impressed with the idea that he had met this gentleman before somewhere, and began to search his memory for the time and place. It soon dawned upon him that his companion was none other than the lieutenant he had often seen at Andersonville, and he asked: "What is your name, may I ask?"

"My name is Cummings, and I live in Canada," replied the Southerner, as he produced a pass or letter permitting him to visit the United States.

"I imagined I had met you before," answered Beverstock.

"Is that so? Where, may I ask?"

"At Andersonville Prison."

"Where is that?"

"It is supposed to be next door to hell," said Beverstock sharply, "but it is in Georgia."

"In what way do you connect me with that place?" asked Davis, as he made an attempt to treat the matter indifferently.

"I think your name is Davis, and that you were the lieutenant that visited the prison every day," replied Beverstock.

"It is one of those cases where one man closely resembles another," answered the lieutenant.

Nothing more was said just then, and presently Beverstock observed Superintendent Stewart, of the S., M., and N. road, and remarked to Davis: "There is a man I do know. Excuse me, I wish to talk to him a few moments."

Davis was quite willing to excuse his inquisitive acquaintance, but began to get uneasy. As Beverstock arose to go to see the superintendent, he caught sight of young Parker motioning to

him. Beverstock and Parker had never met, although both were
in prison at Andersonville at the same time.

"Are you with that man?" asked Parker, as Beverstock drew
near.

"I am not with him, exactly, but I don't intend to let him out
of my sight."

"Neither do I intend to let him out of my sight until something
is done," said the young man.

"Do you know him?" asked Beverstock.

"I do; he was an officer at Andersonville."

"Were you ever in Andersonville?" asked Beverstock.

"You bet I was, and I know that man."

"I know him too, and we'll get him," said the man from Lexington.

The superintendent of the road was informed quietly of the
find, and when the train pulled into Mt. Vernon he went to the
telegraph office and sent word to the provost marshal to be at
the train on its arrival.

Both Beverstock and Parker kept a sharp watch on Davis, and
when Newark was reached the provost official stepped up to the
stranger and said: "You are my prisoner."

The valise owned by Lieutenant Davis was searched, a dozen
pairs of ladies' kid gloves were found, and an old Testament on
the fly leaf of which was written, "Winchester, September 7th,
1862," and on another leaf a mess account dated at a camp near
Charleston, S. C.

He finally owned up, told his name, and was sent to Columbus
for further examination. The next public record found in the
papers concerning Lieutenant Davis was in the *Ohio State Journal* of February 1, which said:

The Rebel spy, Lieutenant Davis, captured on the Sandusky
passenger train, has been tried by court-martial at Cincinnati,
and found guilty of being a Confederate spy and ordered to be
executed on Johnson's Island February 17. The finding of the
court was approved by the President.

On February 3 the Sandusky *Register* announced:

It will be remembered that S. B. Davis, alias Willoughby
Cummings, was arrested some two weeks ago near Newark.
The specifications show that he was a spy in the service of the

Confederacy, and the court so found, and he was sentenced to be hanged between the hours of 10 A.M. and 3 P.M. Friday, February 17. The Lieutenant was brought to the Island from Cincinnati the first of the week. At Monroeville he saw a lady enter the car who closely resembled a relative, and at sight of one who brought back thoughts of home and loved ones his pent-up feelings gave way, and, as if he were a child again and sorrowed at some childish care, the tears streamed down his cheeks.

On arriving at this city he begged the officer in charge to remove the irons from his wrists, which request was at once complied with, and he thus walked through the city and over the ice to the prison.

On the way over he was met by Lieutenant Calver, of the One Hundred and Twenty-Third Ohio Regiment, who recognized him as one of his old prison keepers. Lieutenant Calver said that he knew nothing of the treatment accorded the Union privates by Lieutenant Davis, but that he had been treated with courtesy and kindness by the Southern officers. On arriving at the Island Davis wrote to his personal friends and also to President Lincoln, to whom he stated his case and asked for a reprieve.

January 6, 1865, the Detroit *Tribune* says:

Davis, at the time of his arrest, was on his way to Richmond to get a commission for Young, one of the St. Albans raiders. It was he who went to Richmond and brought back in safety Burleigh's commission, concerning which so much bluster was indulged in during the trial of the latter.

February 13 the Sandusky *Register* states:

The commandant of the Union forces at Sandusky gave notice to the papers that citizens will not receive permission to attend the execution of Lieutenant Davis.

On February 18 the same paper states:

The sentence of Lieut. S. B. Davis, Confederate spy, who was to have been executed yesterday, was changed to imprisonment at Fort Delaware during the war. The order commuting his sentence was not made known to him until nine o'clock yesterday, and at 9:30 he was on the train *en route* to his future place of confinement. He seemed confident from the first that he would not hang, but on Thursday his hopes and fears were about evenly balanced. The manner of making his fate. known to him was conducted so quietly that he had no chance of thanking any one. He is a nephew of General Trimble, for merly President of the B. and O. Railroad, and not a nephew. as asserted, of the President of the Confederacy.

The subsequent fate of Lieutenant Davis is unknown to the writer. That his life was spared is known, and he and his friends owe it to the great heart of Lincoln.

On January 5, 1865, a prisoner, who by some means secured a complete Federal uniform, walked out of the prison with the guards attending the roll call. Of course in due time he was missed, but no one was able to tell where he was, and so the commandant offered a reward of one hundred dollars for his recapture.

Commenting upon this circumstance, the paper remarks:

Last April a search for Union uniforms was made, and several pairs of blue pants were found. Since that time repeated searches have been instituted for clothing and other contraband articles, and on several occasions blouses and fatigue caps were found, and it was supposed that everything had been removed, but at the muster and search yesterday afternoon over a dozen pairs of light blue pants and two fatigue caps were obtained. Some of the pants had recently been provided with stripes by the prisoners in the style of officers of the Veteran Reserve Corps.

The *Register* of January 10 said:

Col. Daniel R. Hundley, Thirty-First Alabama, escaped from Johnson's Island about 9:30 on the morning of the 2d inst., and on the morning of the 6th was captured by Peter Kessler at Fremont, Ohio. A reward of one hundred dollars had been offered by Colonel Hill for the capture of Colonel Hundley, which reward was paid to Mr. Kessler, who was very much pleased with the roll of greenbacks.

The reward of one hundred dollars was offered for the recapture of Lieut. Rufus Jones. These escaping prisoners most always provide themselves with forged orders or passes; doubtless Lieutenant Jones had one.

Colonel Hundley undertook to pass himself off as Private Charles A. Whittier, and in aid of his plans provided himself with a special order on which the signature of Capt. J. F. Huntington, A. A. A. G., was closely imitated, announcing that "Private Charles A. Whittier is hereby detailed for special duty in Detroit. He is ordered to report forthwith to the provost marshal of that place."

The Colonel is a man of great intelligence and of high literary attainments. Kessler had been a member of the old Eighth Ohio, and had seen too many Southerners to be taken in by the Colonel's papers or United States clothing.

The Sandusky *Register* of December 4, 1863, said:

There are now two thousand five hundred and thirty-six officers of the Confederate army at Johnson's Island. Packages for them are daily arriving from all parts of the North containing clothing, boots, game, wine, food, and all kinds of luxuries. In this way their imprisonment has been the most utter farce, while our soldiers have been almost starved at Richmond. These things were permitted for a while, but are changed now. The packages are now confiscated and sold, or given away to the soldiers of the post. All prisoners will be denied any but ordinary rations.

A burying ground for the prisoners has recently been laid out under the supervision of Gen. Jeff Thompson, and has been neatly fenced in. Deaths occur at the rate of from one to three a day. Whenever a prisoner dies, he is buried by six of his comrades, who carry the body to its assigned place, dig a shallow grave (for the limestone strata prevents digging graves more than three feet), and quietly inter their comrade.

The *Register* of April 8, 1865, said:

Thomas F. Berry, the spy who murdered a fellow-prisoner at Johnson's Island sometime ago, together with nine witnesses from the prison, left yesterday for Cairo, from which point he will be sent through the lines for trial in some one of the States in revolt. We may be mistaken, but it seems no more than right that he should be held for trial in the county where the offense was committed. He was taken away in irons, and seemed the most dejected person of the entire party.

No previous notice of this affair could be found in the papers. Who he killed was not mentioned, nor the occasion for the killing. By following the files of this paper closely, one is enabled to gather a deal of the unwritten history of Johnson's Island.

This history was merely local items of occurrences as they happened. Often, as Lieutenant Cunningham, in his interesting story, "Plain Living at Johnson's Island," wrote: "The paper published a story one day and contradicted or changed it afterwards." This was well put, but even at that there is a deal of history gathered in three years by a live daily paper.

The author of the *Century Article* and the *Register* were evidently not of the same opinion concerning the appearance of the prisoners mustered for exchange during the spring of 1865.

The *Register* of February 25, 1865, stated:

Yesterday three hundred prisoners were brought over from

Johnson's Island and were immediately loaded upon the Sandusky, Mansfield, and Newark train for Point Lookout, for exchange. They were a hearty, healthy-looking set of men, giving no evidence of starvation. They embraced all classes, from lieutenants to colonels. They were chosen for exchange in the order of their priority of capture. This squad makes something over five hundred who have left for exchange. There yet remains on the Island nearly two thousand five hundred, many of whom are of high rank. Most of these are anxious to be exchanged, but their anxiety is greater to return to their suffering families than to the army.

But few of them have any confidence in the success of their cause, and these few base their faith not in their own ability to achieve their independence, but upon foreign assistance.

Many of those that left yesterday were well-dressed, and all seemed comfortably clad. For months there had been a great crystal bridge between Sandusky and the Island. That stern king, the north wind, had built it, and marching squadrons in blue and heart-weary hosts in gray passed over it. Then about March 1 the sun broke through the gray clouds, and the south wind laughed at Jack Frost, and the bridge without piers began to give way.

Going from Sandusky to Cedar Point March 1 were four men in a sleigh. One of these was a soldier mail carrier. Horse, sleigh, and all went down into the icy waters. In some mysterious manner three men escaped, but the mail carrier went down to death.

It was on the morning of that day that the commandant of the Island made known to Lieut. Col. Thomas M. Atkins and Capt. Vincent G. Wynne, prisoners of war, that they had been chosen to go to Camp Douglas, near Indianapolis, where was a large depot for Confederate privates, and distribute to them quantities of clothing. This clothing was a portion of the proceeds of a cotton sale at New York, which sale had been made for that purpose. The suggestion was made that the ice bridge was now considered unsafe, and if they were content to wait a few days boats would be running. Naturally the Confederate officers suggested that they must wait his convenience; but if they were to choose they would go at once, as the men in Camp Douglas were suffering for clothing. Colonel Hill thought his men not less daring than the prisoners, and made the detail to accompany the officers to Indianapolis. The facts were, it was not a detail, but a chance for an officer and ten men to accompany these Confederates. Many more volunteers came forward than were needed, but ten were selected, and out they went upon the breaking ice. It was an escape, pure and simple; the ice was creaking, and no one knew what moment a great seam would open, or at what time they might be left upon an island of ice. It was a "heart disease" march, but they finally landed at Sandusky in safety.

On March 5 the *Register* said:

The· great old ice bridge between this city and Johnson's Island commenced to move yesterday about half past two, and in about half an hour it seemed clear water as far as the eye could penetrate. The ice over the bay the past winter has been thicker and stronger than has been known for many years, whilst the length of time it has remained has never been exceeded in the memory of the oldest inhabitant.

April 11, 1865.

There was a salute of two hundred guns fired at Johnson's Island yesterday in honor of the surrender of Lee and his army. The old thirty-two-pound Parrott's jarred every house in the city, rattling the window panes like an earthquake.

While the Federal forces were having a jubilee that the long and desperate war was nearing the end, the faithful men who had waited with weary patience the day of exchange that did not come were listening with sorrowing hearts to the roaring guns and the cheers. A number of their own men who had applied for the amnesty oath ran up a flag of the United States over Block Number One, where were fifty or sixty Confederate officers. "This," said the *Register,* "called forth the impotent wrath of the other class of tenants of the 'Bull Pen.' A large crowd of officers and men stood on the parapet to hear what defeated malice could say when plunged into such humiliating depths of disaster. The amnesty men sent back replies equal in force and wit to the shots from the other side."

The man who is artist enough to get in on the winning side of any great controversy is not confined to any particular locality.

April 15, 1865.

There is gloom in Sandusky to-day.

This brief sentence told the story. The North had won the great struggle, but lost the man who would have made the bitter days in the South less bitter. The sounds of rejoicing suddenly ceased, and there was moaning and weeping in the North. Well

would the South have wept with us could they have known the
reconstruction days—days that could not have been had the
warm-hearted Lincoln lived. How the soldiers of the North
loved him! There were many reasons why they should. If
ever a sleepy boy on picket was sentenced to death for the crime
of going to sleep, and was saved because some heart-broken mother pleaded for his life, it was Lincoln that saved him. The stern,
implacable Stanton, the mighty but stony-hearted War Secretary,
signed every death warrant—eagerly, it seemed—but there was
one higher than Stanton, and rarely indeed did the mother appeal
in vain.

Frank B. Carpenter, the artist, in a book published some twenty-
five years ago, relates a story of Lincoln worthy of being often
told, and it is given in this connection:

A young lad, the last one left to an old mother, had fallen asleep
one night on guard. He had marched and fought, and was worn
out when placed on duty. They found the poor boy asleep and
reported him, and it was the old story—a death sentence. Then
just before the time for his legalized murder the story came
to an old woman at Lancaster, Pa. There was no time for her
to sit and bemoan his fate. Thad Stevens was the Congressman from his district, and out of her scant means she took enough
money to go to Washington. There was little time to lose, and
Stevens was soon found.

"You have no idea, madam, how busy a man Mr. Lincoln is,"
said the Congressman. "It will be almost impossible to see
him."

"O, but, Mr. Stevens, he wouldn't refuse to see me if he knew
that they were going to kill my only boy."

The Congressman and the sorrowing woman were soon waiting at the White House. The doorkeeper knew Stevens well,
and took his card to the President, though there were many
waiting. At once the President asked what he could do for the
Congressman from Lancaster.

"Mr. President," said Stevens sadly, "I could not refuse a
poor old woman from my district who is here to see you. Her
only son"—

"Sentenced to be shot, I suppose?" broke in the President.

"Yes; sentenced to be shot—he is a mere boy. Two older
brothers were killed in battle," replied Stevens.

"Bring her in," said Mr. Lincoln; "I'll give her a moment."
When he looked up, there stood before him a spare woman some
fifty years of age. Her dress was plain, and her queer little
bonnet had crape upon it. He saw that her lips were trembling,

and in her faded eyes there was an appeal so pathetic that he felt a lump rising in his throat. Finally she spoke, "O, Mr. Lincoln, you'll give me back my little boy," and then she shook with sobs and could say no more.

"Mr. Stevens tells me that you have given two boys to your country that were killed in battle."

"Yes, I did; and it seems to me you ought to let me have one."

"You shall have this one," he was saying to himself, but the mother did not hear what the great man murmured. He turned to his desk and wrote hurriedly, rang for a messenger, and a pardon was telegraphed to the front where the boy was awaiting death.

When Mr. Stevens informed her that her son had been saved, she stood for a moment looking at him; and the tall, ungainly-looking man seemed a god, since he had saved her boy. Then she sought to kneel before him, and had he permitted she would have kissed his feet. He spoke to her very gently, saying that he was very busy and she must go.

"I haven't thanked you," she said brokenly, as Mr. Stevens led her to the door. But the President had seen her thanks in the faded eyes that lighted up when they told her her boy was saved.

He was the best man in the world to the poor old woman. He was now dead, and the North was in tears.

The *Register* said editorially on April 17:

Colonel Hill, we understand, has given orders to the guard to shoot down the first Rebel who exults over the death of President Lincoln.

Under the same date Colonel Hill replied, the reply being creditable to the honor and the humanity of the man:

Mr. Editor: The article in your paper [referring to the above] is entirely incorrect, and places me in a position indefensible. In no possible view of the case could I be allowed to forget that the men in my hands are unarmed prisoners, whom it is as much my duty to protect as to retain. If I supposed that any one of them had an actual agency in the assassination, certainly neither the duty nor the privilege would be mine, on my own motion, to shoot him or punish him in any way. Much less could I order men to shoot those whom I could not suspect as having any agency in the assassination; and from the first I felt sure the prisoners would generally disapprove the act. . . . In justice to the prisoners, let me say right here that before I had indicated my purpose to any of them, as far as I could see, every one who heard the news, of the more than two thousand two hundred officers before me, appeared to be depressed and sorrowful over what had occurred. They seemed to realize it as a terrible calamity to them as well as us.

Many of the prisoners had money. The commandant of the post keeps the prisoners' money on deposit at the First National Bank of Sandusky, and the balance there yesterday was $23,-444.87.

In the reminiscences of Camp Chase, the reader will recall the story of Capt. W. H. Herbert, of Sandusky, Ohio, who was a prisoner there in 1862. In conversation with the gentleman in September, 1904, he mentioned a poem that the *Confederate Veteran* published in January, 1901, and which was written by Col. C. W. Frazier, a friend of Mrs. Herbert, then Miss Elizabeth Davis Lea. The copy furnished the author was copied by the lady from the original written on Johnson's Island while Colonel Frazier, of Memphis, was a prisoner there:

THE CAPTIVE ON LAKE ERIE.

A captive on a lake-girt isle
   Looks on the waters sadly,
His thoughts on one whose blessed smile
   Would welcome him so gladly;
But that beneath a Northern sky—
   A sky to him so dreary—
He's doomed to pine and vainly sigh.
   Away out on Lake Erie.

The winds that waft to others bliss
   But mock him with their tone;
The lips are pale they stoop to kiss
   With yearning for his home.
The waves that dash upon the beach
   Keep ceaseless watch and weary;
They chant of joys beyond the reach
   Of him who looks on Erie.

They bear to him his mother's tone,
   His sister's mournful song,
Until he longs to be alone
   Far from that captive throng;
And when he lays him down to sleep,
   With aching heart and weary,
The winds and waves his vigils keep,
   Dear dreamer on Lake Erie.

But all who love him pray to God
To bless his precious life
With patience to endure the rod,
With faith to close the strife,
And look beyond the dreary morn
To brighter days and better,
When native winds shall fan his brow,
And only fond arms fetter.

On June 21 the Sandusky *Register* said.

Several carloads of Confederates left last evening on the Cleve land and Toledo train, and quite a large number awaited the early train on the C., H., and D. road.

No further mention was made of the prisoners on the Island There were a number kept for a time who were not prisoners of war, but men charged with various offenses that only time would settle.

The *Confederate Veteran* of July, 1900, says:

A few years ago Col. Robert Alexander, of Texas, who was making a tour of the lakes, stopped off at Sandusky and went over to Johnson's Island to see the spot where so many of his former comrades in arms had been confined.

As he passed slowly through the cemetery reading the names upon the headstones, he was seen to suddenly lift his hat and fall upon his knees beside one of the low green mounds. There were tears in his eyes as he bent his head over the grave, and they trickled down his furrowed cheeks and fell upon the green sward beneath which rested all that was mortal of one who had been very dear to him and for whose mysterious loss he had been inconsolable. Colonel and Mrs. Alexander were childless. They had years before the war taken as their own the orphaned son of a sister of Mrs. Alexander. The war came on, the boy enlisted, was captured, and died in a Northern prison. Colonel Alexander never knew what his fate had been until he visited Johnson's Island. Inscribed upon the headstone were the words: "James E. Peel, Captain Eighth Arkansas Infantry; aged twenty-four years."

The same article states:

The cemetery where two thousand two hundred and sixty Confederates are buried attracts the most attention. In 1886, when, through the influence of Gov. J. B. Foraker and his adjutant general, Gen. H. A. Axline, an appropriation was obtained from the United States government to inclose Camp Chase, there was sufficient to build not only the wall at Camp Chase, but to build the iron fence around this cemetery and put in order the last resting place of those buried there, who are dear to the South.

Whatever of differences may exist politically toward this distinguished son of Ohio, the South will not forget his great heart in this initial work in preserving the graves of those who died in prison and far from their loved ones.

The view of the cemetery on Johnson's Isalnd (see page 191) was taken September 24, 1904, by Mr. J. T. Gamble, and is a very realistic and natural picture of the cemetery. The reader can form some idea of the quiet beauty of the place.

There lives in Sandusky a gentleman who had been a prisoner at Camp Chase, Capt. William H. Herbert, and the author wrote to him about the condition of the cemetery there. He replied that the cemetery is kept in good condition, and every year he accompanies the Union veterans to their decoration services, and then they take the boat for the Island and put flowers on every Confederate grave and a wreath on each headstone.

Whatever may be done at other Northern cemeteries where lie the Southern prisoners of war, it is with pleasure I record that in this State the Blue (growing gray) and the Gray (growing grayer) go side by side and put flowers on the graves of the men who battled for the South.

When his story began there were flowers everywhere. The chill of autumn is now at hand, and the blooms are fading. It was a beautiful September day, however, when I visited Johnson's Island to see the resting place of the dead and view the old forts and walk over the ground where the prisoners once restlessly paced. I was accompanied by Mr. J. T. Gamble, who had his photographic equipment with him to show the reader what the Island looks like to-day. As Shakespeare said of sleep, "It knits up the raveled sleave of care," and time wears away the angles of the redoubt and levels the frowning breastworks. At present there is little of the Johnson's Island of forty years ago. Two hundred and six Southern soldiers—150 known and 56 unknown—sleep there under the hickory trees. Hawthorn bushes, with their flaming scarlet berries, here and there bend over the graves; but most of the trees in the cemetery are young shellbark hickories with leaves turning yellow and falling with the nuts, bedecking the low mounds as though it were a gala day.

The deep wood lying back of the cemetery is composed almost

entirely of second-growth hickory. The visitor to the Island is prone to sit on the veranda of the pavilion and watch the scene upon the bay until he wearies of its quiet beauty. Then he strolls over into the cemetery and on into the woods, and goes to gathering the waiting nuts.

Cedar Point, three miles across Sandusky Bay, has become quite a summer resort, and Johnson's Island, with its infinitely greater natural attractions, has simply raised its crop of corn and hay, and sleepily dozed through succeeding summers, until this last summer.

The improvements are but beginning, and in a year or two they will doubtless be asking the South to come and visit and loll in the shade where the murmurs of the waters are answered by the whispers of the leaves.

One of the little circulars issued by the Johnson's Island people reads: "When you are in Sandusky don't fail to visit the historical Johnson's Island, and the famous forts and magazines, and where the Confederate officers are buried."

The visitors to the Island are principally young people, who dance awhile or swing, and then go down into the woods near where these Southern men are so quietly lying and talk of life and love until, perchance, the white headstones that the government placed in the little inclosure reminds them that there is awaiting them somewhere something strange and chill, something that inevitably follows the dancing and the laughing and the loving.

The Island is truly a beautiful spot. The trees, lovely in their afternoon dress of yellow and scarlet, and with here and there patches of green, lure the visitor with their ripened charms more readily than the sirens of the laughing lake.

As the vague autumn sun sank that evening behind the forest of gayly turbaned hickories we sailed away regretfully from the "Quick and the Dead."

WM. H. KNAUSS AND FAMILY.

KATHARINE ELIZABETH GAMBLE.

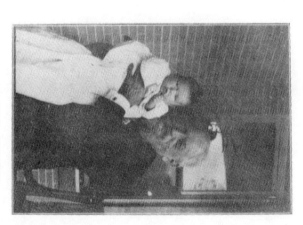

WILLIAM HIRAM PLETCHER.

WILLIAM H. KNAUSS.

MRS. WILLIAM H. KNAUSS.

MRS. JOHN T. GAMBLE   MRS. ORLAND W. PLETCHER.

Daughters of Mr. and Mrs. William H. Knauss.

JOHN T. GAMBLE.   ORLAND W. PLETCHER.

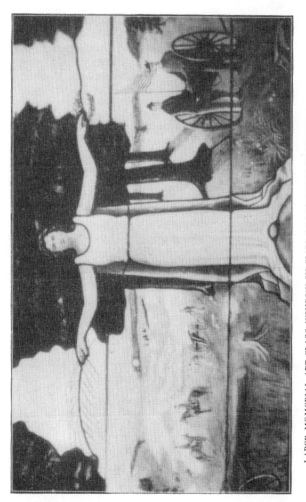

LARGE MEMORIAL ART GLASS WINDOW IN HALL OF RESIDENCE OF WILLIAM H. KNAUSS.

The battle represents War. The clasping of hands of the Blue and the Gray over the cannon and the dove building its nest in the mouth of the cannon represent Peace. The figure or portrait is that of the author's daughter, who, a short time before she died, said to her father: "Those who are opposing and condemning you for your good work don't appreciate the satisfaction and pleasure you are giving to the loved kindred of the dead Confederates, so don't give up your good work." A friend who saw the window writes: "This memorial window is a most fitting tribute to the memory of the loyal, beautiful daughter of Col. Knauss."

EMBLEMS PRESENTED BY COL. BENNETT H. YOUNG, OF LOUISVILLE, KY., TO
THE EX-SOLDIERS AND SAILORS OF FRANKLIN COUNTY,
OHIO, MAY 30, 1898.

THE FLORAL PIECE FROM THE SOUTH TO THE NORTH AT THE MONUMENT
OF EX-SOLDIERS AND SAILORS' ASSOCIATION OF FRANKLIN
COUNTY, OHIO, MAY 30, 1898.

APPENDIX.

APPENDIX.

ANTIETAM NATIONAL CEMETERY.

THE charter of the Antietam National Cemetery granted by the Legislature of Maryland at the January session of 1864, and amended and re-enacted at the January session of 1865, provides for the purchase, inclosing, and ornamenting of ten acres of land—a part of the battlefield of Antietam—as a burial and final resting place for the soldiers who fell in the battle of Antietam. This battle of Antietam was called by the Confederates Sharpsburg.

It sets forth the duty of the Trustees of the respective States who may join the corporation to remove the remains of all the soldiers who fell in that battle and have them properly interred in the aforementioned grounds, and "the remains of the soldiers of the Confederate army to be buried in a part of the grounds separate from those of the Union army."

The charter also provides that the grounds shall be devoted in perpetuity as a burial place for the dead of said battle, and to remain the property of the State of Maryland in fee simple, in trust for all the States which may participate in the work by their appropriations.

For the purpose of carrying into effect the provisions of the charter, the Legislature made two appropriations amounting to fifteen thousand dollars, which has been paid to the trustees, and it has been expended on the work.

Additional appropriations have from time to time been made by other States—namely, New York, Indiana, Connecticut, New Jersey, Minnesota, Maine, Rhode Island, Pennsylvania, Ohio, Wisconsin, Michigan, Vermont, West Virginia, and Massachusetts—which States are represented by trustees appointed by their respective Governors, and who, with those representing Maryland, constitute the corporation.

The Federal dead to the number of nearly five thousand having been removed to the cemetery, Mr. Boullt, of Maryland, at a meeting of the trustees held on the 7th of December, 1867, called attention to the fourth section of the charter of the Association, which makes it the duty of the Trustees to remove the remains of the Confederate soldiers who fell in the battle of Antietam, and he requested that some action be taken to carry into effect the provisions of the charter in this behalf; upon which subject John Jay, Esq., Trustee for New York, read the following communication from Governor Fenton, which was ordered to be entered among the proceedings of the Board:

STATE OF NEW YORK, EXECUTIVE DEPARTMENT,
ALBANY, December 3d, 1867.

Dear Sir: In regard to the payment of the balance of $4,000 still remaining unpaid of the ten thousand dollars appropriated by this State, I beg leave to remark that since my note to you of the 23d October, directing the Commissioner to pay the money in his discretion, my attention has been drawn to the question of the right to have the Confederate dead buried in the Antietam Cemetery, and that I regard the matter as entitled to the gravest attention.

The appropriation of ten thousand dollars was made by our Legislature in these words: "For a contribution to the fund for a National Cemetery at Antietam, to be paid on the certificate of the Governor to the person authorized to receive the same." There is nothing in the legislation of this State that either restricts or enlarges the purpose of the appropriation. It is simply declared to be a contribution to the fund for a National Cemetery at Antietam. We are remitted to the original act establishing the cemetery passed by the State of Maryland. That act, passed March 23d, 1865, recites in the preamble that under a former act passed March 10, 1864, and thereby repealed, the Governor of that State had made purchase of a suitable lot of ground situated on or near the battlefield of Antietam, in Washington County, for the burial and last resting place of the remains of the soldiers who fell in that action.

The second section of the act provides that said lot of ground purchased by the Governor, as set forth in the foregoing preamble, remain in the State of Maryland in fee simple, in trust for all the States that shall participate as hereinafter provided, and said lot of ground shall be devoted in perpetuity for the purpose of the burial and final resting places of the remains of the soldiers who fell in the battle of Antietam, or at other points north of the Potomac River during the invasion of Lee in the summer and fall of 1862, or died thereafter in consequence of wounds received in said battle, or during said invasion.

The third section names four Trustees from the State of Maryland, who, with one Trustee from each of the other States to be appointed by the Governor of their respective States, are created a body politic, under the name of the Antietam National Cemetery, to whom shall be conveyed the ground referred to.

The fourth section intrusts the care and management of the ground referred to solely to said Trustees, and it then declares: "And it shall be their duty out of the funds that may come into their hands, by State appropriation or otherwise, to remove the remains of all the soldiers referred to in the second section of this act, and to have them properly interred in the aforementioned ground. *The remains of the soldiers of the Confederate army to be buried in a part of the grounds separate from those of the Union army.* Also to lay out and inclose said grounds with a good, substantial stone wall not less than four feet high, or with an iron fence as said Trustees may think best, and to ornament, divide, and arrange into suitable plots and burial lots, establish carriage ways, avenues, and footways, erect buildings and a monument or monuments and suitable marks to designate the graves, and generally to do all things in their judgment necessary and proper to be done to adapt the ground to the uses for which it has been purchased and set apart."

From this extract it is clear that the use for which the ground was purchased and for which power was given to the Trustees, and appropriations were made by the State of Maryland, was as a burial ground for all who fell on either side, with the single provision: "That the remains of the soldiers of the Confederate army be buried in a part of the grounds separate from those of the Union army."

It is also clear that the same duty rests upon the Board in respect to each of the two classes of fallen soldiers, and that they are instructed to appropriate one part of the cemetery grounds for the dead of one army, and a separate part for the burial of the dead of the other.

It appears from the second annual report of the President of the Board to the Trustees, dated June 5, 1867, that up to that time the United States Burial Corps, under the superintendence of Lieut. John W. Sherer, had removed to the cemetery and buried therein 3,580 dead from nineteen States (including Maryland and Delaware), and also from the regular army, of whom 2,462 had been identified and 1,118 were interred as unknown. The total number of burials have since been increased, as I learn, to 4,695. I am also advised that no provision has been made by the Trustees for a separate plot in the cemetery to be devoted to the burial of the Confederate dead, and that no Confederate dead have been buried therein to the knowledge of the Board.

It is true that all the burials have been made by order of the Washington authorities, and at the expense of the government; but it does not appear that the Board has drawn the attention of the authorities to the fact that the act contemplated the interment of the Confederate as well as the Union dead, or that they have invoked the assistance of the government in executing this part of their trust.

To this it may be replied that by the eighth section of the act it is provided that "the expenses incident to the removal of the dead, inclosing or ornamenting the cemetery, and all the work connected therewith and its future maintenance, shall be apportioned among the States connecting themselves with the corporation, according to their population as indicated by their representation in the House of Representatives of the United States; and that, inasmuch as the States recently in rebellion had not connected themselves with the corporation nor assumed their share of the necessary expenses, the Board is under no obligation to devote any part of the funds received from the States which furnished no soldiers to the Confederate army for the burial of the dead of that army.

A partial answer to this would be that the States of Maryland and West Virginia have joined the association and contributed to its funds, and that, as many of the Confederates who fell at Antietam and during Lee's first invasion came from the States, they (especially Maryland) have a just right to demand that a separate part of the cemetery shall be appropriated to that class, and that the Board shall take the same steps toward accomplishing this part of their trust as they have done to fulfill that relating to the Union soldiers.

But looking at the matter not from a narrow, technical point of view but from a broad, national standpoint, it seems to me that good faith toward the State of Maryland, which originated the scheme, purchased the ground, enacted the law, and made two appropriations to carry out its object, makes it the clear duty of the Trustees to effectuate as far as lies in their power the known intent of the act, and that such a course will meet the approval of the people of the loyal States who have become parties to the corporation and whose dead repose in the cemetery.

A strong local and individual feeling in the neighborhood of Antietam and other parts of Maryland, naturally engendered by the invasion, may have created some indifference in regard to the remains of the Confederate dead, and an indisposition to see them buried side by side with those who died in the defense of our nationality. But it is confidently believed that no such feeling pervades the breasts of the American people or the surviving officers and soldiers of the Union army.

When we recall the generosity and moderation that marked the conduct of the people, the government, and the army during the war, the

magnanimity that presided at its close; when we remember that our countrymen are now engaged in the work of reconstructing the Union on the
basis of universal freedom and with an earnest desire to restore to the
Southern States a prosperity infinitely greater than that which slavery
and rebellion conspired to destroy, it is impossible to believe that they
would desire to make an invidious distinction against the moldering
remains of the Confederate dead, or that they would disapprove of their
being carefully gathered from the spot where they fell, and laid to rest
in the National Cemetery on the battlefield of Antietam.

Conquerors as we were in that great struggle, our stern disapproval of
the cause in which they fought need not forbid our admiration of the
bravery with which they died. They were Americans, misguided indeed
and misled, but still our countrymen, and we cannot remember them
now either with enmity or unkindness.

The hostility of the generous and heroic ends with death; and, brief as
our history is, it has furnished an early and striking example. The British
and Americans who fell at Plattsburg sleep side by side, and a common
monument on the Plains of Abraham attests the heroism of Wolfe and
Montcalm.

To-day nothing perhaps could sooner awaken a national spirit in the
heart of the South than the thought that representatives of the Northern
States were gathering the remains of its fallen sons for interment in our
National Cemetery; and in future days when our country is one, not
alone in its boundaries but in spirit and affection, and the recent struggle is remembered as a war less of sections than of systems, the cemetery
at Antietam, with its colossal statue of a Union soldier keeping guard
over the ashes of all who fell in the opposing ranks of McClellan and
Lee, will have a common interest for descendants of those who died on
either side in that sad and memorable Civil War.

I think, therefore, that the Trustees of the Antietam Cemetery, especially in view of the fact that the Southern States have not thus far been
in a position to contribute to the general fund, should either set apart
a sufficient plot of ground within the cemetery walls for the burial of the
Confederate dead, or make suitable arrangements for an enlargement of
the present inclosure, if necessary, to the attainment of the end proposed.
I would also recommend that the attention of the War Department be
called to the subject; and I entertain no doubt that the Secretary will
cheerfully coöperate in an object of so much interest.

Very truly yours,   R. E. FENTON.
John Jay, Esq., Special Commissioner, etc., New York.

After reading the above letter, Mr. Jay offered the following resolution.

Resolved, That, in pursuance of the provision of the 4th section of the
Act of Maryland, passed March 23d, 1865, incorporating the Antietam
National Cemetery, this Board do now designate and set apart for the
burial of the Confederate dead who fell in the battle of Antietam in the
first invasion of Lee the southern portion of the grounds not occupied,
and separate from the ground devoted to the burial of the Union dead.

With reference to that part of Governor Fenton's letter which recom-
mends "that the attention of the War Department be called to the
subject," Mr. Jay informed the Board that, in company with Colonel
Selleck, of Wisconsin, Chairman of the Executive Committee, he had
called that morning on General Grant, Secretary of War, and submitted
to him the facts of the case; that General Grant, after consulting with
General Schriven as to the powers of the Department, expressed his cordial approval of the fulfillment by the Trustees of the provisions of the

Act, and his readiness to afford all the assistance in his power, regretting that no act of Congress conferred on the War Department any authority in the matter.

The resolution was then adopted by a vote of 7 to 2.

The Legislature of Maryland at the following January session appropriated the sum of five thousand dollars to assist in carrying out the resolution of the Board.

At a meeting of the Trustees of the Cemetery held May 6, 1868, the superintendent reported that the unoccupied southern portion of the grounds was not sufficient for the burial of the Confederate dead, and recommended the purchase of additional grounds on the south side of the cemetery. The Board resolved to make the purchase, and a committee was appointed for that purpose. The Board met the following month (June 17) and adopted a resolution postponing all action with reference to the removal of the Confederate dead until the next meeting, which was held on the 18th of November, when the question was again postponed till the annual meeting, held December 9, 1868. At this meeting, after discussing the question, the Board resolved to continue the resolution postponing all action for the burial of the Confederate dead.

After the Board adjourned, the Trustees for the State of Maryland addressed a communication to Governor Swann, calling attention to the exposed and neglected condition of the Confederate dead, and informed the Governor that many of the trenches and graves were so washed that the bones were laid bare, and in some instances the remains had been turned over by the plow. They requested that some action be taken to protect the dead till they could be removed to a proper place of sepulture.

In consequence of the extreme illness of Governor Swann and his retiring from the gubernatorial chair, the communication was referred by him to his successor, Governor Bowie, who at once addressed a note to Thomas A. Boullt, Esq., of Hagerstown, Md., one of the Trustees for the State in the Antietam Cemetery, and requested him to employ agents to go over the battlefield and mound up the trenches and graves, and also to make careful notes of their location, and, as far as possible, identify the dead. For the accomplishment of the work, the services of Moses Poffinberger and Aaron Good, Esquires, citizens of Sharpsburg, and gentlemen well acquainted with the battlefields, were engaged. They visited every trench and grave herein described, and from their field notes this descriptive list has been compiled and published by direction of His Excellency, Oden Bowie, Governor of Maryland.

This list, it is believed, embraces, with a few exceptions, all the Confederate dead buried upon the battlefields of Antietam, South Mountain, and the Monocacy.

Friends of the Confederate dead can obtain copies free of charge by addressing Thomas A. Boullt, Hagerstown, Md.

Four unknown; J. Thompson, Co. H, 10th La. (died October 15, 1862); William Clark, 2d La.; M. Little, 6th La.; G. Zeller, Co. E, 6th La.; Philip Bitler, Co. B, 14th La.; P. N. Duplices, 8th La.; W. Wagner, Co.

I, 6th La.; Augustis Canas, Co. E, 6th La.; J. P. M., Co. G, 8th La., disinterred by friends. Buried east of J. C. Grove's warehouse, on hill near a new house; the headboards are all destroyed, but the graves are in good order and can be plainly seen.

J. P. Hudson, 8th La.; M. Anker, Co. H, 5th La.; L. D. Savage, Co E, 7th La.; J. Garnett, 9th La.; P. Oger, 6th La.; Capt. McFarland, Co. A, 7th La ; Capt. H. B. Ritchie, Co. C, 6th La. (died September 17, 1862) ; Capt. Lewis Heintz, 6th La.; J. E. Clay, Co. K, 14th La.; — Charles, 6th La.; one unknown. Buried on right-hand side of road leading to Grove's Warehouse, opposite to a large white oak stump, close along the fence, first field from Sharpsburg.

One unknown. Buried in the above field north of the last-named place not far from a stump along the hillside; been plowed over.

One unknown. Buried in J. C. Grove's orchard, where J. Houser lives; been plowed over.

One unknown. Buried in a hollow west of J. Houser's house and in line with the warehouse, ten feet above a cedar bush.

Four unknown. Buried in J. C. Grove's yard above the cave and close to a peach tree; had boards, but were destroyed and names forgotten.

Capt. James E. Martin, 2d Miss. Buried in Grove's yard near an old bake-oven wall, on right-hand side of road to Shepherdstown.

Six unknown. Buried below J. C. Grove's spring in the flat and between spring and limekiln.

Capt. G. W. Pollard, 53d Va.; one unknown. Buried near the line fence between Grove and Smith, three hundred yards from the tree at the gate in Smith's field, near a large rock.

S. B. Pleasants, B. P. Carlton, of Athens, Ga. Buried near a large walnut tree in Smith's field, but disinterred by friends.

One unknown. Buried in truck patch in front of Capt. D. Smith's house.

One unknown. Buried near the gate at Capt. D. Smith's carriage house.

E. Wood, Co. E, 32d Va.; E. Malicoat, Co. H, 32d Va.; C. S Francis, 15th Va.; W. B. Wicker, 15th Va.; J. B. Rate, 15th Va.; Lieut. James Dye, 32d Va.; W. D. Vinston, 15th Va.; G. W. Otey, 15th Va.; C. Wotz, 15th Va. Buried in Mayer's field in the hollow below Grove's house, toward the canal, under a clump of honey locusts; the graves are in good condition and headboards up.

William Wright, Co. E, 53d Ga.; Dozier Brown, Co. B, 24th Ga.; L. B. Persh, Co. H, 24th Ga.; J. B. Colwell, 53d Ga.; J. A. Keg, Co E, 10th Ga.; J. A. Wiley, 15th N. C.; W. W. Barnes, 15th N C. Buried on west side of Mayer's old graveyard; boards destroyed.

Lieut. L. J. Bozeman, Co. F, 3d S. C. Buried near fence above the company house and among a lot of cedar bushes.

One unknown. Buried in Mayer's yard near an apple tree.

Lieut. J. Anderson, 30th Va.; H. P. Alsop, 30th Va.; Richard Taylor, 30th Va.; T. C. Carmichael, 27th N. C.; S. J. Smith, 27th N. C.; J. Fry, 46th N. C.; Duncan McWilliams, 46th N. C.; J. N. Denson, 3d Ark ; E. L. Hyatt, 3d Ark.; Wesley J. Hogue, 3d Ark.; Serg. Behton Keesee, 3d

Ark.; James Hall, 3d Ark.; Jesse D. Head, 3d Ark. Buried in Samuel Beeler's barn field along the fence, running east from the barn, fifteen feet from a small locust tree and around a rock quarry; some unknown are also buried here; graves have been plowed over.

A. Douglas, Co. G, 6th S. C.; — Rice. Buried in front of Israel Smith's house in peach orchard.

R. D. Crawford, Co. D, 6th S. C.; L. Ria Met, S. C.; A. F. Byrd, Co E, 6th S. C. Buried in the hollow west of Israel Smith's barn, near some locust trees in Smith's field.

H. Hunt, 12th Ga.; one unknown. Buried in Daniel Poffenbarger's field northeast of barn on the hill; buried deep; been plowed over.

B. Rollins, 1st McIntosh Battery; A. W. Spraight, 3d N. C ; W. E. Willingham, Co. F, 12th S. C. Vol.; Col. W. T. Millican, 15th Ga.; Lieut. E. N. Fuller, S. C. Vol.; D. P. Herring, 1st N. C. (died September 16, 1862) ; J. W. Cobb, 12th Ga.; J. H. Williams, 1st Ga.; E. R. Martin, 6th La.; Samuel Lavin, 1st Ga.; H. H. W., 1st Ga.; W. Stone, 3d N. C.; J. Slade, 2d Ga.; P. B. F. Kimpson, 8th Ga.; Maj. Smith, 4th Ga.; V. M. Snyb, — Ga.; J. H., — Ga. Buried in Capt. David Smith's orchard, northeast corner; were buried deep; the orchard has been plowed and graves plowed over, but can all be pointed out; some of the boards have been preserved at the house; some unknown were also buried here.

Two unknown. Buried twenty feet north of an elm tree in Samuel Beeler's field along the line fence between D. Smith and Beeler.

James T. Sullivan, Hughes's Battery; H. Dyeryer, 4th Tex.; W. J. Davis, 4th Tex.; A. C. Robison, 2d Miss.; R. N. Taylor, 11th Miss.; J. M. William, 11th Miss.; H. Turner, 11th Miss.; Capt. J. K. Morton, 11th Miss.; Serg. J. C. Baker, 11th Miss.; F. Kessler, 11th Miss.; R. Harris, 60th Ga.; G. Young, 60th Ga.; W. J. Ieste, 60th Ga.; R. Hoords, 60th Ga.; J. M. Fuller, Co. H, 11th Miss.; J. C. Roher, 11th Miss.; F. Ressler, Tenn. Buried in Benjamin Grave's young orchard on left-hand side of road to Shepherdstown; names cut on apple trees; the orchard has been plowed, but the graves can be seen.

J. F. Fields, Co. A, 14th Tenn. Buried in Benjamin Grave's old orchard close to an apple tree in the hollow, first tree from house and left-hand side of road to Shepherdstown.

— Walton, 23d Va.; J. Booker, 23d Va.; C. W. Keesee, 23d Va.; Benjamin Green, 37th Va.; Serg. W. Walton, Co. I, 23d Va.; J. H. Ieste, 23d Va.; J. W. Noir, 14th N. C.; L. C. Colys, 4th N. C.; W. S. Aspray, 4th N. C.; E. W. Johnson, 14th N. C.; Lieut. D. Platham, 4th N. C.; T. H. Clark, 15th La.; Y. B. Egan, 15th La.; Lieut. J. McBride, 2d La.; L. B. Egan, Asst. Serg. 15th La.; Lieut. D. P. Latham, Co. E, 1st N. C. Buried in northeast corner of Benjamin Grave's garden on right-hand side of Shepherdstown road on inside and outside of fence, beginning at an apple tree; graves have not been disturbed.

— Duber; — Atkins, 3d Co., W. Battery (killed September 17, 1862). Buried at a rock brake in Grave's field west of his house, close to a small cherry tree on right of and sixty yards from Shepherdstown road; have boards.

J. H. Argenbright, 5th Va.; B. A. Carter, Co. C, 23d Va.; John E. Black, Co. F, 23d Va.; Ebenezer Cox, 48th N. C.; William Mann, 48th N. C.; Dr. Shadburn, Co. E, 9th La. (died September 20, 1862) ; Thomas Coughty, 48th Ala.; W. W. Hedrick, 48th Ala.; Lieut. A. Gordon, 9th La.; S. W. Day, Co. E, — N. C.; A. J. Igenhower, Co. D, 4th Va.; Corp. J. H. Coy, — Ga. Buried on Ben. Graves' farm in first field on right-hand side of Shepherdstown road and around a large poplar stump; the farm did belong to J. H. Grove; the graves have never been plowed over; are in good condition; some boards still remaining; a number of unknown are buried there.

Serg. John F. Mayes, Battery (killed September 17, 1862) ; one unknown. Buried on right of hollow leading from Shepherdstown road to the lock, up against the hill by the side of a small locust tree; Mayes has a board.

G. W. Weller, — Ga.; Lieut. Col. Thomas Sloan, 53d Ga. Buried at the back end of Elias Grove's orchard, twenty feet east of a double apple tree near the line fence of Grove and Smith.

Two unknown. Buried on the outside of stone wall along Rev. Douglas's field, above the well at the lock near an old post.

Two unknown. Buried on lower side of the abutment of the bridge, covered deep with drift.

Two unknown. Buried at the abutment of Runnel's dam, but was washed away by freshet.

Two unknown. Buried below Miller's sawmill at lower end of board yard.

C. P., one unknown. Buried below Miller's Basin, between the road and canal, at the lower end of basin; board up.

— Dunlap, Co. C, 12th S. C.; — Roach, Co. H, 12th S. C. Buried in northeast corner of Morgan Miller's orchard.

One unknown. Buried on towpath opposite Miller's sawmill under a sycamore tree.

H. D. B.; John Allen, 48th Va.; Lieut. John Hurnes, 37th Va.; Charles Booker, 32d Va.; Lieut. M. V. B. Swann, 2d La.; A. J. Smith, 53d N. C.; Kertz Harty, 14th N. C.; K. Thiaton, 3d N. C.; J. Ascott, 7th N. C ; Paul Sanford, 7th N. C.; R. B. Tall, 4th Tex.; — Gones, 13th Miss.; C. D. Gardner, 13th Miss.; A. W. Gower, 24th Ga.; Lieut. H. B. Brantlay, 28th Ga ; J. C. Wright, 48th Ga. Buried along the northern edge of Stephen Grove's woods; all had boards; some still have boards.

J. P. Snipes, 15th Ala.; R. Hadmans, 4th Ala ; Lieut D. A. King, 4th Ala.; R. Sigmon, 46th N. C.; Lieut. H. T. Eason, 13th Miss. Buried in Mrs. Lucker's second field south of barn on west side of a large rock brake and near a locust tree and an elm tree.

W. R. Lindsey. 3d S. C.; J. C. Morgan, 3d S. C.; R. A. Wagner, 18th Miss.; R. B. Davis, 13th Miss.; W. O. Cambpell, 18th Miss.; C. H. Clark, Co. D, 18th Miss.; Thomas Wells, Co. F, 21st Miss. Buried below Mayer's barn on flat at side of branch; boards destroyed; graves exposed to stock; no fence.

James Shinp, 3d N. C. Buried in Daniel Poffenbarger's out lot along the line fence, between Poffenbarger and Marker, six feet above a forked sassafras.

J. S. Hudson, 15th Ga. Buried in southwest corner of Stephen P. Grove's orchard, four panels from corner; name cut on fence.

E. Conner, Co. G, 18th Va.; five unknown. Buried in Francis Miller's orchard, next to his wagon shed, close to an apple tree; stump for a stone.

Two unknown. Buried in Henry Blackford's wood, near a sink hole.

Two unknown. Buried in the road near the southwest corner of Mayer's barn.

One unknown. Buried in Henry Blackford's orchard, second row and under the third tree from southeast corner.

One lieutenant, unknown. Buried above a large rock nearly opposite out lot lane, along hillside, first field of H. Blackford's from forge road.

One unknown. Buried thirty yards from the last-named rock in same field and toward the lane.

E. L. Frazier, 12th S C.; six unknown. Buried in H. Blackford's first field, northeast corner at forks of the roads.

Three trenches of supposed thirty unknown. Buried in southeast corner of Mrs. Lucker's barn field; bones exposed.

One unknown. Buried in the hollow in H. Blackford's first field from forge road, twenty-two steps from a large rock in the hollow toward the forge road.

One unknown. Buried in D. Reel's field, back of the Marker field, seventy-six yards from the gate toward S. Reel's shop.

A. J Koontz, 48th N. C.; J. D. Cockran, 17th Miss.; G. F. Shuford, 17th Miss.; E. B. H., 17th Miss.; J. W. Wright, 17th Miss.; J. M. B., 17th Miss.; H. H. Wood, Co. A, 17th Miss.; J. G. W., 17th Miss.; J. S. H., 17th Miss.; C. E. Powe, 13th Miss. Buried along the south side of Mrs. Lucker's barn field, along division fence near a large locust tree; stone on the graves; some boards still here.

Jonathan Sessions, 13th Miss.; W. L. West, 13th Miss.; E. R. Kilpatrick, 13th Miss ; M. Marcon, 48th Miss. Buried along the south side of Mrs. Lucker's barn field, along division fence near a large locust tree; stone on the graves; some boards still here.

J. McDougle, Co. H, 12th Miss.; L. Butler, Co. D, 12th Miss. Buried in David Reel's field, third one from house, southwest corner, eighteen feet from and in front of a rock brake west of Hagerstown Pike.

Five unknown. Buried in David Reel's field along the east side of field; bones exposed; some were scattered.

One unknown. Buried in Mrs. Lucker's barn field opposite the garden near the road.

Fifteen unknown. Buried in a trench in S. Reel's gold mine field, twenty-three steps south of a hickory and near the line fence between Reel and Piper.

One unknown. Buried in second field west of J. Nicodemus's well, on south side of lane and along the western division fence and thirty panels from corner.

One unknown. Buried in S. Reel's gold mine field, seventy-five yards north of southwest corner of field, close to fence; bones exposed.

Col. Strong; ten unknown, — La. Buried in the hollow south of Dunkard Church, seventy-five steps and ten feet east of a walnut stump toward pike.

R. W. Tompkins. Buried in southwest corner of Colonel Miller's woods; name cut on tree; has been disinterred.

Lieut. J. M. Roberts, Co. C, 21st Miss.; W. Blalock, Co. I, 21st Miss.; J. C. Pruitt, 21st Miss.; Lieut. J. O. Kreigner, 21st Miss.; N. M. Hugney, 2d S. C.; F. B. V. Johnson, 2d S. C.; G. Halley, 8th La. Buried in Colonel Miller's woods west of church along the line fence between Miller and Mrs. Lucker on flat under a large walnut tree; some boards are still here; also a number on unknown.

One unknown, Jackson's Brigade. Buried in Mrs. Lucker's orchard, near northeast corner.

Lieut. S. Robinson, 2d S. C.; Serg. J. S. Boyd, 2d S. C. (been disinterred by friends); L. C. Green, Co. A, 8th Ga.; J. L. Denson, Co. K, 3d Ark ; W. H. Ward, 10th Ga.; R. T. Johnson, 10th Ga.; Maj. McIntosh, 10th Ga. (disinterred by friends); S. C. Greer, 8th Ga.; Corp. Sutherland, 10th Ga.; C. O. Morris, 10th Ga.; J. T. Binion, 10th Ga.; E. B. Goin, 3d S. C.; S J. Craine, 3d S. C.; William Franklin, 3d S. C.; M. J. Shuber, Co. I, 3d S. C.; Serg. A. McNeedy, 3d S. C.; Jesse Gary, 3d S. C.; Lieut. Abernathy, 3d S. C.; S. T. McCoy, Co. E, 3d S. C.; Corp. J. R. Harris, 3d S. C.; H. G. G. Gallman, 3d S. C. Buried around the rock brake southwest of Mrs. Lucker's barn; in the barn field the brake is covered with locust and other trees Some boards are here.

P. W. Teter, 32d Va.; T. H. Marrow, 32d Va.; Corp. F. Lunder, 32d Va.; H. Grove, 5th Va.; G. M. Hanger, 27th Va.; D. Coughlin, 27th Va.; Reuben Rodway, 15th La.; T. H. Phifer, 2d La.; J. S Kearney, 2d La.; Corp. T. Skinner, Co. K, 32d Va.; W. A. Snead, 15th Va.; Reuben Badens, 5th La. Buried around first rock brake west of Mrs. Lucker's barn and in the barn field; some boards are still standing.

R. F Davis, 4th Ala.; S. Sutton, 6th Ga.; R. H. Campbell, 4th Ga.; G. F. Davis, — Ga.; Beth Harford, 27th Ga.; W. D. Riskenbecken; W. D. Norwood, 3d Va ; J. H. Marting, 42d S. C.; Lieut. E. F. Dobson, 42d S. C Buried in George Line's orchard; some boards are still here; the graves have not been disturbed.

B. Matheny, 10th Ga.; J. Riley, 10th Ga.; E. N. Gunn, 10th Ga.; John Hanks, 10th Ga.; Brocks Mathering. 10th Ga.; James M. Lowe, 10th Ga.; G. W. C. Allen, 10th Ga.; J Q. H. Mitchell, 10th Ga.; R. B. Hightower, 10th Ga.; J. H. Q. Campbell, Co. E, 10th Ga.; J. C. Butler, 10th Ga. Buried in G. Burgan's field along the line fence between Burgan and Mrs. Lucker and in a direct line with the fence back of Burgan's orchard; some boards still remain; also some unknown board.

John Stokes, 49th Va ; W. A. Renoe, 49th Va.; George Able, 49th Va.; J. G. Rod, 49th Va.; D. N. Johnson, 44th Va.; W. J. Scoggins, 9th La.; Lieut. S. T. Robinson, 9th La.; W. O. Price, 9th La.; E B. Legget, 9th

La.; B. Old, Co. H, 2d La. (killed September 17, 1862); Thomas Chitwood, 42 Va. Buried in northeast corner of Mrs. Lucker's house field, commencing at an old road and running along the southern edge of woods; some boards still here.

L. G. Burditt, 13th Ala.; Lieut. W. E. Cooke, 8th La.; — Fontenet, — La.; W. B. Ayes, 1st N. C.; C. T. Bass, 1st N. C.; J. H. Thompson, 1st N. C.; W. H. Lane, 3d N. C.; F. L. Pollet, 6th N. C.; P. N. Oliphant, 3d N. C.; Elias Sotton, 3d N. C.; — Hatchet, Co. D, 1st N. C.; C. Branch, Co. D, 5th N. C.; Ezra Towle, 10th Miss.; H. Hickman, 2d Miss ; Capt. J. C. Beeks, 27th Ga.; John L. Slaughter, 6th Ga.; Benjamin C. Laprabe, 28th Ga.; W. Bailey, 61st Ga.; W. Bruster, 23d Ga.; — Late, Co H, 23d Ga.; M. Coleman, 38th Ga.; — Jones, 28th Ga.; John Wright, 28th Ga.; G. Summer, 28th Ga.; J. Royal, 6th Ga.; — Sweet; J. Phelps, 1st Tex.; J. Boon, 1st Tex.; A. F. Wolf, 5th Tex. Buried west of George Line's house in his new ground alongside of an old white oak tree near his pond and north of the road leading to his house; the ground is low and wet and has been plowed; graves pretty much exposed.

One unknown. Buried in Mrs. Middlekauff's orchard.

One unknown. Buried in John Poffenbarger's field east of house, twenty steps north of hogpen.

James F. Maxcey, Co. C, 27th Ga. (died December 12, 1862); Joseph P. Pratt, Co. D, 12th Ga. (died October 11, 1862); one unknown (died October 8, 1862). Buried in the Smoketown Hospital graveyard; boards still here and graves have not been disturbed.

One unknown. Buried in northeast corner of garden belonging to the tenant house of S. Poffenbarger's farm.

— Stogner, 49th N. C.; — Simpson, 49th N. C.; L. M. N., 49th N. C. Buried in Colonel Miller's woods in front of Mrs. Lucker's house, ten feet from a hickory tree, along the fence and ten feet from a stump.

Three unknown. Buried in Colonel Miller's woods, third hollow and west side of pike, twenty steps from D. R. Miller's fence and close to a walnut stump with three notches cut in.

One unknown. Buried on top of a little hill on south side of lane and west of J. Nicodemus's well.

W. H. Talbot, 2d Miss.; three unknown. Buried in Jonathan Poffenbarger's orchard along the west side close to the fence and near a small cherry tree.

Four unknown. Buried in J. Nicodemus's new ground.

Two unknown. Buried in Mrs. Lucker's wood.

J. A. J. Tally, 15th Va.; J. A. Talley, 15th Va ; G. W. Brook, 15th Va.; W. E. Rean, 15th Va.; J. M. Leak, 15th Va.; J. G. Hagans, 53d Ga.; W. N. Shrouhart, 53d Ga.; S. Ocrue, 53d Ga. Buried in Mrs. Lucker's field near an old well; have been plowed over.

Capt. T. H. Wynne, 32d Ga.; John Campbell, 10th Ga.; John Mitchell, 10th Ga ; G. W. Callet, 10th Ga.; Lieut. D. J. Downing, 2d N. C.; L. W. Gale, 10th Ga ; James Lowe, 10th Ga. Buried in a stone pile six feet from locust tree near George Burgan's well.

One unknown. Buried in southwest corner of George Burgan's orchard, two panels east of corner.

One unknown. Buried near Mr. Murdock's spring, opposite Money Herr's tavern stand.

Three unknown. Buried along the edge of E. Hoffman's woods at Smoketown, fifty yards from house.

Capt. J. C. Beeks, 27th Ga.; J. S. Ervin, 21st Miss.; Capt. Cooke, 20th Miss. Buried in Euromus Hoffman's field south of barn along the hillside, twenty-three steps east of a large walnut tree.

J. R. Cody, 18th Ga.; N. B. Parker, 27th N. C.; Capt. John Howard, 2d N. C.; Lieut. R. L. Noble, 27th N. C. Buried in Dr. Smith's field, northwest of house in the hollow between two gullies, fifty yards south of a walnut tree; a number of unknown were also buried here, and some have been washed out.

Three unknown. Buried east of H. Neikirk's barn on opposite hill and twenty feet west of a hickory stump.

Two unknown. Buried in D. R. Miller's orchard back of the garden, six steps from northeast corner of garden.

Two trenches of supposed forty-seven unknown. Buried in northwest corner of Michael Miller's meadow, four feet from branch and five feet from board fence.

Henry Perring, 23d Va.; Beneft Laurence, 30th N. C.; Benjamin A Butler, 30th N. C.; William Cox, 7th S. C.; G J. Galaway, 15th Ala.; Lieut. D. H. Hallman, 23d Ga.; Capt. W. F. Plane, 6th Ga. (disinterred). Buried on eastern side of branch in Samuel Poffenbarger's meadow and along the line fence between Poffenbarger and Miller.

J. B. Stegall, 23d Ga. Buried in D. R. Miller's field back of orchard along the woods.

Eighteen trenches supposed to contain two hundred and ninety unknown; Col. Colwell, 27th Ga. (disinterred); Maj. Tracey, 27th Ga.; in east end of trench containing one hundred and fifty. Buried in D. R. Miller's fifty-acre field east side of pike; the trenches can all be seen, although the field has been plowed; buried shallow; bones exposed in places; trappings, etc., can be seen.

Nine trenches supposed to contain two hundred and twenty-five unknown. Buried in D. R. Miller's field east of pike and bordering on Smoketown road; buried shallow; exposed.

Eight trenches supposed to contain three hundred and five unknown. Buried in D. R. Miller's field west of pike and joining the woods; bones exposed.

Two trenches supposed to contain thirty unknown. Buried in northwest corner of Samuel Mummas's field at the junction of Smoketown road and pike.

Four unknown. Buried seventy yards north of walnut tree in S. Mummas's graveyard field.

Three trenches supposed to contain about thirty unknown. Buried near the graveyard in Samuel Mummas's field; exposed.

Twelve unknown. Buried in Samuel Mummas's first field south of meadow.

One unknown. Buried in lower corner of William Rulett's meadow.

One unknown. Buried in William Rulett's orchard close to his house.

Five trenches supposed to contain two hundred and fifty unknown; Capt. Whatley, of Jacksonville, Ala., in one end of trench. Buried in the first field of William Rulett's along Bloody Lane.

Twenty unknown. Buried in Samuel Mummas's field joining Rulett's lane, southeast corner twenty steps from rock brake.

Twenty unknown. Buried in Samuel Mummas's bear hole field.

Three trenches supposed to contain eighteen unknown. Buried in S. D. Piper's field east of his orchard in hollow; bones exposed.

Four trenches supposed to contain twenty-five unknown. Buried in S. D. Piper's eighteen-acre field joining Bloody Lane.

Two unknown. Buried in S. D. Piper's field, bought of Squire Miller.

Twenty unknown in one trench. Buried in S. D. Piper's field west of orchard in the flat near forks of gullies.

Two unknown. Buried in S. D. Piper's field opposite his corncrib, close along the lane fence.

Stephen Credit, — Ga.; two unknown. Buried in Squire Miller's orchard in town.

N. Y. N., 10th Ala. Buried in Samuel Reel's field north of Michael's orchard, fifteen steps from bars.

John B. Smith, 2d Miss.; one unknown. Buried in Samuel Reel's orchard.

Seventeen unknown. Buried in Samuel Reel's twenty-acre field twenty yards from west fence and one hundred yards from back corner.

Two unknown. Buried in Moses Cox's field northeast of his blacksmith shop.

One unknown. Buried in S. Reel's meadow along the line fence between David and Samuel Reel's and near a locust stump.

Two unknown. Buried in Colonel Miller's field opposite S. Reel's lane, six steps northwest of some locust trees.

G. W. Corbin, 13th Miss Buried in Colonel Miller's first field north of Stine's house, close to Mercerville road, six feet from a panel of fence; notches cut in the rail.

One unknown. Buried in southeast corner of Mrs. Lucker's field on the Mercerville road, twenty steps from locust tree; bones exposed.

One unknown. Buried in George Burgan's field on the hill close along the Mercerville road; stone up at head and foot.

James Wright, Co. G, 7th S. C.; — Bishops, 2d Fla.; — Jenkins, 3d N. C.; — Sellus, 2d N. C.; Lieut. J. R Drake, 5th Tex.; J. R. Baker, 15th Va.; F. M. Foster, 10th Ga.; W. O. Brien, 16th Ga.; C. Simms, 15th Miss.; J. W. Shettles, 2d Miss.; J. R. Harper, 14th N. C.; J. Spradling, 13th Ala.; J. Strider, 14th N. C.; C. A. Foult, 48th N. C.; T. S. Gardner, Co. H, 8th La.; D. M. Jones, Co. F, 16th Miss.; Serg Henry, Co. H, 2d Miss.; W. R. Bryant, — Miss.; C. H. McIntyre, 13th Va.; J. Sloan, 10th La.; W.

S. Brazeall, 7th Tex.; C. W. Coleman, 30th N. C.; H. F. Collins, 24th Ga.; Capt. J. E. Buckley, Co. B, 16th Miss.; J. Williams, 6th Ga.; S. Reading, 5th Ga.; three unknown. Buried in Rev. J. J. Adams's town lot back of the M. E. graveyard.

J. W. Weaver, Co. I, 12th Ala. Buried in A. Michael's orchard under fourth tree and sixth row from northeast corner and eastern side; name cut on tree.

J. L. M., 28th Va ; J. Stubbs, 23d S. C.; J. M. Farris, 17th S. C.; three unknown. Buried in Lutheran graveyard in Sharpsburg.

— Wood. Buried in German Reformed graveyard in Sharpsburg.

Two unknown. Buried in southern end and corner of John Highbarger's lot along the forge road.

G. W. Judd, 1st Co. Wash. Art.; one unknown. Buried in Ben Miller's orchard, second pear tree from spring house south.

Two unknown. Buried in Reel's woods on right of the gate leading to S. I. Piper's under a walnut tree.

One unknown; Lieut. C. C. Binn, 53d Ga. Buried in Colonel Miller's woods on left of road to Lafayette; cross cut on tree.

Capt. J. M. Bourn, 4th Va.; T. J. Wilson, 4th Va.; J. Bryson, 7th Va ; four unknown. Buried in H. Reel's field west of his orchard along a stone wall, thirty steps above the gate.

Lieut. J. G. Flemming, 49th N. C. Buried in northeast corner of H. Reel's orchard between second and third tree from corner along the back end.

Two unknown. Buried in southwest corner of Lafayette Miller's woods, west of path and south of hickory tree.

Three unknown. Buried in Daniel Poffenbarger's town lot, where he lives.

W. J. Johnson, 6th La. Buried in D. Rohrback's lot, south of John Grice's lot, close along the forge road and under first tree from gate.

Two unknown. Buried in southwest corner of John Kretzer's lot back of his orchard.

Twenty-eight unknown. Buried in Adam Micheal's field east and south of his pond field.

M. M. B., 11th Va.; J. W. Reed, 11th Va.; S. A. Lucas, 11th Va.; James Phelan, 17th Va.; M. O. Anderson, 7th Va. Buried in Ben Miller's field joining and east of John Highbarger's lot, twenty steps from southeast corner toward and near a small edge of rocks.

Serg. Strobuck, N. 133 N. Buried in northeast corner of Ben Miller's field south of orchard.

S. Mills, R. 89 N ; H. Rimple, H. 108 N.; L. M.; Corp. Walker, 108 N. Buried in Ben Miller's field and along the line fence and stone wall between Miller and Sherrick and north of a locust stump.

Three unknown. Buried west of Benjamin Miller's house, between wood pile and fence.

One unknown. Buried on outside and east of Hiatt's stable, two panels of fence.

Two unknown. Buried in Mrs. Rohrback's orchard field.

T. S. C., two unknown. Buried in Mrs. Rohrback's field along the line fence between Mrs. Rohrback and Snavely, west of a leaning elm and between a stone wall division fence.

One colonel of a Georgia regiment. Buried east of John Benner's barn and thirty steps of a beech tree along an old fence.

Five unknown. Buried in John Benner's stone quarry.

Two unknown. Buried in John Otto's field south of Benner's orchard along the hillside.

One unknown. Buried in gully in northeast corner of Sherrick's little field joining Benner's orchard; probably washed away.

Two unknown. Buried at the east end of Sherrick's barn at the yard fence.

Three unknown. Buried in Samuel Magraw's field joining the A. N. Cemetery

Three unknown. Buried in A. N. Cemetery, and were removed by unknown persons.

One unknown. Buried in Mrs. Kennedy's yard near the pump and between an apricot and plum tree.

Twenty unknown. Buried on Maryland Heights, twenty yards north of fort.

One unknown. Buried south of Mrs. Vandusen's house near where the board and rail go in.

Two unknown. Buried on Dr. Butler's farm in the swamp.

Serg. John Dolan, Co. F, 26th Ga. Buried in T. Bryns's orchard; flowers planted on the grave.

L. McElwer, Yorkville, S. C.; H. Johnson, Co. K, 6th S. C.; W. E. Little, Co. D, P. S. S.; M. C., Co. H, P. S. S.; Newton Petty, Co. M. P. S. S.; George Fink, Co. H, P. S. S.; J. Binks, Co. H, 6th S. C.; C. Golickly, Co. K, 5th S. C.; R. Gritten, Co. F, 6th S. C.; A Tillacum, Co. A, 5th S. C.; one unknown. Buried in Mrs. Kennedy's little orchard opposite her house; the graves are shallow and have never been plowed over.

Three unknown. Buried in Michael Tenant's orchard.

One unknown. Buried along the road from William Wade's barn to the mountain near a grave, inclosed by a fence.

One unknown. Buried in northeast corner of William Crampton's house field, third cedar from corner, along Harper's Ferry road; stone up.

J. M. White, 1st Ga.; W. L. A., 1st Ga. Buried in William Wilson's woods at the back end and south side of a branch near the line fence between Wilson and Byrns; names cut on a chestnut tree; graves covered with stone.

D. B. T., 2d Va. Buried in western side of Grove's graveyard near a peach tree.

Twelve unknown. Buried in the field back of Mr. Staley's barn in the hollow.

One unknown. Buried in northwest corner of Anderson's walnut tree field, twenty steps from corner, near Brownsville schoolhouse.

Five unknown. Buried in J. J. Moore's graveyard on the road to Weverton.

James Lewis, — Va. Buried in Barton Butler's field in corner joining Burns's meadow.

Twelve unknown. Buried in T. Crampton's field, twelve steps south of bars and at the mouth of Remsburg's lane along the woods.

James M. Birdsong. Buried in T. Crampton's field opposite a walnut stump in the lane leading to his house.

One unknown. Buried at the graveyard at Oak Grove Schoolhouse below Rohrersville.

Elijah Lacey, Co. H, 2d Ga.; J. F. Gartaw, Co. A, 8th La.; G. W. Gausnell, Co. E, 5th La.; R. E. Smith, Co. E. 5th La.; four unknown. Buried in hospital graveyard at Russer Spring; still have boards up.

Lieut Col. E. S. James, — N. C.; forty-seven unknown. Buried in Wise's lot on east side of house and lot on top of South Mountain.

Twenty-three unknown. Buried in Wise's lot on west side of house and stable on top of South Mountain.

One unknown. Buried one hundred yards west of the mountain road and a large white oak south of Wise's.

Two unknown. Buried in the woods south of Beekly's field on east side of mountain road and three-quarters of a mile south of Wise's house; bones exposed.

Three unknown. Buried in Smith's field opposite the hotel on South Mountain, ten steps from bars.

Three unknown. Buried on Magill's farm at falling waters.

J. B. Walker, Co. A, Phil. La.; J. W. Bryant, 5th Ga.; Lieut. J. F. Bryant, 6th Ala.; L. Parker, 23d Ga.; C. M. Fontenberry, 26th Ala.; O. Johns, 5th Ala.; Thomas Gee, 5th Ala.; M. Furgison, 23d Ga.; T. Nott, 23d Ga.; J. N. Philips, 28th Ga.; T. J. Ward, 6th Ala.; Lieut. A. A. Scott, 6th Ala.; H. L. Tucker, 26th Ala.; C. H. Moore, 26th Ala.; C. M. Smith, 26th Ala.; M. D. Jackson, 5th Ala.; G. B. Wright, 5th Ala.; J. McBee, 23d Ga.; Thomas McElwie, 23d Ga.; J. Wetherby, 23d Ga.; T. E. Blichington, 28th Ga ; W. Thomas, 23d Ga.; J. B. Lacy, 6th Ala.; A. W. Maxell, 6th Ala.; W. D. Jackson, 5th Ala.; four unknown. Buried in Mrs. Hoffman's barn field near Boonsboro, one hundred and fifty yards northwest of the barn.

Capt. Litchfield, 8th S. C. Buried in Dr. E. Butler's graveyard.

Two unknown. Buried in Russell's graveyard field along the fence against the mountain.

One unknown, — Fla. Buried in the woods west of Phil Pry's house near a white oak tree and along the orchard fence

One unknown. Buried in Christian Keedy's field opposite Mr. Made's shop.

One unknown. Buried in south side of the old Middletown road, midway between two stumps and directly opposite to William Lampert's house at foot of South Mountain.

Fifty-eight unknown. Buried in Wise's well on South Mountain.

Seven unknown. Buried on Mr. Dellinger's farm at falling waters.

Six unknown. Buried on Mr. William's farm, south of Williamsport on east side of Sharpsburg road near a walnut and locust tree close along the road.

John Shuffler, — N. C.; two unknown. Buried on spring field farm near Williamsport.

One unknown. Buried on Mr. Charlton's farm below Williamsport.

Three unknown. Buried in stone quarry in Miller's lot in Williamsport.

Eleven unknown. Buried outside of public graveyard at Williamsport.

W. W. Baily, Co. D, 1st Va.; eight unknown. Buried in first woods below Benevola, three-quarters of a mile east of pike and near the mouth of a lane.

J. T. Hubble, Q. M., 5th Va.; J. R. Latum, — N. C.; Z. P. Henry, Co. D, 5th Tex.; — Boan, — N. C.; Col. J. E. Ayer, S. T., July 3, 1863, 6th N. C.; — Coxanson, — N. C.; J. W. Driskill, Co. G, 6th Ala. (killed July 6, 1863); J. R. Barnes, Co. C, 43d N. C.; W. Gardner, Co. A, 23d N. C.; J. Wiles, — N. C.; forty-three unknown. Buried in the public graveyard at Williamsport.

Samuel Maxwell, — S. C.; one unknown. Buried south of Mr. Embrey's warehouse in a niche of the bank; stone up.

Edward J. Jewell, — La. (tombstone); Capt. J. P. Welsh, Co. B, 27th Va.; three unknown. Buried in Catholic burial ground at Williamsport.

S. P. Moore, 3d Ark.; — Walker, S. C. Art.; twelve unknown. Buried in John Hogne's town lot, nearly opposite the Presbyterian Church in Williamsport.

One unknown. Buried at the mouth of lane in Mr. Finley's woods, thirty feet from lane along stone wall on south side of pike from Williamsport to Hagerstown.

One unknown doctor from Virginia. Buried in front of Suman's house, on pike from Williamsport to Hagerstown.

One unknown. Buried along the fence west of Moler's orchard on pike from Williamsport to Hagerstown.

One unknown. Buried fifty yards west of tollgate on pike from Williamsport to Hagerstown.

One unknown. Buried in Cost's field at locust tree, northeast of bone mill at Hagerstown.

Col. S. P. Lumpkin, 44th Ga. (died September 12, 1863). Buried in Presbyterian graveyard at Hagerstown; has tombstone.

Three unknown. Buried in Episcopal graveyard at Hagerstown.

— Warfield. Buried in graveyard at St. Paul's Church on pike from Hagerstown to Clearspring.

Five unknown. Buried in Lutheran graveyard at Funkstown.

— Riley. Buried on Straub's farm, one mile south of Hagerstown.

W. L. Calhoun, Co. I, 5th Ala.; George Williams, — N. C. Buried in Dunkard graveyard at Funkstown.

One unknown. Buried on Eakle and Newcomer's farm on Sharpsburg road near Funkstown.

One unknown. Buried on Archy McCoy's farm below Funkstown.

One unknown. Buried in Thomas Watt's wood near Mr. Stover's.

One unknown. Buried on John W. Stover's farm near the tollgate on Sharpsburg and Hagerstown Pike.

Capt. Mitchell, — Ga.; Serg. Brooks, — Ga.;· fifteen unknown. Buried on Mr. Stover's farm, one mile southeast of Funkstown.

Two unknown. Buried along the fence back of Mr. Stockslager's garden.

One unknown. Buried in Samuel Williams's field near a locust tree and back of Stockslager's farm.

One unknown. Buried one-quarter of a mile west of Boonsboro and Hagerstown Pike along the line fence between Shindle and Hunter, between two locust trees.

One unknown. Buried in northwest corner of Mr. Hildebrand's woods near a hickory; bones exposed.

J. S. Christian, 28th Va.; J. T. Wise, 23d S. C.; — Reynolds, 28th Va. (died October 27, 1862); J. O. Kounce, 2d Va.; Professor Phinx; James Cole, Co. D, 7th Va. (in Giles Co., Va.); S. S. Keenan, Co. F, 23d Ga.; Serg. T. M. Garland, 50th Ga.; J. J. Carver, Co. F, 50th Ga.; E. F. Johnson; — McClendon, Co. I, 57th Ga.; Thomas Lowell, 8th Fla.; C. L. Atkins, Co. G, 7th Va.; J. H. Hedrick; Winfield Ivey, 51st Ga.; W. S. Hill, — S. C. Buried at the Disciple church in Boonsboro.

One unknown. Buried along the branch at edge of Downey's wood at falling waters.

Three unknown. Buried in Snyder's lane at falling waters.

Lieut. A. Christian, W. Va.; W. H. Naun, Co. B, 20th N. C; E. H. Counts, Co. I, 14th N. C.; F. R. Gregory, — Miss.; Lieut. J. Elliott, 1st N. C. (died July 28, 1863); J. W. Wilson, 5th N. C. (died July 28, 1863); W. H. Dunn, 10th Ala.; Franklin Cunningham, 3d W. Va.; T. B. Giaco, 19th Miss.; H. Watkins, — Va., Ashby's Cavalry; F. M. Canoway, Co. H, 13th Ala.; H. Rowell, Co. E, 4th Ala; Q. D. Gray, 37th Va.; A. B. Nevlin, 13th Va; I. I. Edwards, 55th N. C.; Serg. John McDowell, 55th N. C.; John Reice, 5th Va.; S. V. York, Co. A, 2d N. C.; A. M. Plagason, ·Co. H, 6th N. C.; R. I. Little, Co. E, 13th N. C.; J. D. Smith, — Tenn ; Lieut. J. B. O'Neale, Co. F, 3d S. C.; Alexander Cune, Co. L, 50th Va.; sixteen unknown. Buried in almshouse lot at Hagerstown; some boards :still here.

Two unknown. Buried south of Beekley's barn alongside of pike.

Four unknown. Buried on Mr. Doub's farm on pike above Boonsboro.

One unknown. Buried on George Snavely's farm in orchard at tenant house.

One unknown. Buried along the pike above Boonsboro, opposite a clump of thickets on Mr. Shiffler's farm.

CAMP CHASE CEMETERY.

CONFEDERATE DEAD BURIED AT "CAMP CHASE," FOUR MILES WEST OF
COLUMBUS, OHIO.

No. of Grave.

1977. Abbott, Joseph, Co. B, 26th Va. Sharpshooters, died May 16, '65.
2032. Abie, Simeon, 66th Ga. Inf., died January 7, '65.
256. Adams, B., Texas Legion, died September 20, '64.
785. Adams, J. R., Co. D, 57th Va. Inf., died January 16, '65.
1230. Adams, O. D., Co. A, 8th Ga. Inf., died February 14, '65.
688. Adams, William, Co. H, 6th Ky. Inf., died December 31, '64.
1556. Adamson, James, Co. E, 30th Ga. Inf., died March 5, '65.
1830. Aday, Benton, Co. E, 5th Ala. Cav., died April 8, '65.
63. Adkins, H. A., Co. E, 11th Va. Cav., died Nov. 12, '63. Removed.
2. Adkins, William, citizen of Virginia, died August 14, '63.
515. Adkins, William, Co. B, Witcher's Va. Cav., died November 25, '64.
1987. Agnew, Elijah, Co. A, 16th Ga. Inf., died May 25, '65.
1151. Aiken, W. B., Co. C, 8th Ga. Inf., died February 9, '65.
1747. Aikins, H., Co. G, Moreland's Cavalry, died March 21, '65.
1718. Albert, Frank, Co. F, 20th Ala. Inf., died March 20, '65.
149. Alexander, T. B., citizen of Alabama, died June 12, '64.
119. Alford, J., citizen of West Virginia, died March, '64.
233. Allen, B. L., Co. D, 50th Tenn. Inf., died September 9, '64.
1877. Allen, C. A., citizen of Georgia, died April 16, '65.
81. Allen, J. C., Co. C, 11th Tenn. Cav., died December 15, '63.
392. Allen, Wm. H., Co. B, 5th Ala. Cav., died Nov. 3, '64. Removed.
121. Ambuster, G. P., died March, '64.
1299. Anders, J., Quartermaster Department, died February 10, '65.
1188. Anderson, Abijah, Co. F, 19th S. C. Inf., died February 11, '65.
569. Anderson, Benjamin, Co. C, 6th Ga. Cav., died December 7, '64.
1572. Anderson, D., Co. E, 57th Ala. Inf., died March 6, '65.
1034. Anderson, J., Co. D, 2d Ky. Cav., died February 4, '65.
817. Anderson, L. W., Co. A., 17th Va. Cav., died January 22, '65.
294. Anderson, R. B., Co. E, 34th Ga. Inf., died October 10, '64.
558. Anderson, Robert, Co. D, 5th Tenn. Cav., died December 6, '64.
1012. Anderson, W., Co. G, 29th Ga. Inf., died February 3, '65.
1917. Andrews, Solomon O., Co. I, 63d Ga. Inf., died April 25, '65.
313. Anloniff, E., Co. K, 8th Tenn. Cav., died October 10, '64.
576. Archibald, L. H., Co. B, 36th Ala. Inf., died December 8, '64.
1580. Armstead, J., Co. E, 22d Va. Inf., died March 6, '65.
255. Armstrong, William, Co. K, Adams County, died September 18, '64
352. Arnett, Creel, Co. C, 13th Va. Inf., died October 23, '64.
987. Arnold, Basham, Co. I, 60th Va. Inf., died February 1, '65.
397. Arnold, W. A., Co. A, 2d Ky. Cav., November 3, '64.
1540. Arrants, J. M., Johnson's Conscript, died March 4, '65.
399. Arthur, Luke, Co. A, 36th Va. Cav., died November 4, '64.
622. Arthurs, R. F., Co. I, 19th Va. Cav., died December 16, '64.

No. of Grave.
677. Asbury, H. R., Co. E, 10th Ky Cav., died December 28, '64.
346. Ashtacks, William R., Co. B, 8th Tenn. Cav., died October 22, '64.
2000. Askins, A. J., Co. E, 8th S. C. Inf., died May 25, '65.
802. Atchison, Serg. Wm. J., Co. H, 6th Tex. Inf., died January 19, '65.
137. Atkins, D. C., 6th Va. Cav., died April 13, '64
424. Atkins, William B., Co. I, 24th Ala. Inf., died November 7, '64.
25. Austin, William, Co. F, 10th Ky. Cav., died September 14, '63.
1723. Ayers, B. F., Co. K, 25th Va. Cav., died March 21, '65.
1091. Babin, J., Co. E, 4th La. Inf., died February 7, '65.
1676. Bachelor, W., Co. B, 10th Ala. Inf., died March 16, '65.
875. Bacon, Thomas, Co. D, 25th Ga. Inf., died January 24, '65.
1746. Bagerly, W. B., Co. D, 41st Tenn. Inf., died March 24, '65.
866. Bagwell, S. W., Co. I, 15th Miss Inf., died January 23, '65.
1346. Bagwell, W. W., Co. G, 7th S. C. Inf., died February 19, '65.
659. Bailes, Thomas R., Co. F, 22d Va. Cav., died December 23, '64.
2063. Bailey, J., Co. B, 7th Ala. Cav., died August 9, '65.
1486. Baker, J., Co. D, 12th Ky. Cav., died February 28, '65.
1177. Bailey, James H., Co. A, Miss. Inf., 15th Regt., died February 11, '65.
692. Baker, J. M., Co. G, 46th Ala. Inf., died January 1, '65.
562. Baker, James M., Co. F, 7th Tenn. Cav., died December 6, '64.
1607. Baker, W., Co. I, 4th Tenn. Cav., died March 9, '65.
1646. Baley, B. J., Co. D, 7th Miss. Inf., died March 13, '65.
703. Balkum, James, Co. F, 20th N. C. Inf., died January 4, '65.
974. Balls, James, Co. G, 24th S. C. Inf., died January 31, '65.
781. Banron, Serg. James C., Co. B, 19th La. Inf., died January 15, '65.
59. Barber, John, Co. C, 4th Ala. Inf., died December 31, '63.
835. Barbre, W. O., Co. B, 2d Ark. Cav., died January 22, '65.
2012. Barger, Martin, N. C. Reserves, died June 1, '65.
739. Barker, Lewis, Co. D, 5th Ky. Inf., died January 10, '65.
1400. Barker, N. O., Co. B, 40th Ala. Inf., died February 23, '65.
999. Barnes, David W., Co. B, 7th Fla. Inf., died January 31, '65.
1168. Barnes, F. W., Co. D, 2d Tenn. Cav., died February 9, '65.
1822. Barnes, H., Co. F, 57th N. C. Inf., died April 6, '65.
779. Barnes, J. F., Co. E, 1st Va. Cav., died January, '65.
733. Barnett, S. A., Co. B, 6th Ky. Cav., died January 11, '65.
170. Barrett, J. L., Co. C, 6th Miss. Inf., died May 31, '64.
228. Barrett, John, Co. A, 4th Tenn. Cav., died October 17, '64.
547. Barrett, T. C., Co. B, 15th Tex. Cav., died December 3, '64.
1455. Barrett, T. H., Co. C, 6th Miss. Inf., died February 26, '65.
660. Barrett, William D., Co. I, 8th Tenn Inf., died December 24, '64.
478. Barrett, William F, Co. I, 42d Ga. Inf., died November 16, '64.
98. Barron, F. H., Co. H, 4th S. C. Inf., died January 5, '64.
351. Bartlett, W. R., Co. C, 46th Ga. Inf., died October 23, '64.
1493. Barton, J. W., Co. I, 6th Fla. Inf., died March 1, '65.
1742. Barton, John E, Co. B, 44th Ga. Inf., died March 24, '65.
382. Basham, Serg. David, Storr's Cavalry, died October 30, '64.
155. Bass, J. F., Co. F, 22d Miss. Inf., died May 13, '64.

1445. Bassentine, W., Co. I, 40th Ga. Inf., died February 26, '65.
720. Baswell, G. W., Co. K, 4th Tenn. Cav., died January 18, '65.
1647. Batson, E., Co. E, 16th S. C. Inf., died March 13, '65.
463. Baxder, Jacob, Co. C, 54th N. C. Inf., died November 14, '64.
1349. Bayse, Samuel, 23d Va. Bat., died February 19, '65.
1005. Beasley, B. F., Co. A, 4th Ala. Cav., died February 1, '65.
1732. Beasley, I. A., Co. B, 10th Ala. Cav., died March 22, '65.
1679. Beasley, John, Co. E, 4th Tenn. Cav., died March 16, '65.
771. Beasly, John M., 10th Tenn. Cav., died January 15, '65.
527. Beatty, Thomas M., Co. E, Stewart's Cavalry, died November 28, '64.
1640. Beaucamp, J. A., Co. D, 6th Fla. Inf., died March 13, '65.
874. Beck, Jacob, N. C. Conscript, died January 25, '65.
1623. Beck, W. A., Co. H, 36th Ga. Inf., died March 11, '65.
782. Beckett, James A., Co. I, 8th Conf. Cav., died January, '65.
1167. Bedworth, Thomas, Co. A, 13th Ky. Cav., died February 10, '65.
556. Bell, Ezra, Co. H, 18th Ala. Inf., died December 5, '64.
808. Bell, John G., Co. G, 3d Fla. Inf., died January 19, '65.
818. Bell, Corp. John R., Co. I, 4th Fla. Inf., died January 20, '65.
263. Bennett, J. H., Co. F, 36th Va. Inf., died September 21, '64.
709. Bennifield, John, Beauregard's Battery, died January 7, '65.
1806. Bensley, W. S., Co. H, 4th Tenn. Inf., died April 3, '65.
1406. Bentley, W. J., Co. F, 37th Miss. Inf., died February 23, '65.
1415. Benton, H. E., Co. E, 24th S. C. Inf., died February 24, '65.
530. Berrel, R. D., Co. F, 4th La. Inf., died November 28, '64.
1888. Berry, I. G., Co. E, 30th Ga. Inf., died April 20, '65.
832. Berry, Serg. John F., Co. I, 4th Ky. Cav., died January 21, '65.
1795. Berry, Salathiel, Co. G, 4th Ala. Cav., died March 31, '65.
1327. Berry, W. J., Co. H, 20th Tenn. Inf., died February 18, '65.
1199. Bertram, Pleasant, Co. E, 22d Va. Cav., died February 8, '65.
1890. Bertrand, Andrew, Co. B, 3d La. Inf., died April 18, '65.
1274. Bethea, H. P., Co. G, 8th S. C. Inf., died February 15, '65.
1058. Bettiss, W. J., Co. A, 13th La. Cav., died February 5, '65.
342. Bickerstaff, Serg. Noah, Co. B, 54th N. C. Inf., died October 21, '64.
675. Bickley, James B., Co. A, 22d Va. Cav., died December 27, '64.
89. Bigsby, Frank, Co. B, 4th Ky. Cav., died January 5, '64.
1819. Birchel, George W., Co. A, 1st Ala. Cav., died April 5, '65.
1094. Bird, D., Co. K, 15th S. C. Inf., died February 7, '65.
279. Bird, F., Co. H, 36th Ga. Inf., died October 4, '64.
431. Bisherer, John, Co. C, 57th N. C. Inf., died November 8, '64.
1824. Bishop, M. L., Co. A, 19th Va. Cav., died April 7, '65.
1721. Black, J. W., Co. H, 17th Ala. Inf., died March 20, '65.
210. Black, John, Co. B, 19th Va. Cav., died August 18, '64.
360. Black, John M., Co. D, 5th Ala. Cav., died October 24, '64.
1608. Black, W., Co. B, 51st Va. Inf., died March 9, '65.
275. Blackburn, William M., Co. G, 4th Ga. Cav., died October 1, '64.
1720. Blackman, R. L., Co. C, 1st Fla. Inf., died March 20, '65.
27. Blackwell, M., Co. H, 3d Ky. Inf., died September 24, '63.

No. of Grave.

245. Blackwood, Richard, Co. C, 20th Va. Cav., died September 15, '64.
843. Blair, H. P., Co. D, 1st Ga. Inf., died January 22, '65.
1405. Blair, W. W., Co. C, 28th Miss. Cav., died February 23, '65.
514. Blank, H., Co. C, 34th Va. Cav., died November 24, '64. Removed.
664. Blank, J. W., Co. B, 54th Ala. Inf., died December 24, '64.
1967. Blanton, F. A., Co. H, 4th N. C. Reserves, died May 19, '65.
1331. Blaylock, W. H., Co. B, 5th Ala. Cav., died February 18, '65.
1954. Blount, John G, Co. G, 17th N. C. Inf., died May 11, '65.
2029. Bolton, August R., Co. A, Freeman's Battery, died June 5, '65.
147. Bolton, G. W., Co. D, 44th Ala. Inf., died May 3, '64.
1077. Bolton, John, Bodger's Scouts, died February 6, '65.
1574. Bond, W., Co. H, 3d Miss. Inf., died March 6, '65.
1894. Bonds, G. W., Co. G, 29th Ga. Inf., died April 19, '65.
127. Boone, Serg. E. K., Co. A, 1st La. Cav., died March, '64.
1364. Booth, W. B., Co. G, 21st Va. Cav., died February 21, '65.
842. Boothe, Abijah, Co. H, 36th Va. Inf., died January 21, '65.
390. Boss, Leonard, Co. G, 42d Ga. Inf., died November 2, '64.
1261. Bowers, J. F., Hampton's Legion, died February 15, '65.
759. Bowers, Serg. Charles, Co. D, 24th S. C. Inf., died January 13, '65.
1402. Bowles, H. C., Co. E, Warren's Regiment, died February 26, '65.
1603. Bowlin, E. F., Co. C, 64th Va. Inf., died March 9, '65.
1186. Bowman, James, Co. D, 3d Engineers, died February 11, '65.
231. Boyd, Alex, Co. F, 54th N. C. Inf., died September 8, '64.
1130. Boyd, Robert W., Co. F, 1st Ga. Inf., died February 8, '65.
1500. Boyd, S., Co. K, 3d Miss. Inf., died March 2, '65.
839. Boyd, W. E., Co. A, 7th Ala. Cav., died January 22, '65.
579. Boyles, Charles, Co. G, 55th Ala. Inf., died December 9, '64.
1286. Bradford, J. C., Co. D, 10th Miss. Inf., died February 16, '65.
496. Bradley, John, Co. G, 46th Ala. Inf., died November 20, '64.
319. Brangenly, H., Co. C, 55th Tex. Cav., died October 16, '64.
375. Brantley, M. F., Tullis's Artillery, died October 28, '64.
1971. Brantley, W. W., Co. G, 42d N. C. Inf., died May 11, '65.
1086. Brasham, Eli M., Co. A, 8th S. C. Inf., died February 7, '65.
273. Brasswell, M. P., Co. E, 29th Ga. Inf., died September 28, '64.
83. Brazier, Ellis, 64th Tenn. Inf., died December 16, '63.
1593. Brians, R. H., Co. A, 17th Va. Cav., died March 8, '65.
1643. Briant, R., Co. H, 21st Va. Cav., died March 13, '65.
1036. Bridges, Serg. B., Co. M, 7th Ala. Cav., died February 4, '65.
61. Bridget, Benjamin, Co. G, 4th Ky., died November 9, '63.
1238. Briggs, Henry, Co. D, 29th N. C. Inf., died February 14, '65.
809. Briggins, J. H., Co. G, 22d Tenn. Inf., died January 19, '65.
2043. Brinkley, R., Co. C, Freeman's Battery, died June 14, '65.
713. Brock, C. A. H., Co. E, 50th Ga. Inf., died January 5, '65.
1141. Brock, Calvin, Co. B., 8th S. C. Inf., died February 9, '65.
53. Brock, G. H., Co. G, 2d Ky. Inf., died October 20, '63.
669. Brock, J. D., died December 27, '64.
1074. Brooklin, Isaac V., Co. B, 57th Ga. Inf., died February 6, '65.

No. of Grave.

1542. Brooks, A. G., Co. C, 66th Ga. Inf., died March 4, '65.
858. Brooks, Serg. C. E., Co. F, 2d S. C. Inf., died January 23, '65.
680. Brooks, E. B., Co. K, 1st Ga. Inf., died December 25, '64.
1334. Brooks, J. T., Co. E, 32d Miss. Bat., died February 19, '65.
1223. Brooks, Jesse, Co. I, 40th Miss. Inf., died February 13, '65.
120. Brooks, R., Co. C, 2d Ark. Inf., died March, '64.
486. Brookshire, N. F., Co. G, 1s⁺ Ga. Inf., died November 19, '64.
125. Brown, ——, died March, ʺₙₜ.
435. Brown, A. L., Co. H, 30th Ga. Inf., died November 8, '64.
950. Brown, B. R., Co. K, 52d Ga. Inf., died January 28, '65.
598. Brown, Crockett, Co. H, 18th Tenn. Cav., died December 11, '64.
646. Brown, D. E., government employ, Ala., died December 22, '64.
——. Brown, E. A., Co. E, 7th Va. Cav., died June 21, '65.
1558. Brown, J. J., Co. K, 22d Ala. Inf., died March 5, '65.
1370. Brown, John, Conscript of Tennessee, died February 21, '65.
574. Brown, John M., Co. K, 15th S. C. Inf., died December 8, '64.
1502. Brown, M., Wordais's Cavalry, died March 1, '65.
985. Brown, R. S., Co. G, 11th Va. Cav., died January 31, '65.
472. Brown, Robert, Co. G, 30th Ga. Inf., died November 15, '64.
56. Brown, Russel, 11th Tenn. Cav., died October 28, '63.
1794. Brown, Wiley S., Co. A, 11th Tenn. Inf., died March 31, '65.
432. Brown, William, Co. B, 33d Ala. Inf., died November 8, '64.
1131. Brown, W. S., Madison's Artillery, died February 15, '65.
1206. Browning, B., Co. K, 29th Ga. Inf., died February 12, '65.
868. Browning, Stephen, Co. C, 45th Ga. Inf., died January 25, '65.
643. Bruge, David A., Co. D, 30th Va. Cav., died December 21, '64.
2011. Bryan, J. D., Co. K, 39th Ala. Inf., died June 1, '65.
1750. Bryan, S. W., Co. G, 25th Ga. Inf., died March 25, '65.
430. Bryant, Jesse, Co. A, 66th Ga. Inf., died November 8, '64.
1953. Bryant, P. A., Co. H, 46th Miss. Inf., died May 10, '65.
1496. Buckhart, George, Co. B, Hill's Cavalry, died March 1, '65.
1884. Buckhart, George, 7th Fla. Inf., died March, '65.
1059. Buitt, John, Co. F, 19th S. C. Inf., died February 5, '65.
542. Bullington, T. R., Co. C, 8th Tenn. Cav., died December 2, '64.
449. Bullock, G. K., Co. F, 6th Fla. Inf., died November 13, '64.
1266. Bumgarden, John B., Co. E, 8th Va. Cav., died February 14, '65.
661. Bumpers, D. D., Co. E, 24th Ala. Inf., died December 24, '64.
373. Bumpers, Nath, Co. E, 24th Ala. Inf., died October 28, '64.
2016. Bunch, S. F., Co. E, 29th Tenn. Inf., died June 2, '65.
334. Burgess, George H., citizen of Ohio, died October 18, '64.
2006. Burgess, I. H., Co. B, 8th Ga. Inf., died May 30, '65.
1353. Burgis, R. F., Co. H, Moreland's Battery, died February 20, '65.
1984. Burkett, John A., Co. G, 6th Fla. Inf., died May 19, '65.
929. Burnett, I., died January 28, '65.
1669. Burnett, J., Co. E, 1st Tenn. Cav., died March 15, '65.
381. Burnette, ——, citizen of Louisiana, died October 30, '64.
82. Burns, Andrew, Co. C, 36th Va. Cav., died December 16, '63.

No. of Grave.

1744. Burt, Andy, Co. C, 22d Miss. Inf., died March 24, '65.
1577. Burt, F. J., Co. D, 22d Miss. Inf., died March 6, '65.
1926. Burt, John W., Co. B, 34th Ala. Inf., died April 28, '65.
1209. Burton, J., Co. C, 4th Ky. Cav., died February 12, '65.
174. Burton, J. D., 15th Tenn. Cav., died June 8, '64.
1934. Busby, I. A., Co. E, 31st Ala. Inf., died May 4, '65.
1889. Bush, Daniel, Co. B, 39th Miss. Inf., died April 17, '65.
1439. Bush, J. S., Co. G, 33d Ala. Inf., died February 25, '65.
716. Bush, P. C., Co. E, 6th Fla. Inf., died January 5, '65
1070. Bushby, Matthew B., Co. B, 4th Ky. Cav., died February 6, '65
753. Bustle, W., Co. H, 8th Tenn. Cav., died January 12, '65.
700. Butcher, Evan, Co. B, 46th Bat., Va. Cav., died January 3, '65.
1501. Butler, John, Co. B, 5th Bat. Va. Inf., died March 2, '65.
932. Butts, W. R., Co. F, 11th Tenn. Inf., died January 28, '65.
2037. Byn, J., Co. K, 9th Ark. Inf., died June 11, '65.
1682. Caigle, N. H., Co. D, 17th Ala. Inf., died March 16, '65.
72. Cain, J. D., Co. C, 10th Ky. Cav., died November 27, '63.
2024. Caine, James A., Co. I, 55th Ala. Inf., died June 4, '65.
2020. Caldwell, R. P. C., Co. K, 21st Miss. Inf., died June 2, '65.
1581. Callahan, W. J., Co. F, 63d Va. Inf., died March 5, '65.
1247. Calley, J. W., Co. C, 42d Ala. Inf., died February 14, '65.
776. Calvin, John W., Co. C, 14th Ky. Cav., died January 15, '65.
1550. Cammons, Thomas, Co. C, 12th Tenn. Inf., died March 5, '65.
249. Camp, Joseph M., Co. K, 64th Ga. Inf., died September 16, '64.
955. Camp, William, Co. B, 4th Ala. Inf., died January 29, '65.
1022. Campbell, A., Co. D, 2d Ky. Bat. Cav., died February 3, '65.
1483. Campbell, F., Co. H, 8th Tenn. Cav., died February 25, '65.
1690. Campbell, G. B., Co. B, 17th Ala. Inf., died March 17, '65.
1517. Campbell, J., Co. D, 4th La. Inf., died March 3, '65.
615. Campbell, J. A., Co. H, 20th Tenn. Inf., died December 14, '64.
599. Campbell, J. J., Co. H, 40th Ga. Inf., died December 11, '64.
1621. Campbell, R. B., Co. I, 27th Va. Cav., died March 11, '65.
1095. Campbell, S., Co. E, 1st Ga. Inf., died February 7, '65.
1851. Campbell, T. J., Co. A, 5th Mo. Inf., died April 11, '65.
237. Canada, Thomas F., Co. H, Fornett's La. Bat., died September 11, '64
1587. Canipy, Eli, Co. F, 58th N. C. Inf., died March 7, '65.
840. Cannon, T. E., Co. D, 5th Ky. Cav., died January 22, '65.
788. Canseg, J. L., 3d Bat., Miss. Inf., died January 16, '65.
702. Canterbury, I. N., Co. C, 32d Ala. Inf., died January 3, '65.
877. Cantrell, W. C., Co. K, 21st Tenn. Cav., died January 25, '65.
783. Capdeville, J. B., Co. C, 30th La. Inf., died January 15, '65.
183. Caper, J. B., Co. H, 23d Va. Cav., died July 9, '64.
1993. Carle, T. T., Co. K, 4th La. Inf., died May 23, '65.
1093. Carley, J. A., Co. K, 15th S. C. Inf., died February 7, '65.
1279. Carlisle, G. B. W., Co. H, 18th Ala. Inf., died February 15, '65.
577. Carmichael, William T., Co. H, 8th Tenn. Cav., died December 8, '64
349. Carnett, E. W., Co. G, 1st Ga. Cav., died October 23, '64.

No. of Grave.

458. Carney, J. W., Co. E, 4th Ky. Inf., died November 13, '64.
296. Carpenter, William, Co. K, 8th S. C. Cav., died October 10, '64.
1100. Carr, R., Co. A, 57th Ala. Inf., died February 8, '65.
300. Carr, William, Co. A, 24th Ga. Inf., died October 11, '64.
1829. Carrigan, C. H., Co. D, 8th Tenn. Inf., died April 8, '65.
704. Carroll, B., Co. A, 57th Ala. Inf., died January 5, '65.
1505. Carroll, H., Co. D, 7th Miss. Inf., died March 2, '65.
66. Carroll, H., Walker's Battery, died November 16, '63.
1949. Carroll, James, Co. H, 94th Va. Inf., died May 9, '65.
1818. Carroll, Stephen, Co. C, 22d Miss. Inf., died April 5, '65.
295. Carroll, William F., Co. F, 40th Ga. Inf., died October 10, '64.
1660. Carroll, W., Co. H, 4th Ala. Cav., died March 14, '65.
372. Carson, Robert, Co. B, 37th Va. Cav., died October 28, '64.
2013. Carter, A., Co. E, 24th S. C. Inf., died June 13, '65.
135. Carter, George R., 9th Tenn. Cav., died April 13, '64.
678. Carter, J. W., Co. G, 27th Miss. Inf., died December 29, '64.
1807. Carter, Joel, Co. F, 63d Va. Cav., died April 2, '65.
1324. Carter, Moses, Co. G, 3d Miss. Inf., died February 18, '65.
972. Carter, Robert, Co. A, 1st Md. Cav., died January 30, '65.
1840. Carter, William, Co. E, 1st Tenn. Cav., died April 10, '65.
1891. Casey, Jesse, Dent's Battery, died April 18, '65.
1473. Cass, J., Young's Battery, died February 24, '65.
1010. Cassell, W. B., Co. I, 7th Fla. Inf., died February 2, '65.
324. Caster, Tuck, Co. F, 43d Tenn. Inf., died October 15, '64.
337. Cathcart, Lieut. John H., Co. G, 43d Tenn. Inf., died October 18, '64.
1492. Cavender, William, Co. H, 8th Miss. Inf., died March 1, '65.
848. Cazby, J. J., Co. H, 58th Ala. Inf., died January 23, '65.
1801. Cease, D. J., Co. C, 15th S. C. Inf., died March 18, '65.
436. Chamberlain, R. M., 36th Tenn. Cav., died November 8, '64.
568. Chambers, J. T., Co. G, 37th Va. Cav., died December 7, '64.
2018. Chambers, James, Co. B, 16th Ga. Cav., died June 3, '65.
1163. Chambers, W. L., Co. E, 4th Ala. Cav., died February 10, '65.
723. Chana, P. C., Co. G, 3d Fla. Inf., died January 9, '65.
1442. Channel, T. W., Co. H, 2d Ga. Cav., died February 25, '65.
1697. Chapman, E. T., Co. C, 63d Ga. Inf., died March 18, '65.
1332. Chapman, J. L., Co. E, 37th Ala. Inf., died February 18, '65.
1082. Chapman, L., Co. K, 11th Tenn. Cav., died February 7, '65.
1098. Chappell, A. M., Co. B, 46th Ala. Inf., died February 7, '65.
1221. Cheek, Allen R., Co. I, 41st Ga. Inf., died February 13, '65.
1537. Cheek, P. B., Co. D, 16th Ga. Cav., died March 4, '65.
34. Cherry, F., Co. D, of Tennessee, died October 4, '63.
650. Childers, W. M., Co. A, 43d Ga. Inf., died December 22, '64.
1875. Childs, R. B., Co. H, 30th Ga. Inf., died April 7, '65.
1521. Chillaett, J. W., Co. I, 13th Tenn. Inf., died March 3, '65.
1413. Chitwood, R. O., Roddy's Escort, died February 24, '65.
198. Christian, B., Co. E, 8th Ga. Inf., died August 13, '64.
202. Christian, Jacob, Co. B, 24th Bat., Va. Cav., died August 14, '64.

No. of Grave.
1807. Chudler, Jeff, Co. H, 25th Va. Cav., died March 26, '65.
1595. Church, S. H., Co. D, 30th Miss. Inf., died March 8, '65.
2000. Claiman, James, Co. E, 1st Va. Bat. Inf., died May 26, '65.
1046. Clanahan, W., Co. E, 18th Ala. Inf., died February 4, '65.
1113. Clark, Albert, Marshal's Battery, died February 8, '65.
466. Clark, E. J., Co. A, 4th Ala. Inf., died November 14, '64.
837. Clark, H. Y., Co. A, 54th Ala. Inf., died January 22, '65.
——. Clark, J. J., Co. G, 7th Fla. Inf., died March 3, '65.
1951. Clark, John, Co. B, 4th Ala. Cav., died May 10, '65.
934. Clark, Julius T., Co. H, Moreland's Bat. Cav., died January 28, '65.
1326. Clark, M., Co. B, 2d Ky. Cav., died February 18, '65.
1963. Clark, M. T., Co. C, 29th N. C. Inf., died May 13, '65.
1351. Clark., Robert, Carroll County, Ark., died February 20, '65.
474. Clayborn, Thomas B., Co. C, 56th Ga. Inf., died November 16, '64.
1246. Clayton, R., Co. G, 14th N. C. Inf., died February 14, '65.
1910. Clearman, W. W., Co. D, 3d Miss. Inf., died April 24, '65.
812. Clemens, J. W., Co. I, 52d Va. Inf., died January 19, '65.
1321. Clement, Griffin, Co. D, 30th Ala. Inf., died February 18, '65.
488. Clements, B. F., Co. H, 36th Ala. Inf., died November 19, '64.
405. Clerpuns, M. M., Co. A, 31st Miss. Inf., died November 5, '64.
274. Clipton, H., died September 29, '64.
1020. Cluck, James, Co. C, 31st Tenn., died February 3, '65.
763. Coatney, John, Co. E, 6th Fla., died January 14, '65.
2030. Coble, G., Co. H, 1st N. C. Conscript, died June 5, '65.
87. Cochran, J. D., Co. C, 5th Ky. Inf., died December 23, '63.
370. Cochran, J. S., Co. G, 41st Miss. Inf., died October 26, '64.
762. Cochran, John, Co. F, 39th Miss., died January 14, '65.
1893. Cochran, R. C., Co. F, 46th Miss. Inf., died April 18, '65.
903. Coffee, J. E., Co. B, 5th Ala. Cav., died January 27, '65.
317. Cogee, Christopher, citizen of Virginia, died October 15, '64.
1368. Coggins, J. M., Co. A, 56th Ga. Inf., died February 21, '65.
2028. Cole, David T., Co. K, 56th Ga. Inf., died June 5, '65.
1284. Cole, J. G., Co. C, 37th Ga. Inf., died February 16, '65.
1759. Coleman, John, Co. B, 17th Ala. Inf., died March 26, '65.
——. Colledge, H. P., died January 24, '65.
958. Collins, J. H. (Hospital Steward), 20th Miss. Inf., died Jan. 29, '65.
736. Collins, James, Co. B, 63d Ga. Inf., died January 10, '65.
180. Collins, S., Co. F, 1st Ky. Cav., died June 25, '64.
1985. Colton. E. P., Co. A, 56th Ga. Inf., died May 19, '65.
154. Combs, Peter, Co. B, 8th Ky. Inf., died May 12, '64.
872. Cone, Thomas, Co. D, 21st Tenn. Cav., died January 24, '65.
1935. Coniway, G. W., Co. G, 46th Ala. Inf., died May 4, '65.
182. Conran, Robert, citizen of Virginia, died July 9, '64.
1582. Consert, S. J., Co. I, 47th Tenn. Inf., died March 7, '65.
1071. Cook, David, Co. I, 36th Va. Inf., died February 6, '65.
194. Cook, James, Co. C, 26th Va. Inf., died August 6, '64.
315. Cook, John, citizen of Virginia, died October 15, '64.

No. of Grave.

1435. Cook, J. J., Co. B, 30th Ala. Inf., died February 25, '65.
1302. Cooksey, J. M., Co. K, 1st Ga. Sta., died February 16, '65.
1416. Coonts, J., Co. A, 27th Va. Cav., died February 24, '65.
73. Cooper, Thompson, citizen of Virginia, died November 28, '63.
683. Cooper, William, Co. D, 10th C. S. Cav., died December 30, '64.
1289. Cooper, William S., Co. I, 33d Miss. Inf., died February 1, '65.
1272. Copeland, George A., Co. A, 56th Ga. Inf., died February 15, '65.
652. Cornelius, B., Co. K, 18th Ala. Inf., died December 22, '64.
5. Cornell, J., Co. I, 4th Ala. Inf., died August 10, '63.
944. Corrall, W. W., Co. K, 57th N. C. Inf., died January 29, '65.
1111. Cowan, Samuel, Co. G, 50th Ala. Inf., died February 8, '65.
593. Cowart, A. W., Co. B, 40th Ala. Inf., died December 10, '64.
1861. Cowell, Elias, Co. B, 20th Va. Cav., died April 14, '65.
1733. Cowine, J. W., Co. E, 30th Ga. Inf., died March 22, '65.
1775. Cowinan, H., citizen of Virginia, died March 28, '65.
93. Cox, First Serg. J., 3d C. S. Cav., died January 13, '64.
1270. Cox, M. M., Co. D, 32d Ala. Inf., died February 15, '65.
1081. Cox, Stephen L., Co. B, 4th La. Bat., died February 7, '65.
1424. Coy, Charles W., Co. E, 8th S. C. Inf., died February 24, '65.
270. Coydell, John, Bat. N. C. Inf., died September 28, '64.
953. Crabb, Richard, Co. D, 34th Ala. Inf., died January 29, '65.
1564. Crabtree, H., Co. K, 27th Miss. Inf., died March 5, '65.
1355. Craft, J., Co. B, 10th Ga. Cav., died February 20, '65.
686. Cragle, W. C., Co. D, 51st Tenn. Inf., died December 31, '64.
623. Craig, J. M., Co. K, 48th Tenn. Inf., died December 16, 64.
754. Crane, N. W., Co. C, 38th Ga. Inf., died January 12, '65.
1013. Crane, W. R. D., Co. L, 7th Ala. Cav., died February 3, '65.
1615. Crawford, D., Co. I, 15th Miss. Inf., died March 10, '65.
1456. Crawford, James, Conscript Guards, died February 26, '65.
611. Crawford, John, Co. E, 36th Va. Inf., died December 13, '64.
1930. Crawley, John, Co. G, 66th Ga. Inf., died May 2, '65.
1944. Cree, G. P. H., Co. K, 29th Ala. Inf., died May 8, '65.
591. Creed, Thomas, Co. A, 35th Miss. Inf., died December 10, '64.
1544. Crenshaw, J., Co. F, 7th Fla. Inf., died March 4, '65.
1606. Crenshaw, L., Co. K, 52d Ga. Inf., died March 9, '65.
343. Cress, James H., Co. G, 21st Va. Cav., died October 20, '64.
1525. Cronk, E., Co. D, 54th Va. Inf., died March 3, '65.
1590. Crosswhite, H., Co. G, 10th Ala. Cav., died March 8, '65.
1345. Crow, J. S., Co. G, 14th Miss. Inf., died February 19, '65.
205. Crow, S. H., Co. F, 3d Ala. Cav., died August 15, '64.
1011. Crow, W. L. D., Co. A, 57th Ala. Inf., died February 2, '65.
1767. Crowder, James W., Co. F, 5th Tenn. Inf., died March 26, '65.
1352. Crowley, J. W., Co. H, 32d Tex. Bat., died February 20, '65.
128. Crum, W. R., Stodgalis's Cavalry, died April 7, '64.
1758. Crump, S. S., Co. F, 10th Ala. Cav., died March 26, '65.
1165. Cruse, M., Co. F, 43d N. C. Inf., died February 10, '65.
1346. Cruss, J. W., Co. D, 21st N. C. Cav., died February 19, '65.

No. of Grave.

1062. Crutchfield, P. S., Quartermaster's Dept., died February 5, '65.
1258. Cullan, W., Co. A, 11th S. C. Inf., died February 15, '65.
1052. Cullin, I. M., Co. H, 22d Ala. Inf., died February 5, '65.
841. Cunningham, J. C., Co. I, 3d Conf., died January 22, '65.
353. Cunningham, J. T., Co. G, 54th Ala. Inf., died October 23, '64.
673. Cunningham, S., Co. I, 17th Va. Cav., died December 24, '64.
1896. Cupp, Alexander, Co. K, 7th Ga. Inf., died April 19, '65.
766. Currier, A. J., Co. F, 22d Ala., died January 14, '65.
922. Custer, Madison, Co. F, 22d Miss. Inf., died January 28, '65.
919. Custer, William G., Co. D, 29th N. C. Inf., died January 28, '65.
1532. Cutlipp, Jackson, Co. H, 19th Va. Cav., died March 4, '65.
176. Dagley, Milton, Co. H, 2d Tenn. Cav., died June 12, '64.
1641. Dailey, Patrick, Co. B, 1st Ga. Inf., died March 13, '65.
48. Daniel, Lieut. J. A., 17th Tenn. Cav., died October 12, '63.
1787. Daniel, J. W., Co. C, 15th Miss. Inf., died March 31, '65.
536. Daniels, J. W., Co. A, 54th Ala. Inf., died November 30, '64.
305. Daniels, John, Co. E, 2d Va. Inf., died October 12, '64.
822. Daniels, K., Co. F, 57th Ala. Inf., died January 21, '65.
385. Darby, B. F., Co. A, 57th Ala. Inf., died October 31, '64.
367. Date, T. H., Co. C, 22d Ala. Inf., died October 26, '64.
1428. David (or Daniels), E., Co. B, 4th Ala. Cav., died February 24, '65.
602. Davidson, J., Co. C, 27th Va. Cav., died December 11, '64.
1689. Davis, Charles, Co. K, 8th S. C. Inf., died March 17, '65.
850. Davis, George, Co. F, 20th Va. Cav., died January 23, '65.
1440. Davis, H., Co. C, Engineer Corps, died February 25, '65.
1557. Davis, H. N., Co. K, 14th Tenn. Cav., died March 5, '65.
1597. Davis, J. P., Co. A, 2d Ky. Cav., died March 9, '65.
1638. Davis, M. J., Co. G, 45th Va. Inf., died March 13, '65.
1599. Davis, N., Co. F, 1st Miss. Bat., died March 8, '65.
13. Davis, P. F., 5th N. C. Cav., died September 13, '63.
777. Davis, Pringle, Co. A, 24th S. C. Inf., died January 15, '65.
1469. Davis, Thomas, Co. E, 33d Ala. Inf., died February 27, '65.
1671. Davis, W. R., Co. C, 52d Ga. Inf., died March 15, '65.
285. Dean, W. H., Co. G, 1st Ga. Inf., died October 7, '64.
1329. Deans, A., Co. K, 35th Miss. Inf., died February 18, '65.
629. Deckson, John, Co. K, 1st Tenn. Cav., died December 18, '64.
995. Deiver, J. R., Co. K, 36th Ga. Inf., died February 2, '65.
123. DeLock, J., 10th C. S., died March, '64.
393. Demain, D., Co. B, 7th S. C. Inf., died November 3, '64.
1712. Denniston, P. H., Co. B, 114th Tenn. Inf., died March 20, '65.
107. Derryberry, J. D., Co. B, 11th Tenn. Cav., died February, '64.
855. Dethridge, J. G., Co. D, 8th Va. Cav., died January 23, '65.
166. Dethridge, M., Co. L, 2d Ky. Cav., died May 24, '64.
1253. Dickie, S. W., Co. G, 18th Ala. Inf., died February 14, '65.
695. Dilland, T. E., Co. G, 40th Ala. Inf., died January 2, '65.
1916. Dilley, Thomas, Co. I, 19th Va. Cav., died April 25, '65.
1066. Dillingham, J. A., Co. C, 13th Ky. Cav., died February 6, '65.

No. of Grave.

1758. Dillingham, J. S., Co. C, 13th Ky. Cav., died March 27, '65.
1855. Dillon, Joel, Co. E, Mussy's Battery, died April 13, '65.
524. Dillon, W. D., Co. G, 2d Va. Cav., died November 27, '64.
685. Dills, James, Co. F, 21st Va. Cav., died December 30, '64.
1586. Dinwiddie, David, Co. A, La. Sharpshooters, died March 7, '65.
1128. Dirden, B. W., Co. A, 45th Ala. Inf., died February 8, '65.
1037. Ditto, J., Co. L, 5th Ala. Cav., died February 4, '65.
383. Doig, W. P., Co. C, 40th Ga. Inf., died October 30, '64.
1777. Dolan, Joshua, Co. C, 5th Tenn. Cav., died March 29, '65.
1215. Dorlas, W. A., Co. A, 32d Miss. Inf., February 13, '65.
1004. Dorsett, Philip, Co. H, 46th Ga. Inf., died February 3, '65.
1369. Dougherty, R., Co. D, 4th La. Inf., died February 21, '65.
244. Dougherty, T. R., Co. G, 4th La. Inf., died October 22, '64.
487. Dougherty, W., Co. B, 1st Ga. Art., died November 19, '64.
1967. Dougherty, W. P., Co. H, 22d Va. Cav., died May 15, '65.
799. Douglas, James A., Co. I, 34th Ala. Inf., died January 18, '65.
1374. Dowsing, F. L., Co. F, 8th T. C. S. Cav., died February 22, '65.
167. Doxey, Martin, Co. D, 1st Ky. Cav., died May 27, '64.
1653. Doyle, Charles, Co. H, 2d Tenn. Cav., died March 14, '65.
772. Doyle, J., Co. I, 15th Tenn. Inf., died January 14, '65.
1694. Drake, J. W., Co. K, 4th Ala. Inf., died March 17, '65.
1838. Drake, S. R., Co. G, 20th Tenn. Cav., died April 10, '65.
1465. Driggers, J., Co. B, 8th S. C. Inf., died February 27, '65.
1014. Driggers, J. J., Perry's Battery, died February 3, '65.
1140. Driggers, Simpson, Co. A, 7th Fla. Inf., died February 9, '65.
1235. Drisbach, T. R., Co. F, 7th Ala. Cav., died February 14, '65.
738. Driscoll, W., Co. A, 1st Tenn. Cav., died January 10, '65.
616. Drum, C. H., Co. G, 17th Tenn. Cav., died December 14, '64.
926. Drum, Thomas, Co. B, 19th S. C. Inf., died January 28, '65.
1802. Dubard, Phil C., Co. A, 15th Miss. Inf., died April 1, '65.
50. Dudley, C. H., 10th Tenn. Cav., died October 16, '63.
741. Dudley, Charles W., Co. E, 30th Miss. Inf., died January 10, '65.
1553. Duerson, J. M., Co. E, 34th Ga. Inf., died March 5, '65.
2003. Duke, Stephen, Marshall's Battery, died May 28, '65.
316. Dunaway, David, Co. D, 34th Ala. Inf., died October 15, '64.
1281. Dunbar, T. G., Co. A, 57th Ga. Inf., died February 15, '65.
429. Duncan, George W., Co. G, 3d C. S. Inf., died November 8, '64.
99. Duncan, I., Co. D, 8th Tenn. Cav., died January, '64.
60. Duncan, J. J., Co. I, Forrest's Tenn. Cav., died November 9, '63.
310. Duncan, John W., Co. G, 56th Ga. Inf., died October 12, '64.
892. Duncan, Wm. H., Conscript, Tenn. Guards, died January 26, '65.
200. Dunham, Davidson, Co. D, 3d Fla. Inf., died January 31, '65.
1295. Dupree, Richard, Co. B, 34th Ala. Inf., died February 16, '65.
1655. Eagle, George, citizen of Virginia, died March 14, '65.
1785. Eagle, H. F., citizen of Virginia, died March 29, '65.
241. Eagle, M., Nitre Mining Bureau, died September 14, '64.
1948. Earnhart, James B., Co. K, 1st S. C. Inf., died May 9, '65

No. of Grave.
1612. Easter, T. M., Co. A, 37th Va. Cav., died March 10, '65.
492. Eaton, M. J., Co. F, 8th Va. Cav., died November 20, '64.
461. Eaton, W., Co. A, 4th Tenn. Cav., died November 14, '64.
986. Echols, J. M., Co. C, 66th Ga. Inf., died January 31, '65.
389. Eddins, H. K., Co. C, 3d Tenn. Cav., died November 1, '64.
787. Edgar, Thomas, Co. A, 46th Ala. Inf., died January 16, '65.
420. Edson, Henry S., Citizen of Virginia, died November 7, '64.
998. Edwards, John W., Co. C, 1st Ga. Bat., died January 31, '65.
160. Edwards, Owen, Co. B, 1st Ky. Cav., died May 20, '64.
617. Edwards, W. W., Co. B, 54th N. C. Inf., died December 15, '64.
1291. Egnor, W. G., Co. D, 34th Va. Cav., died February 16, '65.
1446. Elkin, John, Co. K, 4th Ala. Cav., died February 26, '65.
1040. Ellan, W., Co. G, 13th Va. Inf., died February 4, '65.
1050. Ellington, P., Co. E, 5th Miss. Cav., died February 5, '65.
94. Elliot, J. S., Co. F, 62d N. C. Cav., died June 13, '64.
445. Ellis, E. W., Co. D, 6th Fla. Inf., died November 10, '64.
834. Ellis, J. R., citizen of Virginia, died January 22, '65.
17. Ellis, Joseph, Co. B, 5th Ky. ——, died September 30, '63.
51. Elliston, Ed G., Co. H, 62d Va. ——, died October 18, '63.
2049. Eloryge, Hiram, Co. I, 28th Va. Cav., died June 21, '65.
578. Elrod, J. B., Co. F, 39th Ga. Inf., died December 9, '64.
876. Embler, Pusey, Co. C, 29th A. C. Inf., died January 24, '65.
546. Emerson, John M., Co. K, 12th N. C. Inf., died December 2, '64.
1198. Emory, I. H., Co. B, 2d Md. Cav., died February 12, '65.
2004. Enbanks, Al, Co. A, 28th Ala. Inf., died June 28, '65.
2022. Enbanks, E. H., Co. K, 3d Ala. Cav., died June 5, '65.
1579. England, F. M., Co. A, 3d S. C. Inf., died March 6, '65.
1427. England, R. S., Co. A, 2d Mo. Inf., died February 24, '65.
1018. English, Eli, Co. K, 33d Ala. Inf., died February 3, '65.
1001. Erskine, J. C., Co. K, 37th Va. Cav., died February 1, '65.
1372. Ervin, I., Co. E, 10th Ala. Cav., died February 21, '65.
1996. Esell, J. N., Co. H, 59th Ala. Inf., died May 23, '65.
1366. Esmond, R., Co. H, 15th Ala. Inf., died February 21, '65.
284. Estes, B. O., Co. A, 9th Ga. Inf., died October 7, '64.
301. Estes, John, Co. A, 5th Miss. Inf., died October 12, '64.
1614. Estes, John, Co. B, 16th Ga. Cav., died March 10, '65.
1069. Estiss, Allen T., Co. B, 5th Ala. Cav., died February 6, '65.
1494. Evans, William, Co. F, 46th Ga. Inf., died March 1, '65.
1859. Everett, H. M., Co. D, 22d Tenn. Cav., died April 13, '65.
1369. Ewing, J. J., Co. C, 32d Ala. Inf., died February 21, '65.
1379. Ewing, W. W., Co. F, 5th Ala. Cav., died February 22, '65.
1434. Eye, W. M., Co. K, 62d Va. Inf., died February 25, '65.
1234. Faircloth, J. F., Co. G, 57th Ala. Inf., died February 14, '65.
1895. Falkner, H. B., citizen of Kentucky, died April 19, '65.
590. Falsom, ——, Co. F, 6th Fla. Inf., died December 10, '64.
304. Fanclothe, Wilson, Co. G, 6th Fla. Inf., died October 16, '64.
757. Fannin, Theodore, Co. H, — Va. Inf., died January 13, '65.

No. of Grave.

494. Fanom, Miller, Co. C, 5th Ky. Inf., died November 20, '64.
262. Farmier, Jacob H., Co. A, 42d Ga. Inf., died September 21, '64.
289. Farmer, Reuben, Co. K, 43d Ga. Inf., died October 8, '64.
471. Farrell, L., Co. C, 54th Ala. Inf., died November 15, '64.
196. Farris, S., Co. G, 25th Tenn. Inf., died August 9, '64.
931. Farris, Thomas, Co. I, 13th Bat. Va. Inf., died January 28, '65.
895. Farrow, A. H., Co. C, 28th Bat. Va. Cav., died January 25, '65.
813. Farrow, G. W., Co. K, 56th Ga. Inf., died January 20, '65.
1849. Farthing, Paul, Co. A, 11th N. C. Inf., died April 11, '65.
1914. Farthing, R. P., Co. A, 11th N. C. Inf., died April 24, '65.
47. Fenell, Jeff, Co. K, 17th Tenn., died October 10, '63.
192. Fenton, W. E., Co. B, 20th Va. Inf., died August 1, '64.
468. Ferguson, A. P., Co. G, 21st Va. Cav., died November 15, '64.
1503. Fields, J., Co. A, 21st Tenn. Inf., died March 2, '65.
14. Fields, S. A., 3d C. S. Cav., died September 16, '63.
470. Finch, J., Patterson's Battery, died November 15, '64.
879. Fincher, W. C., Co. C, 66th Ga. Inf., died January 25, '65.
1192. Fircley, E. J., Co. H, 31st Miss. Inf., died February 11, '65.
1297. Firney, S. B., Co. K, 54th Ga. Inf., died February 16, '65.
870. Fishbrom, F. B., Co. A, 37th Bat. Va. Cav., died January 25, '65.
49. Fisher, W. H., citizen of Virginia, died October 13, '63.
1032. Fitzgerald, W. C., Co. D, 36th Bat. Va. Cav., died February 3, '65.
1674. Fitzgerald, W. C., Co. E, 36th Va. Cav., died March 16, '65.
211. Flake, S. L., Co. A, 15th Tenn. Inf., died August 19, '64.
786. Fleeman, L. W., Co. F, 54th Va. Inf., died January 16, '65.
374. Fleming, George, Co. I, 18th Tenn. Cav., died October 28, '64.
1300. Fleming, Louis, Co. H, 22d Va. Cav., died February 16, '65.
1961. Fletcher, Newton, Co. G, 25th Va. Cav., died May 12, '65.
756. Flippo, A. Y., Co. K, 49th Ala. Inf., died January 13, '65.
801. Floyd, I. A., Co. K, 49th Ala. Inf., died January 19, '65.
1027. Floyd, Robert, Co. C, 1st Ky. Cav., died February 8, '65.
287. Flurry, Thomas G., Co. D, 42d Ala. Inf., died October 8, '64.
1587. Foly, P., Co. I, 3d La. Inf., died March 4, '65.
172. Fontaine, J. A., Co. F, 12th Va. Cav., died June 2, '64.
465. Fonville, John F., Co. C, 1st Miss., died November 14, '64.
76. Ford, J. D., died December 1, '63.
1347. Ford, W. H., Co. H, 54th Ala. Inf., died February 18, '65.
1965. Fore, Daniel, Co. B, 39th Miss. Inf., died May 14, '65.
97. Fore, F. A., Co. K, 5th Tenn. Inf., died January 18, '64.
1836. Forrest, J. G., Co. I, 29th Ga. Inf., died April 9, '65.
961. Fortenburg, John, Co. H, Lowry's Miss. Inf., died January 29, '65.
103. Foust, E., Co. E, 5th Tenn. Inf., died February 6, '64.
1912. Fowler, E., Co. A, 13th Ky. Cav., died April 24, '65.
1541. Fowler, J. L., Co. B, 13th Bat. Va. Inf., died March 4, '65.
388. Fowler, W., Co. H, 5th Ga. Inf., died November 1, '64.
102. Fox, J. J., Co. B, 11th Tex. Cav., died January 18, '64.
690. Fox, James P., Co. B, 17th Va. Cav., died December 31, '64.

No. of Grave.

640. Francesco, D. B., Co. A, 12th Tenn. Cav., died December 21, '64.
1931. Francis, N. F., Co. E, Thomas's N. C. Legion, died May 2, '65.
522. Francum, W., Co. E, 58th N. C. Inf., died November 27, '64.
648. Franklin, Albert, Co. K, 46th Miss. Inf., died December 22, '64.
1083. Franklin, C. W., Co. H, 23d Tenn. Inf., died February 7, '65.
1061. Franklin, Peter, Co. A, 8th C. S. Cav., died February 5, '65.
724. Frasier, J. S., Co. F, 2d Miss. Inf., died January 9, '65.
302. Frazzell, Thomas, Co. F, 34th Ala. Inf., died October 12, '64.
1049. Free, Malachi, Co. A, 52d Ga. Inf., died February 4, '65.
320. Freeland, J., Co. B, 41st Ga. Inf., died October 16, '64.
1765. Freeling, Finney, Co. A, 4th Ala. Cav., died March 27, '65.
1375. Freeman, A. W., Co. D, 5th Ala. Cav., died February 22, '65.
1448. Freeman, J. M., Co. K, 7th Miss. Inf., died March 13, '65.
1753. Freeman, M. M., Co. B, 70th Ala. Inf., died March 25, '65.
767. Freeman, P. B., Co. E, 28th Tenn. Inf., died January 13, '65.
1097. Freeman, W. F., Co. I, 56th Ga. Inf., died February 7, '65.
1487. Freeman, W. P., Co. C, 31st Ga. Inf., died February 25, '65.
1374. French, J. R., — Ga. Conscript, died February 22, '65.
1902. French, Willis, Co. F, 38th Ala. Inf., died April 23, '65.
1813. Fridley, John, Co. A, 22d Va. Inf., died April 3, '65.
1827. Frier, Newton, Co. C, 4th Fla. Inf., died April 7, '65.
1460. Frierson, Henry, Co. G, 9th Tenn. Cav., died February 27, '65.
1196. Frisbee, M. F., Co. C, 29th N. C. Inf., died February 12, '65.
1233. Fry, B. F., Co. I, 7th Miss. Inf., died February 14, '65.
195. Fuller, M. R., Co. F, 41st Miss. Inf., died August 8, '64.
885. Fuller, S., Co. C, 8th Ga. Inf., died January 25, '65.
682. Furguson, J. K., Co. G, 37th Miss. Inf., died December 30, '64.
302. Furlgam, James F., Co. I, 30th Ala. Inf., died October 16, '64.
2009. Futch, Thomas, Co. D, 25th Ga. Inf., died May 17, '65.
1972. Gable, James, Co. J, Moreland's Ky. Cav., died May 16, '65.
1063. Gaines, A. N., Co. I, 1st Ga. Inf., died February 5, '65.
1610. Galliway, M., Co. B, 18th Ga. Inf., died March 10, '65.
882. Gantlin, J., Co. K, 48th Tenn. Inf., died January 25, '65.
3. Gardner, E. H., 4th Ga., died August 9, '63.
355. Gardner, S. M., Albany Nitre Works, died October 24, '64.
1330. Garner, W., Co. D, 1st Ky. Cav., died February 18, '65.
1504. Garrett, D., citizen of Virginia, died March 1, '65.
596. Garrett, Joshua, Co. B, 40th Ga. Inf., died December 10, '64.
269. Garrett, William, Co. A, 46th Ga. Inf., died September 24, '64.
1008. Garrison, L., Co. K, 57th Ala. Inf., died February 2, '65.
1980. Gaston, R. H., Co. E, 4th N. C. Inf., died May 16, '65.
88. Gaunt, A., citizen of Virginia, died December 26, '63.
2014. Geddie, D. J., Co. A, Freeman's N. C. Bat., died June 3, '65.
230. Gee, James P., Co. C, 15th Tenn. Cav., died September 7, '64.
151. Gellam, W. W., 33d Ala. Inf., died May 7, '64.
422. Germany, H. C., 8th Confederate, died November 7, '64.
800. Gerrold, George A., citizen of Virginia, died January 18, '65.

No. of Grave.

1109. Gibbs, Stephen, Government Employee, died February 8, '65
58. Gibson, Andy, Co. G, 3d Conf. Scouts, died November 6, '63.
1107. Giddons, M. V., Co. G, 29th Ga. Inf., died February 7, '65.
2046. Giger, John H., died June 16, '65.
1357. Gilfoil, M. S., Co. A, 4th La. Inf., died February 20, '65.
1295. Gill, J., Co. K, 1st Ga. Inf., died February 16, '65.
1602. Gill, S. C., Co. D, 13th Ky. Cav., died March 9, '65.
1683. Gilmer, W. J. N., Co. F, 2d S. C. Inf., died March 1, '65.
1381. Gilmore, Morgan, Co. A, 16th Va. Cav., died February 22, '65.
914. Gilpin, W. R., Co. A, 13th Va. Inf., died January 27, '65.
915. Gilsland, F. A., Co. G, 1st Ga. Troops, died January 27, '65.
1388. Gissiner, Adam, Co. B, 3d Va. Inf., died February 22, '65.
449. Gladden, W. A., Co. E, 15th S. C. Inf., died November 11, '64.
1309. Gladdish, A. S., 4th Ala. Cav., died February 17, '65.
2052. Gladstone (or Glasson), J. M., Co. H, 1st N. C. Detailed, died June
     21, '65.
224. Glass, J. M., Co. I, 34th Ala. Inf., died August 28, '64.
1084. Glover, A. A., Co. C, 6th Ga. Cav., died February 7, '65.
1868. Goar, S. B., Co. E, 41st Miss. Inf., died April 15, '65.
1865. Gober, Bradford, — Va. Art., died April 15, '65.
962. Goble, Adam, Co. A, 10th Ky. Cav., died January 29, '65.
354. Godby, James H, Co. C, 17th Va. Cav., died October 24, '64.
804. Godwin, Joseph, Co. C, 29th Ga. Inf., died January 19, '65.
67. Golden, S. C., 20th —— Bat. Cav., died November 18, '63.
1831. Goldon, A. I., Co. D, 17th Va. Cav., died April 8, '65.
557. Goldsby, G. W., Co. B, 28th Tenn. Inf., died December 5, '64.
794. Goldsbury, R. R., Co. D, 13th Ky. Cav., died January 17, '65.
928. Goldsmith, James, Co. G, 14th N. C. Inf., died January 28, '65.
1490. Goodhead, J. C., Co. K, 14th Tenn. Inf., died March 1, '65.
1411. Goolsby, John M., Co. K, 28th Ala. Inf., died February 24, '65.
146. Gordon, H., Co. D, 51st Ga. Inf., died April 27, '64.
356. Gossett, W. M., Co. B, 22d Ala. Inf., died October 24, '64.
1144. Gost, W. H., Co. I, 16th Va. Cav., died February 10, '65.
1551. Gothard, T. G., Co. A, 30th Ala., died March 5, '65.
1856. Gowman, C. C., Co. G, 41st Miss. Inf., died April 13, '65.
1395. Gradick, J., Co. B, Roberts's (Miss.) Cavalry, died February 23, '65.
523. Graham, W. R., Co. G, 2d Ala. Cav., died November 28, '64.
1966. Granger, J. W., Co. A, 15th Ky. Cav., died May 14, '65.
1788. Gray, Alexander, Co. C, 1st Fla. Inf., died March 31, '65.
1772. Gray, William M., Co. A, Tennessee Conscript, died March 27, '65.
143. Gree, James L., Co. F, 2d Tenn. Cav., died April 23, '64.
250. Green, Charles, Co. B, 49th Ga. Inf., died September 20, '64.
1921. Green, John, Co. G, 36th Ala. Inf., died April 26, '65.
845. Green, John F., Co. H, 28th Ala. Inf., died January 20, '65.
1312. Green, L., Co. C, — Va. Bat. Cav., died February 17, '65.
272. Green, Thomas, Co. G, 54th N. C. Inf., died September 28, '64.
350. Green, W. A., Co. K, 18th Tenn. Inf., died October 23, '64.

No. of Grave.

1312. Greener, Thomas, Co. C, 27th Va. Cav., died February 15, '65.
1947. Gregg, John W., Co. H, 8th S. C. Inf., died May 9, '65.
1407. Gregory, W. F., Co. C, 66th Ga. Inf., died February 23, '65.
1321. Griffin, Clement, Co. D, 30th Ala. Inf., died February 18, '65.
883. Griffin, John L., Co. K, 1st Ga. Bat., died January 25, '65.
52. Griffith, Benjamin, citizen of Virginia, died October 18, '63.
362. Griffith, H. H., Co. K, 51st Va. Inf., died October 25, '64.
1391. Griffith, I., Co. F, 46th Miss. Inf., died February 22, '65.
1724. Griffith, James, Co. E, 24th S. C. Inf., died March 21, '65.
1619. Griffith, S., Co. B, 50th Ga. Inf., died March 11, '65.
79. Grigsby, Lieut. Edwin, Co. C, 10th Ky. Inf., died December 9, '63.
532. Grogg, J. B., Co. H, 63d Va. Inf., died November 29, '64.
65. Growin, David, citizen of Virginia, died November 16, '63.
925. Guidney, I. P., Co. A, 30th La. Inf., died January 29, '65.
1728. Gulleht, Asst. Surg. J. W., 15th Ky. Cav., died March 21, '65.
1854. Gunter, D. W., Co. F, 34th Ala. Inf., died April 12, '65.
209. Hackett, P., Co. B, 57th Va. Inf., died August 17, '64. Removed.
1033. Haggerty, James, Co. I, 10th Tenn. Inf., died February 3, '65.
1273. Haines, J. W., Co. B, 46th Ala. Inf., died February 15, '65.
1843. Halder, J. B., Co. E, 17th Ala. Inf., died April 14, '65.
1180. Hale, Thomas, Co. G, citizen of Tennessee, died February 9, '65.
1529. Haleman, D. P., Co. C, 15th S. C. Inf., died March 3, '65.
1554. Haleman, M. L., Co. F, 14th Miss. Inf., died March 6, '65.
1816. Haley, A. J., 36th Miss. Inf., died April 5, '65.
1003. Hall, A., Co. D, 32d Miss. Inf., died February 2, '65.
1498. Hall, E., Co. K, 29th Ga. Inf., died March 1, '65.
750. Hall, E. R., Co. D, 4th Ala. Inf., died January 12, '65.
1506. Hall, J. D., Co. G, 3d Ky. Cav., died March·2, '65.
1212. Hall, J. W., Co. I, 29th Ga. Inf., died February 13, '65.
758. Hall, John L., Co. G, 9th Tenn. Cav., died January 12, '65.
1038. Hall, L. C., Co. E, 42d Tenn. Inf., died February 4, '65.
948. Hall, Thomas J., Co. A, 2d Ky. Mounted Inf., died January 28, '65.
966. Hall, Wiley, Co. H, 23d Ala. Inf., died January 29, '65.
1716. Hall, William M., Co. E, 24th Ala. Inf., died March 20, '65.
1210. Halley, R. H., Co. D, 1st Fla. Inf., died February 12, '65.
1151. Hally, J. O., Co. K, 35th Ala. Inf., died February 10, '65.
69. Hamby, J. W., Co. K, 16th Ky. Cav., died November 21, '63.
281. Hamilton, A. D., Co. K, 6th Va. Inf., died October 5, '64.
1065. Hamilton, E. W., 16th S. C. Inf., died February 6, '65.
564. Hamilton, J., Co. A, 13th Va. Inf., died December 7, '64.
565. Hamilton, J. O., Co. E, 4th Ala. Cav., died December 9, '64.
663. Hamilton, John, Co. K, 60th Va. Inf., died December 25, '64.
1287. Hamilton, Levi, Co. F, 6th Fla. Inf., died February 16, '65.
847. Hamilton, W. M., Co. C, 19th S. C. Inf., died January 23, '65.
1251. Hamilton, W. S., Co. C, 1st Ga. Inf., died February 14, '65.
665. Hamlet, William, Co. G, 35th Miss. Inf., died December 26, '64.
937. Hamley, B., Co. G, 39th Ga. Inf., died January 28, '65.

No. of Grave.

2054. Hammert, E. B., Co. F, 25th Va. Cav., died June 29, '65.
737. Hammock, John, citizen of Virginia, died January 10, '65.
1644. Hampton, J., Co. K, 53d Ala. Inf., died March 13, '65.
1342. Hampton, John S., Co. A, 5th Ala. Cav., died February 19, '65.
1031. Hancock, J. H., Co. C, 2d Miss. Cav., died February 3, '65.
1519. Hancock, J. M., Co. F, 7th Ala. Cav., died March 3, '65.
670. Hand, Thomas, Co. H, 58th Ala. Inf., died December 31, '64.
1365. Hankins, R. M., Co. C, 16th Va. Cav., died February 21, '65.
1161. Hanks, W. S., Co. I, 39th Miss. Inf., died February 10, '65.
921. Hanley, H. C., Co. B, 8th Va. Cav., died January 28, '65.
1232. Harding, Valentine, Co. A, 6th Ky. Cav., died February 14, '65.
1817. Hardon, James, Co. B, 4th Fla. Inf., died April 4, '65.
656. Hardy, John W., Co. I, 40th Ga. Inf., died December 25, '64.
264. Harlow, Albertus, Co. H, 6th Ga. Cav., died September 20, '64.
1820. Harmer, John, Co. A, 13th Ky. Cav., died April 3, '65.
188. Harmon, H. E., Co. B, 3d S. C. Inf., died July 22, '64.
299. Harmon, Rush T., Co. F, 8th Va. Inf., died October 11, '64.
951. Harper, E. W., Co. G, 20th Ala. Inf., died January 28, '65.
1869. Harper, G. W., Co. E, 29th Ala. Inf., died April 15, '65.
11. Harper, W. H., Co. H, 30th Miss. Inf., died August 24, '63.
1178. Harrington, W. G., Co. E, 4th Ky. Cav., died February 11, '65.
687. Harris, F. P., Co. F, 2d Va. Cav., died January 6, '65.
1268. Harris, Hezekiah F., Co. A, 19th Tenn. Cav., died February 15, '65.
1403. Harris, J. C., Co. K, 31st Miss. Inf., died February 23, '65.
1833. Harris, J. K., North Conscript, died April 8, '65.
31. Harris, J. T., Co. H, 39th Ala., died October 4, '63.
1798. Harris, M., Co. D, 32d Ala. Inf., died March 29, '65.
365. Harris, Martin S., Co. C, 17th Ga. Cav., died October 26, '64.
1101. Harris, P. H., Co. E, 1st Ala. Inf., died February 8, '65.
226. Harris, S. R., Co. F, 1st Ga. Inf., died August 30, '64.
587. Harrison, E., Co. F, 31st Ala. Inf., died December 10, '64.
826. Harrison, J. B., Co. B, 36th Ala. Inf., died January 21, '65.
1754. Harrison, Thomas, Co. F, 7th Va. Cav., died March 25, '65.
1463. Harrold, J., Co. F, 19th Tenn. Inf., died February 27, '65.
1792. Hart, Thomas C., Co. I, 28th Ala. Inf., died March 31, '65.
288. Hartman, George R, Co. E, 36th Va. Inf., died October 8, '64.
2062. Hartszoge, Samuel, Co. B, 1st Ky. Inf., died June 29, '65.
1591. Hatch, Thomas, Co. K, 3d Fla. Inf., died March 8, '65.
448. Hatcher, H. F., Co. A, 17th Va. Cav., died November 11, '64.
1736. Hatcher, Thomas, Co. E, 20th Ala. Inf., died March 23, '65.
417. Hathaway, Gus, Co. G, 6th Fla. Inf., died November 6, '64.
339. Hawkins, W. H., Co. F, 1st Ga. Inf., died October 24, '64.
592. Hays, T. W., Co. C, 18th Miss. Inf., died December 15, '64.
1850. Hazlewad, W. H., Co. E, 1st Ala. Cav., died April 11, '65.
689. Head, James, Co. D, 19th Ala. Inf., died January 6, '65.
1444. Hearn, J., Co. I, Fout's Battery, died February 26, '65.
671. Hearn, William H., Co. I, 2d Ga. Cav., died December 31, '64.

No. of Grave.

1205. Heason, J. N., Co. K, 46th Ala. Inf., died February 12, '65.

1401. Heidelberg, D. W., Co. I, 6th Fla. Inf., died February 23, '65.

331. Hellon, Franklin, Co. F, 91st Tenn., died October 17, '64.

852. Helman, Benjamin, Co. F, 54th Ga. Inf., died January 22, '65.

859. Helvey, H. W., Co. L, 8th Va. Cav., died January 23, '65.

1392. Hemphill, W. A., Co. F, 30th Bat. Va. Cav., died February 23, '65.

1685. Henderson, W. F., Co. I, 15th Miss. Inf., died March 17, '65.

——. Hendon, S. Z., Owentown, Ky., died August 10, '64. Sent home.

16. Hendrick, J., Co. C, 13th Tenn., died September 29, '63.

26. Hendrick, W. A., Co. E, 2d Tenn., died September 21, '63.

1149. Hendrick, Wesley, Co. G, 33d Ala. Inf., died February 9, '65.

396. Hendricks, A. R., Co. A, 22d Ala. Inf., died November 3, '64.

1871. Henendon, Wesley, Co. I, 57th Ga. Inf., died April 15, '65.

1237. Henninger, W. I., Co. I, 13th Bat. Va. Cav., died February 14, '65.

1812. Hensted, G. W., Co. A, 26th Va. Cav., died April 3, '65.

1692. Herring, J. B., Co. F, 13th C. S. Cav., died March 18, '65.

905. Herring, Stephen, Co. D, 10th S. C. Inf., died January 27, '65.

996. Herrington, J., Co. G, 29th Ala. Inf., died February 1, '65.

1418. Heron, Asher, Co. K, 10th Ky. Cav., died February 24, '65.

1761. Herron, W. H., Co. K, 13th Ky., Cav., died March 25, '65.

1598. Hester, T. J., Co. C, 65th Ga. Inf., died March 8, '65.

514. Hicks, A. J., Co. C, 34th Va. Cav., died December 6, '64.

1628. Hicks (or Hickox), Benj., Co. G, 3d Miss. Cav., died March 12, '65.

1404. Hicks, D. H., Co. C, 12th Ky. Cav., died February 23, '65.

1119. Hicks, G. S., Co. K, 1st Ga. State Troops, died February 8, '65.

946. Hicks, Samuel S., Co. C, 43d Bat. Va. Cav., died January 29, '65.

2051. Hicks, W. H., Co. H, 23d Ala. Inf., died June 21, '65.

1727. Hicks, William B., laborer, died March 21, '65.

581. Hides, P. E., Co. I, 5th Ga. Cav., died December 10, '64.

1390. Higden, P. W., Co. F, 13th Ky. Cav., died February 22, '65.

84. Hill, Alton, 1st Tenn. Cav., died December 18, '63.

653. Hill, B. H., Co. D, 36th Ala. Inf., died December 23, '64.

434. Hill, F., Co. D, 30th Ga. Bat., died November 8, '64.

1048. Hill, J. C., Co. H, 1st Ga. Cav., died February 4, '65.

711. Hill, J. H., Co. D, 1st Tenn. Inf., died January 6, '65.

1654. Hill, J. M., Co. B, 19th Ala. Inf., died March 14, '65.

1292. Hill, J. W., Co. B, 36th Ala. Inf., died February 16, '65.

453. Hill, Thomas, Co. B, 6th Fla. Inf., died November 12, '64.

949. Hill, Thomas M., Co. B, 10th Ky. Inf., died January 28, '65.

1955. Hill, William, Co. D, 14th Va. Cav., died May 10, '65.

1114. Himbra, S. G., Co. K, 1st Ga. State Troops, died February 8, '65.

497. Himes, W. H., Co. I, 41st Ga. Inf., died November 20, '64.

1634. Hincly, Benjamin F., Co. K, 13th Ga. Inf., died March 12, '65.

1769. Hobbs, Elisha, Co. B, 10th Ky. Cav., died March 26, '65

248. Hobbs, R. C., Co. E, 38th Ala. Inf., died September 16, '64.

1684. Hocter, Benjamin, Co. F, 49th Ala. Inf., died March 17, '65.

901. Hodge, William, Co. G, 29th Ga. Inf., died January 26, '65.

No. of Grave.
1627. Hodges, E. M., Co. D, 1st C. S. Inf., died March 12, '65.
1942. Hoffman, D. J., Co. G, 18th Ala. Inf., died May 13, '65.
796. Hoffman, Jacob, Co. F, 30th Bat. Va. Cav., died January 17, '65.
1662. Hoffman, Joel, Co. B, 37th Miss. Inf., died March 15, '65.
742. Hoffmaster, Louis, Co. B, 36th Va. Inf., died January 11, '65.
199. Hogan, J. C., Co. F, 27th Bat. Va. Cav., died August 13, '64.
159. Holbrooks, J., Co. K, 7th Ala. Cav., died May 12, '64.
1739. Holcomb, A. W., Co. B, 11th Va. Inf., died March 23, '65.
1202. Holden, James, Co. F, 52d Ga. Inf., died February 12, '65.
1796. Holden, James M., Co. D, Moreland's Cavalry, died March 25, '65.
220. Hollis, D., Co. I, 38th Ala. Cav., died August 27, '64.
2042. Hollowey, J. S., Co. C, 37th Ga. Inf., died June 15, '65.
1092. Holman, J. C., Co. C, 7th Ky. Cav., died February 6, '65.
978. Holmes, David, Co. E, 33d Miss. Inf., died January 31, '65.
235. Holmes, M., 1st Ga. State Troops, died September 9, '64.
1843. Holston, Hiram, Co. B, 4th La. Inf., died April 11, '65.
1436. Holton, L., Co. G, 7th Miss. Inf., died February 25, '65.
1481. Homberger, J., Co. C, 2d Ark. Cav., died February 28, '65.
1170. Honeberger, G., Co. B, 13th Ky. Cav., died February 10, '65.
1944. Hood, F. M., Co. G, 54th Ala. Inf., died May 14, '65.
508. Hook, Curtis, Co. D, 59th Ga. Inf., died November 24, '64. Removed.
1755. Hooker, J., Co. K, 19th Va. Cav., died March 25, '65.
203. Hoover, A. S., 19th Va. Inf., died August 14, '64.
878. Hopkins, Ewing, Co. D, 12th Tenn. Inf., died January 25, '65.
1154. Hopkins, Robert B., Co. K, 5th Tenn. Cav., died February 11, '65.
1585. Horton, H., citizen of Alabama, died March 6, '65.
1707. Horton, James H., Co. G, 54th Tenn. Inf., died March 18, '65.
1. Horton, S., 4th Ala., died August 4, '63.
1524. Horton, T. B., Conscript, died March 3, '65.
1174. Horton, T. S., Co. I, 15th Miss. Inf., died February 11, '65.
873. House, William, Co. D, 4th Tenn. Inf., died January 25, '65.
1187. Houston, W. S., Co. H, 1st Ga. Inf., died February 11, '65.
1226. Houton, E. L., Co. B, 12th La. Cav., died February 13, '65.
1726. Howard, Lewis L., Co. A, 26th Va. Cav., died March 20, '65
485. Howell, R. H., Co. H, 18th Ala. Inf., died November 19, '64.
420. Howery, W. J., Co. B, 41st Va. Cav., died November 7, '64.
780. Hoyle, J. P., Co. F, 54th N. C. Inf., died January 16, '65.
1870. Hubbard, John, Co. E, 33d Miss. Inf., died April 15, '65.
886. Hudleson, David, Co. A, 7th Ala. Cav., died January 25, '65.
1810. Hudson, E. W., Co. E, 36th Ga. Inf., died April 3, '65.
846. Hudson, H. L., Co. C, 18th Tenn. Inf., died January 22, '65.
1129. Hudson, W. D., Co. I, 27th Miss. Inf., died February 8, '65.
307. Huesley, A. S., Co. B, 45th Va. Cav., died Nov. 23, '64. Removed.
641. Huff, Amos, Co. F, 4th Ala. Cav., died December 23, '64.
1888. Huff, J. B., Co. E, 18th Ala. Inf., died April 18, '65.
1649. Huff, J. G., Co. D, 36th Va. Cav., died March 14, '65.
1060. Huff, J. W., Co. H, 42d Ga. Inf., died February 5, '65.

No. of Grave.
330. Huffaker, J. D., Co. G, 36th La. Inf., died October 17, '64.
85. Huffman, Henry, Co. C, 20th Va. Bat., died December 19, '63. Shot.
803. Hughes, A. R., Co. K, 1st Miss. Inf., died January 19, '65.
407. Hughes, C., Co. H, 16th Va. Inf., died November 5, '64.
1015. Hughes, C. J., Co. D, 5th Miss. Cav., died February 3, '65.
621. Hughes, D. A., Co. E, Thomas's N. C. Legion, died December 21, '64.
1786. Hughes, George W., Co. C, 8th Ky. Cav., died March 29, '65.
1903. Hughes, James J., Co. K, 1st Miss. Inf., died April 23, '65.
1950. Hughes, J. A., Co. H, 23d Ala. Inf., died May 10, '65.
880. Hughes, Joel, Co. F, 2d Tenn. Cav., died January 25, '65.
1197. Hughes, W. A., Co. C, 22d Va. Cav., died February 12, '65.
1658. Hughes, William, Co. E, 29th Ala. Inf., died March 14, '65.
869. Hughes, William D., Co. D, 31st Ala. Inf., died January 25, '65.
1583. Huie (or Hail), A. A., Co. E, 30th Ga. Inf., died March 7, '65.
1211. Hull, E., Co. B, 15th Miss. Inf., died February 13, '65.
455. Humphries, S., Co. C, 66th Ga. Inf., died November 12, '64.
669. Hundley, I. F., Co. E, 36th Va. Cav., died December 27, '64.
1264. Hunt, Davis, Co. F, 4th Fla. Inf., died February 15, '65.
936. Hunt, H. F., Co. B, 22d Va. Inf., died January 28, '65.
1249. Hunt, W. H., Co. D, 30th Miss. Inf., died February 14, '65.
384. Hunter, A. A., Co. D, 28th Miss. Cav., died October 30, '64.
148. Hurlburt, Cole, citizen of Virginia, died May 3, '64.
1155. Hurt, J. C., Co. D, 19th Ga. Inf., died February 9, '65.
1328. Hutchcourt, James, Co. A, 4th Miss. Inf., died February 18, '65.
1041. Hutchins, J. D., Co. E, 17th Ala. Inf., died February 4, '65.
1108. Hysch, E., Woodward's Battery, died February 8, '65.
1659. Ingraham, B., Co. B, 4th Ala. Cav., died March 14, '65.
1474. Ingram, I. F., Co. C, 7th Ala. Cav., died February 26, '65.
606. Irwin, J. C., Co. B, 3d Fla. Inf., died December 12, '64.
1140. Irwin, William, Co. K, 9th Ark. Inf., died February 10, '65.
187. Isaac, Norman, Co. D, 37th Va. Cav., died July 22, '64.
309. Isen, Charles, Co. K, 10th Ky. Cav., died October 13, '64.
911. Ivers, J. E., Co. C, 18th Tenn. Inf., died January 27, '65.
856. Jacks, James, Co. D, 54th Ala. Inf., died January 23, '65.
1451. Jackson, A., Co. C, 4th Ky. Cav., died February 26, '65.
1423. Jackson, H. I., Co. F, 5th Ga. Inf., died February 24, '65.
1788. Jackson, Henry, Co. I, 4th Miss. Inf., died March 31, '65.
349. Jackson, J., Co. K, 8th S. C. Inf., died October 21, '64.
1596. Jackson, J. E., Co. B, 38th Ala. Inf., died March 9, '65.
1588. Jackson, J. H., Co. K, 5th Miss. Inf., died March 7, '65.
1087. Jackson, John T., Co. C, 66th Ga. Inf., died February 6, '65.
368. Jackson, William, Co. I, 5th Regt., ——, died October 27, '64.
2057. Jacob, W. F., died July 17, '65.
1399. James, G., Co. G, 19th La. Inf., died February 23, '65.
612. James, W. F., Co. F, 1st Tenn. Cav., died December 13, '64.
1560. Janney, W. B., Co. D, 6th Va. Cav., died March 5, '65.
444. Jarett, Abraham, Co. E, 22d Va. Inf., died November 10, '64.

684. Jarold, J. D., 33d Tenn. lnf., died December 30, '64.

800. Jarrett, George, Co. C, citizen of Georgia, died January 18, '65.

468. Jarves, Capt. E. J., Co. A, 46th Va. Cav., died November 15, '64.

1303. Jenkins, A. A., Co. B, 5th Miss. Cav., died February 11, '65.

1588. Jenkins, G., Co. I, 55th Ala. Inf., died March 3, '65.

695. Jenkins, H. W., Co. I, 65th Ga. Inf., died January 3, '65.

1809. Jenkins, John, Co. F, 45th Ga. Inf., died April 3, '65.

1080. Jenkins, William, Co. I, 55th Ala. Inf., died February 5, '65.

1102. Jett, S. E., Co. G, 1st Miss. Art., died February 8, '65.

189. Jetton, R., — Ala. Cav., died July 23, '64.

1882. Jobe, W. M., Co. F, 31st Miss Inf., died April 17, '65.

1166. Johns, L. I., Co. I, 1st Fla. Cav., died February 10, '65.

827. Johnson, A. J., Co. B, 22d Va. Cav., died January 22, '65.

1543. Johnson, A. J., Co. K, 24th Ala. Inf., died March 4, '65.

1675. Johnson, C. A., Co. H, 42d Ala. Inf., died March 16, '65.

657. Johnson, Elijah, Co. D, 8th Tenn. Cav., died December 25, '64.

1122. Johnson, G. M., Co. K, 40th Ga. Inf., died February 2, '65.

1737. Johnson, James L., Co. H, 42d Ga. Inf., died March 23, '65.

1811. Johnson, Moses, Co. B, 46th Ala. Inf., died April 4, '65.

1677. Johnson, R. M., Co. E, 20th Va. Cav., died March 16, '65.

1629. Johnson, S. C., Co. H, 4th Fla. Inf., died March 12, '65.

619. Johnson, S. W., Co. C, 8th Va. Cav., died December 15, '64.

105. Johnson, Samuel, Co. A, 44th Miss. Inf., died February, '64.

676. Johnson, Thomas, Co. A, 40th Ala. Inf., died December 28, '64.

1771. Johnson, T. H., Co. C, 54th Ala. Inf., died March 27, '65.

551. Johnston, B. R., Co. F, 36th Ala. Inf., died December 4, '64.

694. Johnston, Franklin, citizen of Virginia, died January 2, '65.

746. Johnston, H. A., Co. C, 57th Ala. Inf., died January 11, '65.

441. Jones, David, Co. C, 54th Va. Inf., died November 9, '64.

825. Jones, Edwin, Co. B, 52d Tenn. Inf., died January 21, '65.

980. Jones, G., Co. F, 18th Ala. Inf., died January 31, '65.

460. Jones, J., Co. C, 1st Miss. Inf., died November 13, '64.

994. Jones, John, Co. H, 18th Ala. Inf., died February 1, '65.

904. Jones, John M., Co. A, 12th Va. Cav., died January 27, '65.

1341. Jones, Joseph, Co. H, 23d Ala. Inf., died February 19, '65.

941. Jones, M. J., Co. A, 53d Ala. Inf., died January 29, '65.

1448. Jones, R. H., Co. A, 37th Miss. Inf., died February 26, '65.

1051. Jones, R. J., Co. C, 10th Ala. Cav., died February 5, '65.

1116. Jones, Squire, East Tenn. Reserve, died February 8, '65.

509. Jones, Stephen, Co. B, 1st Fla. Cav., died November 23, '64.

1507. Jones, W. A., Co. G, 1st Ga. State Troops, died March 2, '65.

1438. Jones, W. E., Co. H, 20th Va. Cav., died February 25, '65.

552. Jones, W. F., Co. I, 1st Ga. Inf., died December 4, '64.

1664. Jorda, A., Co. F, 30th La. Inf., died March 15, '65.

725. Jordon, W. R., Co. H, 29th Tenn. Inf., died January, '65.

1878. Jumverson, J., Co. G, 21st Va. Cav., died April 16, '65.

2017. Kay, John, Co. C, Moreland's Miss. Cav., died June 3, '65.

No. of Grave.

376. Keadon, William, Co. D, 17th Va. Cav., died October 28, '64.
398. Keaton, W. J., Co. D, 17th Va. Cav., died November 3, '64.
481. Keenea, James M., Co. E, 14th N. C. Inf., died November 18, '64.
1665. Keister, Col., Co. D, 34th Miss. Inf., died March 15, '65.
244. Keith, W. C., Co. I, 7th Ala. Cav., died September 15, '64.
1852. Keleclofy, H. H., Co. H, 56th Ga. Inf., died April 7, '65.
896. Kelley, James M., Co. G, 57th Ala. Inf., died January 25, '65.
1715. Kelly, B. S., Co. A, 46th Ala. Inf., died March 20, '65.
1443. Kelly, G., Co. E, 1st Fla. Cav., died February 25, '65.
959. Kelly, Jacob, Co. G, 57th Ala. Inf., died January 29, '65.
820. Kelly, T. L., Co. G, 5th Ala. Inf., died January 22, '65.
1079. Kelly, W. F., Co. H, 22d Ala. Inf., died February 11, '65.
5. Kelly, William, Co. I, 4th Ala. ——, died August 15, '64.
1693. Kemp, J. L., Co. C, 1st Ky. Cav., died March 18, '65.
1826. Kemp, M. A., Co. I, 16th Tenn. Inf., died April 7, '65.
603. Kenedy, Charles, Co. B, 22d Va. Cav., died December 12, '64.
761. Kenneday, T. N., Co. F, 22d Va. Cav., died January 12, '65.
825. Kennedy, J. C., Co. D, 28th Ala. Inf., died January 22, '65.
1241. Kennedy, W., Co. C, 37th Ga. Inf., died February 14, '65.
1633. Kennedy, W. J., Asst. Enroller's Office, died March 12, '65.
232. Kenney, J., Conscript of Virginia, died September 3, '64.
957. Kenney, James, Co. C, 1st La. Inf., died January 29, '65.
1599. Kent, F., Co. E, 15th Miss. Inf., died March 1, '65.
1652. Kersy, J. G., Co. A, 23d Ala. Inf., died March 14, '65.
1605. Kesse, E. G., Co. B, 20th Miss. ——, died March 9, '65.
193. Kettle, Benjamin, citizen of Virginia, died August 5, '64.
260. Keys, H., Co. B, 40th Ga. Inf., died September 20, '64.
1045. Kight, Henry, Co. K, 58th Ala. Inf., died February 4, '65.
1265. Kiken, A. A., Co. F, 40th Ga. Inf., died February 15, '65.
1075. Kincaid, L. M., Co. B, 55th Tenn. Cav., died February 6, '65.
1373. King, J. L., Co. G, 1st Conf. Inf., died February 22, '65.
278. King, Newton, Co. C, 37th Bat. Va. Cav., died October 4, '64.
1320. King, S., Co. B, 13th Ky. Cav., died February 17, '65.
807. King, Samuel, Co. G, 8th Tenn. Cav., died January 19, '65.
725. King, William, Co. D, 34th Ga. Inf., died January 9, '65.
520. Kirk, James, citizen of Georgia, died November 26, '64.
1763. Kirk, John N., Co. B, 38th Ala. Inf., died March 27, '65.
1520. Kitchen, C. J., Co. I, 23d Ala. Inf., died March 2, '65.
597. Klutts, J. A. C., citizen of Georgia, died December 11, '64.
1531. Knole, William, Co. D, 63d Va. Inf., died March 1, '65.
421. Knoles, D. G., Co. F, 36th Ala. Inf., died November 7, '64.
426. Knotts, John G., Co. F, 13th Tenn. Cav., died November 7, '64.
1976. Knowls, S. V., Co. F, 23d Ala. Inf., died May 16, '65.
721. Knox, John, Co. H, 3d Ga. Cav., died January 8, '65.
1656. Koon, G. E., Co. I, 15th S. C. Inf., died March 14, '65.
600. Koon, John H., Co. G, 32d Ala. Inf., died December 11, '64.
819. Kuhn, John A., Co. A, 2d Md. Cav., died January 20, '65.

APPENDIX. 367

No. of Grave.

638. Lackey, E., Co. G, 21st Va. Cav., died December 20, '64.

971. Lacroy, George, Co. D, 46th Ala. Inf., died January 31, '65.

964. Lagrove, R. W., Co. K, 41st Miss. Inf., died January 30, '65.

1239. Lake, Elisha, Co. G, 42d Ga. Inf., died February 14, '65.

1709. Lake, John R., Co. G, 62d Ala. Inf., died March 18, '65.

2047. Lamb, Alex, Co. B, 4th N. C. Reserves, died June 19, '65.

250. Lamb, I. J., Co. E, 1st Ga. Inf., died September 17, '64.

651. Lamb, W. M., Co. G, 35th Miss. Inf., died December 22, '64.

585. Lamber, A. L., Co. A, 15th Tenn. Cav., died December 9, '64.

1571. Lancaster, A. G., Co. H, 29th Ga. Inf., died March 10, '65.

1096. Landers, J. M., Co. C, 4th Ala. Cav., died February 7, '65.

924. Lane, G. N., Co. B, 5th Ga. Cav., died January 28, '65.

219. Lang, I. F., Co. K, 30th Ga. Inf., died August 26, '64.

1138. Langhorn, John, Co. A, 57th Ala. Inf., died February 9, '65.

1484. Lanson, I. H., Co. A, 4th Ky. Cav., died February 28, '65.

403. Laprude, E. S., Co. G, 1st Ga. Inf., died November 4, '64.

112. Larimore, George, died February, '64.

531. Lark, James R., Co. C, 4th La. Inf., died November 28, '64.

1419. Lasiter, A. W., Co. C, 17th Miss. Inf., died February 24, '65.

990. Lassiter, Henry, Co. E, 1st Ga. State Troops, died February 1, '65.

838. Lassiter, W., Co. G, 58th Ala. Inf., died January 22, '65.

712. Lassiter, Wiley B, Co. E, 1st Fla. Inf., died January 5, '65.

1436. Latimer, T., Co. I, 2d Tenn. Cav., died February 25, '65.

74. Latimer, T. J., Merry's Tenn. Bat., died November 28, '63.

1420. Lavergne, W. J., Co. G, 7th Fla. Inf., died February 24, '65.

1242. Law, J., Co. H, 22d Va. Cav., died February 14, '65.

335. Lawer, Strethers, Co. F, 34th Ga. Inf., died October 18, '64.

1973. Lawson, J. S., Co. A, 4th Tenn. Cav., died May 16, '65.

1703. Lease, D. J., Co. C, 15th S. C. Inf., died March 18, '65.

1508. Lease, G. W., Co. F, 11th Va. Cav., died March 2, '65.

1990. Leavall, John, Co. G, 28th Miss. Cav., died May 21, '65.

1429. Leavall, W. I., Co. K, 1st Ga. Inf., died February 28, '65.

1708. Ledbeater, George, Co. H, 31st Ala. Inf., died March 19, '65.

185. Ledbetter, G., Co. I, 18th Tenn. ——, died July 20, '64.

500. Lee, J. W., Co. G, 16th Ala. Inf., died November 20, '64.

923. Lee, Jesse, Co. E, 19th Ala. Inf., died January 28, '65.

1904. Lee, John, Co. F, 41st Ala. Inf., died April 23, '65.

110. Lee, K., died February, '64.

1535. Lee, Loren, Co. I, 29th Ala. Inf., died March 4, '65.

100. Lee, M. P., Co. A, 2d Tenn. Cav., died January 10, '64.

550. Lee, P. W., Co. A, 4th La. Inf., died December 4, '64.

13. Lee, R. N., citizen of Kentucky, died August 25, '63. Removed.

1491. Lee, R. O., Co. F, 54th N. C. Inf., died March 1, '65.

752. Lee, Randolph, Co. H, 24th Tex. Cav., died January 12, '65.

2053. Lee, Thomas, Co. K, 45th Ala. ——, died June 21, '65.

90. Lee, W. P., 3d S. C. Cav., died January 10, '64.

1860. Leech, John, Co. B, 43d Miss. Inf., died April 13, '65.

No. of Grave.

863. Legg, Franklin, Co. B, 36th Bat. Va. Cav., died January 24, '65.
106. Lemaster, Merida, Co. C, 5th Ky. Inf., died February, '64.
1359. Lemaster, W., Co. C, 5th Ky. Inf., died February 20, '65.
1305. Lemax, R., Co. D, 39th Ala. Inf., died February 17, '65.
23. Lemly, Samuel, Co. A, 19th Va. Cav., died September 17, '63.
400. Lenebaugh, J. F., Co. H, 22d Ala. Inf., died November 4, '64.
1313. Leonard, C., Co. C, 8th Va. Cav., died February 14, '65.
1756. Leonard, John, Co. B, 10th Ala. Inf., died March 25, '65.
1143. Leonard, Thomas J., Co. C, 13th Bat. Inf., died February 9, '65.
2044. Lester, E. W., Co. A, 57th Ala. Inf., died June 15, '65.
1945. Lester, G. R., Co. A, 51st Ala. Cav., died May 9, '65.
549. Lester, John, Co. E, 1st Ga. Cav., died December 5, '64.
976. Lester, J. G., Co. A, 30th Ga. Inf., died January 31, '65.
510. Lester, J. W., Co. A, 23d Tenn. Inf., died November 24, '64.
480. Lester, Lewis, Co. F, 16th Ga. Cav., died November 17, '64.
1344. Lester, M. W., Co. B, 4th Ga. Inf., died February 19, '65.
225. Lestinger, W. H., Co. K, 29th Ga. Inf., died August 30, '64.
186. Letterel, James, 27th Bat. Va. Cav., died July 22, '64.
939. Lewis, K. J., 3d Conf. Cav., died January 29, '65.
1027. Lewis, T. E., Co. G, 6th Miss. Inf., died February 12, '65.
190. Lichty, G. W., Co. H, 4th Ga. Cav., died October 8, '64.
464. Lightfoot, J. M., Co. E, 22d Ga. Inf., died November 14, '64.
1072. Linder, Thomas F., Co. D, 5th Ga. Cav., died February 6, '65.
511. Lindley, T. P., Co. F, 1st Conf. Inf., died November 24, '64.
1620. Lindsey, W. H., Co. I, 26th Ala. Inf., died March 11, '65.
2013. Litiker, Michael, N. C. Troops, died June 6, '65.
312. Lively, Robert, Co. B, 16th La. Inf., died October 14, '64.
1296. Locker, W. N., Co. A, 1st Md. Cav., died February 16, '65.
1526. Lockett, D. H., Co. A, 3d Ky. Cav., died March 3, '65.
699. Lockhart, Benjamin, Co. C, 16th Va. Cav., died January 3, '65.
1256. Lockwood, W. T., Co. B, 1st Ark. Inf., died February 15, '65.
1421. Lofton, W. J., Co. K, 30th Ga. Inf., died February 24, '65.
412. Logan, G. W., Co. D, 2d Ky. Cav., died November 5, '64.
8. Logan, S. C., Co. K, — Ky. Cav., died August 22, '63. Removed.
1959. Long, J. J., Co. D, 30th Ga. Inf., died May 12, '65.
1055. Long, Noah, Co. B, 34th Ala. Inf., died February 5, '65.
1367. Looney, I. J., Co. B, 34th Ala. Inf., died February 21, '65.
963. Loop, Elijah, Co. F, 1st Tenn. Cav., died January 29, '65.
1975. Lovitt, G. W., Co. K, 53d Ga. Inf., died May 16, '65.
1546. Lucas, H. A., Roddy's Escort, died March 5, '65.
594. Ludlow, W. J., Co. D, 16th La. Inf., died December 10, '64.
1651. Luker, Allen, Co. K, 32d Ala. Inf., died March 14, '65.
614. Lumans, G. L., Co. A, 60th Va. Inf., died December 13, '64.
1799. Lynch, J. N. P., Co. H, 21st Tenn. Inf., died March 30, '65.
654. Lynn, A. J., Co. A, Stuart's Cavalry, died December 23, '64.
1989. Lyon, Nicholas, Co. G, 4th Ky. Cav., died May 20, '65.
1711. Lytham, J. H., Co. B, 31st Miss. Inf., died March 19, '65.

774. Maberry, James, died January 14, '65.

1770. Màbery, Thomas T., Co. I, 9th Tenn. Cav., died March 27, '65.

2054. Mackey, Nathaniel, died June 27, '65.

1789. Mackey, William, Co. F, 31st Ala. Inf., died March 30, '65.

1322. Madox, W. J., Co. I, 30th Ga. Inf., died February 18, '65.

1760. Mafors, George W., died March 26, '65.

1459. Mald, J., Co. E, 13th Ky. Cav., died February 27, '65.

1879. Malone, G. W., Co. G, 13th Tenn. Inf., died April 17, '65.

570. Malone, John T., Co. I, 22d Ala. Cav., died December 7, '64.

171. Maning, W. C., Co. E, 1st Ky. Cav., died May 31, '64.

1319. Mann, Henry, Co. C, 7th Ala. Cav., died February 17, '65.

126. Marcum, W., Smith's Virginia Rangers, died March, '64.

1920. Marian, James K., Co. I, 44th Miss. Inf., died April 26, '65.

1707. Markham, I., Co. D, 13th Ky. Cav., died February 17, '65.

1236. Marlin, C. R., Co. B, 13th La. Inf., died February 14, '65.

554. Marlin, O. C., Co. F, 4th Ala. Cav., died December 5, '64.

1163. Marshall, S. J., 7th Miss. Inf., died February 10, '65.

630. Marshall, W. S., Co. I, 8th Miss. Inf., died December 18, '64.

2056. Martin, B., Co. B, Baumbgarnor's Battery, died June 27, '65.

1176. Martin, C. O., Co. F, 1st Ala. Inf., died February 11, '65.

1749. Martin, Isaac, Co. D, 13th Ky. Cav., died March 25, '65.

377. Martin, J. A., Co. C, 2d Ga. Cav., died October 28, '64.

70. Martin, J. C., Co. B, 65th N. C. ——, died November 23, '63.

345. Martin, J. E., Co. K, 36th Va. Inf., died October 22, '64.

308. Martin, Thomas, Co. B, 37th Va. Inf., died October 13, '64.

981. Martin, Zachariah, Co. F, 45th Ala. Inf., died January 31, '65.

479. Mash, J. T. F., Co. C, 8th S. C. Inf., died November 16, '64.

1667. Mason, J., Co. H, 37th Tenn. Inf., died March 15, '65.

1848. Masters, W. L., Co. F, 10th Ala. Inf., died April 4, '65.

2039. Mathews, E. B., Co. I, 41st Ga. Inf., died June 12, '65.

1298. Mathews, G. W., Co. A, 4th Fla. Inf., died February 15, '65.

1148. Matthews, A. F., Co. H, 18th Ala. Inf., died February 9, '65.

1175. Matthews, E., Co. K, 29th Ga. Inf., died February 11, '65.

694. Maxwell, William, Co. I, 1st Ga. Inf., died January 3, '65.

1700. May, R. S., Co. E, 19th Va. Cav., died March 18, '65.

12. McAllister, J. C., unknown, died August 24, '63.

414. McAllister, W. H., Co. E, 34th Va. Cav., died November 6, '64.

477. McArdy, D. A., Co. F, 1st Ga. Inf., died November 16, '64.

2060. McCall, J. B., Co. E, 29th Ga. ——, died July 30, '65.

1301. McCarter, C. I., Co. B, 1st Ga. Troops, died February 16, '65.

475. McCarter, J. M., Co. H, 1st Ga. Inf., died November 16, '64.

1909. McCarty, Brien, Co. E, 7th Miss. Inf., died April 23, '65.

502. McCarty, W. H., Co. E, 3d Ky. Inf., died November 21, '64.

124. McCarver, W. D., Co. I, 59th Tenn. Inf., died March, '64.

537. McClarty, G. W., Co. C, 30th Ga. Inf., died December 1, '64.

1424. McCoy, Charles, Co. E, 8th S. C. Inf., died February 25, '65.

748. McCoy, Davis, Co. A, 57th Ala. Inf., died January 11, '65.

No. of Grave.

1573. McCoy, H. (or T. C.), Co. D, 26th Va. Inf., died March 6, '65.
1530. McCoy, W. F., Moreland's Cavalry, died March 2, '65.
1371. McCracken, W., Co. B, 10th S. C. Inf., died February 21, '65.
1539. McCrary, J. M., Co. E, 65th Ala. Inf., died March 4, '65.
1774. McCreary, Joseph F., Co. H, 18th Tenn. Cav., died March 28, '65.
1112. McCurdy, J. J., Co. F, 1st Conf. Inf., died February 8, '65.
566. McDaniel, A. W., Co. A, 5th Ala. Cav., died December 7, '64.
887. McDaniel, J. L., Co. A, 38th Tenn. Inf., died January 26, '65.
1315. McDaws, T. B., Co. E, 3d Ky. Cav., died February 17, '65.
965. McDonald, R., Co. B, 5th Ala. Cav., died January 30, '65.
1702. McDonald, Richard, Co. D, 29th Miss. Inf., died March 18, '65.
1159. McElrath, J., Co. B, 54th N. C. Inf., died February 10, '65.
1722. McElroy, W. M., Co. F, 46th Miss. Inf., died March 20, '65.
1561. McGaughey, A. I., Co. C, 7th Ala. Cav., died March 5, '65.
1452. McGhee, A. O., Co. I, 46th Ga. Inf., died February 26, '65.
1468. McGhee, Lynn, Co. K, 38th Ala. Inf., died February 27, '65.
744. McGilbury, David, Co. B, 38th Ala. Inf., died January 11, '65.
726. McGinnis, Isaac B., Co. E, 34th Ga. Inf., died January 9, '65.
———. McGlothen, J. P., Co. A, 29th Ga. Inf., died March 6, '65.
1478. McGowen, J. W., Co. I, 25th Ga. Inf., died February 28, '65.
945. McGowin, G. W., Co. E, 54th Ala. Inf., died January 29, '65.
1636. McGuarity, A. L., Co. H, 24th S. C. Inf., died March 11, '65.
1911. McGuire, H. C., Co. D, 46th Ala. Inf., died April 24, '65.
228. McIntosh, ———, Conscript, N. C., died September 3, '64.
1899. McIntosh, James, Co. B, 43d Va. Inf., died April 22, '65.
1617. McKean, John, Co. A, 3d Miss. Inf., died March 11, '65.
525. McKenney, James, Co. F, 20th Va. Cav., died November 27, '64.
992. McKennie, R., Co. E, 29th Ga. Inf., died February 1, '65.
970. McKenzie, John, Co. H, 41st Miss. Inf., died January 30, '65.
1873. McKey, D. A., Co. A, 46th Miss. Inf., died April 15, '65.
1047. McKie, J. P., Co. F, 28th Tenn. Inf., died February 8, '65.
1713. McKowan, J. W., Co. E, 30th Ga. Inf., died March 20, '65.
1780. McLain, L., Co. D, 1st Fla. Inf., died March 30, '65.
1337. McLaughlin, E., Co. I, 36th Ala. Inf., died February 18, '65.
1053. McLaughlin, T. J., Co. B, 51st Va. Inf., died February 5, '65.
572. McMahon, E. L., Co. A, 31st Miss. Inf., died December 7, '64.
586. McMurry, J. B., Co. B, 1st Ga. State Troops, died December 9, '64.
1316. McNeise, W. B., Co. I, 8th Miss. Inf., died February 17, '65.
991. McPherson, W., Co. G, 39th Miss. Inf., died February 1, '65.
780. McQueen, T. S., 1st Ga. Inf., died January 15, '65.
363. McRoe, J. C., Co. A, 3d Ark. Inf., died October 26, '64.
247. McWhorter, S. W., Co. C, 1st Ga. Inf., died September 16, '64.
1190. McWright, J. J., Co. I, 44th Ala. Inf., died February 11, '65.
1380. Meade, John, Co. H, 34th Ga. Inf., died February 22, '65.
1734. Meadow, Joseph, Co. C, 3d Ky. Inf., died March 22, '65.
1960. Meadows, Joshua B., Co. B, Derrick's Bat. Inf., died May 12, '65.
521. Mears, J. M., Co. A, 5th Ga. Cav., died November 25, '64.

No. of Grave.

425. Medows, John, Co. G, 21st N. C. Inf., died November 7, '64.

1220. Meghar, H. C., Co. A, 18th Ala. Inf., died February 13, '65.

378. Mells, Albert, Co. H, 7th Fla. Inf., died October 29, '64.

293. Menar, Thomas, Co. K, 11th Tenn. Inf., died October 19, '64.

208. Meredith, W., Co. C, 1st Ga. Inf., died August 17, '64.

635. Merrill, Joseph H., Co. G, 54th Ala. Inf., died December 19, '64.

1695. Messengale, J., Co. B, 37th Va. Cav., died March 17, '65.

152. Mester, David, Co. D, 34th Bat. —— Cav., died May 9, '64.

791. Metcalf, J. W., Co. I, 54th N. C. Inf., died January 17, '65.

251. Mevers, Joseph, Co. H, 21st Va. Cav., died September 17, '64.

715. Middlebrook, J. P., Co. G, 53d Ala. Cav., died January 6, '65.

938. Miers, William, Co. A, 35th Ala. Inf., died January 28, '65.

1422. Mige, D., Co. E, 25th Ala. Inf., died February 24, '65.

1016. Mikeal, J., Co. G, 58th N. C. Inf., died February 3, '65.

1067. Miles, H. I., Co. C, 29th N. C. Inf., died February 6, '65.

1908. Miller, H. P., Co. C, 35th Miss. Inf., died April 23, '65.

2014. Miller, J. J., Co. F, 39th Miss. Inf., died June 2, '65.

727. Miller, James A., Co. B, 42d Ga. Inf., died January 9, '65.

940. Miller, James F., Co. F, 8th Bat. Ga. Inf., died January 29, '65.

139. Miller, T. D., citizen of Louisiana, died April 15, '64.

1199. Miller, W. H., Co. I, 18th Ala. Inf., died February 12, '65.

1864. Miller, W. N., Co. D, 7th Miss. Bat. Inf., died April 15, '65.

1548. Mills, W. A., Co. F, 12th La. Inf., died March 5, '65.

528. Miner, S. J., Co. E, 3d Ala. Cav., died November 28, '64.

1017. Mitchell, D. C., Co. C, 8th Bat. Ga. Inf., died February 3, '65.

1618. Mitchell, J., Co. A, 13th Ky. Cav., died March 11, '65.

68. Mitchell, J. B., Co. D, 29th Va. ——, died November 18, '63.

144. Mitchell, J. H., Co. D, 1st La. Cav., died April 25, '64.

2027. Mitchell, J. W., Co. E, 5th Ala. Cav., died June 5, '65.

1026. Mitchell, William, Co. D, 55th N. C. Inf., died February 7, '65.

1957. Mixson, W. A., Co. A, 44th Ky. Cav., died May 10, '65.

101. Mixton, Capt. S. R., Co. H, 13th Miss. Inf., died January 18, '64.

975. Moates, W., Co. I, 62d Va. Inf., died January 31, '65.

1710. Mobley, G. W., Co. H, 44th Ala. Inf., died March 28, '65.

912. Mobley, William, 39th Ala. Inf., died January 27, '65.

2009. Moiety, David, Co. B, 11th N. C. Inf., died May 31, '65.

517. Molley, James, Co. E, 36th Ala. Inf., died November 26, '64.

1350. Monroe, John, Co. E, 2d S. C. Inf., died February 20, '65.

1356. Montgomery, Deacon, Co. E, 22d Tenn. Inf., died February 21, '65.

178. Mooney, J. W., Co. A, 1st Ark. Cav., died June 14, '64.

625. Mooney, Robert, Co. F, 43d Ga. Inf., died December 16, '64.

956. Moore, B. J., Co. H, 8th S. C. Inf., died January 29, '65.

1054. Moore, D. W., Francis's Battery, died February 5, '65.

41. Moore, E., Co. E, 8th Tenn. ——, died October 8, '63.

92. Moore, George, Co. G, 16th Va. Cav., died January 12, '64.

1073. Moore, James, Co. A, 20th Ala. Inf., died February 12, '65.

9. Moore, Pleasant, Co. A, 3d Ky. Cav., died August 22, '63.

No. of Grave.

169. Moore, S. B., Co. A, 29th N. C. Inf., died May 28, '64.
891. Moore, W. H., Co. G, 3d Miss. Inf., died January 26, '65.
1820. Moore, William G., Co. H, 3d Miss. ——, died April, '65.
281. Morgan, G. W., Co. G, 8th Va. Cav., died October 5, '64.
1808. Morgan, James, Co. F, 57th Ala. Inf., died April 3, '65.
1575. Morgan, J. J., Co. C, citizen of Georgia. died March 6, '65.
2035. Morgan, M. B., Co. I, 4th Ala. Cav., died June 10, '65.
1536. Morgan, T. J., Co. E, 7th Miss. Inf., died March 4, '65.
1706. Morreston, W. C., Co. D, 20th Va. Cav., died March 18, '65.
439. Morris, Henry, Co. D, 45th Ala. Inf., died November 9, '64.
416. Morris, John, Co. H, 24th Ala. Inf., died November 6, '64.
1657. Morris, W. P., Co. C, 4th Ala. Cav., died March 14, '65.
734. Morrison, A., Co. D, 22d Ala. Inf., died January 11, '65.
1204. Morse, James, Co. A, 20th Ala. Inf., died February 11, '65.
811. Mosely, C., Co. K, 2d Ala. Cav., died January 19, '65.
1158. Mosely, J. W., Co. K, 2d Miss. Inf., died February 10, '65.
1144. Mosely, William, Co. K, 10th Ky. Cav., died February 9, '65.
2045. Moses, E. L., Co. D, 27th S. C. Inf., died June 16, '65.
213. Moss, R. L., Co. K, 1st Ga. Inf., died August 22, '64.
2038. Moss, Zac, Co. G, 33d Ala. Inf., died June 11, '65.
830. Motteron, Samuel, Co. C, 38th Tenn. Inf., died January 21, '65.
221. Mount, G. W., Co. E, 46th Ala. Inf., died August 27, '64.
1889. Mull, W. E., Co. C, 39th N. C. Inf., died April 18, '65.
504. Mullens, S. C., Co. A, 44th Miss. Inf., died November 22, 64.
457. Mullens, T., Co. E, 34th Va. Inf., died November 13, '64.
223. Munsey, J., unknown, died August 28, '64.
1398. Murphy, G., 13th Ky. Cav., died February 23, '65.
1876. Murray, Newton, Co. G, 57th Ala. Inf., died April 16, '65.
493. Myers, A. T., Co. D, 1st Conf. Inf., died November 20, '64.
1145. Myers, F. A., Co. I, 24th S. C. Inf., died February 9, '65.
1255. Myers, F. N., Co. I, 19th Tenn. Inf., died February 15, '65.
1589. Myers, Joseph, Co. D, 8th S. C. Inf., died March 7, '65.
1672. Myers, J. M., Co. E, 62d Va. Inf., died March 15, '65.
1842. Myers, William H., Co. K, 1st Tenn. Cav., died April 10, '65.
387. Naboor, William, Co. C, citizen of Virginia, died October 31, '64.
1699. Nance, Wash P., Co. I, 10th Ala. Cav., died March 18, '65.
1688. Nash, George, Co. B, 46th Ala. Inf., died March 17, '65.
1216. Nash, J. W., Co. F, 36th Ga. Inf., died February 13, '65.
318. Nash, Thomas, Co. C, 29th N. C. Inf., died October 15, 64.
1837. Nash, Thomas J., Co. F, 37th Ga. Cav., died April 10, '65.
1271. Nash, W. P., 36th Ga. Inf., died February 15, '65.
134. Neal, Graham, Co. C, citizen of Tennessee, died April 12, '64.
588. Nealey (or Nealor), W., Co. I, 39th Miss. Inf., died Dec. 10, '64.
1764. Neely, R. S., Co. D, 7th Ala. Cav., died March 27, '65.
1171. Neff, G. B., Co. A, Harrison's Cavalry, died February 9, '65.
827. Neighbors, W., Co. H, 25th Ala. Inf., died January 22, '65.
1549. Nelson, J. P., Co. A, 20th Ala. Inf., died March 5, '65.

APPENDIX.   373

No. of Grave.

732. Nelson, John W., Co. A, 17th Va. Cav., died January 9, '65.

1803. Nelson, John W., Co. C, 29th Ala. Inf., died April 1, '65.

1142. Nelson, Wesley A., Co. B, 34th Ala. Inf., died February 9, '65.

1549. Nettles, G. H., Co. G, 30th Ala. Inf., died March 6, '65.

984. Newson, Henry L., 7th Ala. Cav., died January 31, '65.

544. Newsom, J. D., Co. D, 29th Ala. Inf., died December 2, '64.

2023. Newton, J. B., Conscript N. C. Detailed, died June 3, '65.

418. Nichols, A. S., Co. C, 25th Tex. Cav., died November 6, '64.

1173. Nichols, C. L., Co. E, 46th Miss. Inf., died February 10, 65.

1191. Nichols, G. W., Co. C, 9th Tenn. Cav., died February 11, '65.

1867. Nichols, Robert, Co. H, 6th Tex. Cav., died April 14, '65.

1466. Nidever, A., Co. D, 3d Tex. Cav., died February 27, '65.

605. Nix, David, Co. I, 37th Ga. Inf., died December 12, '64.

419. Noble, Alex, Co. G, 10th Ky. Cav., died November 6, '64.

1710 (or 1210). Nobley, W. S., Co. K, 24th Ala. Inf., died March 19, '65.

437. Norman, Henry, Co. E, 111th N. C. Inf., died November 9, '64.

1900. Norman, P. R., Co. I, 41st Ga. Inf., died April 22, '65.

844. Norris, John, Co. K, 54th N. C. Inf., died January 20, '65.

1193. Northcutt, G. W., 31st Ala. Inf., died February 11, '65.

1480. Northrop, H. H., Co. H, 2d Ky. Cav., died February 28, '65.

1782. Northrop, James T., Co. B, 39th Ala. Inf., died March 29, '65.

1120. Norton, T. S., Co. C, 1st Ga. Inf., died February 8, '65.

1820. Nunn, John, Co. A, 13th Ky. Cav., died April 5, '65.

1883. O'Brian, James, Co. F, 4th Miss. Inf., died April 17, '65.

529. O'Brian, W. S., Co. A, 5th Va. Cav., died November 28, '64.

613. O'Briant, Arch, Co. K, 1st Ga. Inf., died December 13, '64.

190. O'Bryant, J. M., Co. F, 5th Ala. Cav., died July 23, '64.

22. O'Clowd, John, Co. G, 5th Regt. ——, died September 12, '63.

163. Odet, William, Co. C, 5th Ky. Inf., died May 21, '64.

778. O'Donnell, Patrick, Co. K, 10th Tenn. Inf., died January 17, '65.

1576. Offield, J., Co. K, 26th Tenn. Inf., died March 6, '65.

1361. Offield, W., Co. K, 65th Tenn. Inf., died February 21, '65.

1938. Oglesby, G. T., Co. K, 36th Ga. Inf., died May 5, '65.

795. Omans, Wilson, 7th Ala. Cav., died January 17, '65.

639. Omens, W. H., Co. I, 39th Miss. Inf., died December 20, '64.

394. Oney, J. H., Co. C, 16th Va. Cav., died November 3, '64.

1630. Orr, Thomas, Co. I, 43d Tenn. Inf., died March 12, '65.

1533. Orrell, J. W., 5th Ala. Cav., died March 4, '65.

1195. Osborne, John, Co. C, 2d Bat. Ky. Cav., died February 11, '65.

1731. Osborne, W. W., Co. D, 8th Miss. Inf., died March 22, '65.

1845. Osteen, D. D., Co. A, 1st Fla. Cav., died April 9, '65.

1563. Overstreet, L., Co. D, 24th S. C. Inf., died March 5, '65.

175. Owen, J., Co. A, 10th Tenn. Cav., died June 10, '64.

582. Owen, John, Co. G, 3d Conf., died December 9, '64.

1913. Pace, E. I., Co. F, 36th Ga. Inf., died April 24, '65.

707. Pace, John, Co. A, 10th Tenn. Cav., died January 5, '65.

115. Pack, E. S., died November 30, '63.

No. of Grave.

608. Packard, E., Co. A, 40th Ga. Inf., died December 12, '64.

1035. Paine, J. L., Co. I, 8th Conf. Cav., died February 4, '65.

559. Paltatty, J. M., Co. C, 19th S. C. Inf., died December 6, '64.

162. Pardeau, D. L., Co. G, 7th Ala. Cav., died April 20, '64.

20. Park, Joseph, Co. E, 5th Ky. Cav., died May 23, '64.

1970. Parker, F. C., Co. G, 46th Ga. Inf., died May 16, '65.

674. Parker, James, Co. B, 19th S. C. Inf., died December 27, '64.

943. Parker, John M., Co. G, 1st Ala. Inf., died January 29, '65.

823. Parsley, Richard, Co. I, 28th Tenn. Inf., died January 21, '65.

857. Parsons, W. L., citizen of Jackson County, Va., died January 23, '65.

215. Parvett, John, Co. H, 60th Va. Inf., died August 13, '64.

899. Paschal, T. P., Co. C, 53d Ala. Cav., died January 26, '65.

145. Pate, George E., Co. D, 34th Miss. ——, died March, '64.

1078. Pate, Thomas, 4th Ala. Cav., died February 7, '65.

1225. Patrath, S., Co. A, 25th or 35th Ala. Inf., died February 13, '65.

1028. Patrick, Preston, Co. D, 6th Miss. Inf., died February 3, '65.

454. Patrick, Wilsòn, Co. I, 16th Va. Inf., died November 12, '64.

259. Patten, Samuel, 66th Ga. Inf., died September 7, '64.

624. Patterson, Archie, Co. C, 4th Fla. Inf., died December 16, '64.

1835. Patterson, George W., Co. C, 37th Va. Cav., died April 9, '65.

649. Patterson, James, Co. K, 47th Tenn. Cav., died December 21, '64.

1136. Patterson, W. T., Co. F, Thomas's Legion, died February 14, '65.

329. Paulet, W. H., Co. A, 16th Va. Cav., died October 17, '64.

1009. Pauley, Ira, Co. F, 8th Va. Cav., died February 2, '65.

1471. Paulk, W. L., Co. E, 12th Ala. Inf., died February 27, '65.

1604. Payne, Commodore, Co. A, 19th Va. Cav., died March 9, '65.

1566. Payne, W. H., Co. F, 20th Ala. Cav., died March 6, '65.

1244. Payton, W. R., Co. F, 36th Ga. Inf., died February 14, '65.

620. Peacock, J. W., Co. D, 63d Ga. Inf., died December 15, '64.

898. Peacock, W. D., Co. B, 36th Ala. Inf., died January 26, '65.

1240. Peake, Samuel (or L.), Co. G, 24th S. C. Inf., died February 14, '65.

75. Pendry, Richard, Co. B, 10th Ky. Cav., died November 6, '63.

1776. Pennell, J. A., Co. F, 31st Ala. Inf., died March 26, '65.

40. Penney, J. S., Co. A, 1st La. Cav., died October 7, '63.

217. Penniston, C. W., 5th La. Cav., died August 23, '64.

409. Perkins, Elijah, Co. E, Clay's Battery, died November 5, '64.

291. Perkison, W. P., Co. A, 51st Ala. Inf., died October 8, '64.

631. Perry, E. J., Co. F, 28th Miss. Cav., died December 18, '64.

595. Perry, Stephen R., Co. G, 27th Miss. Inf., died December 10, '64.

1023. Peterson, R. B., Co. C, 35th Miss. Inf., died February 3, '65.

916. Petersor, W. B., Co. C, 17th Ala. Inf., died February 2, '65.

225. Petil, N. M., 18th Tex. Cav., died October 13, '64.

1088. Petty, G. W., Co. I, 8th Tenn. Cav., died February 7, '65.

1625. Philips, A. J., Co. H, 5th Ga. Cav., died March 10, '65.

1936. Philips, John S., Co. B, 8th Ga. Inf., died May 4, '65.

1562. Philips, W. E., Co. A, 13th Ky. Cav., died March 5, '65.

336. Phillips, John, Co. I, 37th Va. Cav., died October 17, '64.

No. of Grave.

43. Phillips, P. R., Co. E, 10th Conf., died October 8, '63.

347. Phillips, Robert, Co. I, 54th Ala. Inf., died October 22, '64.

446. Pierce, John, Co. I, 17th Ala. Inf., died November 11, '64.

954. Pierce, R. M., Co. C, 55th Tenn. Inf., died January 29, '65.

910. Pierson (or Parsons), W. G., 34th Ala. Inf., died January 27, '65.

1280. Piles, T. E., Co. H, Tennessee Reserves, died February 15, '65.

681. Pinkston, Richard, Co. B, 27th Ala. Inf., died December 29, '64.

1152. Pitman, John E., Co. A, 6th Fla. Inf., died February 11, '65.

679. Pitmar, John D., Co. H, 66th Ga. Inf., died December 29, '64.

1823. Pitts, Benjamin, Co. G, 27th Miss. Inf., died April 7, '65.

636. Pitzenbarger, A., Co. G, 22d Ala. Inf., died December 19, '64.

1024. Plant (or Platt), W. H., Co. C, 34th Ga. Inf., died February 3, '65.

1132. Platt, I. L., Co. E, 36th Ala. Inf., died February 9, '65.

503. Pledger, Calvin, 23d Ark. Inf., died November 21, '64.

1288. Poe, John, Tennessee Conscripts, died February 15, '65.

200. Poe, Thomas J., Co. B, 28th Ala. Inf., died September 9, '63.

1663. Poindexter, W., Co. D, 20th Tenn. Inf., died March 15, '65.

792. Poling, Jacob, citizen of Virginia, died January 17, '65.

311. Pollard, John, Co. E, 5th Miss. Inf., died October 9, '64.

1686. Pomphrey, G. W., Co. E, 1st Md. Cav., died March 17, '65.

361. Pope, H. L., Co. I, 6th N. C. Inf., died October 25, '64.

1730. Pope, J. R., Co. C, 23d Ala. Inf., died March 21, '65.

655. Pope, W., Co. I, 2d Va. Inf., died December 25, '64.

59. Pope, W. L., Co. A, 9th Tenn. Cav., died Nov. 6, '63. Removed.

54. Porter, J. H., Co. G, 8th Va. Cav., died October 20, '63.

1847. Porter, J. W., Co. H, 19th S. C. Inf., died April 9, '65.

1915. Porter, William E., Co. C, 39th Miss. Inf., died April 24, '65.

2034. Posey, W. T., Co. I, 5th Ala. Cav., died June 7, '65.

1511. Potts, R. P., Co. A, 13th Ky. Cav., died March 2, '65.

348. Powell, Henry, Co. G, 8th Va. Cav., died October 22, '64.

1988. Powell, James W., Co. E, 1st Ga. Inf., died May 20, '65.

1925. Powell, R. W., Co. H, 56th Ga. Inf., died April 28, '65.

411. Pratt, L. P., Co. B, 4th La. Bat., died November 5, '64.

1314. Preacher, W. E., Co. E, 24th S. C. Inf., died February 17, '65.

575. Price, A. B., citizen of Kentucky, died December 8, '64.

286. Price, Daniel, citizen of South Carolina, died September 20, '64.

968. Price, R. C., Co. C, 15th S. C. Inf., died January 30, '65.

490. Price, Thomas B., Co. F, 4th Ga. Cav., died November 19, '64.

806. Pridemore, William, Co. G, 27th Va. Cav., died January 19, '65.

645. Priger, Steve, Co. D, 53d Ala. Cav., died December 22, '64.

716. Pritchard, I. W., Co. A, 1st Conf. Cav., died January 6, '65.

1085. Pritchford, N. W., Co. F, 10th Ala. Inf., died February 7, '65.

226. Probpte, A., 1st Va. Cav., died August 24, '64.

1393. Province, R., Co. A, 35th Ala. Inf., died February 23, '65.

1335. Pruett, W. P., Co. F, 2d Miss. Cav., died February 19, '65.

1139. Pruner, John, Co. F, 1st Conf. Ga. Inf., died February 9, '65.

1570. Pugh, J. W., Co. F, 7th Va. Cav., died March 6, '65.

376   THE STORY OF CAMP CHASE.

No. of Grave.

482. Pugh, T. J., Co. C, 19th Miss. Inf., died November 18, '64.
942. Pullen, John, Co. E, 25th Ga. Inf., died January 29, '65.
229. Pursel, Richard, Co. I, 36th Va. Inf., died August 23, '64.
1450. Puslunth, ——, Co. B, 11th Ky. Cav., died February, '65.
1611. Quadelbum, C., Co. B, 57th Ala. Inf., died March 10, '65.
129. Queen, G. W., Co. F, 20th Va. Cav., died April (or August) 7, '63.
1705. Quickle, A. A., citizen of Virginia, died March 18, '65.
639. Quinn, G. W., Co. A, 34th Miss. Inf., died December 19, '64.
705. Quinn, John R., citizen of Tennessee, died January 5, '65.
2010 Quinn, Patrick, Miss. Bat., died May 30, '65.
1387. Quisenby, R., Co. B, 4th Ky. Cav., died February 22, '65.
1133. Rabon, John, Co. K, 4th La. Inf., died February 9, '65.
861. Rabon, John, Co. G, 24th S. C. Inf., died January 24, '65.
1224. Raborn, Cyrus, Co. H, 30th Miss. Inf., died February 13, '65.
1020. Raborn, Trusley, Co. D, 19th Tenn. Inf., died February 3, '65.
1999. Rader, James B., Co. K, 62d Va. Inf., died May 25, '65.
1194. Radford, I. W., Co. D, 56th Ala. Cav., died February 11, '65.
1497. Ragham, James, Co. D, 16th La. Inf., died March 1, '65.
1488. Rainar, W. C., Co. E, 26th Ala. Inf., died February 28, '65.
21. Rains, Joel, Co. F, 5th Tenn. ——, died September 9, '63.
1646. Raley, B. J., Co. D, 7th Miss. Inf., died March 13, '65.
1245. Ramage, R., Co. H, 46th Ala. Inf., died February 14, '65.
55. Ramney, George, Co. G, 8th Ky. ——, died October 23, '63.
168. Ramsey, A. M., Co. D, 14th Ky. Cav., died May 28, '64.
1839. Ranes, J. W., Co. F, 55th Ala. Inf., died April 10, '65.
1766. Rasberry, James, Co. C, 31st Miss. Inf., died March 27, '65.
952. Ratcliffe, Samuel, Co. E, 22d Miss. Inf., died January 29, '65.
1079. Rathburn, P. A., Co. A, 19th La. Inf., died February 6, '65.
1333. Rawles, J. D., Co. B, 13th Ky. Cav., died February 18, '65.
1429. Ray, F. W., Co. D, 29th N. C. Inf., died February 24, '65.
44. Ray, Henry, Co. D, 5th N. C. Cav., died October 9, '63.
2048. Ray, John, Co. K, 17th Ala. Inf., died June 19, '65.
969. Ray, William, Co. I, 18th Miss. Cav., died January 30, '65.
401. Reade, James M., Co. D, 8th Va. Cav., died November 4, '64.
1650. Redden, Jeff, citizen of Alabama, died March 14, '65.
548. Reed, F., Co. H, 51st Va. Inf., died December 3, '64.
206. Reed, R. T., Co. D, 15th Tenn. Cav., died August 16, '64.
1605. Reese, E. G., Co. B, 20th Miss. Inf., died March 5, '65.
728. Reese, John H., Co. H, 6th Va. Inf., died January 9, '65.
967. Reese, O. H. P., Co. C, 35th Miss. Inf., died January 29, '65.
191. Reese, W. R., Co. C, 11th Tenn. Cav., died July 25, '64.
307. Reeves, D. W., Co. I, 36th Tenn. Inf., died October 13, '64.
1019. Regester, F. M., Co. G, 57th Ala. Inf., died February 3, '65.
1532. Register, G. W., Co. G, 1st Fla. Inf., died March 5, '65.
518. Reville, F. H., Co. E, 29th Ga. Inf., died November 26, '64.
410. Reynolds, Charles, Co. H, 53d Ala. Inf., died November 5, '64.
489. Reynolds, S., Co. K, 29th Tenn. Inf., died November 19, '64.

No. of Grave.

428. Reynolds, Thomas, citizen of Virginia, died November 7, '64.
1626. Rice, Z., Co. H, 30th Ala. Inf., died March 11, '65.
1841. Richards, A. I., Co. A, 1st Tenn. Inf., died April 10, '65.
1884. Richards, George, 7th Fla. Inf., died April 17, '65.
718. Richards, John, Co. G, 37th Bat. Cav., died January 7, '65.
1510. Richards, Thomas, Co. B, 13th Tenn. Inf., died March 2, '65.
24. Richards, Thomas, Co. C, 49th Tenn. ——, died September 17, '63.
1399. Richardson, W. M., Co. D, 8th Ala. Inf., died February 23, '65.
1857. Richardson, William, Co. K, 36th Ga. Inf., died April 13, '65.
1231. Richmond, W. D., Co. F, 4th Ark. Inf., died February 14, '65.
798. Ricks, John W., Co. I, 15th Miss. Inf., died January 18, '65.
1897. Riddle, R. R., Co. A, 10th Ky. Cav., died April 19, '65.
667. Rider, David, Co. I, 43d Ga. Inf., died December 26, '64.
1441. Rinchear, W., Co. A, 1st Ala. Inf., died February 25, '65.
358. Roach, Joseph, Co. H, 7th Fla. Inf., died October 25, '64.
1222. Roach, Robert, Co. C, 6th Fla. Inf., died February 13, '65.
1670. Roach, W. E., Co. E, Armstrong's Cavalry, died March 15, '65.
222. Robenson, W., Co. B, — Miss. Cav., died August 28, '64.
1515. Roberson, N. A., Co. E, 111th N. C. Troops, died March 3, '65.
38. Roberts, Daniel, — Va. ——, died October 5, '63.
301. Roberts, E., Clay's Ky. Bat., died August 14, '64.
1748. Roberts, H. C., Rogers's Escort, died March 25, '65.
333. Roberts, Jackson, — Ala. Cav., died October 18, '64.
1090. Roberts, J. M., Co. H, 36th Ga. Inf., died February 7, '65.
760. Roberts, L. D., Co. D, 3d Fla. Inf., died January 13, '65.
1555. Roberts, M., Co. E, 19th Bat. Va. Inf., died March 5, '65.
506. Roberts, M. A., Co. B, 4th Ga. Inf., died November 22, '64.
849. Roberts, R. R., Co. F, 15th Ky. Cav., died January 23, '65.
271. Roberts, S. J., Co. H, 41st Ga. Inf., died September 28, '64.
1714. Robertson, T. J., Co. L, 3d Ga., died March 19, '65.
1905. Robertson, W. S., Co. I, 36th Ala. Inf., died April 23, '65.
505. Robins, John G., Co. A, 16th Tenn. Cav., died November 22, '64.
824. Robinson, Berry, Co. G, Smith's Va. Home Guards, died Jan. 21, '65.
306. Robinson, Israel, Co. I, 8th Va. Inf., died October 12, '64.
708. Robinson, N. (or James), Co. H, 28th Tenn. Inf., died January 5, '65.
610. Robinson, W. D., Co. D, 4th Ala. Cav., died December 13, '64.
775. Rocketts, James A., Co. I, 8th Conf. Cav., died January 15, '65.
   No such man.
691. Roddy, George, 33d Ga. Inf., died December 31, '64.
1592. Rodenberry, J., Co. K, 7th Fla. Inf., died March 8, '65.
78. Rodgers, John, Co. C, 66th N. C. Cav., died December 4, '63.
933. Rodgers, J. A. B., Co. F, 4th Ala. Cav., died January 28, '65.
1476. Rodgers, J. M., Co. E, 29th N. C. Inf., died February 28, '65.
1467. Rodgers, L. M., Co. A, 57th Ala. Inf., died February 27, '65.
1431. Rodgers, M., Co. H, 57th Ala. Inf., died February 24, '65.
1039. Rodgers, M. T., Co. D, 20th Miss. Inf., died February 4, '65.
467. Rodgers, Peter, Co. I, 8th Tenn. Cav., died November 14, '64.

No. of Grave.

977. Rogers, I. W., citizen of Tennessee, died January 31, '65.

1773. Rogers, James W., Co. H, 18th Ala. Inf., died March 28, '65.

1924. Rogers, J. M., Co. A, 36th Ga. Inf., died April 27, '65.

1751. Rogers, Warren, Co. B, 18th Ala. Inf., died March 25, '65.

456. Roe, David, Co. I, 2d Ky. Cav., died November 13, '64.

402. Roe, James, Co. K, 1st Tenn. Cav., died November 4, '64.

1668. Rolsey, W. H., Co. A, 61st Tenn. Inf., died March 15, '65.

32. Rondine, John, Co. C, 17th Va. Cav., died September 29, '63.

391. Roper, J. M., Co. G, 1st Ga. Inf., died November 3, '64.

862. Rose, E. D. W., Co. B, 51st Va. Inf., died January 24, '65.

1002. Rose, L. J., Co. F, 1st Md. Cav., died February 2, '65.

1024. Rose, R. P., Co. D, 27th Miss. Inf., died February 6, '65.

1021. Ross, J. W. W., Co. E, 11th Ky. Cav., died February 1, '65.

1509. Ross, W. M., Co. G, Moreland's Cavalry, died March 2, '65.

1409. Roundtree, J. S., Co. H, 1st Ga. Inf., died February 23, '65.

443. Rowland, J. G., Co. H, 57th N. C. Inf., died November 9, '64.

447. Rozar, Luke, Co. K, 5th Ga. Cav., died November 11, '64.

132. Rudd, Elijah, Co. A, 2d Ky. Rifles, died April 9, '64.

1939. Runnels, P., Co. C, 7th Miss. Bat. Inf., died May 5, '65.

1992. Rusher, Miles, Co. B, 4th N. C. Inf., died May 22, '65.

62. Russell, A. C., Co. B, 11th Va. Cav., died November 9, '63.

1804. Russell, Edmund, Co. C, 4th Ark. Inf., died April 2, '65.

560. Russell, Isaac, Co. H, 1st Fla. Inf., died December 6, '64.

1013. Russell, J. H., Co. C, 5th Miss. Cav., died February 8, '65.

1026. Ruster, W. H. P., Co. F, 17th Ala. Inf., died February 3, '65.

1135. Rutchford, W., Co. C, 3d Ga. Cav., died February 9, '65.

1680. Ruth, J. C., Co. F, 41st Tenn. Inf., died March 16, '65.

601. Rutherford, W., Georgia Militia, died December 10, '64.

1217. Rutledge, J. M., Co. D, 42d Ga. Inf., died February 13, '65.

535. Rutledge, John O., Co. C, 19th Va. Cav., died November 30, '64.

1784. Rutledge, P. A., Co. C, 25th Ala. Inf., died March 30, '65.

1184. Rutliff, M., Co. K, 18th Tex. Cav., died February 11, '65.

1275. Rutsel, J. H., Co. D, 12th La. Inf., died February 15, '65.

282. Ryan, F. N., Co. C, 17th Va. Cav., died October 6, '64.

1765. Saling, Finney, Co. A, 4th Ala. Inf., died March 27, '65.

1044. Salley, G. W., Co. H, 35th Miss. Inf., died February 4, '65.

913. Salter, A. H., Co. F, 1st Ala. Inf., died February 2, '65.

339. Salmon, W. R., Co. C, 30th Ga. Inf., died October 18, '64.

1343. Sample, James, Co. B, 10th Ky. Cav., died February 19, '65.

369. Sampson, George, citizen of Virginia, died October 27, '64.

1844. Sanders, James A., Co. F, 31st Miss. Cav., died April 10, '65.

1277. Sanders, W. B., Co. A, 23d Ala. Inf., died February 15, '65.

627. Sanders, W. F., Co. C, 15th S. C., Inf., died December 18, '64.

491. Sanders, W. P., Co. K, 46th Miss. Inf., died November 19, '64.

917. Sanderson, David, Co. A, 10th Ala. Cav., died January 28, '64.

988. Sanderson, J. B., Co. H, 10th Ala. Cav., died February 1, '65.

580. Sanford, John, Ward's Battery, died December 9, '64.

No. of Grave.

1637. Sanford, V. A., Co. H, 1st Ala. Inf., died March 12, '65.
888. Sanott, William, Co. A, 5th Conf. Inf., died January 26, '64.
582. Sansey, A. G., 1st Ga. Inf., died December 9, '64.
1568. Satterfield, J. B., Co. A, 6th Ga. Cav., died March 6, '65.
1169. Saucier, N., Co. F, 3d Miss. Inf., died February 10, '65.
1188. Saunders, Moses, Co. G, 39th Ala. Inf., died February 11, '65.
1213. Sayer, D. P., Co. I, 56th Ga. Inf., died February 13, '65.
1458. Scandler, Pat, Co. B, 5th Conf. Inf., died February 26, '65.
947. Scarber, Edgar, Co. D, 38th Ala. Inf., died January 28, '65.
142. Schafer, W. F., 17th Tenn. Cav., died April 21, '64.
1472. Schogan, I. D., Co. I, 33d Miss. Inf., died February 27, '65.
589. Schrader, Chris, citizen of Virginia, died December 10, '64.
889. Schrisopsher, J. P. B., Co. E, 7th Miss. Bat. Inf., died Jan. 26, '64.
30. Schriver, E. L., Co. E, 5th Ky. Cav., died September 28, '63.
1725. Scott, D. H., Co. H, 23d Miss. Inf., died March 21, '65.
2036. Scott, W. B., Co. G, 8th Ga. Bat. Inf., died June 9, '65.
1182. Scriggs, J., Co. E, 48th Tenn. Inf., died February 11, '65.
1687. Scrogan, W. A., Co. C, 56th Ga. Inf., died March 17, '65.
982. Secrease, R. H., Co. B, 4th Mo. Cav., died January 31, '65.
188. Seimpkins, George, died September, '64.
72. Sellard, David, Co. E, 16th Va. Cav., died November 24, '63.
141. Sellers, John, 5th Ky. Cav., died April 19, '64.
1635. Sellers, P., Co. A, 2d Ala. Cav., died March 12, '65.
1487. Senclair, I. A., Co. A, 1st Conf. Cav., died February 28, '65.
415. Seniker, D. B., Co. B, 36th Va. Inf., died November 6, '64.
133. Senles, Capt. W. N., died April 9, '64. Removed.
1121. Sensabaugh, John S., Co. I, 29th N. C. Inf., died February 8, '65.
666. Seopine, Ed, Co. B, 16th La. Inf., died December 26, '64.
717. Sermons, John, Co. G, 29th Ga. Inf., died January 7, '65.
526. Shamel, Jacob W., Co. B, 6th N. C. Inf., died November 27, '64.
1923. Shane, E. B., Co. B, 1st Fla. Inf., died April 27, '65.
2041. Shanton, M. D., Co. B, 24th S. C. ——, died June 13, '65.
1043. Sharp, F., Co. I, 1st Tenn. Cav., died February 4, '65.
23. Sharp, G. B., Co. A, 10th Va. Cav., died September 25, '63.
1704. Sharp, James A., Co. A, 2d Ky. Cav., died March 18, '65.
735. Sharp, James L., Co. F, 19th Va. Cav., died January 9, '65.
1183. Shaver, Elijah, Conscript of Tennessee, died February 11, '65.
893. Shaw, A. L., Co. A, 18th Ala. Inf., died January 26, '64.
1201. Shawber, John A., Co. F, 22d Va. Cav., died February 12, '65.
658. Shealey, L., Co. C, 15th S. C. Inf., died December 23, '64.
815. Shearouse, J. W., Co. I, 54th Ga. Inf., died January 20, '64.
1340. Shelton, Isaac, Co. K, 56th Ga. Inf., died February 19, '65.
1514. Shelton, J. H., Co. A, Hays's Cavalry, died March 2, '65.
1613. Shephard, H., Stewart's Escort, died March 10, '65.
906. Shephard, John, Co. A, 45th Ala. Inf., died January 27, '64.
973. Sheppard, Philip, Co. B, 38th Ala. Inf., died January 30, '65.
109. Sherault, J., died February, '64.

No of Grave.

865. Sherrew, John, Co. K, 16th La. Inf., died January 24, '64.

404. Shields, John, Co. B, 19th La. Inf., died November 4, '64.

1516. Ship, R., Co. F, 39th Ala. Inf., died March 2, '65.

1449. Shirly, Hampton, Co. G, 24th S. C. Inf., died February 26, '65.

1104. Shoemaker, J., Co. I, 15th Tenn. Inf., died February 8, '65.

1477. Sholer, W. A., Co. L, 10th Ala. Cav., died February 27, '65.

519. Shoop, J. W., Co. E, 31st Va. Cav., died November 26, '64.

1928. Shrouse, I. F., Co. K, 52d Ga. Inf., died April 30, '65.

1430. Silas, E., Co. I, 34th Ala. Inf., died February 24, '65.

918. Sills, S. J., Co. E, 38th Miss. Inf., died January 28, '65.

444. Silver, L. P., Co. I, 29th N. C. Inf., died November 9, 64.

1263. Simmes, W. C., Co. A, Camper's Battery, died February 15, '65.

533. Simmons, J. L., Co. E, 54th Ala. Inf., died November 29, '64.

1290. Simmons, J. W., Co. K, 5th Miss. Cav., died February 16, '65.

327. Simpson, John, 1st Ga. Cav., died October 17, '64.

1336. Singleton, H. B., Co. E, 34th Ala. Inf., died February 19, '65.

2005. Singley, John, Co. I, 30th Ga. Inf., died May 29, '65.

1462. Sinkins, L., Co. E, 23d Ark. Inf., died February 27, '65.

864. Sinn, William, Co. H, 18th Ala. Inf., died January 24, '64.

499. Sisenore, David, Co. K, 37th Va. Cav., died November 20, '64.

116. Sizemore, G. (or W. C.), Co. F, 7th Ala , died February, '64.

1645. Skinner, F. E., Co. A, 13th Ky. Cav., died March 13, '65.

2026. Skinner, N. S., Co. I, 30th Ga. Inf., died June 4, '65.

1317. Slaughter, J. W., Co. K, 2d Miss. Cav., died February 17, '65.

1994. Small, James, Co. C, 19th Va. Cav., died May 23, '65.

1814. Smallwood, C. S., Co. F, 4th Ga. Cav., died April 3, '65.

1123. Smith, A. H., Co. F, 22d Ala. Inf., died February 8, '65.

2040. Smith, A. M., Co. D, 1st Ga. Bat. Inf., died June 13, '65.

1752. Smith, Alex, Co. B, 8th Va. Cav., died March 25, '65.

563. Smith, Alex J., Co. E, 29th Ga. Inf., died December 6, '64.

1512. Smith, B. A., Co. G, 57th Ala. Inf., died March 2, '65.

935. Smith, C. C., Co. E, 34th Va. Bat. Cav., died January 28, '65.

1412. Smith, C. N., Co. A, 36th Va. Inf., died February 24, '65.

1815. Smith, C. T., Co. A, 17th Miss. Cav., died April 3, '65.

1257. Smith, E. H., Co. G, 58th Ala. Inf., died February 15, '65.

1219. Smith, Elfred, Co. B, 3d Miss. Inf., died February 13, '65.

539. Smith, F. B., Co. C, Dobbin's Ark. Cav., died Dec. 1, '64. Removed.

1110. Smith, Gasper, Co. C, 1st Ark. Inf., died February 8, '65.

894. Smith, Hilliard, Co. B, 46th Ala. Inf., died January 26, '64.

1185. Smith, Howell S., Co. A, 18th Miss. Inf., died February 11, '65.

108. Smith, J. B., 66th N. C. Cav., died February, '64.

1432. Smith, J., Co. E, 1st Fla. Cav., died February 24, '65.

326. Smith, J. H., Co. D, 1st Ga. Cav., died October 17, '64.

1285. Smith, J. O., Co. D, 24th S. C. Inf., died February 16, '65.

359. Smith, J. P., Co. D, 29th Miss. Inf., died October 25, '64.

1538. Smith, J. W., Co. A, 6th Fla. Inf., died March 4, '65.

96. Smith, John, citizen of West Virginia, died January 16, '64.

No. of Grave.

1378. Smith, L. T., Co. H, 21st Ga. Inf., died February 22, '65.
831. Smith, Morgan, Co. D, 6th N. C. Inf., died January 20, '64.
290. Smith, Noah B., Co. I, 42d Ga. Cav., died October 9, '64.
1940. Smith, R. N., Co. C, 21st Tenn. Cav., died May 6, '65.
29. Smith, Robert, Jr., Co. G, 2d Tenn. Cav., died September 25, '63.
698. Smith, Shemorick, Co. C, 2d Ala. Cav., died January 3, '65.
1741. Smith, Simeon, Co. A, 20th Miss. Inf., died March 23, '65.
1800. Smith, S. S. (or S. P.), Co. G, 29th Ga. Inf., died March 31, '65.
131. Smith, Virgil, Co. B, 2d Md. Cav., died April 8, '64.
1968. Smith, W. D., Co. G, 8th N. C. Inf., died May 16, '65.
545. Smith, W. G., Co. B, 33d Miss. Inf., died December 2, '64.
122. Smith, W. S., Co. E, 26th Va. Cav., died March, '64.
1513. Smotherman, J. W., Co. D, 11th Tenn. Cav., died March 2, '65.
1661. Snipes, J. B., Co. A, 46th Ga. Inf., died March 14, '65.
1874. Sorrulls, W. H., Co. A, 42d Miss. Cav., died April 3, '65.
1218. Spain, Thomas, Co. F, 66th Ga. Inf., died February 13, '65.
1447. Sparkman, C. I., Co. A, 4th La. Inf., died February 26, '65.
234. Sparks, J., Co. C, 18th Ala. Inf., died September 9, '64.
406. Spears, J. B., Co. E, 1st Ga. Inf., died November 5, '64.
1433. Speers, I. H., Co. C, 4th Ga. Cav., died February 24, '65.
561. Spencer, B. H., Co. H, 5th Ga. Cav., died December 6, '64.
1394. Spencer, W. A., Moreland's Cavalry, died February 23, '65.
2007. Spere, James, Co. D, 17th Ala. Inf., died May 29, '65.
1383. Spicer, I. S., Co. K, 2d Tenn. Cav., died February 23, '65.
863. Spriggs, Andrew, Co. F, 13th Bat. Va. Inf., died January 24, '64.
10. Sproul, S. H., 10th Conf. Cav., died August 22, '63.
111. St. Clair, J., died February, '64.
371. St. John, Abner, Co. D, 18th Tenn. Inf., died October 28, '64.
1068. Staff (or Stapp), J. W., Co. I, 7th Ala. Cav., died February 5, '65.
1982. Stafford, Louis, Co. H, 1st N. C. Detailed, died May 18, '65.
451. Stafford, S. J., Co. F, 8th Va. Cav., died November 11, '64.
632. Stafford, W. B., Co. F, 8th Va. Cav., died December 19, '64.
1306. Stakes, W. W., Co. E, 58th Ala. Inf., died February 17, '65.
1797. Stalwker, R. P. W., Co. A, 46th Ala. Inf., died March 27, '65.
177. Stamper, Joel, Co. I, 2d Ky. Cav., died June 12, '64.
153. Stanton, W. H., Co. D, 35th Ala. Inf., died May 12, '64.
1639. Staub, Mike, Co. F, 13th La. Inf., died March 13, '65.
80. Stead, J. D., White's Va. Bat., died December 11, '63.
1793. Steal (or Stiles), R. W., Co. K, 44th Miss. Inf., died March 31, '65.
2008. Stearnes, W. W., Co. I, 23d Ala. Inf., died May 31, '65.
1791. Steel, Joseph B., Co. K, 33d Miss. Inf., died March 31, '65.
1527. Steel, J., Co. A, Tenn. Reserve Troops, died March 3, '65.
——. Stenett, Summerson, Co. A, 40th Miss. ——, died March 24, '65.
884. Stephen, Cyrus, 39th N. C. Inf., died January 25, '64.
1818. Stephens, Casal, Co. I, 22d Miss. Inf., died April 3, '65.
1624. Stephens, I. H., Co. E, 1st Conf. Cav., died March 11, '65.
1156. Stephens, J., Co. H, 33d Ala. Inf., died February 9, '65.

No. of Gra e.
1042. Stephens, J. D., Co. H, 17th Va. Cav., died February 4, '65.
740. Stephens, Marsback, Co. I, 4th Tenn. Cav., died January 9, '65.
512. Stephens, T. J., Co. B, 16th La. Inf., died Nov. 24, '64. Removed.
1453. Stephens, William, Co. B, 38th Ala. Inf., died February 26, '65.
442. Sternes, Thomas W., Co. D, 2d Ark. Inf., died November 9, '64.
1872. Steward, Hazell, Co. I, 40th Miss. Cav., died April 15, '65.
1862. Steward, William W., Co. F, 36th Miss. Cav., died April 14, '65.
1283. Stewart, B. F., Co. H, 46th Ala. Inf., died February 15, '65.
1056. Stewart, Charles, W., Co. F, 25th Ga. Inf., died February 5, '65.
433. Stewart, Douglas, Co. E, 24th Ala. Inf., died November 8, '64.
1248. Stewart, G. C., Co. I, 35th Ala. Inf., died February 14, '65.
1339. Stewart, J., Co. D, 29th Tenn. Inf., died February 19, '65.
37. Stewart, Robert, Co. E, 19th Va. Cav., died October 5, '63.
268. Stewart, S., Co. C, 24th Va. Cav., died September 24, '64.
197. Stickler, A. M., Co. F, 26th Va. Inf., died August 9, '64.
1545. Stickney, J. E., Co. E, 19th S. C. Inf., died March 4, '65.
1600. Stiles, T., Co. A, 13th Ky. Cav., died March 8, '65.
42. Stinnett, S. A., Co. I, 2d Ky., died October 8, '63.
283. Stizer, E. A., died October 6, '64.
900. Stoggsdale, Thomas, Co. I, 55th Ala. Inf., died January 26, '64.
1117. Stokely, W. G., Co. E, 1st Fla. Cav., died February 8, '65.
745. Stone, B. F., Co. H, 35th Miss. Inf., died January 11, '65.
1937. Stone, James R., Wheeler's Scouts, died May 4, '65.
136. Stone, P. T., 9th Ky. Cav., died April 13, '64.
452. Stone, William T., Co. C, 12th Tenn. Inf., died November 12, '64.
1389. Stovell, A. J., Co. H, 5th Conf. Inf., died February 22, '65.
——. Stratton, ——, — Ark. ——, died June, '65.
890. Strawl, J. B., Co. C, 41st Tenn. Inf., died January 26, '64.
1740. Strickland, C., Co. A, 29th Ga. Inf., died March 23, '65.
1228. Strikland, J., Co. B, 1st Ga. Inf., died February 14, '65.
1475. Strother, G. M., Co. K, 46th Ala. Inf., died February 27, '65.
276. Studer, J. B., Co. A, 43d Ga. Inf., died October 2, '64.
1886. Sturdevant, Thomas F., Co. A, 31st N. C. Inf., died April 17, '65.
1408. Suddeth, I. L., Co. F, 54th Ala. Inf., died February 23, '65.
1030. Suggs, D. W., Co. C, 6th Tenn. Inf., died February 3, '65.
797. Sullivan, Dennis, Co. D, 5th Conf. Cav., died January 18, '64.
805. Sullivan, George, Co. L, 4th Tenn. Cav., died January 19, '64.
816. Summerall, John, Co. C, 7th Bat. Miss. Inf., died January 20, '64.
789. Summers, Robert, Co. H, 46th Ala. Inf., died January 16, '65.
1991. Summersett, John W., Co. H, 18th Ala. Inf., died May 21, '65.
1601. Suppington, D., Co. K, 14th Miss. Cav., died March 9, '65.
2033. Sutlora, A. B., Co. A, 22d Miss. Inf., died June 8, '65.
989. Sutton, James C., Co. K, 12th Ark. Inf., died February 1, '65.
1131. Sweley, John M., Nitre Mining Bureau, died February 9, '65.
1997. Swope, Henry, Co. D, 27th Va. Inf., died May 25, '65.
1260. Sykes, A. C., Co. C, 30th Miss. Inf., died February 15, '65.
1622. Sylvester, Serg. W. M., 6th Fla. Inf., died March 11, '65.

No. of Grave.

538. Syree, John S., Co. D, 34th Miss. Detailed, died December 1, '64.

1025. Tabor, I., Co. F, 14th Va. Cav., died February 3, '65.

729. Taggart, E. H., Co. G, 29th Ga. Inf., died January 9, '65.

902. Talbot, I. F., Co. G, 19th S. C. Inf., died January 27, '65.

1089. Talbot, John W., Co. E, 34th Ga. Inf., died February 7, '65.

252. Talliman, H. F., Co. C, 45th Va. Inf., died August 24, '64.

501. Tally, Jonas, Co. B, — N. C. Inf., died November 21, '64.

149. Talton, T. E., Co. F, 36th Ga. Inf., died May 8, 6'4.

6. Tanilin, H., 2d —— Cav., died August 15, '63.

1943. Tappley, J. P., Co. I, 39th Miss. Inf., died May 8, '65.

1901. Tarrb, Robert M., Co. H, 7th Ala. Cav., died April 22, '65.

1522. Tate, J., Co. D, 11th Tenn. Cav., died March 3, '65.

498. Taylor, Daniel S., Co. G, 17th Va. Cav., died November 21, '64.

1125. Taylor, J. B., Co. B, 14th Va. Cav., died February 5, '65.

1308. Taylor, J. M., Co. F, 1st Conf. Ga. Inf., died February 17, '65.

1200. Taylor, J. W., Co. C, 25th Ga. Inf., died February 12, '65.

854. Taylor, James A., Co. D, 35th Miss. Inf., died January 23, '65.

408. Taylor, James J., Co. B, 12th Tenn. Cav., died November 5, '64.

133. Taylor, John, Co. I, 1st La. Cav., died January 15, '64.

214. Taylor, K., Co. A, 33d Tenn. Inf., died August 4, '64.

1888. Taylor, Robert R., Co. B, 4th Ala. Cav., died April 19, '65.

161. Taylor, W., Co. G, 31st Tenn. Inf., died May 15, '64.

218. Taylor, W. I., Co. K, 22d Va. Inf., died August 23, '64.

1064. Taylor, W. L., Co. E, 36th Ala. Inf., died February 6, '65.

1386. Tell, G. W., Co. B, 46th Ala. Inf., died February 22, '65.

1470. Templeton, J. N., Co. E, 35th Miss. Inf., died February 27, '65.

634. Templeton, W. N., Co. A, 5th N. C. Bat., died December 19, '64.

979. Tennison, W. H., Stuart's Escort, died January 30, '65.

1729. Terry, Thomas, Co. F, 17th Ala. Inf., died March 21, '65.

730. Terry, W. T., Co. B, 24th S. C. Inf., died January 9, '65.

157. Tevalt, P. W., Co. H, 11th Va. Cav., died May 6, '64.

1833. Thacker, Martin J., Co. F, 28th Tenn. Inf., died April 8, '65.

784. Thede, James J., Co. F, 34th Ala. Inf., died January 16, '65.

261. Thigpen, J., Co. I, 20th Ala. Inf., died September 18, '64.

960. Thomas, J. N., Co. M, 8th S. S. Inf., died January 29, '65.

332. Thomas, James G., Co. B, 5th Ala. Cav., died September 9, '64.

731. Thomas, S. M., Co. E, 29th Ga. Inf., died January 9, '65.

1105. Thomas, William S., Enrolling Officer, died February 8, '65.

722. Thompkins, A., 37th Va. Cav., died January 8, '65.

2021. Thompson, B. N. (or N. N.), Co. F, 41st Miss. Inf., died June 3, '65.

851. Thompson, Charles R., Co. E, 1st Md. Cav., died January 23, '65.

1326. Thompson, G., Co. C, 27th Bat. Cav., died February 17, '65.

1118. Thompson, I. J., Co. I, 14th Tenn. Cav., died February 8, '65.

584. Thompson, J. D., Co. H, 28th Ala. Inf., died December 9, '64.

1410. Thompson, J. H., Co. G, 66th Ga. Inf., died February 25, '65.

253. Thompson, N. S., Co. K, 7th Fla. Inf., died September 17, '64.

541. Thompson, O. D., Co. H, — Conf. Cav., died December 1, '64.

No. of Grave.

1362. Thompson, P., Co. E, 8th Va. Cav., died February 21, '65.
908. Thompson, Simeon, Co. B, 18th Ala. Inf., died January 27, '65.
1584. Thompson, W. J., Co. B, 3d Conf. Cav., died March 7, '65.
853. Thomson, G. W., Co. E, 40th Ga. Inf., died January 23, '65.
1421. Thorn, E. B., Co. K, 25th Ga. Inf., died February 24, '65.
———. Thorn, P. H., Co. D, 6th Miss. Inf., died March 14, '65.
1267. Thornhill, William, Co. C, 23d Ala. Inf., died February 15, '65.
1762. Thornton, F. D., Co. I, 10th Miss. Inf., died March 27, '65.
277. Thornton, J. W., Co. G, 1st Tenn. Cav., died September 23, '64.
829. Tice, Fleming, Co. G, 21st Va. Cav., died January 21, '65.
516. Tille, George, Co. D, 24th Tex. Inf., died November 26, '64
609. Tincher, Albert, Co. B, 21st Va. Cav., died December 12, '64.
1335. Tipton, R., Co. K, 4th Ala. Cav., died February 18, '65.
1983. Tobias, B. R., Co. B, 37th Ala. Inf., died May 18, '65.
1922. Tolan, James H., Co. C, 49th Tenn. Inf., died April 27, '65.
1076. Tolson, George W., Co. K, 1st Ga. Inf., died February 6, '65.
204. Tolton, W. M., Co. F, 16th Va. Cav., died May 21, '64.
909. Tomley, G. H., Co. K, 28th Tenn. Inf., died January 27, '65.
1681. Tomlin, Wesley, Co. B, 10th Ala. Cav., died March 16, '65.
1701. Tomlinson, W. B., Co. A, 17th Ala. Inf., died March 18, '65.
881. Tousley, I., Co. I, 3d Conf. Cav., died January 25, '65.
1146. Townsend, J. R., Co. I, 15th Miss. Inf., died February 9, '65.
96. Tracy, Peter, citizen of Virginia, died August 15, '63.
697. Trainum, J. F., Co. C, 17th Ala. Inf., died January 3, '65.
267. Trapp, John C., Co. G, 1st Ga. Inf., died September 20, '64.
236. Tricket, Michael E., Co. A, 20th Va. Cav., died October 2, '64.
1006. Triplet, J. J., Co. H, 19th Tenn. Inf., died February 2, '65.
1115. Tripp, S. I., Co. K, 3d N. C. Cav., died February 8, '65.
292. Trotten, J. W. B., Co. E, 5th Va. Cav., died September 10, '64.
1029. Trusley, J., Co. B, 19th Tenn. Inf., died February 3, '65.
897. Tucker, J. L., Co. C, 23d Ala. Inf., died January 23, '65.
162. Tunstill, W., Co. D, 7th Ala. Cav., died May 20, '64.
1323. Turnage, W. J., Co. G, 16th La. Inf., died February 18, '65.
1743. Turner, Benjamin, Co. D, 7th Fla. Inf., died March 24, '65.
1696. Turner, George, Co. E, 40th Miss. Inf., died March 18, '65.
764. Turner, I. D., Co. F, 19th S. C. Inf., died January 14, '65.
476. Turner, M. L., Co. F, 14th Tenn. Cav., died November 16, '64.
1735. Turner, S. P., Co. B, 13th Ky. Cav., died March 22, '65.
1941. Turner, William, Co. A, 28th Bat. N. C. H. G., died May 7, '65.
1338. Tylar, Pleasant, Co. H, 4th Ala. Cav., died February 19, '65.
1047. Tyler, J. S., Co. I, 47th Tenn. Inf., died February 4, '65.
1354. Tyson, C., Co. G, 41st Ga. Inf., died February 20, '65.
303. Umphrey, John, Co. F, 40th Ga. Inf., died October 12, '64.
1927. Underwood, W. J., Co. A, 10th Ala. Cav., died April 29, '65.
46. Unknown soldier, — Conf. ———, died October 11, '63.
19. Upchurch, Calvin, Co. G, 5th N. C. Cav., died September 4, '63.
1010. Upchurch, John, Co. I, 39th Miss. Inf., died January 5, '65.

No. of Grave.

1946. Upright, John, N. C. State Reserves, died May 9, '65.

749. Valentine, Joseph C., Co. H, 46th Miss. Inf., died January 11, '65.

987. Vance, David E, Co. B, 8th Tenn. Cav., died January 27, '65.

1461. Vandike, C. E., Co. H, 21st Tenn. Cav., died February 27, '65.

1779. Vanhoosar, L., died March 20, '65.

1385. Vansant, W., Co. B, 23d Va. Cav., died February 22, '65.

1698. Vaugh, R., Co. B, 10th Ky. Cav., died March 18, '65.

701. Vaughan, B., Co. B, 1st Ga. Inf., died January 3, '65.

1106. Vaughan, I. M., Co. K, 25th Va. Cav., died February 8, '65.

1887. Vaughn, Ambers, Co. E, 10th Ala. Cav., died April 17, '65.

1523. Vaughn, J. A., Co. E, 16th S. C. Inf., died March 3, '65.

747. Venable, W. T., Co. E, 55th Ala. Inf., died January 10, '65.

810. Vesey, E. F., Co. K, 5th Miss. Inf., died January 19, '65.

28. Vetulol, A. G., Co. G, 1st Tenn. Cav., died September 24, '63.

1208. Vick, Charles, Co. G, 27th Ala. Inf., died February 12, '65.

1377. Vickers, S., Co. H, 20th Miss. Inf., died February 22, '65.

1489. Victory, L., Co. E, 12th Ga. Inf., died February 28, '65.

64. Vincent, Osmon, 3d Conf. Cav., died November 15, '63.

1051. Vining, J. C., Co. C, 16th Ga. Cav., died February 5, '65.

743. Vowell, Joseph H., Co. C, 1st Ark. Inf., died January 11, '65.

1691. Wade, Solomon, Co. C, —— Battery, died March 17, '65.

1254. Wade, W. F., Co. I, 1st Mo. Cav., died February 14, '65.

647. Wagoner, Henry, Co. H, 54th N. C. Inf., died December 22, '64.

207. Wain, M., Co. A, 19th Va. Cav., died August 16, '64.

91. Wait, George, Co. K, 24th Tenn. Inf., died January 12, '64.

1717. Walch, John, Co. H, 6th Fla. Inf., died March 20, '65.

1459. Wald, J., Co. E, 13th Ky. Cav., died February 27, '65.

1417. Waldon, J., Co. E, 13th Ky. Cav., died February 24, '65.

1262. Walker, B. F., Co. D, 1st Ga. Inf., died February 16, '65.

1885. Walker, D. O., Co. I, 8th Tenn. Inf., died April 17, '65.

227. Walker, J. H., Co. C, 23d Tenn. Inf., died September 2, '64.

765. Walker, J. P., Co. I, 14th Tenn. Cav., died January 14, '65.

1642. Walker, John, citizen of Alabama, died March 13, '65.

379. Walker, Levi, Co. D, 60th Va. Inf., died October 29, '64.

1781. Walker, O. P., Co. K, 2d Ky Cav., died March 29, '65.

793. Walker, Stanley, Co. D, 8th Ky. Cav., died January 17, '65.

1534. Walker, T. J., Co. K, 13th Miss. Inf., died March 4, '65.

321. Walker, W., Co. F, 36th Va. Inf., died October, '64.

1363. Walker, W. M., Co. E, 1st Miss. Inf., died February 21, '65.

113. Walket, Capt., Co. E, 4th Tenn. Cav., died February 6, '64.

1834. Wallace, R. H., Co. C, 32d Miss. Inf., died April 9, '65.

150. Wallkall, J. N., Co. E, 25th Ark. Inf., died May 6, '64.

181. Walls, J. P., Co. C, 12th Tenn. Cav., died June 29, '64.

1974. Walstonhome, Thomas S., Co. B, 43d Miss. Inf., died May 16, '65.

1928. Ward, A. E., citizen of East Tennessee, died May 1, '65.

1134. Ward, W. W., Co. D, 12th La. Inf., died February 9, '65.

607. Warden, Wilson, Co. C, 36th Va. Inf., died December 12, '64.

No. of Grave.

484. Ware, G. W., Co. C, 23d Va. Cav., died November 18, '64.
773. Warfield, W., Co. A, 1st Md. Cav., died January 14, '65.
212. Warren, J. W., conscript of N. C., died August 20, '64.
571. Warren, James H., Co. D, 18th Tenn. Inf., died December 7, '64.
618. Warren, William J., Co. F, 47th Tenn. Inf., died December 15, '64.
1358. Warrick, I. H., Co. K, 46th Ala. Inf., died February 20, '65.
340. Waruble, Henry, Co. A, 56th Ga. Inf., died October 19, '64.
1278. Washburn, S., Co. D, 11th Ky. Cav., died February 15, '65.
2015. Waters, E. F., Co. D, 46th Ga. Inf., died June 2, '65.
814. Watkins, O. R., Co. C, 37th Tenn. Inf., died January 20, '65.
254. Watson, A. M., Co. K, 29th N. C. Inf., died September 18, '64.
33. Watson, J. A., citizen of Virginia, died October 4, '63.
626. Watson, J. M., Co. E, 1st Ga. Inf., died December 17, '64.
534. Watson, Thomas, Co. G, 1st Tenn. Cav., died November 29, 64.
86. Watts, J. A., Co. A, 10th Ky. Inf., died December 19, '63.
364. Waul, W. F., Co. B, 4th Ala. Cav., died October 26, '64.
1942. Waydell, Addison, Co. I, 25th Va. Cav., died May 7, '65.
644. Weaver, David, Co. A, 43d Ga. Inf., died December 21, '64.
755. Weaver, J. W., died January, '65.
1958. Weaver, John B., Co. E, 54th Ga. Cav., died May 12, '65.
1932. Webb, John J., Co. I, 13th Va. Inf., died May 2, '65.
266. Weese, A., citizen of Virginia, died September 23, '64.
386. Weese, Isaac, Co. C, 1st Ga. Inf., died October 31, '64.
1745. Weldon, D. C., Co. D, 20th Ala. Inf., died March 24, '65.
709. Wells, Columbus, 42d Ala. Inf., died January 5, '65.
114. Wells, J., died February 6, '64.
1158. Wesley, J. W., Co. K, 2d Mo. Inf., died February 10, '65.
1243. Wesson, L. L., Co. I, 35th Ala. Inf., died February 14, '65.
993. West, C. S., Co. I, 18th Miss. Inf., died February 1, '65.
1559. West, J. H., Co. B, 30th Tenn. Inf., died March 5, '65.
541. West, W. O., Co. E, 20th Va. Cav., died December 1, '64.
1666. Whaley, A., Co. I, 17th Ala. Inf., died March 15, '65.
156. Whatley, A. C., Co. D, 3d Ga. Cav., died May 13, '64.
1866. Wheeler, A. J., Co. I, 10th Tex. Inf., died April, '65.
410. Wheeler, J. S, Co. A, conscript from Tenn., died November 6, '64.
298. Wheetley, George, Co. D, 15th Miss. Inf., died October 11, '64.
15. Whetmore, H., Co. K, 4th Ala. Cav., died September 27, '63.
117. Whettle, A., citizen of Virginia, died February 6, '64.
2025. Whidden, Bennett, Co. B, 6th Fla. Inf., died June 4, '65.
1181. White, B. W., Co. H, 3d Tex. Inf., died February 11, '65.
1304. White, H., Co. I, 1st Fla. Cav., died February 16, '65.
1153. White, J. M., Co. B, 7th Fla. Inf., died February 11, '65.
1853. White, L. N., Co. K, 39th Ga. Inf., died April 11, '65.
1464. White, Leonidas, Co. F, 16th Ala. Inf., died February 27, '65.
395. Whitefield, Charles, Co. E, 18th Tex. Cav., died November 3, '64.
1906. Whitfield, B. I., Co. A, 13th Ky. Cav., died April 23, '65.
1828. Whitfield, J. S. M., Co. A, 13th Ky. Cav., died April 7, '65.

No. of Grave.

1027. Whitfield, W., Co. D, 44th Tenn. Inf., died February 3, '65.
1482. Widham, B. F., Co. E, 38th Ala. Inf., died February 28, '65.
1995. Widham, S. W., Co. F, 23d Miss. Inf., died May 22, '65.
1632. Widner, Elijah, Co. A, 21st Va. Cav., died March 12, '65.
1294. Wiggins, E. H., Co. L, 11th Ala. Cav., died February 16, '65.
555. Wiggins, R. L., Co. F, 36th Ala. Inf., died December 5, '64.
294. Wilbourn, John F., Co. F, 22d Va. Cav., died October 10, '64.
173. Wilcox, S. B., Co. E, 1st Ky. Cav., died June 3, '64.
314. Wilder, W., Co. K, 4th Fla. Inf., died October 15, '64.
1805. Wildman, W., Co. G, 55th Ala. Inf., died April 2, '65.
2002. Wilfong, C. S., Co. E, 3d N. C. Inf., died May 26, '65.
633. Wilkes, John W., Co. F, 8th S. C. Inf., died December 19, '64.
1150. Wilkinson, J. B., 57th Ala. Inf., died February 9, '65.
1986. Willard, John, Co. H, 23d Bat. Va. Inf., died May 19, '65.
1565. Willcox, J. P., Co. A, 49th Tenn. Inf., died March 5, '65.
1528. Willet, William, Co. D, 18th Ala. Inf., died March 3, '65.
1979. William, George F., Co. E, 63d Ala. Inf., died May 17, '65
246. Williams, A. P., Co. H, 15th Tenn. Cav., died September 16, '64.
1495. Williams, A. S., Co. I, 59th Tenn. Inf., died March 1, '65.
1547. Williams, B. F., conscript of Kentucky, died March 5, '65.
1227. Williams, B. T., Co. I, 15th Tenn. Cav., died February 14, '65.
1382. Williams, E. F., Co. D, 5th Ga. Cav., died February 22, '65.
164. Williams, E. J., Co. K, 36th Ga. Inf., died May 22, '64.
1846. Williams, E. M., Co. I, 10th Ky. Inf., died April 9, '65.
1952. Williams, G. A., Co. C, 5th Miss. Cav., died May 10, '65.
1007. Williams, G. W., Co. B, 1st Mo. Cav., died February 2, '65.
1673. Williams, J., Co. F, 19th Va. Cav., died March 15, '65.
1425. Williams, J. B., Dardon's Bat., died February 25, '65.
1907. Williams, John B., Co. B, 56th Tenn. Inf., died April 23, '65.
366. Williams, John D., Co. D, 42d Ala. Inf., died October 25, '64.
1269. Williams, Luke B., Co. C, 1st Bat. S. S. Troops, died Feb. 15, '65.
1892. Williams, Nelson, Co. F, 65th Ga. Inf., died April 17, '65.
1609. Williams, O., Co. F, 20th Ala. Inf., died March 9, '65.
1396. Williams, R. J., Co. C, 2d Ala. Cav., died February 23, '65.
338. Williams, Serg. W. L., Co. D, 16th Tenn. Cav., died October 18, '64.
495. Williams, Samuel, Co. A, 23d Va. Cav., died November 20, '64.
1259. Williams, W. H., Co. F, 6th Mo. Inf., died February 15, '65.
7. Williamson, I., Co. I, 8th Ky. Cav., died August 17, '63.
132. Willis, Rice, 1st Ky. Cav., died '65.
1998. Willis, J. L., Co. I, 31st Ala. Inf., died May 25, '65.
836. Willoughby, Andrew, Co. A, 54th Ala. Inf., died January 22, '65.
604. Wilson, A., Co. F, 42d Ala. Inf., died December 12, '64.
1384. Wilson, G. W., Co. G, 33d Ala. Inf., died February 22, '65.
628 Wilson, George, Co. E, Gilmore's Bat., died December 18, '64.
1451. Wilson, I. F., Co. A, 40th Ala. Inf., died February 26, '65.
920. Wilson, J. C., Co. C, 24th S. C. Inf., died January 28, '65.
1719. Wilson, Jackson, Co. B, 13th Ky. Cav., died March 23, 65.

388   THE STORY OF CAMP CHASE.

757. Wilson, John A., Co. A, Lewis's Ala. Bat., died January 5, '65.
833. Wilson, Joseph R., Co. E, 1st Fla. Inf., died January 21, '65.
1454 (or 1434). Wilson, L. M., Co. B, 24th Tenn. Inf., died Feb. 26, '65.
759. Wilson, Owen, Co. K, 7th Ala. Cav., died January 17, '65. Erased.
795. Wilson, Owen, Co. K, 7th Ala. Inf., died March 17, '65.
997. Wilson, P. P., Co. A, 66th Ga. Inf., died February 17, '65.
104. Wilson, S., Co. B, 8th Va. Cav., died February 6, '64.
323. Wilz, Samuel P., Co. I, 5th Conf. ——, died October, '64.
533. Windson, James M., Co. H, 18th Ga. Inf., died December 4, '64.
1137. Wines, Hayton, Co. C, 19th Va. Cav., died February 9, '65.
983. Wines, Jackson A., Co. C, 19th Va. Cav., died January 30, '65.
1172. Winfield, William, Co. A, 37th Bat. Va. Cav., died February 10, '65.
257. Wingond, J. B., Co. H, 63d Ga. Inf., died September 20, '64.
1858. Winnet, A. I., Co. I, 4th Tenn. Cav., died April 13, '65.
142. Winstud, Ellis G., Co. E, 4th Ark. Inf., died April 22, '64.
543. Wirt, Henry, Co. C, 34th Va. Inf., died December 2, '64.
930. Wisdom, J. W., Co. B, 11th Tex. Cav., died January 28, '65.
573. Wisecarver, W. H., Co. H, 11th Va. Cav., died December 8, '64.
927. Wiseman, S. C., Co. A, 29th Ga. Inf., died January 28, '65.
473. Wissing, Henry, Co. G, —— Ga. Inf., died November 16, '64.
184. Wolfe, J. N., Co. C, citizen of Virginia, died July 11, '64.
1203. Wood, Jonathan, Co. B, 4th Ala. Cav., died February 12, '65.
1616. Wood, N. D., Co. H, 10th Ala. Cav., died March 11, '65.
1282. Woodall, J. A., Co. K, 4th Ala. Cav., died February 15, '65.
1919. Woodall, William A., Co. A, 29th Ala. Inf., died April 26, '65.
'1738. Woodrad, T. A., Co. E, 10th Ky. Cav., died March 23, '65.
1250. Woodruff, B. H., Co. G, 6th Ga. State Troops died February 14, '65.
-214. Woodruff, Greene, Co. E, 46th Miss. Inf., died February 12, '65.
483. Woodrum, John, Co. I, 6th Ga.' Cav., died November 18, '64.
138. Woodrum, R., 22d Va. Bat., died April 15, '64.
438. Woods, R., 36th Miss. Inf., died November 9, '64.
567. Woods, W. A., Co. A, 37th Va. Cav., died December 7, '64.
662. Woodson, T., Co. A, 9th Tex. Cav., died December 25, '64.
1631. Woodward, B. E., Co. A, 13th Ky. Cav., died March 12, '65.
36. Woodward, ——, died October 3, '63.
35. Woodward, Thomas, 10th Ky. Cav., died October 4, '63.
871. Woville, J. C. (or Wm.), Co. B, 43d Miss. Inf., died January 25, '05.
1981. Wright, G. Y. M., Co. H, 4th Ala. Cav., died May 17, '65.
450. Wright, Uriah, Co. G, Baltimore Art., died November 11, '64.
63. Wright, W. B., Co. C, 6th Cav., died December 24, '63.
1229. Wyatt, J. H., Co. I, 52d Tenn. Inf., died February 14, '65.
380. Yancey, William, Co. H, 1st Ark. Cav., died October 29, '64.
860. Yarborough, Haz, Co. G, 16th Ga. Cav., died January 23, '65.
1783. Yarbrough, A. I., Co. I, 4th La. Inf., died March 30, '65.
1594. Yargin, W. F., Co. E, 34th Ga. Inf., died March 8, '65.
158. Yeager, J. E., Co. K, 7th Ala. Cav., died May 17, '64.
1956. Yeates, Green J., Co. I, 1st Ala. Inf., died May 11, '65.

No. of Grave.
1310. Yerby, W., Woodward's Ala. Cav., died February 17, '65
1522. Yete, J., Co. B, 11th Tenn. Cav., died March 3, '65.
462. Yonan, J., Co. K, 1st Fla. Inf., died November 14, '64.
1567. York, E. A., Co. K, 26th Tenn. Inf., died March 6, '65.
642. Yost, E. L., Co. F, 22d Va. Cav., died November 21, '64.
1318. Yother, T. J., Co. E, 65th Ga. Inf., died February 17, '65.
1678. Youst, Francis, Co. B, 20th Va. Cav., died March 16, '65.
423. Young, Peter, Co. G, 37th Va. Cav., died November 7, '64.
1918. Young, W. H., Co. B, 5th Miss. Cav., died April 28, '65.
1521. Young, William A., Co. K, 46th Miss. Inf., died April 6, '65.

CONFEDERATE DEAD BURIED AT CAMP CHASE.

Aggregate of Confederate dead buried at Camp Chase Cemetery
from the following States: Alabama, 419; Arkansas, 23; Florida,
63; Georgia, 301; Kentucky, 130; Louisiana, 45; Mississippi, 202;
Missouri, 8; Maryland, 12; North Carolina, 86; South Carolina,
69; Tennessee, 213; Texas, 18; Virginia, 267.................... 1,856
Burial of citizens from the following States: Virginia, 37; West
Virginia, 11; Alabama, 4; Georgia, 5; Ohio, 1; Louisiana, 2; Tennessee, 9; Kentucky, 8; South Carolina, 1....................... 78
Burials from different organizations, State not given............... 101
                                                              _____
                                                              2,035
Buried in early part of the war in city cemetery, southeast of Colum-
bus, from the following States: Kentucky, 16; Virginia, 22; Ten-
nessee, 7; Alabama, 3; Texas, 8; South Carolina, 1; Arkansas, 3;
Louisiana, 5; Mississippi, 2; Florida, 1; and marked as citizens
from Virginia, 14; West Virginia, 4; Kentucky, 4; Tennessee, 1;
from commands, States not given, 8............................. 99
Removed by their kindred and taken South...................... 31
                                                              _____
Remainder removed and buried at Camp Chase.................... 68

Buried at Camp Dennison, about twenty-five miles from Cincinnati,
Ohio 116
Removed by kindred and taken South........................... 85
                                                              _____
Remainder taken to Camp Chase and reburied, from the following
States: Alabama, 8; Tennessee, 1; Texas, 5; Arkansas, 2; Louisi-
ana, 11; Mississippi, 4.. 31

Total number now buried at Camp Chase....................... 2,134
Removed from Camp Chase at close of war..................... . 126
                                                              _____
Making total buried at Camp Chase............................ 2,260

CAMP DENNISON CEMETERY.

CONFEDERATE DEAD BURIED AT CAMP DENNISON, OHIO.

No. of Grave.

4. Baldwin, ——, unknown.
72. Bergman, A., Co. C, Texas Rangers, died May 9, '62.
25. Caraway, 1st Lt. James, 11th La., died April 27, '62.
5. Carter, 1st Lt. P. S., Co. I, 3d Miss., died April 20, '62.
49. Cohoon, 1st Lt. J. H., Co. N, Orleans Guard, died May 1, '62.
110. Copland, 1st Lt. Wm., Co. B, 21st Ala., died May 26, '62.
115. Field, E. R., Co. C, 18th La., died June 11, '62.
20. Galier (N. T.), 1st Lt. H. J., 18th La., died April 23, '62.
15. Henry, James H., Co. F, 1st Ark., died April 23, '62.
53. Hubbard, Serg. Maj. T. H., 8th Ark., died May 3, '62.
114. Jaco, Jeremiah, Co. B, 5th Tex., died June 18, '62.
74. James, C. E., Co. C, Texas Rangers, died May 10, '62.
17. Johnson, 1st Lt. Edw., Co. H, 20th La., died April 29, '62.
105. Jones, 1st Lt. A. B., Co. A, 17th La., died May 21, '62.
6. Lampie (or Sample), Serg. Maj. B., 2d Tex. Rangers, died April 21, '62.
48. Larey, 1st Lt. S. C. P., Co. G, 9th Miss., died May 1, '62.
1. Martin, Henry, Co. F., 17th Ala., died May 17, '62.
116. McClellan, J. R., Co. C, 55th Tenn., died June 17, '62.
13. McNair, D., Co. D, 17th Ala.
111. Mims, David L., Co. D, 15th Miss., died May 31, '62.
27. Mirley (or Worley), W. H., Co. F, 17th Ala., died April 27, '62.
58. O'Brian, 1st Lt. Jerry, Co. N, 1st La., died May 5, '62.
46. Pevy, 1st Lt. Allen, 16th La., died April 30, '62.
41. Robinson, 1st Lt. A., Co. F, 17th Ala., died April 29, '62.
99. Rogarmore, 1st Lt. T. M., Co. G, 17th La., died May 17, '62.
7. Senley (or Sealey), E. G., 2d Tex. Rangers, died May 21, '62.
104. Spaulding, 1st Lt. Felix, Co. E, 17th Ala., died May 19, '62.
76. Sylvester, 1st Lt. Wm., Co. D, 16th La., died May 9, '62.
37. Tighlman, William, Co. I, 21st Ala., died April 27, '62.
60. Tippits, 1st Lt. John M., Co. E, 17th La., died May 5, '62.
87. Turney, 1st Lt. J. R., Co. K, 2d Miss., died May 11, '62.

COLUMBUS, OHIO.

CONFEDERATE DEAD BURIED IN THE CITY CEMETERY, SOUTHEAST OF COLUMBUS, OHIO.

82. Albert, Joseph, Co. B, 6th Fla. ——, died March 1, '63.
74. Allen, Lieut. E. R., 1st Tex. Inf., died Feb. 11, '63.
12. Allen, 2d Lt. John F., 1st Ala. Inf., died May 24, '62.
8. Ausbourne, 1st Lt. W. C., Ark. Heavy Art., died May 15, '62.
124. Barnes, Math., citizen of W. Va., died June 23, '63.
115. Barnes, Thomas J., citizen of Virginia, died June 13, '63.
42. Basham, A., 45th Va., Peterstown, died Oct. 5, '62. Rifled.

18. Bean, J. G., 14th Va. Inf., died July 7, '62.
5. Black, Lieut. Leonidas, 3d Tenn. Inf., died April 24, '62.
84. Briden, Lieut. D. F., 24th Tex. Cav., died March 5, '63.
    (Taken by mistake and removed to Glover's Gap, Marion Co., Va.)
73. Candy, James, Hampshire Co., Va., died Feb. 9, '63.
23. Caylor, T. J., Hampshire Co., Va., died July 28, '62.
88. Cheatham, Marcellus, prisoner of war, died May 13, '63.
1. Chields, Lieut. J. M., 3d Miss. Vols., died April 6, '62.
96. Clark, John, Co. C, 3d Va. Cav., died April 6, '63.
45. Clarke, Stephen, Randolph Co. prisoner, died Oct. 14, '62.
116. Collins, Edwin, Co. B, 51st —— Inf., died June 16, '63.
51. Cooper, G. F., prisoner Taylor Co., Va., died Nov. 5, '62.
16. Cummins, John C., Harrison Co., Ky., died June 4, '62. Removed.
118. Duninitz, William, citizen of Ky., died June 16, '63.
77. Ellis, Taylor, Co. B, 1st W. Tenn. Reg., died Feb. 16, '63.
54. Falkington, Geo. W., Marion Co., Va., died Nov. 23, '62.
46. Ferguson, T. B., Simpson Co., Ky., died Oct. 14, '62.
49. Fetterl, Benjamin, 3d Va. Cav., died Oct. 31, '62.
29. Flint, Joseph, Co. I, Adger's Vol. Bat., died Sept. 16, '62.
129. Ford, M., citizen of Virginia, died July 11, '63.
53. Fuller, William, citizen of Kentucky, died Nov. 14, '62.
121. Gelford, Thomas, citizen of W. Va., died June 19, '63.
55. Gellin, William, died November 24, '62.
17. Graves, S. W., 9th La. Inf., died June 13, '62.
64. Halliburton, John A., prisoner of war, died Jan. 31, '63.
126. Hamilton, John, 5th Ky. Inf., died June 30, '63.
131. Hanna, Nathan H., citizen of Virginia, died July 16, '63
133. Hays, Corp. Lawson, prisoner, died July 20, '63.
80. Henry, Lieut. L. F., 19th Ark. Inf., died Feb. 26, '63.
22. Hill, G. W., citizen of Monroe Co., Va., died July 28, '62.
50. Jones, William, citizen of Va., died November 2, '62.
128. Jordon, Daniel, citizen of Virginia, died July 2, '63.
72. Kennedy, John, 23d Ky. Vols., died Feb. 8, '63.
57. Ketterman, Abraham, Hardy Co., Va., died Dec. 15, '62.
111. Kieser, William, prisoner of war, died May 28, '63.
34. Lake, Jacob, Co. G, 90th Tenn. Inf., died Sept. 24, '62.
130. Lawler, J. F., 8th Con. Cav., died July 15, '63.
108. Leslie, J. U., Co. D, 65th Va. Inf., died May 3, '63
19. Lilley, James, citizen of Mercer Co., Va., died July 12, '62.
67. Lindsey, Capt. J. S., 4th Tenn. Cav., died Feb. 6, '63.
132. Lindsey, William, Co. G, 36th Ala. Inf., died July 18, '63.
60. Lykins, James, Co. A., 12th Ky. Cav., died Jan. 9, '63.
98. Lynch, W. H., Co. H, 1st S. C. Cav., died April 7, '63.
86. Malone, Lt. W. S., Co. E, 6th Tex. Inf., died May 11, '63.
48. Malott, Reyon, citizen of Marion Co., Va., died Oct. 30, '62. Removed.
94. McKeon, Lieut. F. G., 19th Ark.——, died May 26, '63.
10. McMurry, 1st Lt. Robert, Co. F, 53d Tenn. Inf., died May 23, '62.
    Removed.

No. of Grave.

7. Mooney, Jacob, 18th La. Inf., died May 13, '62.
13. Mundy, Thomas, 9th La. Inf., died May 28, '62.
87. Murray, 2d Lt. W. T., Co. D, 24th Tex. Cav., died May 11, '63.
32. Osburn, Wm., Bullitt's Ky. Inf., died September 22, '62.
90. Palmer, John, prisoner of war, died May 17, '63.
69. Parker, 1st Lt. W. S., Co. I, 7th Tex. Cav., died February 7, '63.
59. Paul, Joseph B., died December 25, '62.
79. Philips, Capt. W. W., 6th Tex. Inf., died Feb. 13, '63.
28. Phophet, J., 2d Va. Inf., died September 3, '62.
113. Pintzer, Wm., citizen of Wayne Co., Va., died June 4, '63
78. Rankin, Isaac, citizen of Tenn., died Feb. 19, '63.
123. Ravinscroft, Humphrey, citizen of Ky., died June 23, '63.
85. Roberts, I. S., Co. K, 9th Ky. Inf., died May 7, '63.
120. Roberts, J. A., citizen of Virginia, died June 16, '63.
119. Roberts, William, citizen of Virginia, died June 16, '63.
106. Rucker, James, 1st Va. ——, died April 26, '63.
11. Runner, Isaac, citizen of Frederick Co., Va., died May 26, '62.
37. Russell, J. W., 21st Va. Inf., died September 28, '62.
47. Rutherford, John, Taylor Co., Va., died Oct. 26, '62.
107. Sandefur, Charles, Co. B, 4th Ky. Inf., died May 3, '63. Removed.
110. Simonise, Josiah, Co. A, 6th Ky. Inf., died May 21, '63.
127. Sloas, Franklin, — Ky. ——, died July 2, '63.
117. Smith (or Jonas), James, citizen of Va., died June 16, '63.
122. Smith, William, died June 20, '63.
112. Spere, Wm., citizen of Floyd Co., Ky., died May 30, '63.
25. Standiford, Geo., prisoner from Va., died August 12, '62.
27. Steagall, B. F., 9th La. Inf., died August 30, '62.
92. Stilzer, J. A., Co. A., 9th Ky. Cav, died March 20, '63.
125. Tato, T. S., 2d Ky. Cav., died June 20, '63.
68. Thomas, 3d Lt. John, 25th Tex. Cav., died Feb. 6, '63.
4. Thompson, Albert, 36th Va. Inf., died April 9, '62.
134. Tidwell, G., 22d Ala. Inf., died July 27, '63.
3. Tipps, Lieut. Thomas J., 41st Tenn. Inf., died April 9, '62.
20. Tolar, William H., 9th La. Inf., died July 20, '62.
15. Walantine, George, citizen of Va., died June 3, '62.
109. Walker, James, Co. G, 16th Va. Cav., died May 4, '63.
41. Wallace, Corp. M. W., 17th Batt. Va. Cav., died October 4, '62.
39. Warner, J. W., citizen of Ky., died September 30, '62.
52. Weans, James, Co. C, 7th Ky. Inf., died Nov. 5, '62.
75. Weatherbee, Lieut. Jas. M., 3d Tex. Inf., died Feb. 11, '63.
135. Wells, J., Co. E., 1st Ky. Cav, died July 27, '63.
2. White, 2d Lt. R. B., 14th Miss. Inf., died April 9, '62.
6. Willes, Capt. J. H., 51st Va. Inf., died May 3, '62.
56. Windsor, Isaac, prisoner of war, died December 11, '62.
93. Wygant, J. W., citizen of W. Va., died May 23, '63.

JOHNSON'S ISLAND, NEAR SANDUSKY, OHIO.

CONFEDERATE DEAD BURIED IN THE "CONFEDERATE CEMETERY" AT JOHN-
SON'S ISLAND, NEAR SANDUSKY, OHIO.

No. of Grave.

160. Alexander, Lieut. F. (or T.) J., Co. C, 4th Ala. Bat., died Feb. 15, '64.
33. Anderson, B., Mo. S. C., died February 14, '63.
156. Archibald, Capt. A. B., Co. D, 8th Conf. Cav., died February 6, '64.
115. Armfield, Capt. M. D., Co. B, 11th N. C. Inf., died December 3, '63.
123. Arrington, Lieut. J. D., Co. H, 32d N. C. Inf., died December 26, '63.
78. Asbury (or Ashby), J., Kentucky ——, died October 27, '62.
90. Bacon, Capt. Mark, Co. D, 60th Tenn. Inf., died December 8, '63.
131. Barnes, Capt. N. T., Co. E, 10th Conf. Cav., died January 9, '64.
13. Barnett, Lieut. Col. Joel, 9th Bat. La. Cav., died November 7, '63.
159. Baya, Lieut. Francis, Co. H, 2d Fla. Inf., died February 23, '64.
168. Bisell (or Mizell), Capt. Joshua, Co. G, 8th Fla. Inf., died April 10, '64.
122. Blount, Lieut. B. J., Co. H, 55th N. C. Inf., died December 20, '63.
180. Brigham, Lieut. John F., Co. E, 14th Tenn., died June 1, '65.
93. Cabble (or Gabble), Private Hugh, Co. E, 5th Ky., died Nov. 2, '63.
152. Campbell, Col. J. B. (or J. P.), 27th Miss. Inf., died February 4, '64.
105. Canoway, Private J. D., 16th Va. Cav., died January 14, '64.
94 Cash (or Gash), Lieut. J. B., 62d N. C. Inf., died October 30, '63.
22. Cassaway, J. D.
126. Chormley, Samuel, Blount Co., Tenn., died January 9, '65.
72. Christian, D., Co. E, 128th Va., died October 12, '62.
47. Cole, Private Peter, 6th Va. Inf., died November 23, '62.
119. Coleman, Lieut. F. G. W., 7th Miss. Art., died December 8, '63.
61. Collier, Lieut. J. W., 10th Ky. Inf., died December 3, '63.
191. Colter J. (or C. Colter), citizen of M'sville, Tenn., died Sept. 23, '64.
3. Confederate soldier, unknown.
4. Confederate soldier, unknown.
5. Confederate soldier, unknown.
6. Confederate soldier, unknown.
7. Confederate soldier, unknown.
9. Confederate soldier, unknown.
11. Confederate soldier, unknown.
12. Confederate soldier, unknown.
14. Confederate soldier, unknown.
17. Confederate soldier, unknown.
23 Confederate soldier, unknown.
27. Confederate soldier, unknown, died September 30, '63.
35. Confederate soldier, unknown.
36. Confederate soldier, unknown.
37. Confederate soldier, unknown.
39. Confederate soldier, unknown.
39. Confederate soldier, unknown.
40. Confederate soldier, unknown.

No. of Grave.

41. Confederate soldier, unknown.
42. Confederate soldier, unknown.
43. Confederate soldier, unknown.
44. Confederate soldier, unknown, died November 21, '63.
45. Confederate soldier, unknown.
46. Confederate soldier, unknown.
48. Confederate soldier, unknown.
49. Confederate soldier, unknown.
50. Confederate soldier, unknown.
52. Confederate soldier, unknown.
52. Confederate soldier, unknown.
53. Confederate soldier, unknown.
54. Confederate soldier, unknown.
55. Confederate soldier, unknown.
56. Confederate soldier, unknown.
57. Confederate soldier, unknown.
58. Confederate soldier, unknown.
62. Confederate soldier, unknown.
64. Confederate soldier, unknown.
65. Confederate soldier, unknown.
66. Confederate soldier, unknown.
71. Confederate soldier, unknown.
76. Confederate soldier, unknown.
77. Confederate soldier, unknown.
80. Confederate soldier, unknown.
81. Confederate soldier, unknown.
85. Confederate soldier, unknown.
87. Confederate soldier, unknown.
88. Confederate soldier, unknown.
91. Confederate soldier, unknown.
97. Confederate soldier, unknown.
202. Confederate soldier, unknown.
203 Confederate soldier, unknown.
204. Confederate soldier, unknown.
205. Confederate soldier, unknown.
206. Confederate soldier, unknown.
141. Cooper, Capt. F. F., Co. K, 52d Ga. Inf., died February 2, '64.
21. Copass, Lieut. R. D., Co. E, 6th Tenn. Inf., died August 29, '63.
145. Coppege, Lt. F. T. (or F.), — Tenn. Inf. or 10th Mo., died Dec. 20, '64.
190. Cresswell, Lieut. Henderson H., Freeman's Reg., died Sept. 12, '64.
1. Cruggs (or Scroggs), Col. J. E., 85th Va., died November 8, '63.
102. Davis, Private M. W., 35th Miss. Inf., died January 14, '65.
111. Dawson, Lieut. H. B., Co. A, 17th Ga. Inf., died December 22, '63.
184. Day, Capt. J. W., Co. D, 55th Ga. Inf., died May 7, '64.
157. Dean, Lieut. J., Co. H, citizen of Tenn. or 28th Tenn, died Feb. 14, '64.
29. Dotson, Lieut. J. M., 10th Tenn. Cav., died September 30, '63.
68. Dow, John, Pulaski, Ohio.

No. of Grave.

146. Dungan (or Duncan), Private J. L., 22d Va. or King's Art., died December 21, '64.

75. Fox, Col. Samuel, died October 22, '62.

143. Frazier, A. F. (or A. J.), Co. H, 15th Miss. or 2d Ky., died Dec. 12, '64.'

195. Gamble, 2d Lt. Robert, Co. G, 9th Ala. Inf., died November 2, '64.

70. Gibson, Lieut. E., 11th Ark. Inf., died August 12, '62.

32. Gillespie, Capt. C. W., Co. D., 66th N. C. Cav., died September 9, '63.

148. Gobeau (or Gobo), Lieut. J. J., Co. B, 10th Miss. Inf. or King's Art., died February 26, '65.

83. Graham, 1st Lt. S. R., Co. I, 3d Tex. Cav., died September 28, '63.

38. Gregory, Capt. J. W., 9th Va. Inf., died November 21, '63.

154. Hamilton, Capt. S. V. (or J. E.), Co. B, 2d Choctaw or Ind. Cav., died February 4, '64.

98. Handy, M. R., citizen of Hopkins Co., Ky., died February 28, '63.

19. Hansin, Lieut. W. E., 1st Ga. Inf., died August 20, '63.

28. Harden, Lieut. W. P., 5th N. C. Inf., died September 30, '63.

92. Hardy, Capt. J. B., 15th Ark., died November 12, '63.

113. Hardy, Capt. J. B., Co. I, 5th Ark. Inf., died November 12, '63.

135. Harp, Lieut. R. C. (or B. J.), Co. I, 25th Tenn., died January 12, '64.

107. Hazzard, Capt. J. B., 24th Ala. Inf., died December 31, '63.

183. Helton (or Hilton), Capt. W. L., Co. F, 23d N. C. Inf., died May 7, '64.

177. Henagan, Col. John W., 8th S..C. Inf., died April 25, '65.

178. Henken, 1st Lt. J. M., Co. K, 12th S. C. Inf., died May 12, '65.

84. Henry, Capt. S. W., 19th Tenn. Cav., died October 9, '63.

60. Herrin, Daniel (or John), Poindexter's Mo. Cav., died Jan. 16, '63.

133. High, Lieut. J. Q., 1st Ark. Bat. Inf., died January 12, '64.

197. Hill, Capt. J. M., Co. G, Dobbin's Ark. Cav., died January 18, '65.

151. Hill, Lieut. John W., Co. L, 9th or 19th Va. Inf., died February 3, '64.

69. Hodges, R. (or J. B.), Memphis, Tenn., died July 24, '62.

174. Holt, Lieut. E. B., Lexington, N. C., died April 22, '65.

125. Holt, Lieut. John (or James C.), Co. G, 61st Tenn., died Jan. 6, '65.

201. Hood, Adjt. J. L., 59th Va. Inf., died May 1, '65.

15. Hudson, Lieut. William J., 2d N. C. Inf., died August 5, '63.

25. Huffstettler, Lieut. J., 1st Bat. Ark. Inf., died September 14, '63.

89. J. R. H.

24. Jackson, C. B., Guerrilla, Va., died September 8, '63.

110. Jackson, Capt. James R., Co. H, 38th Ala. Inf., died December 20, '63.

187. Jacques, Lieut. J. W., Co. F, 24th Tenn., died June 25, '64.

31. Jetter (or Jeters), S. G., Co. H, 31st Ala. Inf., died September 10, '63.

95. Johnson, Capt. J. W., Green's R. (Mo.) S. G.'s., died October 31, '63.

51. Johnson, Private Wm. (or W. J.), Poindexter's Mo. Cav., died Dec. 13, '62.

112. Johnston, Lieut. D. D., Co. A, 48th Tenn. Inf, died December 3, '63.

63. Kean. Capt. John M., 12th La. Bat. Art., died November 21, '63.

30. Keller, D. D., 2d Tenn. Cav., died September 12, '63.

104. Kelley, Lieut. A., 10th Ark. Inf., died January 4, '64.

144. Killem, Lieut. W. E., Co. H, 45th Va. Inf., died December 13, '64.

No. of Grave.

96. King, J. N. D., Co. K, 9th Ga. Inf., died November 5, '63
130. Land, Lieut. J. L , Co. A, 24th Ga. Inf., died January 11, '64.
167. Lane, Lieut. P. W., 23d Ark. Inf, died March 30, '64.
179. Lash, Maj. J. A., 4th Fla. Inf., died May 21, '65.
116. Lewis, Capt. E. (or G.) W., Co. C, 9th Bat. La. Cav., died Dec. 3, '63.
118. Ligon, Lieut. J. T., 53d Va. Inf. or 23d Ark., died December 9, '63.
166. Lock, Lieut. B. F., Co. E, 4th Ark., died March 18, '64.
134. Long, Lieut. J. C. (or J. P.), Co. I, 62d N. C. Inf., died Jan. 12, '64.
162. Love, 1st Lt. R. C., Co. K, 1st Miss. Art. or 6th Ga., died March 3, '64.
150. Lowis (or Lewis), Capt. T. J., Co. C, 3d Va. Inf., died April 25, '65.
124. Lowshe, Lieut. Jos. (or Jas.), Co. C, 18th Miss. Cav., died Dec. 25, '64.
176. Mackin (or Mankin), Lieut. Peter, Co. I, 16th Miss. Inf., died May 17, '65.
100. Matlock, Col. Charles H., 4th Miss., died December 9, '64.
82. McBride, Lieut. J. A., Co. H, 60th Tenn. Inf., died September 22, '63.
132. McElroy, Lieut. John F., Co. F, 24th Ga. Inf, died October 26, '62.
109. McKay, Lieut. D. H., Co. D, 46th Ala. Inf., died January 1, '64.
188. McRae, 2d Lt. J. W., Co. E, 67th Ga., died August 6, '64.
67. McWhirter, Capt. S. W., Co. H, 3d Miss. Inf., died August 29, '62.
199. Michael, Lieut. W. H., 59th Va. Inf., died June 18, '65.
106. Middlebrooks, Capt. J., 40th Ga. Inf, died January 2, '64.
194. Miller, 3d Lt. J., Williams's Ark. Cav., died October 1, '64.
127. Moore, Lieut. J. W., Co. B, 25th Ala. Inf., died January 21, '65.
147. Moore, 2d Lt. S. T., Co. F, King's R. Ala. Inf. or King's Art., died January 6, '65.
59 More, E. L.
193. Morris, Lieut. C. B., Co. I, 9th Ala. Inf. or 9th La., died Sept. 27, '64.
99. Morrison, Private E , 8th Ala. Inf., died February 11, '63.
158. Nash, Lieut. C. B. (or C. E.), Co. H, 30th Miss. Inf. or 6th La., died February 15, '64.
163. Nichols (or Nicholas), Capt. P., Co. B, 11th Bat. N. C. Inf., died February 28, '64.
170. Nickell, Surg. J. J., 2d Ky. Mounted Rifles, died September 2, '64.
196. Noland (or Nolan), Lt. P. J., English's Miss. Bat., died Nov. 6, '64.
189. Norton, Lieut. W. P., Co. D, 22d N. C. Inf., died September 4, '64.
136. Norwood, Lieut. W. S., Co. E, 6th S. C. Inf., died January 17, '64.
18. Nullins (or Mullins), Lieut. J. W., 1st Miss. Inf., died Sept. 7, '63.
86. Orr, Lieut. E. M., 62d N. C. Inf., died October 21, '63.
169. Pankey, Lieut. S. H., 49th Ala. Inf, died April 12, '64.
129. Peal, Lieut. William, Co. C, 11th Miss., died February 17, '65.
10. Peden, 2d Lt. J. P., Hamilton's Bat., died November 19, '63.
161. Peel, Capt. M. C., 8th Ark. Inf, died February 26, '64.
173. Phillips, 2d Lt. W. E., 4th Ala. Cav. or Forrest's Cav., died Feb. 18,'65
200. Pitt, 2d Lt. A. G., Co. K, 20th Tenn. Inf., died April or May 4, '65.
175. Porter, Capt. W. J., Co. D, 61st Ala. Inf., died April 23, '65.
186. Puckett, Lt. E. N., Co. K, 12th Ark. Inf. or 21st Ark., died June 18,'64.
101. R. E. M.

No. of Grave.
139. Rabenan, Capt. P. J., 5th Ala. or La. Inf., died January 31, '64.
172. Randall, Lieut. Willis, Co. G, 52d N. C. Inf., died December 31, '64.
72. Rasins (or Rains), T., Co. C, 46th Va., died October 14, '62.
79. Reeves, J. (or M.), Co. I, 1st Ga. Cav., died October 30, '62.
198. Reidy (or Reading), M. C., Co. G, 11th Ky. Cav. or 1st Ky., died February 27, '65.
164. Rolling (or Bowling), Lieut. R. P., Co. H, 6th Ga. Cav. or Miss. Art., died March 3, '64.
192. Ruffin, Lt. Thos., Co. D, 4th N. C. Cav. or 59th N. C., died Sept. 23, '64.
74. S. W. C.
128. Scott, 2d Lt. D. L., Co. I, 3d Mo. Cav., died February 11, '65.
121. Shuler, Capt. J. G., Co. H, 5th Fla. Inf., died December 11, '63.
140. Sisk, R. H., citizen, died February 1, '64.
114. Skidmore, Lieut. W. T., Co. D, 4th Ala. Cav., died November 27, '63.
185. Starns, Lieut. or Capt. B. B., Co. B, 9th Ala. Cav. or 9th La., died May 21, '64.
149. Stephens, Lieut. W. A., Co. K, 46th Ala. Inf., died March 15, '65.
20. Stephenson, Capt. H. D., Co. A, 15th Ark. Inf., died August 21, '63.
138. Sullins, Capt. S. P., 1st Ala. Inf., died January 21, '64.
103. Swift, Lieut. W. N., 34th Ga. Inf., died January 1, '64.
155. Swink, Lieut. G. W. (or E. W.), Co. K, 8th Va. Inf., died Feb. 13, '64.
120. Threadgill, Lieut. J. E., Co. H, 12th Ark. Inf., died December 8, '63.
2. Tuggle, Capt. C. M., Co. H., 35th Ga. Inf., died November 6, '63.
8. Upchurch, Capt. A. E., 55th N. C. Inf, died November 9, '63.
108. Vaun, Capt. J. P., Co. E, Bell's R. Ark. Inf., died December 25, '63.
34. Veasey (M. W.), W. W., 10th Ky. Cav., died February 11, '63.
142. Watson, Adjt. W. E., 1st Tenn. Inf., died February 7, '64.
16. Webb, Capt. D. C., 1st Ala. Cav., died July 26, '63.
171. Webb, Capt. James E., 8th Ark., died December 24, '64.
137. Weeks, 2d Lt. R. K. C., Co. F, 4th Fla. Inf., died January 17, '64.
153. Welch, Lieut. John, Co. B, 40th Va. Inf., died February 4, '64.
182. Wilkinson, Lieut. H., Co. B, 9th Va. Inf., died April 21, '64.
117. Williams, Lieut. J. N., 6th Miss. Inf., died December 8, '63.
26. Williams, Lieut. L. B., 63d N. C. Inf., died September 29, '63.
165. Wood, Lieut. J. B, Co. G, 10th C. S. Cav. or 10th C. Cav., died March 16, '64.
181. Wynn, Capt. W. W. (or W. H. Winn), Co. G, 64th Va. Inf., died April 20, '64.

Buried at Johnson's Island, near Sandusky, Ohio: From Kentucky, 7; Virginia, 18; Georgia, 13; North Carolina, 17; South Carolina, 3; Louisiana, 3; Alabama, 19; Mississippi, 16; Arkansas, 16; Tennessee, 17; Missouri, 5; Ohio, 1; Texas, 1; Florida, 5 141
Names unknown marked as Confederate soldiers 56
Miscellaneous commands, States not mentioned 9

206

FREDERICK COUNTY, MARYLAND.

LIST OF DEAD BURIED IN FREDERICK COUNTY, MD.

Forty unknown in two trenches. Buried on top of Crampton Gap, in Paget's field, east of a little house.

Lieut. Col. Lamar, Legion of Georgia; Lieut. Thompson; two unknown. Buried in northeast corner of graveyard back of German Reformed Church, at Burkittsville.

Two unknown. Buried under a large oak tree, southeast of Mr. Horine's house, near Burkittsville.

Fifty-nine unknown. Buried in Samuel Whitnight's lot, on east side of Crampton's Gap.

Two unknown. Buried twenty rods west of road on Manuel Fink's land and east side of Crampton Gap.

One unknown. Buried one hundred and fifty yards north of African Church, near a log along the road.

Two unknown. Buried on top of Crampton Gap, on south side of and near the forks of the road.

Benjamin Mell, 1st Georgia, died October 21, 1862; Lieut. Thrasher, Legion of Maryland. Burned in northwest corner of Episcopal graveyard, east of Petersville.

One unknown. Buried near Persimmon Spring, above Weverton, close to cedars.

One unknown, of Virginia. Buried in Weverton Hospital graveyard.

One unknown. Buried near Ogleton's house, a colored man living along the east side of mountain north of Weverton.

One unknown. Buried in the old tobacco patch above Ogleton's.

Franklin Black and Seamore Hammond, of Virginia; one unknown. Buried in M. E. Graveyard in Buckeyestown.

One unknown. Buried on towpath at Nolend's Ferry, supposed to be washed away.

Adam Eberly, of Virginia, and one unknown. Buried on J. T. Worthington's farm, near Monocacy bridge, and on east side of creek.

One box of bones of unknown. Gathered by Mr. Thomas on his farm and interred by him on his farm, near Monocacy bridge, and on east side of creek.

One unknown. Buried in John Hagan's garden, one mile west of Frederick, along the pike.

John McCausland, of Georgia. Buried one hundred yards west of Reel's Mill and near a locust stump and flint stone and one mile east of Frederick Junction on right-hand side of railroad near a run.

Two unknown. Buried in Peter Beekley's uppermost field.

Fifty unknown in two trenches. Buried in southeast corner of John H. Beekley's field, on north of old Middletown road

Three unknown. Buried in John H. Beekley's field, close along the fence and directly opposite to Martshouse.

Four unknown. Buried in Lewis Hutzel's lot, below Wise's.

One unknown. Buried in John H. Beekley's field and directly opposite Coffman's house.

Dr. Joe, of North Carolina. Buried one hundred and fifty yards below Coffman's house and close along the fence and in John H. Beekley's field.

Four unknown. Buried in Jonas Beekley's field.

One unknown. Buried in John H. Beekley's meadow.

Two unknown. Buried in Keplinger's woods, near a large white oak along the road and just below Jones's house.

Lieut. Marshall Kolbs, of Georgia. Buried ten feet east of a locust tree and near a gully in Michael's meadow, three miles south of Middletown, and on east side of Catoctin Creek.

Two unknown. Buried in Mount Tabor Church graveyard, close along the road and opposite to a large, white oak tree.

One unknown. Buried in northeast corner of Joseph Gaver's orchard field along the road.

Ten unknown. Buried along the stone pile twenty steps southwest of Solomon Houpt's stable.

Six unknown. Buried on Dean's mountain lot, south of Mumford's lot; bones scattered and skulls exposed.

Six unknown. Buried on north end of Conrad Beekley's mountain lot, near the line between Beekley and Houpt; skulls and bones scattered about.

Six unknown. Buried on Philip Flook's mountain land, on northwest of and joining Koogle's land.

Seventeen unknown. Buried on Adam Koogle's mountain field, joining pike, covered nicely and not been disturbed.

G. Rowe, Co. B, 26th Ga.; O. M. Fontwot, Co. F, 8th La.; O. Crisolin, Co. E, 5th La.; C. W. Clark, Co. H, 13th Ga.; H. J. Hobson, Co. D, 12th Ga.; W. A. Lewis, Co. G, 13th Ga.; W. J. Sanders, Co. E, 9th La.; J. Higgins, Co. I, 6th La.; T. B. Heath, Co. E, 12th Ga.; T. Kanghorm, Co. F, 12th Ga ; G. W. Miller, Co. E, 8th La.; W. A. French, Co. A, 17th Va.; W. D. Coleman, Co. D, 21st Va.; Z. G. Collins, Co. K, 61st Ga.; W. McBride, Co. H, 8th La.; G. S. Roberts, Co. H, 26th Ga.; W. H. Candles, Co. D, 12th Ga.; M. Joiner, Co. E, 12th Ga.; J. M. Ritchie, Co. B, 9th La.; J. K. Dilworth, Co. G, 17th Va.; J. E. Fulgum, Co. E, 12th Ga.; J. Eason, Co. H, 30th N. C.; Capt. J. P. Graves, Co. B, 1st La.; W. Belcher, Co. C, 22d Va.; T. W. Stamps, Co. A, 12th Ga.; J. Anderson, Co. F, 9th La.; D. Curry, Co. K, 6th La.; A. Allen, Co. H, 17th Va. Cav.; A. G. Park, Co. G, 17th Va. Cav.; E. Slay, Co. C, 12th Ga.; Z. Stanford, Co. A, 12th Ga ; H. H. Hardney, Co. K, 13th Ga.; J. H. Gary, Co. G, 38th Ga.; G. W. Boldwright, Co. E, 12th Ga.; T. Dix, Co. K, 13th Ga.; C. B. Smith, Co. F, 45th N. C.; F. Loferty, Co. F, 9th La.; W. T. Goodman, Co. D, 48th Va.; G. Miller, Co. F, 21st Ga.; J. H. Knight, Co. B, 12th Ga.; W. R. Wise, Co. K, 13th Ga.; S. M. Jackson, Co. F, 20th N. C.; D. McDonald, Co. C, 7th La.; M. Montgomery, Co. G, 8th La.; A. J. Tamming; A. Holder, Co. H, 20th N. C.; E. Lay, Co. C, 12th Ga.; J. D. Langferd, Co. G, 13th Ga.; J. D. Show, Co. D, 60th Ga.; W. Davis, Co. A, 60th Ga.; P.

McGee, Co. A, 4th Ga.; G. Link, Co. D, 9th La.; Patrick McGuire, Co. C, 7th La.; S. Kirkard, Co. C, 5th Ala.; D. W. Harvey, Co. A, 21st Va.; T. W. Pope, Co. G, 31st Ga.; J. A. Page, Co. A, Nelson's Va. Bat.; A. S. Gardner, Co. A, Nelson's Va. Bat.; W. Haggard, Co. B, Nelson's Va. Bat.; Johnson Suit, Co. G, 5th Ala.; W. Dancy, Co. G, 18th N. C.; L. T. McKee, Co. G, 42d Miss.; John Langford, Co. E, 60th Ga.; W. B. Watts, Co. C, 1st S. C.; R. Seldon, Co. H, 9th Va.; J. M. Royster, Co. C, 47th N. C.; Capt. J. T. Lane, Co. G, 4th Ga.; L. Grigg, Co. K, 43d N. C.; Capt. G. M. Allbright, Co. F, 53d N. C.; Serg. G. R. Bowles, Co. F, 42d Va.; H. Gossell, 53d N. C.; H. H. West, Co. A, 3d N. C.; T. J. Dunn, Co. E, 18th Miss.; Daniel Kelley, Co. B, 3d N. C.; Robert Reeves, Co. G, 27th Ga.; W. H. Powell, Co. I, 3d S. C.; M. Sullivan, Co. K, 6th La.; Corp. P. K. Williams, Co. E, 2d Ga.; S. P. Mabry, Co. G, 6th Ala.; David Abricht, Co. A, 7th La.; H. D. Howell, Co. H, 26th Ala.; John R. Langford, Co. F, 10th Ga.; E. F. Ard, Co. G, 15th S. C.; Riley Davidson, Co. G, 4th Tex.; E. Power, Co. K, 6th Ga.; W. T. Goode, Co. K, 2d Miss.; Henry London, Co. D, 15th N. C.; A. M. Paget, Co. M, 7th S. C.; Henry C. Baker, Co. H, 30th N. C.; William A. Parker, Co. H, 4th Tex.; Joseph Lahart, Co. C, 16th Miss.; A. V. Kennedy, Co. H, Hampton's Legion, S. C.; T. J. Rountree, Co. K, 7th S. C.; D. M. Kirkley, Co. G, 2d S. C.; M. A. Gammel, Co. G, 3d Ark.; M. T. Strickland, Co. G, 50th Ga.; Aquila Todd, Co. F, 5th N. C.; J. Lane, Co. F, 27th N. C.; R. R. Hughes, Co. D, 50th La.; John Bonds, Co. B, 20th N. C.; Oscar D. Sharp, Co. H, 1st N. C.; A. Thigson, Co. B, 3d N. C.; A. N. Anslen, Co. F, 8th La.; M. M. Cottonginn, Co. A, 2d Miss.; John Boles, Co. B, 48th N. C.; J. Mc-Neal, Co. G, 8th Fla.; Joseph Stacy, Co. F, 27th N. C.; H. D. Lewis, 1st N. C.; William Harman, 37th Va.; L. Reeves, Co. B, 3d N. C.; A. Boyd, Co. C, 38th Ga.; J. McNain, Co. C, 31st Ga.; R. M. Brown, Co. B, 2d S. C.; John Leyden, 7th La.; Jacob Boger, 20th N. C.; B. W. Bell, Co. K, 1st N. C.; E. H. Robinson, Co. G, 14th N. C.; Serg. Henry J. Owen, Co. I, 14th Tenn.; Charles D. Maden, Co. G, 12th S. C.; L. S. Philips, Co. G, 3d S. C.; W. E. Lans, Co. E, 23d N. C.; Serg. August Owen, Co. G, 19th G.; Bernard O. L. Young, 23d Ga.; John Hawkins, Co. A, 38th Ga.; W. H. McPherson, Co. D, 50th Ga.; W. P. Hamby, 22d S. C.; Elihu Adams, 3d Ark.; George H. Cowan, Co. H, 3d N. C.; C. Davis, Co. D, 5th Fla.; William Hartley, Co. C, 6th Ga.; Peter Wimbish, Co. I, 24th Va.; Joseph H. Hicklin, 6th S. C.; G. L. Eason, Co. H, 15th Ala.; J. L. Moss, Co. G, 61st Ga.; J. B. Grantsham, Co. G, 6th Fla.; Nathaniel Perry, Co. F, 22d N. C.; John Murphy, Co. E, 27th Ga.; George Knupp, 7th Va.; Thomas Bryant, Co. B, 14th N. C.; B. M. Stedman, Co. G, 48th N. C.; Lieut. Benjamin Anderson, Co. D, 19th Va.; —— Fitske, Co. I, 12th Ala.; J. R. White, Co. H, 8th Fla.; Marks Henry, Co. B, 23d N. C.; Allen Jones, Co. D, 18th Ga.; G. W. Myers, Co. B, 14th N. C.; J. B. Creamer, Co. G, 27th Ga.; Peter Box, 26th Ga.; James Ray, 3d N. C.; A. W. Ponrick, Co. F, 4th Ga.; John A. Michaels, 27th Ga.; James Landron, Co. E, 6th Ga.; William T. West, Co. K, 51st Ga.; W. J. Walter, Co. G, 23d N. C.; J. P. Conaugh, Co. I, 17th S. C.; William F. Biggs, Co. K, 2d Miss.;

Albert Womack, Co. G, 48th N. C.; Wyatt S. Miles, 3d Ark.; Allen T. Demming, Co. D, 13th Ga.; William T. Gill, Co. D, 30th N. C.; John Wallace, Co. G, 18th S. C.; John Brooks, Co. E, 18th Ga.; R. J. Hestely, Co. G, 12th Ala.; John Stephens, Co. B, 51st Ga ; Samuel Jackson, Co. H, 49th Ga.; John Nickles, Co. I, 3d Ala.; John K. Mason, Co. K, 22d S. C.; J. W. Rintz, 13th Ala.; J. A. Bowers, Co. I, 15th S. C.; J. A. Moore, Co. D, 6th Ga.; J. L. Evans, Co. B, 51st Ga.; J. H. Hargrowe, Co. D, 12th N. C.; M. Mark, Co. A, 23d N. C.; Hints Monk, Co. A, 24th N. C.; Benjamin Bangston, Co. D, 6th Ga.; John McHarper, Co. H, 2d Fla.; F. C. Hernicle, Co. D, 16th Miss.; Robert Harris, Co. C, 2d Miss.; E. T. Shiver, Co. A, 35th N. C.; Daniel Bird, Co. C, 5th N. C.; David Jones, Co. E, 51st Ga.; W. McCloud, Co. E, 61st Ga.; William Eitson, Co. H, 30th Ga.; William G. Coleman, Co. G, 60th Ga.; Alfred Green, Co. C, 33d Ga.; N. T. Nix, Co. F, 50th Ga.; A. D. Kelley, 26th Ala.; James M. Johns, Co. F, 5th Fla.; James McGee, Co. H, 1st N. C.; Benjamin Stembridge, Co. D, 6th Ga.; William Hill, Co. A, 26th Ala.; Joseph Jerningan, — S. C.; Joseph Stewart, Co. E, 34th S. C.; James Hagan, Co. C, 10th Ala.; A. D. Collins, Co. H, 17th S. C.; John Michaels, Co. E, 12th Ala.; Charles G. Williams, Co. G, 8th La.; Henry Miller, Co. C, 3d Md.; G. R. Roberts, 32d Miss.; Manning Gisbot, Co. G, 50th Ga.; Ambrose Blanton, Co. G, 15th S. C.; R. Stewart, 14th N. C.; John C. Young, Co. A, 18th S. C.; Charles R. Bartley, Co. B, 12th N. C.; Solomon Tillyville, Co. E, 1st S. C.; N. T. Griffin, Co. B, 3d S. C.; William S. Legrist, Co. B, 3d S. C.; S. J. Jones, Co. A, 6th Ala.; F. M. Tuck, Co. C, — S. C.; John Sidty, Co. F, 7th S. C.; Baxter Smith, Co. K, 8th Fla.; Lieut. E. M. Penn, 22d S. C.; H. W. Crumby, Co. C, 5th Ala.; Joseph Budd, Co. K, Hampton's Legion, S. C.; Otho Fransch, Co. F, 50th Ga.; J. S. Robertson, Co. H, 26th Ala.; William P. Hunt, Co. B, 12th N. C.; David Sloan, Co. F, 50th Ga.; James Shines, Co. F, 51st Ga.; Jacob Hicks, Co. F, 21st N. C.; Emanuel Roberts, Co. E, 10th La.; J. H. Horne, Co. C, 3d N. C.; M. Easteds, Co. E, 27th S. C.; Serg. Alex Raper, Co. H, 12th Ala.; J. H. Hammerick, 6th Ala.; Lieut. Col. T. S. Watkins, 22d S. C.; Raisin Pitts, 6th Ala.; John Murick, 17th C. V.; J. A. Davis, Co. I, 3d Ala.; Alex Potter, 12th Ala.; Andrew Shuman, Co. E, 50th Ga.; Emanuel Sherman, Co. E, 50th Ga.; David F. Rooker, Co. A, 5th N. C.; Alfred D. Miller, Co. K, 4th N. C.; C. Churchill; John R. O. Steen, 50th Ga.; Barney Castel, North Ga. Vol.; J. J. McGahery, Providence, Ala.; William R. Wiley, Co. F, 50th Ga.; Charles Trubick, Co. F, 50th Ga.; William Sourbro, Co. I, 1st N. C.; J. M. Summeall, Co. G, 50th Ga.; Richard Smith, Co. E, 14th S. C.; G. N. Daniel, Co. E, 19th Ga.; J. N. Hill, Co. K, 14th N. C.; John Register, Big Creek, Dale County, Ala.; J. E. Johnson, Mississippi Tigers; one hundred and fifty-eight unknown. Buried on west side in the cemetery at Frederick; boards up.

Thirty unknown. Buried on Richard Mumford's mountain lot, along the hillside south of Sol Houpt's house; were buried under wood, stone, brush, and logs; bones scattered about.

Benjamin G. Davis, of Barboursville, W. Va.; Harvey Wilson, of Nelson County, Va., Co. D, 8th Va. Cav.; Robert Mitchell, Co. B, 8th Va. Cav.; H. L. Moore, Co. B, 8th Va. Cav.; G. R. Stockton, Co. I, 8th Va. Cav.; Jasper Russ, — N. C. Buried in M. E. graveyard in Middletown.

One unknown. Buried in Wash Horine's corner field, along the old Hagerstown road, southwest corner of field and six steps northeast of a large cherry tree.

Dr. Braddock, one unknown. Buried on Gaver's mountain lot, near Mrs. Main's fence and at west end of a trench of disinterred United States soldiers.

Seventeen unknown in two trenches. Buried on east side of Mrs. Main's farm and fence and midway between stump and high rocks.

One unknown. Buried on south side of road and Mrs. Main's fence, thirty feet below a white oak tree; buried under brush and log.

One unknown. Buried on south side of road and Mrs. Main's fence and twenty feet east of a rocky bluff and a large white oak tree.

Three unknown. Buried in northeast corner of Palmer's old locust field.

Two unknown. Buried along the south side of Palmer's old locust field; bones scattered about; were not buried at all.

Three unknown. Buried on Green's mountain lot, two hundred yards south of Key's house; bones exposed.

Ten unknown. Buried in southeast corner of George J. Smith's mountain field.

Two unknown. Buried in corner of Solomon Houpt's lot, one hundred and fifty yards southwest of his house.

Three unknown. Buried in Solomon Houpt's woods, south of his fence; bones exposed.

Fifty unknown. Buried on Daniel Rentz's farm; bones exposed.

H. L. Swiler, Co. D, 7th La.; Capt. J. W. Morris, 16th Va. Cav.; Lieut. S. M. Peedro, 16th Va. Cav.; J. R. Woolridge, Co. C, 144th Va.; James D. Webb, Co. D, 5th Ala.; O. Hales, Co. F, 51st Ga.; L. Pence, Co. F, 60th Ga.; T. J. Ivey, Co. E, 31st Ga.; G. Lowe, Co. D, 5th La.; J. W. Bachus, Co. A, 12th Ga.; E. H. Lucass, Co. F, 14th Va.; S. Patten, Co. G, 31st Ga.; B. H. Fuller, Co. D, 12th Ga.; W. A. Davis, Co. A, 12th Ga.; H. W. Lynch, Co. F, 13th Ga.; George Cross, of North Carolina; W. J. Bourn, Co. F, 12th Ga.; G. McClung, Co. K, 14th Va. Cav.; W. Allen, Co. G, 8th Va. Cav. Buried along the west side in the cemetery at Frederick; boards up and graves all in good condition.

Three unknown. Buried on hill on Smith's land at mountain house.

B. F. Manny, 51st Ga.; John Pratt, north end of second row; R. W. McSparran, of Ivey Depot, Albemarle County, Va., Co. K, 19th Va., died September 21, 1862; Capt. A. A Holland, of Danville, Va., died September 22, 1862; six unknown. Buried in the common near the academy in Middletown.

Dr. Bradox, of South Carolina; Thomas Sander, Co. G, 10th Ga.; Capt. N. Reeder, Co. H, 16th Ga.; E. H. A., — Ga.; Benjamin Matthews, Co. F, 16th Ga.; William Smith, Co. B, 16th Ga.; Thomas Hobbs, Co. K, 16th

Ga.; Benjamin F. Gillmore, Co. F, 16th Ga.; M. Grubne, Co. C, 16th Ga.; James Light, Co. I, 16th Ga.; John Args, Co. C, 1st Ga. Legion; J. J. McWilliams, Co. C, 1st Ga. Legion; John Dunlap, Co. D, 15th N. C.; J. L. Russell, Co. G, 15th N. C.; Ayel Batten, Co. I, 15th N. C.; J. R. Gaar, Co. C, 1st Ga. Legion; J. R. Argo, Co. C, 1st Ga. Legion; A. J. Bice, Co. F, 1st Ga. Legion; Victor W. Mayott, Co. G, 4th Va.; Manillas B. Johnson, Co. G, 4th Va.; J. A. Farmer, Co. E, 16th Va.; R. F. Moore, Co. F, 15th Va.; B. F. C., Co. F, 2d Va.; ten unknown. Buried close along the fence on west side of woods back of graveyard in Burkettsville; graves in good condition and boards still here.

Names and Burial Places Reported Since the Foregoing Was Put in Type.—Reference (page 13) : Capt. James E. Martin removed to the family burial lot of Hon. James H. Grove, Hagerstown. "John Newton, H. H. A., S. C. V., died July 6, 1863." Square and compass and the letter "G" in angles of the square upon a board placed at the head of his grave. Buried in Bowery Woods on Springfield Farm, near Williamsport, Washington County. Removed by Friendship Lodge No. 84, A. F. and A. M, of Hagerstown, to the cemetery at Williamsport. Head and foot stones put up and inscribed with the same marks and letters found upon the board where the body was first buried. "Thomas W. Metcaff, of Natchez, Miss." Buried by the side of Colonel Lumkin in Presbyterian Cemetery, Hagerstown. Myrtle planted on both graves.

Summary of the Number Identified from Each State, and Those by Names, Letters, Location, etc.—Louisiana, 69; Mississippi, 61; Virginia, 106; Georgia, 210; North Carolina, 119; South Carolina, 71; Arkansas, 10; Texas, 9; Tennessee, 6; Alabama, 54; Florida, 10; Maryland, 2; identified by name, 23; by batteries, 5; P. S. S., 63; unknown, 2,481. Total, 3,239 (as by this report made May 1, 1869).

MONUMENT AT SHEPHERDSTOWN.

Inscription on the monument: "Erected to the memory of our Confederate dead by the Shepherdstown Southern Memorial Association June 6, 1870. True patriots. A nation's tears embalm their memory. To the unknown dead. Though nameless, their deeds are not forgotten. We lie here in obedience to the commands of our sovereign States."

The monument is fifteen feet high.

LIST OF CONFEDERATE DEAD AT SHEPHERDSTOWN.

Boyd, Lieut. H. M., Co C, 5th Tex.
Mercer, W. H., La. Guard Art.
McKee, John, 2d S. C.
March, Rev. E. L., 31st La. Vol.
Cook, W. A., Co. G, 31st La.
Ireland, W., Co. C, 60th La.
Edwards, J., Co. H, 2d N. C.
Wilkerspoon, T. J., North Carolina.

Newall, W. J., Co. K, 12th Ala
Hood, D. S., Louisiana.
Riggs, J., Co. F, 4th Tex.
Gordan, J., Co. F, 48th N. C.
Patten, W. D., Co. C, 1st N. C.
Barnhart, A., 20th N. C. Regt.
Durank, E. D. B., 26th La. Vol.
Willis, Pittsylvania County, Va.
Fountain, Corp M. J., 13th La. Vol.
Goroin, T. J., 2d S. C. Rifles.
Spohr, H., 9th La. Vol.
Davenport, Lieut. Charles E., Charleston, S C.
Crim, T. L., 1st S. C.
Agnew, J. C., 6th S. C.
Banks, M., Co. C, Hampton's Legion.
Tucker, J, 21st La.
James, Lieut. John, 17th Miss. Vol. Died at Sharpsburg, Md.
Ferrell, S. K., Louisiana.
Jones, Serg. S.
Stone, J. B.
McOnon, J., Co. C, 12th La
Rinehart, J., Co. B, 59th N. C.
Daniels, W. B., Co. C, 55th N. C.
Williams, Lieut. N. J, Co. K, 3d N. C. Inf.
Feamster, J. B., 11th Miss. Regt.
Ganty, S., Co. D, 16th S. C.
Wilson, Lieut. C.
Harvey, Lieut. W: H., Co. H, 21st Va.
Ogletree, G. A., Co. I, 13th La.
Gay, John, 31st La.
Connell, R. P., Co. I, 50th La.
Layton, Capt. R. E., Co F, 2d Miss.
Jebbo, William.
Easton, C., Co. E, 33d N. C.
Williams, John, Rockbridge County, Va. Died August 12, 1877.
Holliday, E. P., 5th N. C.
McBride, William F., Co. C, 3d La.
Thompson, S. J., Co. K, 5th N. C.
Elliott, J. M., Huntsville, Ala.
Rattler, A.
Slaughter, M. B., 11th La.
Slandiffer, W. E., Louisiana.
Mabin, M. G., 15th La.
Lemon, Alex, Co. B, 2d Va. Inf.
Johnson, J. Newman. Born December 27, 1832; died July 4, 1864.
Waters, P., Co. A, 8th La.
Jones, Isaac T., 50th La.
Hoffler, G. M., 4th Tex.

CONFEDERATE CEMETERY, SHEPHERDSTOWN, MD.

Miller, Collins, White's Battalion. Killed near Winchester, Va., September 3, 1864, aged twenty years.

Harris, George W., Co. F, 1st Va. Cav., Shepherdstown, W. Va.

Pratt, J. H., 30th Va.

Farnham, N. L., Co. D, 5th Fla.

Thompson, F. M., 1st La.

Hood, D. T., 5th Ala. Art.

Warburton, G. T., Park's Artillery.

Smith, W. T., Co. I, La.

Kipley, Andrew, Co. I, 14th N. C.

Williams, Lieut., Black Horse Cavalry

Rogers, C. R., South Carolina.

Hoey, Edward P., Louisiana Guard Artillery.

Lee, Capt., South Carolina.

Robison, J., Brook's Artillery.

Anderson, Serg. Map, 5th Fla.

Irvin, Louisiana.

Lyon, Lieut C. E., Co. A, 48th Va.

Perry, J. M., Louisiana.

Willis, Alabama.

Baudy, J., 21st Miss.

Vaughan, W.

Tew, O., Co. C, 2d N. C.

Lee, J.

Vespot, A. T.

Smith, Capt. H. J., Co. D, Hampton's Legion.

Deakins, J., Union District, S. C.

Hornbuckler, T. W., 13th N. C.

Eason, W., Co. D, 2d N. C.

Howell, William, Co. K, 19th Miss.

Cotton, Capt. R. W., 1st Tex. Vol. Died October 30, 1862.

Smith, Conrad C., Co. B, 2d Va. Regt. Born April 5, 1819; died November 14, 1886.

Hawn, David, Co. F, 1st Va. Cav. Died July 2, 1900.

Younty, George R., Co. F, 1st Va. Cav. Died January 1, 1885.

Robison, James B., Co. H, 2d Va. Cav. Born March 27, 1837; died June 22, 1885.

Grigsby, Capt. R, Co. A, 8th La.

Monaghan, Col. William, 6th La.

Parham, Dr. William S. Killed at Sharpsburg September 17, 1862.

Overton, W. G.

Porter, Eli, N. C. Troops.

Roup, George L., Co. C, 5th Va., Supt. Stanibon, Va.

Clark, C. M., Co. F, 5th Fla.

Tanner, Paddy.

Wright, Amassa P., Co. C, 21st Va.

Allen, J., Co. K, 6th N. C.

Miller, A., Co. B, 52d N. C.

Wallack, Capt. D., Co. A, 22d La.

Thompson, Serg.

Leopold, Andrew, Maryland. A noted guerrilla along the Potomac.

Burke, Capt. Redman, Jefferson County, W. Va.

Thompson, B., 2d N. C.

Taylor, J. W., Jenkins's Brigade.

Graceby, J. M., 1st Va. Cav. Died July 6, 1876.

Harlin, Serg. J.

York, S. M., Co. K, 8th Miss.

Beazeley, Lieut. James A., Co. C, 9th Va. Cav., C. S. A. Born in Spottsylvania County, Va., July 1, 1833; killed at Boonsboro, Md., September 15, 1862.

Douglas, Gen. Henry Kyd, one of General Lee's staff officers, is also buried in Shepherdstown Cemetery.

Morgan, Col. William A., 1st Va. Cav., C. S. A. Died in 1899.

Hill, George F., 1st Va. Cav. Died at Harrisonburg, Va., Dec. 18, 1864.

Also fifty-eight unknown are buried in the same ground in the Shepherdstown Cemetery.

LEFT ALONE IN THEIR SLUMBERS, CAMP CHASE CEMETERY.

408

411

Garfield, 96
GAR Post, 39
Garrett,G.W., 124
GAR Veterans Drum Corps, 41
Gassarvay,S.W., 150
Gauley Mt., 279, 289
George, 165
George,J.H., 271
George,J.Z., 124
Georgia Editors, 38
Georgian, Propellor Steamer, 218
Gettysburg,Pa., 2, 6, 7, 28, 29, 110, 234, 270
Giboret,J.G., 135
Gibson,A.J., 124
Gibson,Lieut., 244
Giddings Street, 254, 255
Gilland, 153
Glass,Mrs., 249
Goodale Park, 111
Goodloe,Hayward, 81
Goodloe,John J., 81
Goodman,L.H., 47
Gordon, 18, 46
Gordon,John B., xiv, xviii, xix, 62, 64, 65, 71, 82, 84
Gose,W.H., 259
Goshen Bridge, 163
Governors Island, 215, 241
Grafton,WV, 250
Graham,R.H., 124, 198, 199
Graham,T.B., 124
Grant,Mr.,Government Inspector, 90
Grant,Mrs., 174
Grant,General U.S., 7, 8, 24, 28, 29, 46, 58, 60, 69, 71, 72, 168, 257, 269, 289
Grasty,S.G., 264 ,265, 266
Grauger,J.W., 156
Gray,J.F., 151
Gray,N.A., 125
Gray-Beard Brigade, 201
Greary,W.S., 150
Great Northwestern Conspiracy, The, 218
Great Southern Hotel, 94, 96
Green, 151
Green,Capt. Provost Marshall, 170
Green,J., 124, 127
Greene Co.,Tenn., 169
Greeney,E.S., 156
Green Harber, 164
Greenlaw,W.O., 163
Green Lawn Cemetery, 61, 94
Green Springs, Ohio, 189
Greenville, 300
Greenville,Tenn., 260
Greenup, 172
Gresham,J.F., 161
Griffin,B.R., 127
Griffin,James, 154, 169
Grim,J., 94
Grimm,J., 56
Groyn,W.H., 124
Grub,W.H., 35
Gubbins, 203
Guild,G.B., 84
Guin,T.J., 129
Guiton,W., 174
Gundey,Bill, 287

Guthrie,J.Z., 163
Guthrie,Mrs.J.Z., 163

-H-

Hackney,R.B., 111
Haddox,E.C., 156
Hahurst, 284
Hailey,Miss., 170
Hale, 173
Hale,Col. Regiment, 173
Haley's Creek, 151
Halifax, 138, 235
Halison,J.B., 156
Hall, 147
Hall,A.G., 164
Hall,Dick, 153
Hall,J.B., 164
Hall,J.G., 144, 150
Halterman, 256
Hamilton,R.V., 135
Hamilton,W.D., 41, 42, 43, 294
Hamilton Co.,Oh., 135 , 175, 177, 296, 297
Handley,D.R., 307
Hanis, 164
Harbin,M.P., 124
Hardie,John T., 193
Harfiss,S., 111
Harper, 82
Harper,Hattie, 82
Harper,Mary, 82
Harpers Ferry,W.V., 7
Harris,E.A., 174
Harris,Elizabeth, 174
Harrison, 91
Harrison,J.K., 141
Harrison,Mrs.Benjamin, 177
Harrison,R.A., 216
Harrison,T., 135
Harrison,T.H., 124
Harrison,W.P., xvii, 72, 73
Harwood,J.T., 135
Hathorn,T.W., 127
Haurst, 283
Havana, 162
Hawkes, 126
Hawkins,W.S., 38, 114, 258, 261
Hayes,R.B., xix, 3, 11, 13, 206
Haynes,L.C., 151
Haywood, 80
Headquarters of Conf.Spy on W.Broad Street, 277
Heironimus,Bob, 267
Heironimus,Jake, 267
Helmick,J.N., 127
Henderson, 124
Henderson,Gen., 60
Henderson,H.A.M., 60
Henderson,Howard, 56
Henephile,J.R., 124
Henney,J., 157
Henry,J., 135
Henry Co.,Ky., 266
Herald, 156
Herbert, 254, 267
Herbert,Capt., xx
Herbert,Mrs., 313

412

418

419